WELLINFORMED

MEDICAL AND HEALTH CONTRIBUTORS AND REVIEWERS

William B. Baun, M.S., F.A.W.H.P.
Susan Blair, M.B.A., F.A.W.H.P.
John M. Carpenter, M.D.
David L. Chesler, M.D.
William C. Clair, F.A.W.H.P.
Camille F. Deckert, M.Ed.
Robin Fuller Foust
Carolyn Helmly, M.D.
Don S. Hillier
Alan L. Kimmel, M.D.
Ronald M. Lather, M.D.
R. Michael Morse, M.D.
George J. Pfeiffer, M.S.E., F.A.W.H.P.
Michael E. Pfeiffer, D.D.S.
Marti Remmell, R.N.
Andrew Scibelli, M.S.E.
Judith Webster, R.N., M.S.
Michael Wood, M.S., M.P.H.

A publication of
The WorkCare Group, Inc.® and Vitality®
Charlottesville, Virginia
Second Edition

WELLINFORMED

WorkCare Press

P.O. Box 2053

Charlottesville, Virginia 22902

ISBN Number: 0-9634986-5-7
Printed in the United States of America

Publisher:	George J. Pfeiffer
Editors:	Julie Gay, Sandra Werner
Production Manager:	Catalina McChesney
Production Assistant:	Safiyyah Affinnih-Smith
Graphics and Design:	Valerie L'Herrou
Internal Illustrations:	Scott Emond
	Catherine Rose Crowther
Cover Illustration:	Ron Chan

Distributed in the United States by The WorkCare Group, Inc.® and Vitality®.

Limits of Liability: *Well INFORMED: Your Guide to Health and Vitality* **is intended to increase awareness of health and medical care issues. None of the information in this text is intended to be a substitute for appropriate physician diagnosis and medical care.**

Contents

Contents

Contents

Welcome to Well INFORMED

"An ounce of prevention is worth a pound of cure" rings as true today as it did more than 200 years ago. In fact, even though medical technology has improved our chance of living to a ripe old age, the health decisions we make day-to-day still have a greater influence on our future health than medical science does. When you think about your health care, consider not only your access to quality medical care but also that you must take personal responsibility in managing your health. This means practicing positive lifestyle behaviors and making informed health decisions. As you assume an active role in your health care, the *Well INFORMED* self-care guide will be a ready resource. Consult *Well INFORMED* often to improve your and your family's overall health and the health care you receive.

Taking Charge of Your Health: One Step at a Time

Believe it or not, it's never too late to take positive steps to improve your health and well-being. In fact, research has shown that even modest changes in your lifestyle habits—such as increasing your physical activity and reducing the total fat in your diet—can reduce your risk for heart disease and certain cancers. The important first step is committing yourself to change, no matter how small. For each success leads to greater confidence in taking control of your health.

Another step in taking charge of your health is becoming involved, with your doctor, in the medical decisions that impact you. This may include deciding when medical interventions are necessary.

The bottom line? Regardless of your health status, be it well or ill, it's important to be actively involved and informed in your health care decisions. This includes:

- Knowing and practicing self-care skills that help prevent and/or manage lifestyle-related disorders.
- Being able to select a doctor based on your needs.
- Having the basic skills to know when medical care is necessary and when common problems can be treated at home.
- Being able to talk to your doctor comfortably, including questioning available treatment options and their benefits, risks, and costs.
- Discussing with your doctor the need for hospitalization when outpatient services may be just as effective.
- Knowing your rights as a patient.

How Well INFORMED Can Help You

Well INFORMED is designed to give you a basic introduction to the principles of prevention, medical self-care, and medical consumerism. When you use *Well INFORMED*, you will:
- Have greater health and vitality.
- Prevent and/or manage major problems such as heart disease, diabetes, and cancer, through positive lifestyle practices.
- Learn to treat common medical complaints through medical self-care.
- Have greater confidence and skills in dealing with medical care decisions.
- Improve the quality of health care you receive.

You're encouraged to use *Well INFORMED* as part of your overall health management plan. When faced with a health problem, make consulting this book your first step. However, this book is not intended to replace professional medical treatment when it's needed or replace treatment already recommended by your doctor. If you have any questions or concerns, consult your doctor first.

Remember, "when it comes to your health, you can't be too informed."™

An Ounce of Prevention

By using this section you will learn:

- What behaviors have the greatest influence in reducing your risk of illness and disease.

- How to add regular physical activity to your life.

- How to eat right for good health.

- Ways to reduce stress and tension in your life.

- Specific skills for losing weight.

- Which medical screening tests are appropriate for you.

- About good dental care.

- Which immunizations are appropriate for you and your family members.

- How to prevent or manage high blood pressure and high cholesterol.

- About substance abuse and how to get help if you or a loved one has a problem with alcohol or drugs.

- About family planning.

- About AIDS and other sexually transmitted diseases.

- How to keep your child healthy and safe.

Building Blocks of Prevention

....

The cornerstone of health is practicing appropriate behaviors that not only increase your vitality and independence, but reduce your risk for disease and disability. The following chart summarizes key lifestyle behaviors that have the greatest influence on your health and longevity.

BUILDING BLOCK	IDEAS THAT WORK	BENEFITS	RESOURCES
Staying Active	• Be physically active a minimum of five days/week—30 minutes/day. • Activities involving large muscles, e.g., walking, cycling, swimming, and yard work, are recommended. • Also, try resistance exercises that strengthen the shoulders, arms, back, abdomen, and leg muscles. Recommended twice a week. • Maintain adequate levels of joint flexibility through daily stretching.	• Protects against heart disease, cancer, diabetes, osteoporosis, and depression. • Best for weight control. • Increases your energy level. • Maintains adequate levels of muscular strength and endurance needed to perform everyday activities. • Protects major muscle groups and joints. Enhances performance.	• Local YMCA/YWCA • Recreation centers • Health clubs • Company fitness center • Home "gym" • Refer to pages 6-15
Eating Right	• Keep total fat intake below 30 percent of total calories per day. • Limit saturated fat to less than 10 percent of total calories. • Consume 55 to 60 percent of total calories in carbohydrates. • Keep protein intake below 15 percent. Eat leaner cuts of red meat and substitute with fish (unfried) and poultry. • Eat more fruits, vegetables, and grains. • Moderate your use of salt (sodium).	• Protects against heart disease, hypertension, cancer, diabetes, and obesity. • Provides energy for mental and physical activities.	• American Cancer Society • American Dietetic Association • Refer to "Food Pyramid" on page 18 • Refer to 5-A-Day Plan on page 16 • American Heart Association
Watching Your Weight	• Keep your weight within 10 percent of ideal. • Avoid crash diets. • Increase your physical activity. • Reduce your total intake of fat. • Decrease high-fat foods and increase low-fat foods.	• Improves appearance. • Reduces risk of heart disease, hypertension, and diabetes. • Reduces stress on joints. • Enhances self-esteem/ self-image.	• American Dietetic Association • Refer to page 22
Drinking Alcohol in Moderation or Not at All	• A maximum of one to two drinks per day if you do drink. • Don't drink and drive. • Don't operate equipment or machinery while under the influence of alcohol. • Family history of alcoholism puts you at greater risk for alcoholism.	• Lowers risk of liver disease and certain cancers. • Reduces risk of on-the-job accidents and motor vehicle accidents. • Moderate alcohol use is linked to a lower risk for heart disease.	• Your company employee assistance program (EAP) • Alcoholics Anonymous • Refer to page 39

Building Blocks of Prevention

BUILDING BLOCK	IDEAS THAT WORK	BENEFITS	RESOURCES
Staying Drug-Free	• Use prescription and over-the-counter medications only as directed. • Don't use illicit drugs or someone else's prescription medications.	• Prevents dependence on drugs. • Helps prevent the spread of AIDS. • Prevents adverse drug reactions.	• Narcotics Anonymous • Refer to pages 35-38
Practicing Safe Sex	• Maintain monogamous relationships. • Use condoms with the spermicide nonoxynol-9.	• Helps prevent sexually transmitted diseases such as HIV/AIDS, gonorrhea, and chlamydia.	• Your personal physician • Local health department • Refer to page 50
Using Your Seat Belt	• Use your seat belt all the time. • Small adults should sit as far from an air bag as possible. • Have all passengers buckle up before you start your vehicle. • Secure children under age 12 in back of car, in child safety seat or buckled up, as appropriate.	• Reduces vehicular death and injury.	• National Safety Council • Local police
Following Scheduled Immunizations and Medical Tests	• Follow recommended schedules based on age, sex, and health status.	• Identifies health risks. • Prevents and/or manages disease. • Prevents infectious diseases.	• Your personal physician • Immunizations, page 44 • Tests, page 43
Staying Out of the Sun	• Avoid sun during peak hours. • Apply sunscreen: SPF 15 or higher. • Cover up: Wear a hat and other protective clothing. • Protect your children—a single significant burn before age 5 increases their lifetime risk for skin cancer.	• Prevents skin cancer. • Prevents premature aging.	• American Cancer Society
Not Using Tobacco (cigarettes, pipes, cigars, or smokeless tobacco)	• Establish a quit date no more than 30 to 45 days away. • Before you quit, practice positive behaviors such as exercising, eating right, watching your weight, and managing stress. • Seek support from family, friends, and possibly a group smoking-cessation program. • Once you quit, avoid situations that trigger your old habit. • Those who try to quit and fail have a better chance of quitting if they try again. Don't give up!	• **Significantly** reduces the risk of lung cancer, emphysema, oral cancers, heart disease, hypertension, and stroke.	• American Cancer Society • American Lung Association

Walking: The Best Exercise?

Whether you want to lose weight, manage stress, or reduce your health risks, walking is perhaps the best way to add regular exercise to your life. Walking is inexpensive, requires little equipment, can be done almost anywhere, and is good for young and old alike. In fact, research shows that older men who walk regularly have lower overall mortality rates. Here are a few tips on starting your own walking program.

Ideas that Work

- **Use the proper footwear.** Sneakers and running shoes may not give you adequate support and cushioning. There are several "walking shoes" on the market that are designed to help the heel-to-toe motion of walking and provide good support for the heel. Go shoe shopping in the afternoon, when feet are larger from the day's activities. When trying on shoes, make sure that you have enough room in the front (toe box) to allow the toes to spread out as you push off from the ground.

- **Use proper form.** Walk tall, but keep your upper body relaxed. Foot contact with the ground should be heel to toe. You should feel a gentle rocking motion as you transfer your weight from your heel to the final push-off with your toes. Pump your arms in a bent-arm position with elbows kept close to the body. Avoid crossing your arms in front of you as you swing. Avoid using hand weights while walking.

- **Map your course.** To ensure personal safety and increase enjoyment, find a walking route that is out of the way of traffic, offers pleasant scenery, has an even surface, and is safe and well-lit at night. If you must walk in the street, always walk facing traffic. Nearby shopping malls are excellent places to walk, especially in cold climates.

- **Shine on.** If you walk at night, wear reflective clothing (e.g., vest).

- **Start on the right foot.** If you are over 40 years old and have been inactive or, regardless of your age, have a medical condition such as high blood pressure, heart disease, or joint problems, discuss your exercise plans with your doctor before starting. Begin your program slowly. Gradually increase the time (duration) of your walk before increasing the speed (intensity).

  Also, be sure to carry an ID and change for a pay phone.

- **Buddy up!** You don't have to walk alone. Walk with a family member, friend, or co-worker. Ideally, try to walk with someone at your fitness level.

- **Schedule your walk.** If it's been hard for you to exercise because you haven't had the time, schedule your walk and make it a habit. When was the last time you did something for you?

- **Add variety.** Though it's wise to have a regular walking route, try to vary your walking course once you've reached a level of comfort and regularity. Map out additional walking routes that vary in distance, terrain, and scenery, and are safe.

- **Start slowly, then build.** To begin feeling health benefits, walk at least five days a week, for a total of 30 minutes per day. You may find that you can walk for only 10 minutes before needing a rest—that's OK. Three 10-minute walks spread out over the day are just as beneficial. Over time, add a few minutes to the length of your walk until you're able to walk for 30 minutes without stopping. A rule of thumb is that if you can carry on a normal conversation without being out of breath, then you are exercising at an acceptable level of effort.

- **Move it, lose it.** If weight loss is your goal, research suggests that you need to walk for at least 40 minutes, five days per week to experience significant results. Studies also have shown that walking for 20 to 40 minutes seems to be the threshold for reducing anxiety and tension.

- **Refresh yourself.** On hot, humid days, be sure to drink at least 12 ounces of water before start-

Walking: The Best Exercise?

ing. It's also wise to carry a water bottle while exercising and drink before you become thirsty. Use sunscreen, and on sunny days wear a brimmed hat and sunglasses.

• **Have fun!** Once you reach a level of activity that is comfortable, vary your walking routes, change the distance, play with the tempo, walk through city parks or botanical gardens, have a company noon-hour walk program, or participate in a community "walkathon" for charity.

• **Reward yourself or your walking group.** Establish an incentive program for your progress or set up an office walking or family fund. For every mile walked, contribute to the "walk fund." Once the fund has reached a certain amount, treat yourself or the group to movie tickets or lunch at a local restaurant, or donate the money to charity.

Walking through the Day

• **Ride and walk.** If you commute by mass transit, get off earlier than your usual stop and walk the additional distance.

• **Park and walk.** Park your car farther from your place of work or at the back of the parking lot.

• **Break walk.** Instead of running to the vending machine or smoking a cigarette, get out of the office and walk during your scheduled breaks.

• **Lunch and walk.** If you "brown bag," walk to a nearby park that's five to seven minutes from the office. Sit and enjoy your lunch and walk back.

• **Form a walking group.** Form a noon-hour walking group. Have members alternate in choosing the route of the day.

• **Walk after dinner.** Take a stroll for 20 to 30 minutes by yourself or with a family member(s).

Resources

Fitness Walking, by Robert Sweetgall. New York: Perigree Books, 1985.

Rockport Walking Program, by James M. Rippe. Englewood Cliffs, N.J.: Prentice-Hall, 1989.

F.Y.I

FIT ACTIVITY INTO YOUR DAY

The Surgeon General's Report on Physical Activity and Health recommends that people of all ages engage in 30 minutes of physical activity of moderate intensity on most, if not all, days of the week. Recommended activities include brisk walking, jogging, cycling, dancing, swimming, and "lifestyle" activities such as gardening, raking leaves, and doing household chores. See page 8.

Rating Popular Fitness Activities

Regular physical activity is an important component of a healthy lifestyle. The Surgeon General's Report on Physical Activity and Health recommends that adults engage in moderate physical activities for a total of 30 minutes per day for most days of the week, if not every day, in order to experience health benefits.

Daily physical activity may include manual labor; household chores such as housecleaning, raking leaves, and gardening; and participating in a structured fitness program or favorite recreational or sports activity. For most individuals, engaging in a combination of activities (e.g., household chores, basic physical conditioning, and participating in sports) will not only provide health benefits, but also improve the overall fitness level. What's more, by mixing your activities, you avoid the seasonal peaks and valleys of any one pursuit (e.g., softball, skiing)—plus, you'll reduce boredom and achieve a higher level of fitness.

To help you choose which activities will suit you best, consult the chart below. It ranks popular activities and their influence on key fitness components. Activities are ranked 1 through 10, with 10 having the greatest benefit (except for the "Risk of Injury" column).

NOTE: Benefits can vary greatly among individuals. Personal skill levels and the intensity, duration, and frequency of the activity influence its effects. Therefore, use the chart only as a guideline. And remember: If you have been physically inactive or have a health problem, consult your doctor before engaging in any physical activity.

RATING POPULAR FITNESS ACTIVITIES

Activity	Aerobic Fitness**	Muscle Toning	Flexibility	Weight Control	Risk of Injury***
Aerobics (low impact)	6	7	7	6.5	5
Cycling*	6	6	3	6	5-9
Cross-Country Skiing*	9	8	7	9	5-7
Golf (walking)	5	5	6	4	5
In-Line Skating	5	6	6	5	8
Jogging	8.5	6	3	8	7
Rowing*	7	8	6	7	5
Singles Tennis	6	6	7	6	6-7
Stair-climbing exercise	7	6	6	7	4
Swimming (lap)	8	7	7-9	8	3
Walking (4 MPH)	5	5	4	5	3
Weight Training	4	8-10	6	5	7
Yoga	2	6	8-10	2	2

* Includes both stationary equipment and outdoor activity. Outdoor activity increases the chances of injury.

** Approximates exercising at a moderate intensity for 30 minutes.

*** Rates the chances of experiencing soft-tissue injuries such as strains, sprains, abrasions, and bruises due to falls. Injury can be reduced through proper conditioning, warm-up and cool-down, practicing proper technique, using appropriate equipment, and following proper safety procedures.

Improving Your Flexibility

Flexibility is the range of motion within a joint. This range is dependent upon a number of factors such as joint structure and the condition of supporting tissues—ligaments, tendons, and the muscles that move the joint. Outside of acute injury or chronic conditions (e.g., arthritis), the biggest reason for lack of flexibility is disuse. Unless a joint area is stretched through its range of motion on a regular basis, mobility will decrease and the risk of injury will be greater.

Flexibility is especially important for those involved in sports and recreational activities that place repeated stress on muscles and joints. In fact, many athletic careers have ended prematurely because the participant didn't take the time to properly warm-up, cool-down, and stretch key muscle groups.

But, even if you're not an athlete, joint flexibility is a key part of physical health. This is especially important as you age. By doing the exercises on the following pages, you can improve and maintain your range of motion, reduce stiffness in your joints, reduce post-exercise soreness, reduce the risk of injury, and improve your overall mobility and performance.

General Guidelines for Stretching

- If you have a health condition that limits your activity, consult your doctor before doing these exercises. Take this book with you and show your doctor what you intend to do.

- Do a large muscle warm-up such as brisk walking for five to 10 minutes before stretching.

- Don't bounce and jerk when you stretch. Gently stretch to a point of tension.

- Hold the stretch for 15–30 seconds. Concentrate on relaxing the muscles when you're stretching.

- Breathe normally. Don't hold your breath.

F.Y.I EXERCISE TO YOUR HEART'S CONTENT

People often wonder how hard is hard when it comes to exercise. A major gauge of exercise intensity is your heart rate. To maximize your workout, your heart rate should be elevated and maintained within your exercise heart rate zone for a total workout time of 30 minutes. You can calculate your zone by subtracting your age from 220. Then multiply that number by .6 to find the low end of your zone; multiply the first number again by .8 to find the high end of your zone. Where you exercise within that range depends on your physical condition: For example, a beginning exerciser should work out at the low end of his or her zone and increase intensity as his or her fitness level improves. You can find out if you're exercising at the appropriate intensity level by checking your pulse immediately after finishing your workout. Gently place your ring and middle fingers just below your jaw or on your wrist below your thumb. Count the number of beats—the first beat is zero—for 10 seconds and then multiply by six. Adjust the intensity of your next exercise interval or workout appropriately.

Stretching for Health

Back Extension

- Stand with your feet shoulder-width apart and your knees relaxed.
- Place your hands on the small of your back.
- Slowly extend your shoulders back to a point of tension. Hold for 15 seconds and then relax.
- Repeat three times.

Sitting Back Stretch

- Slowly bend over, sliding your hands to your feet.
- Lower your head between your arms.
- Relax your shoulders and neck until you feel the stretch.
- Do not bounce to extend your reach.
- Hold for 15 seconds.
- Repeat three times.

Head Rotation

- Sitting or standing, slowly turn your head, first to the right (hold) and then to your left (hold).
- Repeat three to five times.

Neck Stretch: Chin to Chest

- Sitting or standing, slowly lower your chin to your chest.
- Hold for 15 seconds, then lift your head up.
- Repeat three to five times.

Stretching for Health

Side Stretch

- Sitting or standing with hands together, reach overhead.
- Keeping your back straight, slowly bend from the waist to the right.
- Hold the stretch for 15 seconds. Breathe normally.
- Repeat three times on each side.

Tricep and Shoulder Stretch

- Place your right palm on your back, just below your neck, with your elbow pointing toward the ceiling.
- Place your left hand on your right elbow and gently push to a point of tension.
- Hold for 15 seconds.
- Repeat three times on each arm.

Shoulder/Arm Stretch

- Sit or stand with your back straight.
- Place your hands above your head—arms behind your ears—with fingers interlaced and palms facing the ceiling.
- Slowly press your hands toward the ceiling until you feel the stretch.
- Hold the stretch for 15 seconds. Repeat three times.

"Rack" Stretch

- Lie on the floor with your arms extended overhead.
- Slowly stretch by extending your arms and legs. Hold for 15 seconds. Breathe normally.
- Repeat three times.

11

Stretching for Health

Back Press (pelvic tilt)

- Lie on the floor with knees bent and feet flat on the floor.
- Slowly press the small of your back to the floor.
- Don't hold your breath.
- Hold for 15 seconds.
- Repeat three times.

Hip/Gluteal Stretch

- Lie on the floor with both knees bent.
- Keep your head on the floor.
- With your hands behind and slightly above your knee, slowly pull your right knee toward your chest.
- Hold for 15 seconds. Repeat three times with each leg.

Hamstring/Lower Leg Stretch

- Lie on the floor with both knees bent.
- Slowly raise your left leg until it is perpendicular to the floor. Stretch to a point of tension and hold for 15 seconds.
- Next, flex your foot to stretch your calf, then point your toes to stretch the front of your lower leg.
- Repeat three times with each leg.

Building Strong Muscles

Strength training usually has been reserved for younger and middle-aged adults rather than older adults because doctors have feared that lifting weights could be dangerous to those with such problems as arthritis, heart disease, and hypertension. However, research now shows that strength training can provide significant benefits to most adults. These benefits include increasing muscle mass, protecting the major joints from injury, improving balance, reducing falls, and improving a person's ability to do work.

The exercises on the following pages are designed to condition the major muscle groups of the body. Equipment is limited to dumbbells and ankle weights and can be done in your home. Other equipment options for upper body toning can include using empty detergent bottles (with handles) that can be filled with water or sand to a desired weight or even soup cans that can provide adequate resistance.

Finally, consider joining a local fitness facility (e.g., health club, YMCA/YWCA, company fitness center) that has a variety of resistance equipment and trained supervision to help you develop a safe and effective weight-training program.

General Guidelines for Strength Training

• If you have any chronic health conditions such as heart disease, high blood pressure, or arthritis, or any other health problem, talk to your doctor before starting.

• Be sure to properly warm-up the areas you will exercise and perform flexibility exercises after the strength-training session.

• Use hand or ankle weights that are not too heavy and you can handle with control. Better yet, join a health club that has circuit training equipment and trained supervision.

• Do each movement slowly with control (keep steady tension on the muscle; jerking weights will increase risk of injury) through the full range of motion for 10 to 15 repetitions. This is called one set.

• Breathe naturally, out on exertion and in on recovery.

• Initially, try one set per exercise for at least two weeks. As you gain strength and if you have no soreness or injury, add another set. Rest two to three minutes between sets. You'll know you're working the muscle hard enough when at the end of the set you feel almost as though you couldn't do another repetition; your muscle should feel challenged but not burn.

• If you injure a specific muscle or have significant muscle soreness, don't exercise this muscle group until discomfort is gone.

• Weight training should be done two to three days per week on alternate days.

Building Strong Muscles

Tricep Fly

Strengthens the shoulders and the backs of the upper arms

- Hold a weight or soup can in each hand with elbows bent at shoulder level.
- Extend both arms away from your body until they are parallel to the floor.
- Repeat 10–12 times for two to three sets.

Upright Row

Strengthens the shoulders

- Hold a weight in each hand at the front of the thighs.
- Raise both weights to armpit level, keeping your elbows higher than your hands. (If you shrug while doing this, you'll work trapezius muscles as well.)
- Next, lower the weights to the starting position.
- Repeat 10–12 times for two to three sets.

Shoulder Press

Strengthens the upper back and shoulders

- Sit on a bench with a weight in each hand at shoulder level.
- Slowly push one weight upward to full extension, then lower and push the other one upward.
- Alternate 10-12 repetitions with each arm for two to three sets.

Building Strong Muscles

Bicep Curl

Strengthens bicep, located at the front of the upper arm

- Sit on a bench or sturdy chair with a weight in each hand and arms straight down at your sides.
- Bending your left elbow, slowly raise the weight to your shoulder. Return to the starting position.
- Alternate arms.
- Do 10–12 repetitions.
- Repeat for two or three sets.

Standing Leg Curl

Strengthens hamstring, located at the back of the thigh

- Stand upright, holding on to the top of a chair.
- With an ankle weight on each ankle, slowly raise your right heel toward your buttocks. Then lower it to the starting position.
- Do 10–12 repetitions with each leg.
- Repeat for two or three sets.

Leg Extension

Strengthens quadricep, located at the front of the thigh

- Sit on a bench with an ankle weight on each ankle.
- Slowly extend both legs until they are parallel to the floor.
- Lower your legs with control.
- Do 10–12 repetitions.
- Repeat for two or three sets.

15

Abdominal Crunch

Strengthens abdominal muscles

- Lie on the floor with knees bent and feet flat on the floor.
- Place your arms across your chest.
- Without bending your neck, slowly raise your head and shoulders while pressing your lower back against the floor, then return slowly to the starting position.
- Don't hold your breath. Exhale as you lift up; inhale as you lower to the starting position.
- Do 15–20 repetitions.

Eating Right: Building Blocks of Nutrition

It is said that "we are what we eat," and science is beginning to back this statement with hard facts. As we better understand the effect dietary practices have on such conditions as heart disease, diabetes, and cancer, nutrition is becoming one of the most important building blocks for health longevity. And though the eating habits of Americans have slowly improved over the past 30 years, there's still significant room for improvement when you consider that half of all Americans are overweight.

The following nutritional guidelines can help you and your family develop and practice better dietary habits that will not only help you lower the risk for disease, but also help you control body weight and give you more energy.

Food for Thought

• **Eat a variety of foods.** Eat more breads, cereals, fruits, and vegetables and less meat, dairy, and fatty foods to reduce your risk of heart disease, cancer, diabetes, and obesity. Refer to the Food Pyramid on page 18.

• **Balance the food you eat with regular physical activity and maintain or improve your weight.** Besides good nutrition, regular physical activity is a powerful tool for controlling excessive body weight. Obesity is a significant risk factor for such conditions as hypertension, diabetes, and heart disease.

• **Choose a diet low in fat, saturated fat, and cholesterol.** Cut down on the amount of fat you eat, especially saturated fats found in marbled red meats, whole milk, many cheeses (e.g., cheddar and brie), and coconut and palm oils. The more fat you cut out of your diet, the more calories you save and the lower your health risks become. For example:

–Choose lean meats, poultry, and fish.

–Increase your consumption of fish and skinless poultry to two to three servings per week.

–Trim away visible fat.

–Try low-fat cooking methods such as broiling, baking, and steaming.

–When oils are needed, use those with monounsaturated fat such as canola and olive oils.

–Substitute high-fat foods with lower-fat foods. Refer to page 23.

Contrary to what many people believe, only 25 percent of cholesterol is attributed to cholesterol-laden foods found in animal products. But animal fats are the primary cause of elevated cholesterol for most people. Besides reducing your total fat

F.Y.I   EAT 5-A-DAY

A simple way to eat for health and reduce your risk of heart disease, cancer, and hypertension is the so–called "5-A-Day for Better Health" program. It's recommended that all Americans consume a variety of fruits and vegetables daily in these categories:

1. Eat five servings of fruits and vegetables every day.

2. Eat at least one vitamin A-rich selection every day: e.g., apricots, cantaloupe, carrots, spinach, squash.

3. Eat at least one vitamin C-rich selection every day: e.g., orange, grapefruit, tomato juice, broccoli.

4. Eat at least one high-fiber selection every day: e.g., figs, prunes, dried peas, beans.

5. Eat cabbage family (cruciferous) vegetables several times per week: e.g., broccoli, cabbage, cauliflower.

Source: U.S. Department of Agriculture

Eating Right: Building Blocks of Nutrition

intake as described earlier, control your intake of cholesterol-rich foods. Limit your consumption of animal fats, organ meats (such as liver), lobster, shrimp, and eggs to reduce your risk of heart disease.

- **Choose a diet with plenty of grain products, vegetables, and fruits.** Eat more whole grains (e.g., barley and rice), fruits (e.g., apples and pears), vegetables (e.g., peas and carrots), cereals (e.g., raisin bran and oat bran), legumes (e.g., kidney and lima beans), and whole-wheat breads. To help you add more of the above to your diet, use the "5-A-Day for Better Health" program outlined on page 16.

- **Choose a diet moderate in salt and sodium.** Limit salt-cured, smoked, and nitrite-cured foods, and sodium-laden processed foods and snacks.

- **Moderate your alcohol consumption.** If you drink alcohol, limit your intake to fewer than two drinks per day if you are a male and no more than one drink per day if you are a female (pregnant women should not drink). Moderate alcohol use has been linked to a lower risk of heart disease. Overconsumption of alcohol increases the risk of cancer, liver disease, osteoporosis, and alcoholism.

F.Y.I

CALCIUM-RICH FOODS

Healthy eating includes having adequate levels of dietary calcium for the prevention of osteoporosis and, perhaps, hypertension. The following chart lists calcium-rich foods. It's recommended that adult men and women consume a minimum of 1,000 milligrams (mg) per day and postmenopausal women 1,500 mg.

Food	Serving Size	Calcium (mg)
Plain, low-fat yogurt	8 ounces	415
Canned sardines, with bones	3 ounces	371
Part skim-milk ricotta cheese	1/2 cup	334
Skim milk	1 cup	302–316
Two percent low-fat milk	1 cup	297–313
Swiss cheese	1 ounce	272
Soft-serve ice cream	1 cup	236
Non-fat dry milk	1/4 cup	209
Cheddar, muenster, or part skim-milk mozzarella	1 ounce	203–207
Raw oysters	4–6 medium	226
Slivered almonds	1/2 cup	179
Cooked, chopped collards	1/2 cup	178
Pasteurized, processed American cheese	1 ounce	174
Cooked broccoli	3/4 cup	108

Eating Right: Building Blocks of Nutrition

The ancient Egyptians built the pyramids from the bottom up. The U.S. government recommends that modern Americans apply that same principle to their eating habits.

The Department of Agriculture issued a "Food Pyramid" that lays out the U.S. Dietary Guidelines in graphic form. You should eat more servings of foods listed at the base of the pyramid—breads, cereals, fruits, and vegetables—and fewer servings of high-fat foods listed at the top (see illustration below).

The focus of the Food Pyramid is on the prevention of disease. The guidelines are based on the latest scientific research from organizations such as the National Institutes of Health, the American Heart Association, and the American Diabetes Association. Scientific studies show that good nutritional habits can lower your risk of heart disease and some cancers.

Following are some ideas about how to build the pyramid principle into your everyday life.

- **Breakfast:** Don't neglect breakfast! It's your most important meal of the day. Eating breakfast helps you feel alert and can save you from mid-morning snack binges. Try these tips:
  - Instead of high-fat eggs, bacon, and doughnuts, try cereal, low-fat yogurt or cottage cheese, or a bagel with a low-fat spread. Always try to include a piece of fruit.
  - If it's hard to find time for a sit-down breakfast at home, you can eat fruit and a bagel in the car or on the bus. Or try getting to work a little earlier and eating a "brown-bag" breakfast.
  - Experiment: If you don't like regular breakfast foods, try lunch or dinner food instead.
  - If you're at a fast-food restaurant, order the pancakes instead of the high-fat croissant or biscuit sandwich.

- **Lunch:** No matter where you eat lunch—your desk, the cafeteria, a restaurant—you can make it nutritious and enjoyable. A bonus: A lunch that's lower in fat will help you avoid mid-afternoon sluggishness. Here are a few suggestions:
  - Try packing a balanced brown-bag lunch: a vegetable like cut-up celery; a sandwich with turkey, chicken, or tuna (hold the mayo!); a piece of fruit; fig bars or graham crackers. Or instead of the sandwich, bring leftovers from home.
  - If you eat in the cafeteria, try the salad bar. Be sure not to load up your plate with hidden fats: salads made with mayonnaise; heavy dressings. Your cafeteria also may offer special "health plates" that list total calories, percentage of total and saturated fats, cholesterol, protein, and carbohydrates, and that conform with recommended levels.
  - If you're eating out, try to select main dishes that are broiled or steamed instead of fried. Also, try to include a vegetable side dish or order a main-dish salad. Most fast-food restaurants now post nutritional information—some of it may surprise you.

FAT
Use Sparingly.

DAIRY
2 servings per day for adults.

BEEF, PORK, POULTRY, FISH AND EGGS
2 to 3 servings at 2-3 ounces per serving.

FRUITS AND VEGETABLES
5 to 6 servings per day. Each serving equals 1/2 to 1 cup.

BREADS, CEREALS, GRAINS, PASTAS AND STARCHY VEGETABLES
6- 6-11 servings per day. The more active you are, the more servings you need.

Eating Right: Building Blocks of Nutrition

- **Snacks:** Snacking can help you meet your daily dietary requirements and give you a satisfying pick-me-up in the mid-morning or late afternoon. Try these ideas:
  - –raisins or other dried fruit
  - –low-fat crackers, pretzels, popcorn
  - –fresh fruit or vegetables, canned fruit packed in water
  - –unsweetened cereal, bagels

  If you make regular trips to the vending machine, find out what's in the food you select. Is it high in fat (greater than 30 percent of total calories)? Is it high in sodium (one serving is large in proportion to your daily limit of 2,000 mg of sodium)?

- **Dinner:** With today's busy schedules, it's often hard to plan for dinner. But try doing so before going to the grocery store. Stock up on fruits, vegetables, pasta, rice, whole-grain breads, and lean meats to have on hand for quick meal preparation. Also, consider these suggestions:
  - –To cut down on fat, broil meats instead of frying them. Be sure to trim all visible fat from meat before cooking.
  - –Try to round out your daily recommended servings of fruits and vegetables (at least five servings). Microwave cooking is great for vegetables: It helps to preserve nutrients.
  - –Eat two to three meatless meals per week: You can reduce your intake of high-fat foods by preparing two to three plant-based meals per week with no meat, poultry, or fish.
  - –Be aware of hidden fat in cheeses, sauces, gravies, dressings, and nuts.

- **Beverages:** Drink six to eight 8-ounce glasses of water daily, to aid in digestion and weight control. Also, try to moderate your consumption of caffeine, alcohol, and sugary drinks. Fruit juice, sparkling water, and decaffeinated tea make good substitutes.

- **Vitamins:** Research has begun to support the regular use of specific "anti-oxidant" supplements, namely vitamins C and E, in counteracting so-called free radicals. Free radicals are natural byproducts of oxidation (the use of oxygen in the production of energy) and are associated with cell damage that may increase the risks of such health problems as heart disease and certain cancers. "Optimal" daily dosages are still being debated, but many experts recommend the following intake ranges: 500 to 1,000 milligrams of vitamin C and 400 to 800 IUs of vitamin E. Don't overdo it: Megadoses of vitamins C and E can cause such side effects as diarrhea and headache.

  A word of caution: Recent studies have shown that beta-carotene (vitamin A) supplements do not reduce the risk of cancer or heart disease. In fact, megadoses of beta-carotene may increase the risk of lung cancer among smokers (those with at least a pack-a-day habit) and asbestos-industry workers. Therefore, vitamin supplementation should first be discussed with your doctor, especially if you are a heavy smoker, drinker, or use certain medications that thin the blood.

Resources

Eat for Life, Catherine Woteki and Paul Thomas, eds. Washington, D.C.: National Academy Press, 1992.

"USDA's Food Pyramid Guide"
USDA Home and Garden Bulletin No. 252
Consumer Information Center
Dept. 159-Y
Pueblo, CO 81009
$1 per copy
Make check payable to "Superintendent of Documents."

Reading Food Nutrition Labels

Is one cookie really one serving? What is the Recommended Daily Allowance? Is the food I am eating really good for me?

To help consumers make healthful food choices, the Food and Drug Administration requires that all packaged foods have a nutrition label that assesses the "percent daily value" of the food. The following diagram will help you learn how to read a food label. It's easy when you know what to look for:

Nutrition Facts

Serving Size 1 cup (228g)
Servings Per Container 2

Amount Per Serving

Calories 260   Calories from Fat 120

	% Daily Value *
Total Fat 13g	20%
Saturated Fat 5g	25%
Cholesterol 30mg	10%
Sodium 660mg	28%
Total Carbohydrate 31g	10%
Dietary Fiber 0g	0%
Sugars 5g	
Protein 5g	

Vitamin A 4%	• Vitamin C 2%
Calcium 15%	• Iron 4%

* Percent Daily Values are based on a 2,000 calorie diet. Your daily values may be higher or lower depending on your calorie needs:

	Calories:	2,000	2,500
Total Fat	Less than	65g	80g
Saturated Fat	Less than	20g	25g
Cholesterol	Less than	300mg	300mg
Sodium	Less than	2,400mg	2,400mg
Total Carbohydrate		300g	375g
Dietary Fiber		25g	30g

Calories per gram:
    Fat 9   •   Carbohydrate 4   •   Protein 4

Tells you the serving size in both household and metric measures.

This line tells you the total calories per serving and the total calories of fat per serving.

The left column lists key nutrients that are important to overall health. Next to each is an indication of the total amount of each nutrient. The % Daily Value tells you how much this food (one serving) contributes to your overall daily diet.

This section also tells you how much of key vitamins and minerals are in the food, measured in terms of the recommended daily allowance.

This table helps you determine how much of a certain nutrient you need on a daily basis, depending on your calorie needs. For example, active individuals need more calories per day and need to adjust accordingly.

This line helps you calculate total calories in certain foods: one fat gram has nine calories, one gram of carbohydrates has four calories, one gram of protein has four calories. For example, a food that has 10 grams of fat has 90 calories from fat, since there are nine calories in one fat gram. (10 g x 9 calories/g = 90 total calories from fat)

Understanding Food Labels

In the past, it was difficult to keep track of all we needed to know about nutrition. Food labels didn't always help: Is "lite" really light? What's considered "high fiber"? In the past, the food industry was liberal in how they labeled their products—many times stretching their claims. To bring standards to food labeling, the Food and Drug Administration now requires that all packages conform to a set criteria before they can use such terms as "sodium free" or "fat free." Below are some common label descriptions and their requirements.

TERM	DEFINITION
"Light"	One-third fewer calories than in the regular product
"Fresh"	Raw; never frozen, processed, or preserved
"Free"	Per serving: Calorie free: less than 5 calories Sugar free: less than 0.5 g of sugar Sodium free: less than 5 mg of sodium Fat free: less than 0.5 g of fat Cholesterol free: less than 2 mg of cholesterol Saturated fat free: less than 2 g of saturated fat
"High"	Provides more than 20 percent of the recommended daily consumption of the nutrient, as in "high fiber"
"Lean"	Cooked meat or poultry with less than 10.5 g of fat, of which less than 3.5 g is saturated fat, and with less than 94.5 mg of cholesterol per 100 g
"Extra Lean"	Cooked meat or poultry with less than 4.9 g of fat, of which less than 1.8 g is saturated fat, and with less than 94.5 mg of cholesterol per 100 g
"Less"	At least 25 percent less sodium, calories, fat, saturated fat, or cholesterol than in the regular product
"Low"	Per 100 g or 3.5 ounces: Low sodium: less than 140 mg of sodium Low calorie: less than 40 calories Low fat: 3 g or less of fat Low saturated fat: 1 g or less of saturated fat and not more than 15 percent of calories from saturated fat Low cholesterol: 20 mg or less of cholesterol and 2 g or less of saturated fat
"More"	At least 10 percent more of the nutrient than in the regular product
"Source of"	Provides 10 percent to 20 percent of the recommended daily consumption of the nutrient

Source: U.S. Food and Drug Administration

Watching Your Weight

Losing weight—and keeping it off—can benefit your health as well as your appearance, helping to lower cholesterol and blood pressure and reducing the risk of stroke, heart disease, and diabetes. Many people try to lose weight through crash diets or programs that promise quick weight loss. The fact is, there's no really effective quick-fix diet plan. Instead, you need to focus on successful weight management, which involves three key concepts.

Avoid Crash Dieting

Permanent weight loss doesn't result from drastic methods: Losing weight rapidly through crash diets usually leads to a gradual return of body fat within six months. For many people, weight loss and gain becomes a repeating cycle. Research suggests that this practice, called "yo-yo dieting," increases the risk of coronary heart disease, especially among men. To keep weight off permanently, experts recommend that you lose no more than two pounds per week.

For most people, weight gain can be traced to three main factors: 1) food choices that are too high in fat; 2) too much food intake; 3) lack of physical activity. In most cases, successful weight management comes from making small changes in your everyday eating and activity patterns.

Make a Long-Term Commitment

A successful weight-management program involves long-term behavior change that aims for a gradual reduction in body fat rather than body weight. Inches lost serves as a better measure than pounds lost, since it indicates that you are increasing your lean body mass (muscle) and reducing your total percentage of body fat. Approaching weight loss as a gradual process instead of a crash program is a safer and more effective way to get rid of unwanted fat.

Have a Positive Imagination

Someone once said: "When it comes down to willpower vs. imagination, imagination always wins." Most people blame their weight problems on a lack of willpower, when they may need to do some positive thinking. During any behavior change, it's important to focus on the positive benefits of your change (e.g., more energy, better appearance, improved health) and not on what you're giving up. Believe that you can and will change. Treat any progress toward your goal as a mini-victory. And don't get discouraged if your progress levels off for a time—it happens. Stick to your plan and focus on the positive.

Ideas that Work

- **Eat less fat**. A diet that gets 30 percent or fewer of its calories from fat can help you avoid a variety of health problems and shed excess pounds, too. (The average for American diets is 34 percent.) Try these suggestions for reducing fat in your diet:
  - Choose foods that have fewer than three grams of fat for every 100 calories. Watch serving sizes that tend to be small—they may be loaded with calories from fat. See page 22.
  - Watch your snacking. Try to select low-fat foods. Good choices: low-fat yogurt, fig bars, raisins, popcorn, fresh fruit, and cut-up veggies.
  - Be prepared. Watch how you prepare and cook your foods. Trim excess fat from meats. Remove skin from poultry. Try to broil or bake rather than fry meat selections.
  - Undress. A low-fat baked potato or salad "dressed-up" can quickly become a fat and/or calorie nightmare. Try low-fat yogurt instead of sour cream and cheeses on your baked potato. Try vinegar and oil or low-fat dressings instead of regular high-fat salad dressings.
  - Substitute high-fat, high-calorie foods with low-fat, lower-calorie alternatives.
- **Increase your daily physical activity.** Physical activity will increase your success in losing fat and maintaining ideal weight—and will improve your overall health. Exercise not only burns calories and fat during your activity, but also keeps your body burning calo-

Watching Your Weight

ries for hours after you stop. Exercise also increases your lean body mass (e.g., muscle), which, unlike fat, burns calories while the body is at rest. Physical activity includes walking, cycling, and swimming, as well as manual labor, gardening, and other household chores.

Your exercise program doesn't need to be strenuous. For example, moderate, sustained activity such as 40 minutes of walking five days a week can produce significant weight loss within 12 weeks. See "Walking," page 6.

NOTE: If you're over age 40, have been inactive, or have a medical condition such as high blood pressure, heart disease, diabetes, or joint problems, consult your doctor before starting a weight-loss and exercise program.

- **Eat smaller portions and more often.** This will help your body use calories more efficiently.
- **Look at the mirror, not the scale.** As fat decreases and lean body mass (which is heavier than fat) increases, your weight may actually go up for a while. That's OK. You're becoming trimmer.
- **Keep a diary.** Write down your eating habits: when and what you eat, who's with you, your mood (e.g., bored, nervous, hurried). This helps you identify common eating triggers that most likely are not related to hunger but to habits.
- **Drink plenty of water**–six to eight 8-ounce glasses a day. Ironically, if you drink sufficient water, your body won't try to retain so much of it.

Resources

The Duke University Medical Center Book of Diet and Fitness, by Michael Hamilton, et al. New York: Fawcett Columbine, 1993.

The Fast Food Guide, by Michael F. Jacobson and Sarah Fritscher, eds. New York: Workman Publishers, 1991.

Your Body Mass Index (BMI)

It's important not to have too much fat around your waist. Your health risks—such as diabetes, high blood pressure, osteoarthritis, gallbladder disease, certain cancers, sleep apnea, respiratory problems, stroke, and coronary artery disease—are a lot higher if:

- your waist measures more than 40 inches around if you're a man or 35 inches if you're a woman
- your body mass index (BMI) is high (see below).

BMI shows how body weight relates to height. A high BMI usually means extra body fat—although some people who have a lot of muscle may have a high BMI without having higher health risks.

Use the chart to the right to find your BMI. Draw a line from left to right from your "height." Next, draw a line up from your "weight" to the top of the chart. The point where the two lines cross will show you the category you are in.

SOURCE: National Heart, Lung and Blood Institute

How Does Your Weight Rank?

Height: 6'6", 6'5", 6'4", 6'3", 6'2", 6'1", 6'0", 5'11", 5'10", 5'9", 5'8", 5'7", 5'6", 5'5", 5'4", 5'3", 5'2", 5'1", 5'0", 4'11", 4'10"

Healthy Weight / Overweight / Obese

Weight in Pounds: 50, 75, 100, 125, 150, 175, 200, 225, 250

Watch Your Blood Pressure

Blood pressure is the amount of force blood exerts against artery walls as it flows through them. It is measured and recorded as two numbers: systolic pressure, the peak force when the heart beats (contracts); and diastolic pressure, the force against the artery walls when the heart is between beats.

The American Heart Association defines acceptable blood pressure as below 130/85 mmHg. The lower the numbers, within reason, the lower your risk. Blood pressure of 120/80 mmHg is considered optimal.

People with high blood pressure (140/90 or higher) or with readings in the "high normal range" (a systolic reading of 130 to 139 or a diastolic reading of 85 to 89) should take steps to manage their hypertension.

"Essential hypertension," where the cause cannot be determined, accounts for 90 percent of hypertension cases. The remaining 10 percent are caused by such conditions as kidney disease and tumors. Left untreated, high blood pressure increases the risk of stroke, heart disease, kidney failure, and blindness.

Risk factors for high blood pressure include previous family history; gender (affects more males than females); race (affects African-Americans more than other ethnic groups); being overweight; high alcohol consumption; a sedentary lifestyle; uncontrolled stress; and excessive sodium (salt) consumption.

Blood pressure is easily measured through a pressure cuff, gauge, and stethoscope or computerized instrument. It's recommended that you have your blood pressure measured once a year by a health professional. You may want to buy a test kit for home monitoring. The American Red Cross or your health care provider can teach you the proper way to measure your blood pressure.

Ideas that Work

- **Prevention is the key.** Reduce your risk of developing hypertension with the following self-care practices: maintain your ideal weight; exercise most, if not all, days of the week; avoid eating prepared foods that are high in sodium; throw away the salt shaker; eat foods rich in potassium (e.g., bananas, oranges, potatoes, and green vegetables) and calcium (e.g., low-fat milk and yogurt). If you smoke, try to quit. If you already have high blood pressure, the same strategies are recommended to manage and reduce it. In fact, regular exercise, such as cycling for a minimum of 20 minutes five times per week, has been shown to reduce the need for blood pressure medication by up to 40 percent.

- **Follow your doctor's recommendations.** In general, if you have been diagnosed with hypertension, your doctor will not only recommend lifestyle changes (see above), but also will put you on a medication schedule. Your treatment usually is "stepped." With a stepped care plan, you begin by taking a small dose of a specific anti-hypertensive drug or drugs. You and your doctor carefully monitor blood pressure changes and any side effects and adjust dose accordingly. Refer to pages 271-272 for a further discussion of high blood pressure.

- **Stick to it.** Don't change your treatment schedule without your doctor's prior approval. Tell your doctor about any side effects, such as headaches, fatigue, and extra or skipped heartbeats.

Resources

Your doctor

The American Red Cross. Check your phone directory for the chapter nearest you.

Check Your Cholesterol

Cholesterol is a waxy substance found in the tissue and blood stream of the body that is critical for maintaining healthy cell function. Our bodies manufacture cholesterol, and we also get it by eating certain foods, especially saturated fats. Within the body, cholesterol is transported through the blood stream by being attached to protein packages called lipoproteins. The two main lipoproteins are low-density lipoproteins (LDLs) and high-density lipoproteins (HDLs). HDLs are called the "good cholesterol," since they act as "garbage men" that prevent cholesterol from binding to the inner linings of blood vessels. The action of HDLs helps prevent the development of atherosclerosis, the major culprit in clogged arteries, which leads to coronary artery disease and stroke. LDLs, on the other hand, are considered the "bad cholesterol" because high levels of LDLs in the body promote the development of atherosclerosis.

How Is Cholesterol Measured?

Cholesterol is measured through blood analysis. First, a sample of blood is taken, either through a simple finger prick or by drawing blood from a vein. The sample is analyzed for total cholesterol and for LDLs and HDLs.

Cholesterol is measured in milligrams per deciliter (mg/dl). The chart below summarizes generally accepted values.

Ideas that Work

- **Restrict your total intake of saturated fats.** Limit such foods as butter, hard cheeses, meat fat, and coconut, palm, and hydrogenated vegetable oils. Replace saturated fats with monounsaturated fats found in olive and canola oils. Read food labels carefully. Try to keep your total intake of fats below 30 percent of daily calories and total intake of cholesterol below 300 mg.

- **Keep moving.** Increase your daily physical activity through aerobic exercise such as brisk walking, jogging, cycling, and swimming. Regular physical activity increases the level of HDL, the good cholesterol, in your body.

- **Bulk up.** Increase your intake of soluble fiber, found in oat bran, apples, legumes, and other vegetables. A good guideline is to try to eat a minimum of five servings of fruits and vegetables daily. Refer to page 16.

- **Maintain your ideal weight.** Obese people have been found to have lower HDL concentrations and higher levels of LDL.

- **Learn to manage stress.** Some studies have shown that people who exhibit so-called "Type A" personality traits, such as free-floating hostility, extreme competitiveness, time urgency, and impatience, have a higher rate of heart disease.

TYPE	DESIRED LEVELS	MODERATE RISK	HIGH RISK
Total Cholesterol	Below 200 mg/dl	200 mg/dl to 239 mg/dl	240 mg/dl and higher
HDL	Above 60 mg/dl	35 to 59 mg/dl	Below 35 mg/dl
LDL	Below 130 mg/dl	130 to 159 mg/dl	Above 160 mg/dl

Check Your Cholesterol

• **Follow your physician's advice.** Individuals who have cholesterol readings over 240 mg/dl may be advised by their physician to take a cholesterol-lowering medication, combined with following the lifestyle practices listed on page 25. As with any medication, it's important to follow the recommended schedule and dosage requirements in order to see results.

• **Give me an "E"!** Taking a daily supplement of vitamin E (400 International Units) may help reduce the effectiveness of LDL cholesterol (the bad cholesterol) in damaging the artery walls. However, this does not replace the other strategies listed on page 25 in controlling your cholesterol.

• **Watch your numbers.** Experts recommend that all adults have their cholesterol measured every five years after age 35 for men and after age 45 for women.

On the other hand, if you have a family history of heart attack before age 50 or exhibit other risk factors such as diabetes, high blood pressure, obesity, smoking, and a sedentary lifestyle, your doctor may recommend more frequent screening and at an earlier age. Otherwise, you can follow the standard guidelines.

Resources

Your primary care physician

Your local chapter of the American Heart Association. Check the white pages of your phone book.

Stopping Smoking

Mahatma Gandhi once said, "Don't give up anything until you don't need it anymore." Well, when it comes to smoking, you don't need it anymore.

Nicotine is highly addictive, so it's hard to give up, even for people with strong willpower. (In fact, chewing tobacco is 12 times more addictive than the smoked form. The same quitting principles apply for chewing tobacco.)

True, quitting "cold turkey" may be the only program some people need. Others, however, need group support or self-help materials. And heavy smokers may do best with nicotine-replacement therapy (NRT), combined with behavior modification.

Here are the five basic phases in a typical stop-smoking program:

Phase One: Pre-Conditioning

Get in shape before you quit. Research suggests that people who adopt healthy lifestyle habits have a better chance of staying smoke-free once they stop.

- Exercise most, if not all, days of the week: Walk briskly, ride a bicycle, swim, or pursue other aerobic activities you enjoy.
- Reach your ideal weight by reducing your fat intake. Choose snacks wisely.
- Learn relaxation techniques and put them into your daily routine.

Phase Two: Establishing Your "Quit Date"

Don't stretch your smoking cessation out over a number of months. Reducing how many cigarettes you smoke or switching to a low-tar, low-nicotine brand may only prolong your withdrawal symptoms. Instead, set your quit date and allow only 30 to 45 days to cut down. Once your quit date arrives, stop.

Phase Three: Preparing to Quit

During the 30-to-45-day Quitting Period, keep a record of how much you smoke each day.

Develop alternatives to smoking that you can use when you crave a cigarette: Drink a glass of water, chat with a friend, chew sugarless gum, play with a pencil or paper clip. Do whatever it takes. Explore available resources that can help you in your quitting efforts—convince a friend to quit with you, enroll in a smoking cessation class, or talk to your doctor about using NRT or other medication options. (Caution: Pregnant women and people with heart or blood vessel problems should not use NRT.)

Phase Four: On Your Quit Date

This is a day to celebrate! Give yourself a reward: a special meal, a new outfit, or tickets to a sports event or concert. Discard any remaining cigarettes. You are now a nonsmoker.

Phase Five: Living Life as a Nonsmoker

Take credit for a job well done. Continue to get regular exercise, eat right, and use relaxation techniques. Other strategies for staying with your program:

- Avoid places or events where many people will be smoking.
- Chew sugarless gum or eat natural snacks for a healthful "fix."
- Don't tell yourself that just one won't hurt. And if you find yourself smoking—stop right away. You can quit permanently.
- If you do fail at your first attempt to quit, don't be discouraged! Most people make five to seven attempts before they quit. Each attempt moves you closer to success. So try again!

Resources

American Cancer Society. Contact your local chapter for information and stop smoking programs.

American Lung Association. Contact your local chapter about their "Freedom from Smoking Program."

Sharpen Your Stress Management Skills

Stress is your body's response to what it understands to be a threat. Stress begins as a physical reaction that makes you behave and think in ways that will help you handle the threat. In itself, stress is not unhealthy; in fact, it is one of the many responses your body uses to help you survive.

Things that you perceive as threats are called stressors. In general, physical threats create stress in all of us. But threats don't have to involve physical harm to be stressful. The threat could be to your self-esteem, as when somebody verbally abuses you, but you may have the same feeling as if you were being physically attacked.

Stressors vary from person to person. Something that you consider threatening might not bother your co-worker at all. For example, you might not like to work under deadline pressure; your friend doesn't mind deadlines, but hates it when his supervisor looks over his shoulder.

Getting Physical: Fighting "Imaginary Tigers"

Whenever you think that something is a threat, your body instantly gets ready for physical danger. It automatically takes steps to help you deal with that danger, either by fighting off the attack or running away. This reaction, called the "fight-or-flight response," has been handed down from your earliest ancestors. You share it with all animal species.

Imagine that someone is shouting and starts running toward you. You might hesitate for a second as you sort out the signals, but your body has sensed the threat of trouble and has begun preparing for action:

–Your nervous system releases powerful chemicals that result in extra physical strength.

–You start breathing harder and faster.

–Your fatty tissues release energy stored as fat and your liver releases blood sugars to give your muscles more power.

–Your brain orders the release of hormones that make you more alert and keep your first burst of strength going. It also releases chemicals that ease pain.

–Within a couple of seconds, you have extra strength, alertness, energy, and endurance to protect yourself from an attack.

The fight-or-flight response also is called the "stress response," because the dangers that trigger it don't have to be physical. Anything that your brain and nervous system see as a threat will put you on the same "red alert" status. *Is this reaction needed when you're faced with most day-to-day stressors? Probably not.* Many times we overreact to what we think are threats, when a calmer, problem-solving approach would be more effective—and cause far less tension and stress.

Some other thoughts on stress:

- **Stress can be helpful.** The extra resources provided by the stress response can be useful in many situations. On the job, for example, the stress response can give you the inspiration that helps you perform at your best when making an important sales presentation or meeting a tough production goal. But too much stress that's not controlled can limit your concentration, make you more prone to accidents, and negatively affect your physical and mental well-being.

- **How chronic stress affects you.** In the normal course of the stress response, your body relaxes and goes back to its normal level of arousal after the threat has passed. If stress doesn't go away, you can get stuck in high gear; your body doesn't slow down and you're in a constant state of tension. In fact, some people get to a point where they barely notice this constant state of tension—until their symptoms get too bad to ignore. *Their stress has become chronic.*

- **Watch out.** When stress is frequent or chronic, the effects can quickly build up and take a serious toll on every part of your body and on every aspect of your life.

28

Sharpen Your Stress Management Skills

For example, chronic stress:

– Elevates blood cholesterol, a major risk factor for stroke and heart disease. Other risks include high blood pressure and the sudden closing (spasm) of the blood vessels that supply the heart with oxygen. Repeated stress reactions can damage other organs, including kidneys, stomach, skin and lungs, leading to ulcers, chronic gastritis, skin rashes, and asthma.

– Can affect your mental state. The self-protective reactions of alertness, fear, and aggression may slowly become long-term conditions of anxiety, anger, and other mental disorders, such as depression. Some people try to relieve these problems with food, alcohol, cigarettes, tranquilizers, painkillers, or other drugs. These kinds of behavior are not only harmful in their own right, they also keep you from addressing the real cause of the problem.

– Can affect your relationships with your loved ones and your ability to enjoy your leisure time.

– Can affect your concentration or make it difficult for you to deal with others.

– Often leads people to arguments with family, friends, co-workers and supervisors, as well as absenteeism and burnout.

– Can undermine the way you feel about yourself, leading to poor self-esteem, chronic fatigue, and depression.

• **Taking control of stress.** You don't have to be a victim of uncontrolled stress. In fact, you have the power to reduce the effects of stress in your life.

The following pages provide a basic overview of stress management techniques. These can help you develop an understanding of your own stressors and how you react to them, and give you some strategies to reduce their impact.

How Do You Handle Stress?

This worksheet will help you assess how you currently respond to stress. Look at your answers again after you've read this section to see what changes you could make to better handle the stressors in your life.

• **How much stress do you think you currently have in your life?**
❏ Constant
❏ Too much
❏ Occasional
❏ I wish I had some

• **What are your most common sources of stress? (check all that apply)**
❏ Other people
❏ Family problems (children, parents, spouse)
❏ Health problems
❏ Money problems
❏ Separation or divorce
❏ Job security
❏ Change
❏ Not enough authority to do my job
❏ Conflicts between work and family needs
❏ Lack of confidence in my own abilities and self-worth
❏ Boredom
❏ Overwork
❏ Loneliness
❏ Name your own:_____
_____
_____

Sharpen Your Stress Management Skills

- **Identify one of the previously listed stressors that is the most stressful to you.**

    My main stressor is:

    _____

- **Who's at "fault"?** What's the source of your main stressor? To what degree do you feel you create it or contribute to it?

    _____
    _____
    _____

- **Who's in control?** How much influence do you have in controlling the situation?
    - ❏ A lot of control
    - ❏ Some control
    - ❏ A little control
    - ❏ None at all

- **How do you normally react?** What emotions do you feel when you're faced with the stressor (e.g., anger, hurt, frustration, anxiety)? Do you hold them inside or do you express them? Are you usually glad or sorry that you did?

    _____
    _____
    _____
    _____
    _____

- **How do you feel physically?** Do you feel tense or fatigued? Do you have headaches, insomnia, stomach problems, or trouble eating?

    _____
    _____
    _____

- **How do you act?** What do you do when you're faced with the stressor (e.g., ignore it, run away from the problem, deal with it directly)? How do you normally try to reduce the "threat" or pressure (e.g., use alcohol or drugs, exercise, overeat, try relaxation techniques)?

    _____
    _____
    _____
    _____
    _____

- **Do you think your reactions and actions help or hurt the situation and yourself?** Do you consider your emotions and actions positive or negative? Would you do anything different the next time you experience the same stressor?

    _____
    _____
    _____

- **Do you need help?** Do you think you need help or support in trying to cope with this problem? Who do you think can help you?

    _____
    _____
    _____

What Does this Mean?

This exercise is intended to help you begin to identify the key stress in your life, its main sources, and how you normally respond.

By taking this self-assessment, you may have discovered that you help create stress in your life by overreacting to situations and act in a manner that's counterproductive. Go back and list other important stressors in your life and see how you normally face each situation.

Taking Charge of Stress

Two people who work side by side or who have been married for 10 years experience different kinds and amounts of stress. Why? Because the stress they experience is actually the result of a constantly changing relationship between two kinds of stressors:

1. *Job Stressors* that "come with the territory" of the work itself.
2. *Personal Stressors* that are the result of issues, opinions, and attitudes that are related to family and other personal matters.

It's very difficult to leave your problems either at home or at the office. Therefore, your personal and job-related stress can easily spill into each other and negatively affect both areas of your life. Even if you can't control every stressful situation, you can have a big impact on how your stressors affect you. How? By identifying both your job stressors and your personal stressors, and understanding how they influence your behavior on and off the job.

Job Stressors

There are many issues and problems on the job that may call up your stress response: deadlines, work conditions, an irritating boss or co-worker, a tragic or frightening event. Some jobs have more stress than other jobs, but every job produces at least some stress.

Some of that stress is helpful, of course. Deadlines help make sure you get the work done. A tough but fair supervisor can inspire you to achieve much more than you expected. In fact, having too little stress on the job has been shown to be just as stressful as being overloaded.

Experts have discovered that the most stressful jobs have one striking thing in common: They make you feel as if you have no control over the work that you're trying to do. Here are some of the ways you can recognize a job that makes you feel helpless or out of control:

- It makes too many—or too few—demands on you.
- It is basically boring or routine, but you need to pay attention anyway; for example, assembly-line work, data entry, and office reception.
- You have no say as to how your time or your work is managed.
- The job duties are not well-defined.
- Management gives you no reason to feel valued or supported.
- You don't have the necessary resources or the authority to do the job.
- You get conflicting orders or mixed messages from supervisors.
- You have no guidance on how to do the job.
- You can suffer serious consequences for failure.

On the other hand, the feeling that you are in charge of your work has been identified as the greatest source of job satisfaction.

Personal Stressors

Personal stressors are problems and feelings that you bring from home to work. Some, like a desire to earn more money, can motivate you to do a better job. Others, like a health problem or worries about your family, can make every part of your job even more difficult.

Every person brings different stressors to the workplace, but many of them fall into these groups:

- **Competence.** Lack of skills to do the job. Fear of learning new things.
- **Health.** Not enough energy to get through the shift. Effects of alcohol or drug use. Physical problems, such as back pain or chronic illness.
- **Interpersonal relations.** Shyness. Quick temper or lack of trust. Impatience. Inability to work on a team. Inability to actively listen.

Sharpen Your Stress Management Skills

- **Work/family.** Overwork at home. Elder-care or child-care problems. An abusive or unsupportive partner. Money problems. Upcoming move or divorce.
- **Self-image.** Lack of confidence. Feeling of over-importance. Identifying too much with the job. Always seeing yourself as a victim.
- **Finances.** Worries about money. Living from paycheck to paycheck. Upcoming retirement.
- **Attitude.** Bored with job. Only interested in paycheck. Looking for easy way to do things. Believe that quality is someone else's problem.
- **Fears.** Afraid of change or of learning new skills. Avoiding something necessary to the job, like flying or public speaking. Fear of failure.
- **Poor coping behaviors.** Dealing with problems through drugs or alcohol. Avoiding stress by vegging out in front of the TV; taking out stress on friends or family members.

Once you have identified your stressors, you have begun to take steps to understand your "stress style"—the way you react and act in stressful situations.

A major key to stress control is being able to manage day-to-day stressors before they reduce your personal effectiveness. The following self-care skills can be used to help you avoid overload and reduce tension in your everyday life. When the cause of your stress is more serious, quick fixes are not enough. Refer to "Resources" on page 34 for additional assistance.

Ideas that Work

- **Change your perception.** Do you make a habit of "making a mountain out of a mole hill?" When faced with a "stressful situation," ask yourself: "What's the worst thing that can happen?"
- **Stop that thought!** When you have a stressful or negative thought, try this technique:
  - Stop the thought in midstream. Actually say to yourself: "Stop!"
  - Take a deep breath and exhale slowly.
  - Mentally, take a step back—look at the situation objectively.
  - Ask yourself: "Is my reaction (perception) overblown?"
  - Then ask yourself: "What's a more positive, constructive way to approach this problem?"
- **Learn to accept and use change to your advantage.** Build flexibility into your work and personal life. Try to accept the fact that life doesn't stand still. Adapting to change can be a healthy experience that helps you grow, though there will be bumps in the road. Also, anticipate change and prepare for it (e.g., pay off credit card bills, develop an emergency savings fund, research community elder-care services) before the change takes place.
- **Become a good communicator.** Poor communication is one of the main causes of stressful situations. Learn to be an active listener—try to understand what the other person is saying without interrupting. ("Try to walk in the other person's shoes.") When responding, address the behavior or the problem; avoid attacking the individual.
- **Take charge of the home front.** Take steps to get problems at home under control. Seek counseling for marriage or financial difficulties; work out a reliable solution for child-care or elder-care needs.
- **Keep your job skills up-to-date.** Boost your job skills so that you can be more confident about doing a good job.
- **Appreciate yourself and your abilities.** Increase your personal self-esteem so that you have the courage to take chances and handle the risk of failing. Before you leave work, name at least one thing that you feel good about in that day's work—zero reworks, paving a section of road, helping a customer handle a difficult problem, closing a sale, etc.

Sharpen Your Stress Management Skills

- **Pace yourself.** Pace your workflow—on and off the job—whenever you can, by staying organized, setting realistic timelines, and having needed resources available before you begin any project. Try to set aside 20 percent of your time for unplanned events or problems.

- **Avoid overloading on caffeine.** Coffee, tea, and cola drinks are stimulants that increase your heart rate and can make you more irritable. Try caffeine-free beverages instead.

- **Use your imagination to relax.** When you're feeling tense, find a space where you can sit quietly for 10 to 15 minutes. Try this visualization exercise:

  –Close your eyes.

  –Breathe normally.

  –Visualize yourself as a burlap bag full of sand, full of tension.

  –Your feet are the bottom corners of the bag.

  –The corners suddenly burst open, and the sand begins to run out.

  –Feel the sand run out of your feet, and all the tension that you feel run out, too.

  –Completely empty the bag of all the sand … all the tension.

  –Resume your normal activity.

- **Control your breathing to relax.** Most meditation exercises use breathing techniques to help relax the body and the mind. Try this simple relaxation technique:

  –Find a private spot where you can be quiet for 10 to 15 minutes.

  –Sit erect, with your hands in your lap.

  –Close your eyes.

  –Inhale deeply, hold your breath for five seconds and exhale slowly.

  –Sit quietly, concentrating on your breathing. Breathe through your nose.

  –On every exhale, say the word "calm."

  –With every exhale, feel your mind becoming more still.

  –Don't fight other thoughts or distractions; let them come … let them go.

  –Just concentrate on your breathing.

  –After 10 to 15 minutes, open your eyes. Remain seated for two to three minutes.

  –Resume your normal activity.

- **Tense, then relax.** Progressive relaxation is a popular relaxation technique that has been used for years. The idea is first to tense, then to relax, specific muscle groups in a regular order. Try this technique when you begin to get tense:

  –If possible, find a private, quiet room.

  –Lie on the floor. (If that's not possible, sit comfortably in an armchair.)

  –Loosen any tight clothing: belt, necktie, collar. Remove your shoes.

  –Close your eyes and breathe normally.

  –For each muscle group, tense the muscles for six seconds, then relax. Repeat three times before going to the next group of muscles.

  –The sequence: feet, calves, thighs, buttocks, shoulders (bring shoulders to ears if sitting, up off the floor if lying down), hands, forehead, jaw (make a face, stick out your tongue).

  –Reverse the sequence.

- **Walk it off.** A simple 20- to 30-minute walk has been shown to reduce muscular tension as much as some tranquilizers.

- **Stretch it out.** Simple stretching exercises are an effective way to reduce built-up tension in the neck, shoulders, and back. See pages 10-12.

- **Have a good belly laugh.** Some experts call a good laugh "inner jogging." Keep a book of jokes or humorous short stories close by. If you begin to feel angry or tense, take a humor break.

- **Tune up!** Playing classical or other selections can help you relax and concentrate. There are

Sharpen Your Stress Management Skills

also a number of relaxation tapes that combine nature sounds or soothing music with self-suggestive instructions that either ask you to visualize a specific scene or teach you to relax specific muscle groups.

- **Keep a journal.** A popular and effective way to manage stress is to keep a daily journal. Journal writing allows you to note your feelings on a given day: problems, insights, solutions, and outcomes. Many journal keepers find the exercise of journal writing a means of blowing off steam. Your journal also can be a record of personal growth.
- **Pray.** Many experts have shown that prayer is a very effective calming technique, comparable to other relaxation and meditation techniques.
- **Game it.** Simple mental diversions such as puzzles and video and computer games can take the edge off seriousness, ease tension, and even release a creative urge or two.

Resources

Your company or union employee assistance program

Your health care provider

Your local mental health agency

You Don't Have to Go Home From Work Exhausted!, by Ann McGee-Cooper, Duane Trammell and Barbara Lau. Dallas: Bowen & Rogers, 1990.

Mind as Healer, Mind as Slayer, by Kenneth R. Pelletier. New York: Dell Publishing, 1992.

The Seven Habits of Highly Effective People, by Stephen R. Covey. New York: Simon and Schuster, 1989.

Stress Map: Personal Diary Edition, by Esther Orioli, Dennis Jaffe, and Cynthia Scott. New York: Newmarket Press, 1987.

Stress Management for Wellness, by Walt Schafer. New York: Harcourt Brace Jovanovich, 1992.

Total Life Management Profile, by Marc Michaelson. San Francisco, Calif.: Lifeworks International, 1992.

Drug Abuse

Turn on the television or read the newspaper, and the impact of drugs on our society will be very evident. But contrary to what you may hear or see, drug abuse is not limited to the crack houses of the inner city or the glamorous "jet set." In fact, you may be working or living with a person who has a drug problem. Victims of drug abuse include:

- **The users themselves.** Drug abuse leads to physical and/or psychological addiction. If people share needles for intravenous drug use, they put themselves and sexual partners at risk of HIV or hepatitis infection.
- **The family.** Families of drug users may suffer neglect and physical and mental abuse. Pregnant women who use drugs such as heroin and cocaine place their unborn children at a greater risk for birth defects and infectious disease.
- **Co-workers.** Employees who work with a drug abuser may be victims of unsafe work practices and the abuser's unreliable job performance.
- **Companies.** Employees who abuse drugs cost companies money through increased health and disability claims, defective products, and a damaged reputation in the marketplace.
- **Society.** Consumers may suffer from defective products or services; people who use public transportation are at risk from operators who may use drugs on the job. Drug abuse costs taxpayers billions of dollars for treatment and law enforcement—money that could be spent on education, job training, and other needed services.

How Do Drugs Work?

Drugs that alter the chemistry of the brain and nervous system are called psychoactive agents. A psychoactive agent can act as a stimulant, a depressant, or a hallucinogen. Psychoactive substances are not limited to illegal "street drugs" such as cocaine, heroin, and marijuana, but also include prescription and over-the-counter medications, as well as the most widely used drugs: alcohol, nicotine, and caffeine. Each drug has a unique effect on the mind and body of the user, and can lead to a physical and/or psychological dependence.

Stimulants: Stimulants, or "uppers," raise the metabolism of the user. People use stimulants to stay alert, to get a rapid surge of energy, and to lose weight. "Household" stimulants include coffee, tea, cola drinks, and tobacco. Caffeine and nicotine both stimulate the central nervous system. Commonly used stimulants that are "controlled substances" (drugs that are strictly controlled or banned by federal laws) include cocaine and its highly addictive derivative, crack; amphetamines; and methamphetamine (speed).

Depressants: Commonly known as "downers," depressants slow down the activity of the central nervous system and alter people's perception of the outside world by narrowing their field of focus. Users commonly become withdrawn and "spaced out." Depressants include sedatives, sleep aids, and painkillers.

Alcohol is the most widely used depressant, although many people think it's a stimulant since it decreases people's inhibitions (see page 39). Controlled substances that are classified as depressants include barbiturates; narcotic agents such as heroin, morphine, opium, and codeine; and synthetic drugs such as Percodan,® Demerol,® and Darvon®.

Hallucinogens: Hallucinogens are chemical agents that alter a person's sense of reality. "Tripping" is the common term used to describe the effect of hallucinogens in enhancing and intensifying perception. LSD, mescaline, peyote, and magic mushrooms are substances that are normally ingested to produce hallucinogenic effects. An especially dangerous hallucinogen is PCP, or "Angel Dust," which often produces violent and unpredictable behavior in users. PCP usually is combined with marijuana or other leafy substances such as oregano or parsley, rolled in a cigarette, and smoked.

Drug Abuse

Common household items—such as glue, butane, gasolines, felt-tip marker fluid, propane, room odorizers—produce chemical vapors that can be inhaled to produce mind-altering effects. Young people are the most common abusers, probably because these inhalants are readily available and are inexpensive. Use of these substances can lead to heart failure or suffocation as oxygen is displaced in the lungs and central nervous system.

Cannabis: Cannabis products are taken from the leaves of the hemp plant and usually are sold as marijuana (grass), hashish (hash), hashish oil, or the chemical derivative THC (tetrahydrocannabinol). Usually smoked, cannabis products relax the user and create a mild sense of euphoria. In specific cases, cannabis has been prescribed to cancer patients to counteract the effects of chemotherapy.

Long-term use of cannabis has been linked to lung disease and a weakening of the immune system. Cannabis also affects memory, judgment, coordination, and other sensory motor skills, and can impair a person's ability to drive and operate machinery.

Do You Need Help?

Our message is simple: The use of illicit or other drugs is the quickest way to destroy your career and personal life. Unfortunately, many abusers wait to get help until their problem has compromised their life to such an extent that they have lost everything they value. If you think you have a drug problem, it's important to get help right away.

Getting Help...
The First Step to Recovery

The first step to overcoming a dependence on drugs is admitting that a problem exists and that change can't happen without the help of others. Most drug abusers say that this first step is the most difficult. Rehabilitation programs have up to a 70 percent success rate, and can help the person in recovery realize that he or she doesn't need drugs to cope or for instant gratification.

The following are resources that can provide professional support for drug treatment and recovery:
- If available, your company employee assistance program
- Local or national drug hotlines
- Anonymous Groups; e.g., Narcotics Anonymous (listed in the white pages)
- Local community drug rehabilitation centers (listed in the yellow pages)
- Your personal physician
- Your priest, minister, or rabbi

Recognizing Substance Abuse in Others

It's common for many people to attribute a person's erratic behavior to anything but drug abuse, especially if the individual is a professional or celebrity. When a person has a drug problem, he or she usually is sending out signals for help. Some signs are hard to detect, while others are more obvious. The following are indications that a person may have a drug problem:
- Increased absences or tardiness at work
- Poor health habits
- Physical symptoms such as red eyes and sleepiness (marijuana); a chronic runny nose and bad breath (cocaine); scars or needle marks and constricted pupils that don't respond to light (heroin)
- Presence of drug paraphernalia such as roach clips, pipes, rolling papers, syringes, razor blades, and straws
- Behavioral symptoms such as confusion, hyperactivity, excitability, mood swings, and explosive bouts of anger
- Taking extended breaks or being absent from workstation
- Complaints about money; requests to borrow money from co-workers, friends, or family
- Strained or abusive relationships with co-workers, friends, or family

Drug Abuse

How to Help Drug Abusers Quit

It's very difficult to confront someone about their drug use. Family members and friends often become "enablers": They enable the drug user to continue his or her behavior by ignoring, denying, or covering up the problem.

If you suspect that someone you know and care about has a drug problem, but don't know how to address the problem, try the following strategies:

- **Learn about the problem** by contacting such resources as your company employee assistance program, local drug rehabilitation center, or drug hotline. The professional will advise you how to communicate your concerns to the drug user and will provide you with possible options for referral.

- **You may want to try the intervention method.** In an intervention, a trained drug counselor joins family, friends, and, sometimes, co-workers to confront the drug user about his or her behavior. The goal of an intervention is to get the person to realize that he or she has a problem and to agree immediately to rehabilitation.

- **Expect denial when confronting the individual.** It's common for drug users to deny their problem until the bitter end. In fact, the threat of job loss may be the only thing that pushes a person to seek help; without income there's no money to pay for drugs.

- **If your efforts fail to convince the person to seek help,** be persistent in voicing your disapproval of the individual's behavior, but share your interest in supporting a decision to quit. Avoid becoming or remaining an enabler.

Working through the Treatment Process

Experts agree that recovery from drug dependence is a lifelong challenge. Although treatment depends on each person's individual needs and situation, the rehabilitation process usually follows these basic steps:

- **Assessment.** An assessment is conducted to evaluate the person's physical and psychological needs. The assessment usually is done by a team of health professionals, such as a physician and a mental health professional specializing in addictions. The team recommends a treatment plan based on the results of the evaluation.

- **Determining treatment.** Depending on the severity of the problem, health professionals may advise an in-house treatment program in a local hospital or residential treatment center. In-house programs usually are recommended if the person has immediate medical needs (e.g., overdose, withdrawal) or psychological needs (e.g., threat of suicide) that place him or her in danger.

  Warning: Because of the high costs of residential drug rehabilitation programs (up to $15,000 for a 12-day stay), make sure that the person's health insurance plan approves treatment before he or she is committed for a non-emergency. Check other options, such as outpatient care.

- **Most drug treatment is done on an outpatient basis.** Some outpatient programs require the person to attend an immersion program, in which he or she attends all-day sessions for two to four weeks while living at home. The program usually combines one-on-one counseling, therapist-led group sessions, and instruction in appropriate self-care skills.

- **Transitions.** The recovering person usually progresses from professionally led group therapy sessions to community-based self-help groups such as Narcotics Anonymous. Participants often follow a 12-Step Program that relies heavily on group support and commitment to lifelong recovery.

- **Follow-up.** The therapist or physician will schedule periodic visits to assess the person's progress and his or her need for further therapy.

37

Drug Abuse

Resources

Your company employee assistance program, if available

American Council for Drug Education
164 W. 74th St.
New York, NY 10018-0862
(800) 488-3784

Narcotics Anonymous. Check your phone directory's white pages.

National Clearinghouse for Alcohol and Drug Information
P.O. Box 2345
Rockville, MD 20847
(800) 729-6686

National Cocaine Hotline: (800) COCAINE

National Institute on Drug Abuse Hotline: (800) 662-HELP

Alcohol Use

Since the beginning of civilization, alcohol has been used for religious rituals and celebrations by rich and poor alike.

Classified as a depressant, alcohol is immediately absorbed through the stomach and affects every cell in the body. The brain, kidneys, and lungs are especially affected by alcohol consumption.

How your body reacts to alcohol depends on a number of factors:

- **Dosage:** The higher the alcohol concentration, the faster the blood alcohol level will increase.
- **Drinking rate:** The more drinks taken within an hour, the faster the blood alcohol level will rise. The liver can normally metabolize one drink per hour with limited physical and mental effects on the user.
- **Alcohol and food:** Eating a meal will slow the absorption of alcohol through the stomach, whereas drinking on an empty stomach will accelerate absorption.
- **Alcohol tolerance:** Since alcoholics burn alcohol at a faster rate than non-alcoholics do, they need more alcohol to get the same effects.
- **Body weight:** Usually the greater the body weight, the more alcohol needed for a person to become intoxicated. However, even amounts of alcohol that are perceived as modest (e.g., three beers within an hour for a 180-pound person), can significantly impair judgment and motor skills such as driving a car. In fact, a 180-pound person who drinks three beers in one hour would have a blood alcohol level of .05, which in many states is grounds for being arrested for "driving while under the influence" (D.W.I.).

WHAT'S YOUR ATTITUDE ABOUT ALCOHOL?

The following self-test is designed to assess your attitudes and behaviors regarding alcohol.

How many of these statements do you agree with?

- ❏ I use alcohol to feel good.
- ❏ I often drink by myself.
- ❏ I use alcohol to forget my problems.
- ❏ As long as nobody gets hurt, it's nobody's business how much I drink.
- ❏ I drink and drive.
- ❏ I need a drink first thing in the morning.
- ❏ I often wake up from a heavy drinking session and don't remember where I was or what went on before I passed out.
- ❏ I have frequent hangovers after I drink.
- ❏ I like to boast about my ability to "tie one on."
- ❏ I feel I need to sneak a drink in order to calm my nerves.
- ❏ I have been told I have a drinking problem.
- ❏ I have been arrested for D.W.I. (driving while under the influence).
- ❏ I have been warned by my supervisor about my drinking.
- ❏ I can't enjoy a social function unless alcohol is served.
- ❏ My drinking behavior leads to arguments with family members.
- ❏ I have become violent toward my family or others while under the influence of alcohol.
- ❏ I have felt angered and annoyed when someone criticized my drinking.
- ❏ I often feel guilty or embarrassed about my drinking behavior once I'm sober.
- ❏ I feel I have a drinking problem, but I refuse to get help.

What does this quiz mean?

If you found you agreed with one or more of these statements, you may have a problem with alcohol. It's recommended that you seek professional assistance. Start with your company or union employee assistance program, if available, or refer to the resources on page 42.

Alcohol Use

Three Kinds of Drinkers

Millions of Americans are social drinkers: Their use of alcohol is responsible and not habitual. When it comes to drinking, they can take it or leave it.

Why a person becomes a problem drinker or alcoholic is still debated. Problem drinkers are those individuals whose use of alcohol interferes with their interpersonal relationships, health, and well-being. They also put themselves and others in danger due to their risky behaviors, e.g., driving while under the influence.

Alcoholics are individuals whose use of alcohol has gone out of control. When they take their first drink on any particular day, they cannot predict whether they will be able to stop before becoming drunk or passing out. They have developed a psychological, and sometimes a physical, dependence on alcohol. Alcoholics can suffer withdrawal symptoms such as DTs (delirium tremens) or severe alcohol poisoning. Both conditions can be fatal.

Getting Help...
The First Step to Recovery

The first and most critical step in treating alcohol dependency is getting the problem drinker to admit that a serious problem exists and that change cannot happen without the help of others.

Another critical step in the treatment process is getting the problem drinker to realize that he or she has a behavioral problem as well as a medical condition. It's not uncommon to hear about an alcoholic receiving a liver transplant, only to go back to the bottle after surgery. The bottom line: Unless a problem drinker can admit that he or she has a problem with alcohol, and begins to adopt more positive coping skills, long-term recovery is questionable.

Start with These Resources

- If available, your employee assistance program
- Local or national alcohol hotlines
- Local community alcohol rehabilitation centers (listed in the yellow pages)
- Anonymous groups; e.g., Alcoholics Anonymous (listed in the white pages)
- The person's personal physician
- The person's priest, minister, or rabbi

How to Help a Person with a Drinking Problem

It's very difficult to confront someone about his or her drinking, especially if there is a risk of mental and physical abuse. Friends, co-workers, and "drinking buddies" are often reluctant to confront the person; they become "enablers" by ignoring or denying the problem and encouraging it to continue. The more drinking behavior a person is exposed to, the more difficult it is for him or her to recognize normal behavior. This may be one of the reasons children of alcoholics will marry alcoholics; in the dating process they don't notice that the partner's drinking is abnormal.

Ideas that Work: Getting Involved

If you wish to help an individual who has a serious drinking problem, be prepared for an up-hill climb. It's not easy. In the short term you may be perceived as the enemy, especially if you persist. Here are some suggestions:

- **Learn about the problem.** Contact such resources as your company employee assistance program, alcohol rehabilitation center, and Alcoholics Anonymous (AA).
- **Confront the person when he or she is sober.**
- **Focus on behavior only.** Focus on how the person's drinking affects his or her behavior in relation to work, family, and friends. Be objective and stick to the facts: "When you were drunk last night, you threw a shoe at me. Do you remember that happening?"

Alcohol Use

- **Expect denial.** It's common for problem drinkers to deny their problem until some event forces them to face it.
- **Ease up.** If your first efforts fail to convince the person to seek help, ease up on your feedback. There will be another opportunity.
- **Offer support.** Reinforce your interest in supporting the problem drinker when he or she decides to quit.
- **Avoid abuse.** Never tolerate mental or physical abuse, either as a recipient or observer. Get help before someone really gets hurt.
- **You may want to try the intervention method.** In an intervention, a trained alcohol counselor joins family, friends, and, sometimes, co-workers to confront the person about his or her drinking behavior. The goal of an intervention is to get the person to realize that he or she has a problem and to agree immediately to rehabilitation.
- **Expect denial when confronting the individual.** It's common for alcohol abusers to deny their problem until the bitter end. In fact, the threat of job loss may be the only thing that pushes a person to seek help; without income there's no money to pay for alcohol.

Working Toward Sobriety

Experts agree that staying sober is a lifelong commitment. Treatment depends on each person's situation, and can range from a "lay network" such as Alcoholics Anonymous (AA) to outpatient or inpatient care using an intensive medical and behavioral approach.

- **Inpatient programs.** An in-house treatment program through a local hospital or residential treatment center usually is recommended if the person with an alcohol problem has immediate medical needs (e.g., overdose, withdrawal) or psychological needs (e.g., suicidal thoughts) that place him or her in danger.

  Warning: Because of the high cost of residential alcohol rehabilitation programs (up to $15,000 for a 12-day stay), make sure that the person's medical benefit program approves treatment before he or she is admitted for a non-emergency. Discuss other treatment options such as outpatient care.
- **Outpatient programs.** These community-based programs combine one-on-one counseling sessions and group sessions. Usually patients are referred to a local AA group for ongoing support and assistance.
- **Alcoholics Anonymous.** Many alcoholics have been successful in staying sober through AA. This self-help approach guides a person through 12 carefully designed steps to becoming and remaining sober. In AA, there is continual emphasis on the need for recovering alcoholics to support and help one another in maintaining sobriety. Studies show that the longer people attend AA, the longer they stay sober.

41

F.Y.I

DEPRESSION HARMS RECOVERY

Men and women who are diagnosed with major depression at the time that they are admitted for inpatient treatment of alcohol dependence have shorter times to first drink and alcohol relapse. If you notice the signs of depression (refer to pages 264–265), alert your, or your loved one's, doctor.

Archives of General Psychiatry

Alcohol Use

- **Family assistance.** There are many support organizations and services that can assist family members in coping with a problem drinker. The first resource, if available, should be your company or union employee assistance program. Other organizations such as Al-Anon or Alateen can assist family members in dealing with the stresses of living with an alcoholic. MADD (Mothers Against Drunk Driving) sponsors programs against drunk driving (e.g., designated driver programs) and local support groups for families who have lost family members because of a drunk driver.

Remember, if you or someone you know has a drinking problem, help is available. Please seek it now!

Resources

Your company or union employee assistance program, if available

Alcoholics Anonymous (AA)
General Service Office
P.O. Box 459, Grand Central Station
New York, NY 10163
(212) 870-3400

Al-Anon/Alateen
Family Group Headquarters
P.O. Box 862, Midtown Station
New York, NY 10018-0862
(212) 302-7240

National Institute on Alcohol Abuse and Alcoholism (NIAAA)
6000 Executive Blvd., Suite 409
Bethesda, MD 20892-7003
(301) 443-3860

Mothers Against Drunk Driving (MADD)
511 E. John Carpenter Freeway
Suite 700
Irving, TX 75062
(800) 438-6233

Check your phone book's white pages for AA and Al-Anon groups near you.

42

F.Y.I

ALCOHOL AND HEALTH

For years, the scientific community has been reluctant to condone the use of alcohol as a technique for lowering the risk of heart disease. However, evidence now supports the value of moderate alcohol use in heart disease prevention because it's believed that alcohol increases HDL (good cholesterol). Moderate use is defined as no more than two servings per day for men and one serving per day for women. A serving is defined as 12 ounces of beer, 1 1/2 ounces of alcohol, or 5 ounces of wine. Going beyond these levels eliminates the cardiovascular benefits and increases the risk of liver disease, cancer, and alcoholism. Finally, these recommendations do not encourage non-drinkers to start, and no one should drink alcohol and drive.

Preventive Health Screenings

COMMON HEALTH SCREENING TESTS: RECOMMENDED SCHEDULES

TEST	AGE			
	20–29	30–39	40–49	50 and over
Blood Pressure	• Every one to two years, unless part of a doctor visit for another purpose.			
Cholesterol/HDL			• Once every five years from age 35 for men, 45 for women. See page 25.	
Dental Exam	• Dental cleaning and exam recommended every six to 12 months. • X-rays are not recommended unless the patient has cavities or pain.			
Pap Test and Pelvic Exam	• Every one to three years once sexual activity begins or at age 18 (depending on your risk factors). If test is negative after three consecutive yearly tests, every three years. Depending on risk factors, exams may be more frequent. Consult your doctor.			
Mammography*			• Every 1 to 2 years.	
Breast Exam By Physician	• Every one to three years at time of Pap test and pelvic exam.		• Every year from age 40.	
Breast Self-Exam	• Breast self-exam should be performed every month.			
Testicular Self-Exam	• Monthly examination after shower when scrotum is relaxed.			
Fecal Occult Blood (for rectal cancer)				• Every year.
Prostate Screening				• African-American men and men with a family history of prostate cancer may want to consider beginning PSA (prostate-specific antigen) testing and getting an annual digital rectal exam (DRE) before the age of 50. All men over 50 should discuss the need for regular PSA testing and DREs with their health care provider. See pages 279-280.
Sigmoidoscopy				• Every three to five years.

* Physicians may determine that there are significant risk factors (e.g., a first-degree relative with breast cancer) that would warrant performing mammography at an earlier age.

Source: *Guide to Clinical Preventive Services: Report of the U.S. Preventive Services Task Force,* American Cancer Society

Immunizations

....

RECOMMENDED IMMUNIZATION SCHEDULE FOR COMMON INFECTIOUS DISEASES

Protection from:	Abbreviation	Age
Diphtheria, pertussis, tetanus	DPT	2 months 4 months 6 months 12–18 months (or DTaP) 4–6 years (or DTaP)
Polio	OPV (oral)	2 months 4 months 6–18 months 4–6 years (booster)
Bacterial meningitis* (Hemophilus Type B)	Hib	2, 4, and 6 months* 12–15 months (booster)
Measles, mumps, rubella**	MMR	12–15 months 4–6 or 11–12 years
Tetanus/adult diphtheria	Td	11–12 or 14–16 years of age Every 10 years thereafter
Hepatitis B	Hep B	All infants—birth–2 months, 2–4 months and 6–18 months Individuals at high risk
Varicella Zoster Virus (Chicken Pox)	VZV	12–18 months of age Children under 13 who have not had chicken pox or vaccine Two doses 4–6 weeks apart for those over age 13 without history of disease or vaccine
Influenza (yearly strain)	Influenza	Yearly for adults who are 65 or older, or anyone over 6 months old who suffers from such chronic conditions as diabetes, heart disease, or lung disease, or has impaired immunity
Pneumonia	Pneumovac	For adults who are 65 or older, or anyone who suffers from certain chronic conditions, or has impaired immunity. One-time shot in many cases; however, revaccination sometimes indicated.

* Depending on which vaccine is used, an additional Hib may or may not be needed at 6 months. Also, Hib may be combined with DTP and given as Tetraimmune vaccine.

** Women and teenagers of childbearing age should be tested for antibodies against rubella (German measles). Immunization should be done if no antibodies are found. Talk to your health care provider.

Source: *Guide to Clinical Preventive Services: Report of the U.S. Preventive Services Task Force*, Centers for Disease Control and Prevention

Self-Examination: Breast and Testicular

Self-Examination for Breast Cancer

Doing a regular breast self-examination is one of the most important self-care investments you can make. Indeed, tumors that are found in the earliest stage are curable more than 90 percent of the time. For breast self-exams to be most effective, do them every month, preferably a few days after your period. If you are past menopause, perform your self-exam on the same day every month.

Following are three easy steps that make up a thorough breast self-exam.

Step 1

Stand in front of a mirror and relax with your arms to your sides. Visually inspect the skin of your breasts for signs of puckering, dimples, or changes in the size and shape. Notice whether either nipple has become inverted recently or, if you normally have inverted nipples, whether either one is no longer inverted. Do the same visual inspection with your hands on your hips, and then with your hands behind your head.

Step 2

In the bath or shower, work up a good lather in your hands. Place your left hand behind your head and use your right hand to examine your left breast. Use the flat surfaces of your fingers (not your fingertips) to feel for any unusual lumps or thickened tissue. Work in a clockwise spiral from the outer portion of your breasts (including your armpits) inward to your nipple. Finally, gently squeeze your nipple and check for any discharge. Repeat the procedure with your left hand on your right breast.

Step 3

Repeat the self-exam lying on a flat surface. Place a pillow or folded towel under your shoulder to slightly elevate one breast and then the other. Place your free hand behind your head.

Report any unusual lumps, thickened tissue, surface abnormalities, or nipple discharge to your doctor immediately.

Self-Examination for Testicular Cancer

Although relatively rare, testicular cancer is the most common cancer in men between the ages of 20 and 35. It also is one of the most curable cancers, especially if it is detected and treated early.

Following are two easy steps to a thorough monthly testicular self-examination.

Step 1

During or after a warm bath or shower, examine each testicle. With your index finger and middle finger underneath the testicle and your thumb on top, gently roll the testicle between your fingers and thumb.

Step 2

As you examine each testicle, look for any lumps, swelling, hardness, or other abnormalities you have not noticed before. It's normal for one testicle to be larger or slightly higher in the scrotum than the other. In addition, the cord-like structure on the back of the testicle (the epididymis, which is used to transport sperm) also is normal.

Report any lumps or abnormalities to your doctor immediately.

Dental Health

"Be true to your teeth or your teeth will be false to you," is an often-quoted dental proverb that should be heeded. Making a commitment to spend just 15 minutes a day to properly care for your teeth can mean the difference between keeping your teeth for the rest of your life, or keeping your teeth in a glass next to your bed at night.

Checkup Time?

The best way to turn over a new leaf when it comes to dental hygiene is to get a fresh start. See your dentist every six months for a thorough cleaning and checkup. Take care of any teeth that need to be filled or repaired. Once you've made the investment, it'll be easier to stick with a daily dental care regimen.

During a dental exam, your dentist will check for dental decay and signs of gum disease and oral cancer, and examine your teeth for bite problems.

A good dentist will tell you what all of your options are—from the top-of-the-line, state-of-the-art care and repair, all the way down to what the consequences will be if you do nothing. If he or she recommends more dental work than you can afford, take care of the most pressing concerns first and get to the others as soon as you can afford to have the work done. Any recommended treatment should be accompanied by an itemized summary of the charges for any work your dentist recommends.

Brush Up

Brushing your teeth is your first line of defense against the plaque buildup that hardens into tartar (which only your dentist can remove) and leads to tooth decay, gum disease, and tooth loss.

- **Use the right brush.** A brush with a small head is best: It can fit into your mouth's tight spaces better than a big one. Bristles should be soft and rounded. Buy a new toothbrush every two months, since bristles tend to wear down with use.

- **Use the right paste.** Always use fluoride toothpaste. Tartar-control varieties are a good choice.

- **Use the right touch.** The white-knuckle approach may get your teeth clean, but it will damage your gums in the process. Hold your toothbrush as you would a pencil, with the tips of your thumb and two or three fingers. Tilt the brush at a 45-degree angle toward your gums, then use a small, circular motion to clean the entire surface of each tooth, cheek-side and tongue-side.

- **Brush your tongue.** It only takes a few seconds to clean your tongue, which harbors bacteria just as gums and teeth do.

The entire brushing process should take two to four minutes. Brush at least twice a day, and definitely brush before going to bed.

Floss Away Plaque

Think of flossing as your anti-plaque insurance policy: Whatever plaque your toothbrush misses, your floss will get—if you floss correctly.

- **Work the curves.** While it's important for you to clean out the debris between your teeth, the most important place for your floss to reach is the area where your gums curve around each tooth, where plaque harbors bacteria and hardens into tartar. With floss wrapped around each middle finger, gently work the floss between your teeth to the gumline, then sweep the floss under the gumline around the curve of each tooth. Never use a sawing, back-and-forth motion, which can damage gums.

- **Any floss will do.** There are a number of dental flosses to choose from. Thin floss may work better if your teeth are very close together. Dental tape may be more comfortable for people whose teeth are not so tight-fitting. Waxed or unwaxed, flavored or plain, buy one you like and use it every day. Rinse to finish a job well done.

Dental Health

- **Water works.** Swish a mouthful of water around your teeth after you brush and floss. If you can't brush or floss after eating, a quick water rinse will at least remove food particles and wash away mouth acids. Water-jet appliances (e.g., WaterPik) can do a lot to remove food particles from teeth, but they don't replace flossing or brushing.
- **Mouthwash is optional.** Use it if you like the taste or the feel. Some studies have shown that rinsing with antiseptic mouthwash daily can reduce plaque buildup significantly. As well, you can use a fluoride-containing mouthwash if your tap water doesn't contain fluoride.

Get a Better Bite

Teeth that don't fit together properly can be hard to clean and will often place undue pressure on the structures that support the teeth, leading to dental problems later in life. If your dentist recommends braces or some other appliance to straighten your teeth, consider taking his or her advice. It can mean the difference in keeping and losing some or all of your teeth.

Be Teethwise

- **Chew sugarless gum.** Chew a stick after you eat, especially if you can't brush right away. Chewing gum neutralizes mouth acids and removes food particles from teeth. Don't chew gum all the time, though: You can damage the joint where your lower jaw is attached to your skull.
- **Don't use tobacco.** Besides giving you stained teeth and bad breath, tobacco—especially smokeless tobacco—can cause severe damage to gums and has been implicated in a number of oral cancers.
- **Keep away from sweets.** Candy and sweetened drinks increase acid in your mouth and contribute greatly to tooth decay.
- **Never use your teeth as a tool.** Don't open bottles or try to tear things with your teeth. If you do break a tooth or have one knocked out, see your dentist immediately.
- **Get an early start.** You owe it to your children to give them a good start when it comes to their teeth. Talk to your dentist about how to care for your children's teeth even before their first tooth comes in. He or she also can tell you how to teach your children the proper way to brush and floss, once your kids are old enough to handle the responsibility. Until then, it's up to you to do it for them.

Resources

Your dentist

American Dental Association
211 E. Chicago Ave.
Chicago, IL 60661
(312) 440-2500

Birth Control

One of the most important decisions that responsible, sexually active adults make is what method of birth control they will use. Although most methods are "female oriented," both partners need to be involved in the decision and fully supportive of it. That's why it's important to carefully assess your sexual attitudes and practices before choosing one method over another.

The following discussion defines the various options and provides some background information. Refer to the chart on the next page for failure rates.

Hormones

Oral contraceptives: Birth control pills (oral contraceptives) contain man-made forms of female hormones (progestin only or progestin and estrogen). Birth control pills are designed to be taken daily in order to stop a woman's ovaries from releasing an egg.

Injections: Depo-Provera® is a progestin-only (non-estrogen) hormone shot that provides highly effective contraception for three months. Depo-Provera® inhibits ovulation.

Implants: The longest-acting continuous contraceptive is Norplant®, a set of thin, hormone-containing capsules that are surgically implanted under the skin. Effective for up to five years, Norplant® is ideal for women who do not want to think about birth control. However, many women have experienced unpleasant side effects.

Lactational amenorrhea method (LAM) or breast-feeding: This method is effective if you nurse your baby every two to three hours around the clock with no breaks. Another method of birth control should be used once menstruation resumes, the baby reaches 6 months of age, or the woman begins nursing less often or for shorter periods of time. Talk with your health care provider.

The "morning-after" pill: This is not a primary method of birth control; it is a backup contraceptive option you may try if your regular birth control method fails. High doses of birth control pills are given to bring about changes in the lining of the uterus that help prevent pregnancy. This method may work if pills are taken within 72 hours of unprotected intercourse. Talk to your health care provider if you need "emergency" contraception.

Intrauterine Device (IUD)

The IUD is a small plastic device that contains copper or hormones. Although it does nothing to stop sperm from entering the uterus, the IUD creates changes in the physical environment of the uterus to make it inhospitable to a fertilized egg. An IUD must be inserted into the uterus by your health care provider.

Barrier Methods

Male condom: The male condom is an effective barrier against pregnancy and sexually transmitted diseases. Some men complain that condoms reduce penile sensitivity during intercourse. Ultra-thin, non-latex condoms can be used when both partners are HIV-negative, though they are more likely to break. Many condoms include the spermicide nonoxynol-9, which not only provides further protection from pregnancy but also may protect against HIV.

Female condom: Composed of a lubricated polyurethane sheath with a flexible ring on each end, it is inserted into the vagina as you would insert a diaphragm. One ring remains in place at the opening of the uterus (cervix) while the other partially covers the outside of the vagina. The female condom is much less effective at preventing pregnancy (in practice) than the male condom, although it does offer some of the same protection against sexually transmitted diseases.

Birth Control

Diaphragm: The diaphragm is a soft latex cup stretched over a flexible ring. Up to three hours before intercourse, a woman can fill the diaphragm with spermicide and insert it into the vagina to cover the cervix. It is available only through your health care provider, who can ensure a proper fit.

Cervical cap: The cervical cap covers the cervix like a diaphragm, but it's smaller and somewhat more difficult to insert or remove. It also must be fitted by a health care provider.

Spermicides: Spermicides provide a chemical barrier to conception by killing sperm on contact. Available in foam, jelly, cream, foaming tablets or vaginal suppositories, spermicides are most effective when used in combination with one of the physical-barrier methods described above.

Natural Family Planning

Also known as the rhythm method, natural family planning involves not having intercourse when a woman is likely to become pregnant. A combination of daily body temperature measurements, the calendar of the menstrual cycle, and the day-to-day changes in vaginal mucus give a general indication of a woman's fertile periods each month. Illness, stress, and other biochemical factors can throw off calculations by days or even weeks.

Sterilization

Male sterilization: Sterilization in males (vasectomy) involves cutting and sealing the tube that carries sperm from the testicles to the urethra during ejaculation. The only effect of this simple, outpatient operation is that sperm no longer make their way out of the body. The intensity of ejaculation and the quantity of semen ejaculated during sexual climax remain the same.

Female sterilization: Sterilization in females (tubal ligation) is more invasive than a vasectomy and requires a few days' recovery period. The operation involves cutting and sealing the fallopian tubes so that eggs cannot make the journey from the ovaries to the uterus for fertilization and implantation. Tubal ligation can be done right after a woman has given birth (when the abdomen is still relaxed) or before the abdomen is closed during a Caesarean section.

Because both tubal ligations and vasectomies are difficult to reverse (and their reversals do not guarantee a return to fertility), sterilization is a birth control option best suited for couples who know that they will not want to have another child in the future.

FAILURE RATES OF CONTRACEPTIVE METHODS

The effectiveness of any birth control method depends on how carefully it is used. This chart gives failure rates (estimated percentage of women experiencing an unintended pregnancy in the first year of use) based on real, not theoretical, use.

Method	Rate	Method	Rate
Norplant®	0.05	Male condom (without spermicide)	16.0
Male sterilization	0.2	Diaphragm	18.0
Depo-Provera®	0.4	Cervical cap	18.0
Female sterilization	0.5	Natural family planning	19.0
LAM (breast-feeding)	2.0*	No birth control method	20.0*
Intrauterine device (IUD)	4.0	Spermicide only	30.0
Birth control pill	6.0	Female condom (without spermicide)	n/a

Source: Alan Guttmacher Institute; Planned Parenthood*

Sexually Transmitted Diseases

DISEASE	TYPE OF INFECTION	SYMPTOMS
Chlamydia	Bacterial	Men—usually no symptoms. Painful, burning urination; discharge from penis Women—painful urination, stomach pain, vaginal discharge; most women have no symptoms until chlamydia progresses to pelvic inflammatory disease
Genital warts	Viral	Small, hard, fleshy bumps on the genital or anal area. Warts inside the vagina are softer and reddish
Pubic lice	Parasitic	Severe itching that worsens at night; lice visible in pubic hair and on skin; eggs, called "nits," attached to pubic hair; hives
Acquired Immune Deficiency Syndrome (AIDS)	Viral	Swollen glands; unexplained weight loss and loss of appetite; weakness and fatigue; night sweats; unexplained, prolonged fever; chronic diarrhea; dry cough not associated with a cold or flu; tissue changes of the mouth, tongue, or vagina; shingles (a red, blistery rash); unusual illnesses; development of rare diseases (e.g., tuberculosis, certain cancers, pneumonia)
Gonorrhea	Bacterial	Men—painful, burning, and frequent urination; thick, milky discharge from penis Women—painful and frequent urination; thick vaginal discharge; many women have no symptoms
Syphilis	Bacterial	Painless, open sores on the genitals, mouth, or anus; swollen lymph nodes, especially in the groin. Secondary symptoms include rash (especially on the palms or soles of the feet), fever, headache, and joint pain
Genital herpes	Viral	Intense itching in the genital or anal area, followed by the development of small, red bumps that blister, ulcerate, and then scab over. May be accompanied by fever, headaches, or flu-like symptoms. Women may have swollen labia and pain on urination
Hepatitis B	Viral	Chronic flu-like symptoms, yellow skin and eyes, discolored urine
Trichomoniasis	Parasitic	Heavy (sometimes frothy) green or yellow vaginal discharge with a very strong, foul odor

DIAGNOSIS	TREATMENT	SPECIAL CONCERNS
Microscopic examination and culture of vaginal or penile discharge; antibody test	Treated with antibiotics	Left untreated, chlamydia can cause infertility and pelvic inflammatory disease, urethritis, conjunctivitis, and arthritis-like swelling of the joints in men
Physical examination	May be removed surgically or with medication	Recurrence following treatment is common. Genital warts are linked with a higher incidence of some types of reproductive cancers in men and women
Physical examination	Medication to kill lice	None
Blood test	No cure. Drug therapy that combines azidothymidine (AZT), 3TC, and indinavir sulfate, a new protease inhibitor, has shown promising results	AIDS is fatal, although many patients live for years with the virus (HIV) before showing symptoms of full-blown AIDS
Microscopic examination	Treated with antibiotics. However, new strains are becoming resistant to many common drugs	Left untreated, gonorrhea can cause infertility or arthritis-like joint pain, or it can develop into pelvic inflammatory disease
Physical examination; microscopic examination of fluid from sores; blood test	Treated with antibiotics. However, new strains are becoming resistant to many common drugs	Left untreated, syphilis can cause heart disease, blindness, brain damage, shortened life expectancy, or (in unborn children whose mothers have the disease) birth defects and fetal death
Physical examination and culture of fluid from blisters	No known cure, but medication (especially acyclovir) can relieve symptoms or suppress the virus to limit recurrence	If mother is infected, baby may get disease during childbirth, resulting in blindness, retardation, or even death
Physical examination and blood test	Restricted physical activity and dietary modifications; hospitalization	Left untreated, hepatitis B can lead to severe liver damage and even death. Hepatitis B can be prevented through immunization
Physical examination and microscopic examination	Metronidazole tablets. Sexual partners may need to undergo treatment with metronidazole to prevent re-infection	None

AIDS Facts

A IDS, or acquired immune deficiency syndrome, is a disease that frightens most people. Anyone can get AIDS, but the chances of you becoming infected are rare, unless you're involved in risky behaviors (see below) or are exposed to the virus accidentally.

Today, there is hardly anyone who doesn't know at least something about this tragic illness. However, knowing and understanding often are two vastly different things. Many people are afraid of AIDS and individuals infected with HIV (human immunodeficiency virus), the cause of AIDS, because they don't understand the facts.

Understanding what this disease is, how it is spread, and who is at risk can reduce your risk of getting it. Having the right information also can help you support for individuals you may know who have AIDS.

HIV causes AIDS and gradually damages the body's natural defenses against disease. It also can infect cells in the brain. People who have AIDS develop unusual, life-threatening illnesses that do not affect people with normal immune systems.

Most persons with HIV infection go through a series of stages:

• **Acute Primary Infection.** This stage usually lasts four to 12 weeks. The person experiences mono-like symptoms such as sore throat, fever, fatigue, and swollen lymph glands. During this period, the body is producing antibodies, indicating it is trying to fight the infection. Antibodies usually are present within three to six months of infection. A blood test (Elisa) is used to detect HIV antibodies. A positive test (HIV positive) indicates the likelihood of HIV. A second, more sensitive test, called the Western blot, is done to confirm the first positive test. Infected persons can infect others. See "How is the AIDS virus spread?"

• **Latent Phase.** This period lasts 10 to 12 years, during which the infected person has no symptoms. However, the person can transmit HIV. See "How is the AIDS virus spread?"

• **Active Phase.**

– ARC: Some individuals develop a condition that is called "AIDS-related complex" (ARC). Symptoms include fever, feeling tired, loss of appetite, weight loss, diarrhea, night sweats, and swollen lymph nodes in the neck, armpits, or groin. Persons can have ARC-related symptoms for weeks or years, die from complications, or develop full-blown AIDS.

– AIDS: The severe end stage of the disease, with a variety of complications that further compromise the body's immune system. Two of the illnesses most often seen in AIDS patients are pneumocystis carinii pneumonia (a parasitic infection of the lungs) and Kaposi's sarcoma, a rare type of cancer.

It's estimated that between one million and 1.5 million Americans are HIV positive and carry the virus in their bodies (this is in addition to those known to have AIDS). Many people who are recently infected and are HIV positive show no signs of illness and do not know they carry the virus. However, they can spread it to others through sexual contact or contaminated blood products.

If a person tests positive for HIV through a special antibody test of the blood, it doesn't mean that the person has AIDS or will go on to get AIDS or an AIDS-related illness in the near future. It can take up to 10 years for someone to show symptoms of HIV infection and progress to AIDS. Though there is no cure, new treatments are becoming available that are helping individuals manage their condition, extend their lives, and lead a more independent life.

Work with These Facts

How is the AIDS virus spread?

• The virus is NOT spread through casual contact. The virus dies very quickly when it comes in contact with air or light.

• The virus is spread through direct transmission to the bloodstream during unsafe (unprotected) sexual contact, through sharing needles, from contami-

AIDS Facts

. . . .

nated blood products, and by an HIV-positive mother to her baby during birth and breast-feeding.

- Casual kissing carries a low risk; deep kissing (french kissing) hasn't been linked to transmittal of the virus, unless the infected person passes blood to the partner.

- You can't catch AIDS from donating blood. All needles used for blood donation are sterile and are never reused.

- AIDS has never been shown to be transmitted through insect bites.

- AIDS can't be spread by shaking hands, hugging, or other forms of casual contact.

- Once outside the body, the AIDS virus dies quickly, so you can't catch it from drinking glasses, drinking fountains, or toilet seats.

Who is at risk for catching AIDS?

- Individuals with the highest risk for carrying HIV have been homosexuals and bisexuals, intravenous drug users, male and female prostitutes, and individuals who have sex or share needles with individuals from these high-risk groups. However, heterosexual risk is climbing. The World Health Organization reports that 90 percent of all new AIDS cases worldwide are from heterosexual contact.

- Anyone who has unprotected (unsafe) sex and who has not been in a mutually monogamous relationship for at least the last 10 years (HIV can exist for up to 10 years without symptoms) may have an increased risk for getting AIDS.

- Anyone who received blood transfusions before early 1985 is at risk. Since that time, all blood used for transfusions has been screened for HIV and has reduced the risk within the United States to almost negligible levels. However, if you are scheduled for surgery, you may want to donate your own blood in advance of the procedure.

- Infants born to HIV-infected mothers have a 20 to 30 percent chance of developing AIDS.

- People working in certain professions, such as police, firefighters, funeral home workers, emergency medical workers, dental personnel, prison staff, and medical workers, who are routinely exposed to possibly contaminated blood and body fluids, have a higher risk for contracting the disease, although the risk is small if proper precautions are followed.

How can I reduce my risk of catching AIDS?

- Do not have unsafe (unprotected) sex. If you do, make sure your partner is not infected. Otherwise, use a latex condom. For added protection, buy condoms that contain the spermicide nonoxynol-9 (condoms alone are not 100 percent effective against infection).

- Consider abstinence or a monogamous relationship with an uninfected partner when evaluating your own sexual behavior.

- If your job involves exposure to blood and body fluids, wear personal protective equipment such as gloves, masks, gowns, and face shields. Make sure the equipment is the right type of material and is in good condition.

- Do not share needles if you are an IV drug user. Get some help to kick the habit.

Resources

AIDS toll-free hotline: (800) 342-AIDS

AIDS Education Office
American Red Cross
1730 D St., N.W.
Washington, DC 20006
(202) 434-4074

53

21 Tips for Your Child's Good Health

The key to good health is helping your child practice appropriate behaviors that not only improve his or her health, but also reduce the risk of disease and disability as your child grows to adulthood. The following 21 tips will help your child live a healthier and longer life.

1. **Make sure your child gets regular medical checkups,** including "well-child" or preventive care. Don't just bring your child to see the doctor when he or she is sick. Preventive visits as your child is growing and developing are important to record milestones such as height, weight, and developmental level, as well as to review immunization schedules, test hearing and vision, and to talk about health concerns you, your child, or family may have.

2. **Get your child immunized.** You should be sure your child completes all his or her scheduled immunizations (see page 44 for the recommended schedule). This helps protect your child from infectious diseases that could affect his or her health and well-being. County and city health departments and community clinics are sources for immunizations, in addition to your doctor's office. Keep a record of your child's immunizations; you will need it when he or she enters school.

3. **Learn infant and child CPR.** Check with your local hospital or chapter of the American Red Cross for information on classes they offer.

4. **Have your child get regular dental checkups.** Teach him or her how to brush and floss his or her teeth. Be sure your child brushes regularly, not only to take good care of the "baby" teeth but to establish good dental care habits as he or she grows older.

5. **Keep your child away from secondhand smoke.** Don't allow your child's caregiver to smoke around him or her. If you or anyone in your family smokes, quit if you can. If you can't, smoke outdoors or somewhere away from your child. Don't smoke in the enclosed space of your car when traveling with your child.

6. **Home injuries are a leading cause of death in young children.** Do a safety audit of your home. Check to be sure that smoke detectors are working and that household chemicals and cleaners are stored where a child can't get at them. Store all medications away from your child. Install stairway gates, cabinet and drawer locks, electric outlet covers, and window guards. Check to be sure swimming pools are fenced in. Have your child wear a safety helmet when riding a bicycle. Store guns away from children and lock them up in a safe place. Refer to "Keeping Your Child Safe," on page 56, for more information.

7. **Take time out when you become frustrated by the stresses of parenting.** Never shake a baby or child as this can cause brain injury and death.

8. **Transport small children in approved child safety seats** when driving your car. Buckle up your child at all times!

9. **Encourage your child to be physically active.** Try to interest him or her in playing sports rather than video games. Cut down on the amount of TV that you and your children watch. Exchange an hour of exercise for one hour in front of the TV. Make exercise a family affair. Walking, biking, swimming, running, or any other activity that increases heart rate is a good activity.

10. **Do not excessively expose your child's skin to the sun.** Have him or her wear a hat, play in the shade or indoors during the peak hours of sunlight, and wear sunscreen to minimize his or her future risk of skin cancer.

11. **Start your child's day with breakfast.** After a night without food, it fills your child up and gets him or her going for the rest of the day.

21 Tips for Your Child's Good Health

12. **Feed your child healthy foods** including whole-grain breads and cereals, fresh fruits and vegetables, dairy products, and lean meats, poultry, and fish. Steer them away from high-fat, high-sugar foods. Teach them how to snack smart. Keep the cupboard stocked with pretzels, low-salt crackers, graham crackers, and fresh fruit.

13. **Make sure your child gets enough rest and sleep.** Tired children are irritable, have more behavior problems, and have more difficulty concentrating when learning tasks.

14. **Allow your child to have some quiet time each day,** time when he or she can read or do creative activities.

15. **Help your child maintain a body weight** that is right for him or her through exercise and healthy eating habits.

16. **Make mealtime fun and pleasant.** Often it may be the only time your family is together during the entire day. Do not dim the enthusiasm of your child's day by discussing the pressures of daily life or arguing at meals.

17. **Demonstrate appropriate self-care** for minor medical conditions at home. Teach your child not to expect that a drug or medicine is always the answer when something is wrong. This helps him or her learn good self-care skills and attitudes for later life.

18. **When you do need to seek medical care,** prepare your child ahead of time. Tell your child what to expect and that it's all right for him or her to ask questions of the doctor, too. This prepares your child to be a better and more active partner in his or her own medical care as an adult.

19. **Be a good role model.** Children imitate what they see adults do. Don't smoke, exercise sensibly, maintain an appropriate body weight, and eat healthy foods. Your child will follow your example.

20. **Take time to talk with your child each day.** Arrange for a special time that you spend together, uninterrupted. Encourage him or her to let you know how things are going, and what problems he or she is having. Keep the lines of communication open. Let your child know it's OK to speak up and talk about his or her feelings. And then, make sure you really take time and listen to your child. Reinforce and praise positive behavior and achievements. Avoid being overly critical and negative.

21. **Last, but definitely not least, love your child** and show him or her that you care. This will help your child develop healthy, loving relationships later in life.

Keeping Your Child Safe

Injury-producing accidents may indeed happen by accident, but keeping your child safe from harm is not. Accident-prevention planning is a skill that every parent should possess. Children often are oblivious to the dangers around them. It is up to you to help keep your child safe. The following table outlines some common danger areas, as well as some preventive measures you can take to keep your child safe.

AGE	DANGER	SAFETY MEASURES
Birth to 1 year	Suffocation in crib	Keep pillows, plastic, extra blanket out of crib Put baby to sleep on his or her back
	Strangulation by objects around neck	Keep cords and string away from infant Do not hang pacifier by ribbon or cord
	Choking from food, milk, or foreign objects	Don't leave alone when eating Avoid feeding popcorn or peanuts Check toys for small parts that can come loose Keep small objects out of reach; everything goes in an infant's mouth. If it's small enough to fit inside a toilet paper roll, it's small enough to choke on.
	Falls	Keep sides of crib up when baby is unattended Always keep contact with (hand on) baby Don't leave alone on bed, in bath, etc. where baby can fall, slip, or roll off Place guard rails at top of stairs; guards on windows Do not leave alone in swing, walker (can tumble down stairs), or high chair
	Automobile accidents	Always use approved car safety seat
	Burns	Test bath water before using; turn hot water heater temperature down to 120 degrees F or less Use back burners on kitchen stove; turn pot handles in Don't smoke or drink hot beverages around infant Protect from excess sun exposure Keep floor heaters out of reach
	Cuts and bruises	Pad crib bars Keep baby's fingernails short Use plastic cups and bottles Check toys for sharp edges Keep fans, humidifiers, etc. out of reach
	Electrical shock	Coil electric cords to keep out of reach Cover electrical outlets
	Poisoning	Lock or put childproof latches on cupboards Keep poisonous substances and plants out of reach Post Poison Control number next to phone
1 to 3 years	Falls, cuts, banging into objects	Keep furniture with sharp edges (glass-topped tables) out of traffic flow Place knives and sharp objects out of reach Keep windows and balconies screened Keep child under supervision

56

Keeping Your Child Safe

AGE	DANGER	SAFETY MEASURES
1 to 3 years	Motor vehicle accident	Place child in car safety seat in back of car Teach child not to ride tricycles in street or around cars
	Burns	Keep matches out of reach Teach danger words ("no," "don't," "hot") and make sure child obeys Teach child about danger of fires, including charcoal fires Test water before child's bath Put pots on stove on back burners
	Poisoning	Check house for lead paint Keep medicines, cleaning supplies, pesticides, antifreeze locked in cupboard Teach child not to take medicine except when parent or caregiver OKs Teach child not to put objects in mouth
	Drowning	Do not leave child alone in tub or pool Keep water in tub to minimum level Fence in pools Do not let child play near deep ditches or wells Teach child to swim Put locks on toilets
	Electrical shock	Keep outlets covered
4+ years	Choking, putting foreign objects in ears and mouth, suffocation	Don't let child run with objects (candy, gum) in mouth Teach child not to put small objects in ears, nose, or mouth Remove doors from old freezers, refrigerators, etc., which can trap and suffocate child
	Injury from traffic	Teach child to play in the grass or sidewalk rather than driveway, street, or railroad tracks Show child how to obey traffic signals and cross streets safely
	Playground injury	Teach child not to walk in front of swings Do not let child push others off playground equipment Encourage child to put toys away
	Poisoning	Check Halloween candy Teach child not to eat any objects or plants from outdoors Remind child not to take pills without parental permission
	Drowning	Same as for ages 1 to 3 years
	Fire and burns	Teach child the danger of playing with matches or near fires
	Harm from other people	Teach child to avoid strangers and require child to keep parent informed of whereabouts Keep child supervised
	Harm from animals	Teach child to act and move quietly around animals Don't let child approach strange animals
	Firearm accident	Teach child not to play with guns or other weapons

57

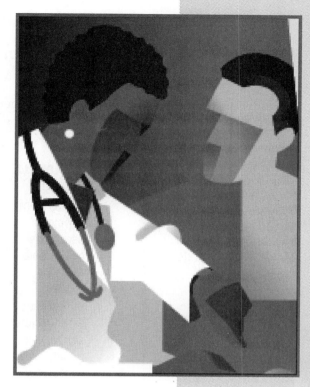

Understanding the Basics of Medical Care

By using this section you will learn:

- Common health care terms.

- How to select a primary care physician.

- How to talk to your doctor and what key questions to ask.

- How to locate health information and resources to make better informed decisions.

Medspeak: Made Easy

From arthroscopy to nephritis, medical terms don't have to be a mystery if you know a few simple prefixes and suffixes.

The following list will help you piece together some of medicine's more puzzling vocabulary.

PREFIX:	REFERS TO:	EXAMPLE:
adeno-	gland	adenoid
angio-	blood vessels	angina
arterio-	artery	arteriosclerosis
arthro-	joints	arthritis
broncho-	windpipe	bronchitis
carcino-	cancer	carcinoma
cardio-	heart	cardiovascular
cephalo-	head	hydrocephaly
cranio-	skull	craniotomy
cysto-	bladder	cystitis
denti-	tooth	dentures
derma-	skin	dermatitis
dys-	impaired	dyslexia
entero-	intestines	enteritis
en- or endo-	inside, within	endoscopy
epi-	attached to	epidermis
gastro-	stomach	gastritis
geronto-	old age	geriatric
hemo-	blood	hemorrhage
hepato-	liver	hepatitis
hyper-	excessive	hypertension
hypo-	inadequate	hypoglycemia
intra-	within	intravenous
lipo-	fat	liposuction
masto-	breast	mastectomy
melano-	dark, black	melanoma
myelo-	bone marrow or spine	myelitis
myo-	muscle	myocardium
narco-	numbness, sleep	narcotic
nephro-	kidney	nephritis
neuro-	nerves	neuralgia
ortho-	straight, normal	orthopedic
osteo-	bone	osteoarthritis

PREFIX:	REFERS TO:	EXAMPLE:
ov-	eggs	ovaries
peri-	around	pericardium
poly-	many	polycystic
psycho-	mind	psychosis
pulmo- or pneumo-	lungs	pneumonia
radio-	ray	radiology
rhino-	nose	rhinoplasty
scler-	hardening	arteriosclerosis
sero-	blood	serology
uro-, urino-	urine	urinalysis
vas-	vessel	vasectomy

SUFFIX:	REFERS TO:	EXAMPLE:
-aholic	addiction	alcoholic
-algia	pain	neuralgia
-cele	tumor	hydrocele
-ectomy	removal of	hysterectomy
-emia	blood condition	leukemia
-itis	inflammation	bursitis
-lysis	breaking down	dialysis
-natal	birth	prenatal
-oma	tumor	melanoma
-opia	sight	myopia
-opsy	medical examination	biopsy
-oscopy	viewing	athroscopic
-osis	abnormal condition	cirrhosis
-pathy	abnormality	psychopathy
-plasia	growth	dysplasia
-plasty	rebuilding	rhinoplasty
-pnea	breathing	apnea
-rrhea	flow	diarrhea
-tomy	cutting	vasectomy
-uria	urine substances	pyuria

Health Care Terms to Understand

As employers, insurance companies, and the government try to manage exploding health care costs, new terms are becoming part of the health care vocabulary. Here are some of the most common terms.

Terms to Work with

- **Allowable charges:** The approved amount an insurance carrier or company will pay for a specific medical or dental procedure. Charges above this amount are the responsibility of the individual.

- **Capitation:** A set dollar limit that a health plan pays to a group of physicians, regardless of how much you use medical services.

- **Case management:** A service that assigns a health professional (usually a nurse) to monitor, with the physician and the hospital, the care plans of individuals who require extensive medical treatment. The case manager's primary responsibility is to make sure that the individual receives the most appropriate and reasonable care.

- **Coinsurance:** The amount patients are required to pay through their insurance plan for reasonable medical expenses after a deductible has been paid (also referred to as a "copayment" in some plans). Often insurance plans require 20 percent to be paid by the patient, with 80 percent paid by the insurance company.

- **Copayment:** A flat fee that is paid by the patient on a per-visit basis. For example, HMOs may require a $5 to $10 "copay" for each office visit or prescription.

- **Deductible:** A minimum payment made by an individual and/or family before the company or insurance carrier begins to pay for medical expenses.

  Example: John Wright broke his leg during a softball game. He has a deductible of $150, a coinsurance of 80/20 percent, and an out-of-pocket maximum of $2,500. His entire medical bill was $850.

–John's total medical bill	$850
–John's deductible	$150
–Total bill minus deductible	$700
–John's coinsurance percentage	X 20%
–Coinsurance charge to John	$140

John is required to pay: $150 (deductible) + $140 (coinsurance) = $290.

His company pays $850 (total medical bill) – $290 (John's charges) = $560.

- **Health Maintenance Organization (HMO):** A "pre-paid" medical system in which members receive medical services for *one monthly fee,* regardless of the severity of the problem or number of visits. HMOs usually are either a Staff Model, an Independent Practice Association (IPA), or network model.

  In the Staff Model, specified clinics and staff are located within the community and treat subscribers only and/or employees of the HMO. In the IPA or network model, physicians are contracted to provide services out of their own offices or clinics and can treat non-HMO patients.

- **Indemnity health plan or "fee-for-service" plan:** Under this plan, the employer or insurance company pays a percentage (often 80 percent) of the reasonable cost of each medical service received by the eligible patient. The patient's contribution is called coinsurance. Indemnity plans usually require the employee to pay a certain deductible before the employer or insurance company begins to contribute.

- **Managed care:** A medical care delivery system that manages health care and costs through a variety of services designed to provide quality care appropriate to patients' needs. Most managed care programs (HMOs and PPOs) involve a network of primary care physicians, specialists, and hospitals.

- **Maximum dollar limit:** The maximum amount of dollars the employer or insurance company will pay within a specified period of time.

61

Health Care Terms to Understand

Maximum dollar limits can be for a lifetime ($1 million) or for a year, or can be illness-specific, such as for psychiatric care or cancer treatment.

- **Out-of-pocket maximum:** The maximum amount that a patient is required to pay through coinsurance before the employer or insurance company pays 100 percent of reasonable medical expenses. Common in fee-for-service plans.

- **Point-of-service (POS):** A managed care system in which all the benefits of the HMO are received when participants' care is managed by their primary care physician. However, when they self-direct their care and/or use non-network providers, their costs are subject to a deductible and coinsurance.

- **Pre-certification or pre-admission review:** A process that requires patients with certain medical conditions to contact their insurer for prior authorization in order to have payment approved for the services.

- **Preferred Provider Organization (PPO):** A network of physicians and hospitals that agree to give discounts to companies when employees use their services.

- **Primary care physician (PCP):** A physician who is responsible for monitoring and treating your general health needs. This includes performing periodic health screenings and immunizations and treating common medical problems. Typical PCPs are internists (who treat adults only), family physicians (who treat adults, children, and infants), and pediatricians (who treat infants, children, and adolescents up to age 18). See page 64.

- **Nurse practitioner:** A Registered Nurse (RN) with advanced training that prepares him or her to provide routine checkups and to help manage certain minor, acute, and chronic health problems, under a physician's supervision.

- **Physician's assistant:** A health care professional with medical training that allows him or her to provide routine health maintenance checkups and to manage certain minor, acute, and chronic health problems, under a physician's supervision.

- **Second opinion programs:** A cost-management process that requires patients to seek the counsel and opinion of a second physician in certain situations: for specific medical procedures that are elective; when other accepted options for treatment exist; when the diagnosis is still in question; or when hospitalization or surgery is recommended.

- **Specialist:** A physician trained and/or certified to treat a specific body system such as a cardiologist (problems of the heart), gynecologist (woman's reproductive system), or dermatologist (skin problems).

Understanding Managed Care

The majority of Americans are now covered by managed care plans, yet polls suggest that many still are confused about what managed care is. The term managed care describes a method of financing, organizing, and delivering health care services. Don't be confused by all the terms (see "Health Care Terms to Understand" on page 61): Whether your plan is a PPO, POS, EPO, or HMO, the foundation of managed care is the primary care physician (PCP).

Similar to the old family doctor, the PCP provides and coordinates all care for a patient. Your personal physician gets to know a patient over time, providing consultation and services to maintain a person's health, not just treat a disease. This is consistent with managed care plans' focus on health promotion.

More than 80 percent to 85 percent of all medical conditions or concerns can be treated by a PCP. If your condition does require the services of a specialist, your PCP will make an appropriate referral and consult with the specialist as necessary. Not only will you receive better care when the treating physician—whether your PCP or a specialist—has your whole health picture in view, but he or she will be better able to design a treatment plan that best meets your specific needs.

The bottom line: By working with a PCP, you receive better quality care. Quality care means treating a condition with the greatest benefit and the least risk at the most appropriate cost. The most appropriate cost does not necessarily mean the least cost. Together, you and your personal physician determine what set of strategies and initiatives will work best for you.

The thing to remember about managed care is that the care is being managed, not you. You and your doctor should work in partnership, no matter how the health care delivery system is organized. The information in "Finding Doctor Right," "The Quality Office Visit," and "Communicating with Your Doctor" on the following pages should help you develop a strong working relationship.

F.Y.I

IS AN HMO RIGHT FOR YOU?

Health Maintenance Organizations (HMOs) are gaining popularity as an alternate way to provide health care services. However, you may have many questions concerning whether an HMO is the right health plan for you and your family. The following key questions may help you assess an HMO plan:

☐ Is the HMO a Staff Model or an IPO (Independent Provider Organization)? A staff model requires you to go to a central clinic; an IPO is a network of contract physicians who provide services from their own offices.

☐ How do the premiums and copays compare to those of other health plans in your area?

☐ What preventive screenings and programs are part of your coverage?

☐ How extensive is the HMO's network of primary care physicians (PCPs) and specialists? For an IPO, are there a number of PCPs close to your home? Is your current doctor a member?

☐ How difficult is it and how long does it take for you to get an appointment?

☐ How difficult is it for you to change your primary care physician?

☐ How many of the HMO's PCPs and specialists are "board certified"? (Board certification is one indication of the quality of the physician network.)

☐ With what hospital is the HMO affiliated? What is the reputation of the hospital?

☐ What is the HMO's reputation among your friends and associates who may be members?

☐ What types of value-added services does the HMO offer?

Finding Doctor Right

Medicine has changed a lot over the last 40 years. The house call has been all but eliminated. It has been replaced by urgent care centers, 24-hour clinics, and the office visit. Most Americans don't have a "Dr. Welby" who treats them from cradle to grave. Instead, more than 50 percent of Americans meet their doctor for the first time during a time of medical need or emergency. This meeting in a crisis is not the best way to build a relationship, especially as you are trusting someone with your own or your family member's care and well-being. An important first step in being a good medical consumer is finding a doctor you can relate to and trust.

Ideas that Work

- **Find a primary care physician (PCP).** Your primary care physician is responsible for your "primary care"—caring for your general health needs, such as performing periodic health screenings and immunizations, and treating common problems that don't require a specialist. Approximately 80 to 85 percent of all medical problems can be treated by a well-trained PCP.

  It's to your advantage to find a PCP. Because your PCP knows you and the two of you have developed a good relationship, he or she can help you avoid unnecessary tests and procedures that can be expensive and possibly place you at greater risk. When a medical problem is more serious, your PCP may refer you to a specialist, but he or she is still involved in your total care plan.

- **Select your primary care physician according to your needs.** Shop for a doctor who can meet most of your medical needs and those of your family. As a first choice, a doctor certified in family practice or as a general practitioner may be able to meet your needs and provide a cohesive care plan that includes lifestyle management. However, your family may need more than one PCP. For example, in a young family of three, the husband may have an internist, the wife an obstetrician-gynecologist, and the child a pediatrician. If this is the case, physician selection should be based on the qualities listed below.

Look for a PCP who:

- ❏ is a person you feel confident about and respect.
- ❏ has good communication skills: He or she is an active listener and takes time to talk and explain things.
- ❏ believes in prevention and provides information to assist you.
- ❏ chooses tests and procedures carefully, and prescribes medication carefully.
- ❏ is willing to accept payment for "allowable charges."
- ❏ has a reasonable waiting time for appointments (e.g., less than five days).
- ❏ can be and is willing to be contacted by phone.
- ❏ has established office hours after regular work hours.

- **Use your network.** Ask friends, family members, and co-workers to suggest doctors. Find out why they like a specific doctor or why they dislike others. Do not automatically rule out someone based on a negative comment. For example, a doctor may have a poor "bedside manner," but be excellent in his or her specialty.

- **Ask the pros.** Contact your local medical society, teaching hospital (talk to the chief resident for recommendations), or your preferred hospital. Whenever possible, talk to nurses, who usually have excellent views of a doctor's professional reputation, skills, and attitude toward patients. If a specialist is needed, ask your PCP for at least two recommendations.

Your local Better Business Bureau can tell you if there are malpractice claims filed against a certain physician. Also, your State Department of Health can tell you if a physician is licensed in your state to practice medicine.

Finding Doctor Right

- **Call a physician line.** A number of "physician referral services" are currently available. When you call an advertised phone number, a consultant will help match you to a doctor based on your health needs, location, and personality preferences. Beware: Though these services can provide you with a list of doctors or even schedule an appointment for you, they usually are paid for and run on the behalf of the doctors who join the service.

- **Is he or she certified?** Some studies suggest that doctors who are "board certified" may provide more appropriate care. A board-certified physician has passed a national standardized test of competency.

- **Refer to your insurance plan.** If you belong to a Health Maintenance Organization (HMO), you may select or be assigned a PCP or be referred to a doctor, depending on your medical needs. If you do not like your assigned physician's performance, request another doctor.

If your company health plan is part of a Preferred Provider Organization (PPO), you may want to select a PCP from a "preferred list" of doctors. You will receive discounts if your doctor is part of the PPO. Use the suggestions above to help you select a PCP from the list.

- **How's the office staff?** How are you treated on the phone and in the office? A friendly, responsive office staff usually reflects a doctor with a similar manner.

- **How long do you need to wait?** How are appointments scheduled: for example, four patients per hour or 10? Ask about the usual waiting time. Look at how many people are waiting in the reception area; this can give you a pretty good hint on office scheduling procedures.

The Quality Office Visit

The visit to the doctor's office has been a source of jokes for many comedians and TV shows. Many Americans are frustrated by the long waits, the impersonal way patients are herded between examining rooms, the short time allowed for them to talk to their doctor, questionable tests, and, of course, the high costs. The medical establishment is not insensitive to these issues. In fact, surveys indicate that doctors want to spend more time with their patients. By following the strategies below, you can improve the quality of the office visit for yourself, the doctor, and other patients, too!

Ideas that Work

- **Question the need.** Estimates show that approximately 25 percent of all visits to the doctor are not needed. Either there is nothing the doctor can do—as in the case of uncomplicated colds—or other health professionals can provide care, as in the case of routine screenings for blood pressure or cholesterol. The first question you should ask is: "Do I need to see my doctor, or do I have other options such as applying self-care?"

- **Be prepared.** If you are going to your doctor with a new problem, it is important to provide the right information. Don't be embarrassed or scared. Try to share your thoughts and observations on the cause of your problem or other medical concerns (past or present). This will help your doctor narrow down the diagnosis and develop a treatment plan. If possible, write down the answers to the following questions before your visit:

  ❑ **What is your primary problem?** Be specific by listing your key symptoms, for example: I have had stomach cramps and diarrhea.

  ❑ **When did your problem begin?** Try to give the exact time. If you cannot pinpoint the exact date that a symptom appeared, try to remember the general period that you began to notice you weren't feeling well.

  ❑ **What do you think may have caused the problem?** Did you eat some unusual food? Do any family members or co-workers have similar symptoms?

  ❑ **Know your family history.** Is there a history of such diseases as heart disease, high blood pressure, diabetes, and breast cancer among your immediate family: parents, grandparents, brothers, or sisters?

  ❑ **What have you done to try to relieve the problem?** Have you used any medications? What kind? What happened?

  ❑ **Did you have this problem before?** When? What happened?

  ❑ **What makes the problem worse?** List what activities, medications, foods, or other situations make your problem more serious.

  ❑ **Are you allergic to any medications?** If yes, what are they?

- **Answer questions as best you can.** Your doctor may ask you detailed questions by body system (e.g., symptoms related to your skin, head, eyes, ears, throat, etc.) to see if there are any patterns to your problem. You also will be asked about your family life, emotional health, potential job-related exposures, and general health behaviors such as alcohol consumption, drug use, tobacco use, exercise habits, and sexual activity. Though these questions are personal, it is important to be direct and honest with your responses.

- **Cooperate during the checkup.** When your doctor has finished his or her questions, you usually receive a focused physical examination. Once again, it is important to answer directly any questions that you may be asked. You have the right to question or refuse any recommendations. State your concern. Listen to your doctor's reasons.

- **Diagnostic tests.** Doctors often use diagnostic tests to better determine either the cause of an illness or how serious it is. Ask questions about the benefits (e.g., "Will it change my treatment if I have this test?"), risks, and costs.

The Quality Office Visit

• **Use the INFORMED Process.** If your problem is complex and requires intensive testing and treatment, it's to your advantage to use a more formal way of deciding on your care plan. The INFORMED Process, explained in detail on pages 78-81, can help you and your doctor consider your treatment options.

• **Follow through with treatment.** To avoid more serious and expensive procedures and treatments, it is important to understand and follow the treatment plan you have agreed to. Many recurring medical problems are caused by patients taking shortcuts in treatment. A common cause is not following through on medications: taking the wrong dosage; stopping medication too early; and not adhering to the daily schedule. Another cause is over-medication. A common belief is, "If one pill is good, then two must be better." Medications are of value only when taken as directed. If you are concerned about your medication, discuss it with your doctor.

Finally, don't ignore suggestions that seem too simple, such as drinking plenty of fluids, getting bed rest, eating a balanced diet, stopping smoking, exercising, or losing weight. These recommendations are just as sound as other high-tech medical advice, and, in fact, are often the best medicine you'll ever give yourself.

F.Y.I   UNDERSTANDING YOUR CARE PLAN

As outlined above, it's important to follow through with your care plan as directed by your doctor. Because most of us tend to forget details over time, it's recommended that you write down what your doctor tells you:

• Write your care plan on the same sheet of paper where you listed your symptoms.

• Write down the diagnosis.

• Write down your treatment plan: medications (see "Medication Use Record," page 287), nutritional needs, activity restrictions, special exercises, and other specifics.

• Question your doctor if any alternative therapies can be used (e.g., chiropractic). See page 71.

• Have your doctor identify any possible medication side effects.

• List what warning signs (e.g., infection, high fever) require further medical evaluation.

• Finally, don't be afraid to ask your doctor to clarify a point you don't understand.

Communicating with Your Doctor

Most patients don't question their doctor. They may feel they have no right to challenge someone who's had at least 11 years of formal medical education, or they feel embarrassed or "stupid," especially when the problem is serious. Instead of giving up control, most experts believe, it's important for you to become *more involved* in your care plan. *The more information you have, the more active you can become in making decisions concerning your health.* Remember that the first skill in being a good medical consumer is asking the right questions. But don't expect to get all your questions answered completely all the time. Medicine is a complex science, and uncertainty is a fact of life.

Basic Communication Tips

The following are some basic guidelines for improving your communication skills with your doctor. When more complex medical procedures (e.g., surgery, hospitalization, diagnostic tests) are recommended, it's suggested that you use the INFORMED Medical Decision-Making Process™ and Worksheet (see pages 78-81).

- **Write down your questions.** Organize your questions and concerns before you visit your doctor.
- **Don't feel intimidated or "stupid."** Ask questions when you don't understand an explanation. Ask your doctor and other health professionals to simplify their responses by stating them in non-technical terms.
- **When tests are prescribed, question their value and need.** For example: "If I have this test, how will it change the outcome of my problem?"
- **When a treatment is prescribed, ask what other options are available.** For each option, have your doctor explain the risks, benefits, and total expense.
- **When medication is prescribed, ask about signs of adverse reactions.** Be sure you understand the recommended dosage and schedule.

68

F.Y.I   THE SECOND OPINION

In cases of elective surgery, or when you aren't sure about your treatment plan, it makes sense to get a second opinion. Check with your insurance company or your primary care physician to find a specialist.

Your insurance carrier may require you to contact them before you proceed with certain procedures. This **pre-certification process** helps ensure that your surgery or treatment plan is the right one for your needs. If a second opinion is required, your insurance carrier usually will pay the bill.

Talk to your doctor and hospital before an elective medical procedure is done to make sure they will accept what is considered an **"allowable"** cost for the procedure. If they agree, you won't have to pay anything above what your insurance agrees to pay. If not, you will be required to pay the difference between what your insurance covers and the cost of the procedure.

Choosing Mental Health Services

Depression, anxiety, drug and alcohol abuse, grief, marital problems, feelings of helplessness and hopelessness, loss of control. Everyone handles life's less-than-perfect moments differently. Most of the time, you can get through tough times with coping skills you've learned along the way. You "talk it out" with friends or family. You take up a new hobby or start exercising to release stress. You take a vacation to give yourself a fresh perspective on the things that trouble you most.

However skilled you are at managing your emotions, there may be times when you could benefit from an objective point of view—someone who can act as a sounding board and offer solid, professional advice. But locating the best source for support can often be difficult. It helps not only to know what mental health services are available to you, but also what type of professional or organization can best serve your immediate need.

Who's Who?

The labels—psychotherapist, counselor, psychiatrist, and so on—can be confusing. Following is a quick run-down of how the National Institute of Mental Health defines the roles of mental health professionals:

- **Psychiatrists** are medical doctors who specialize in mental disorders. They are licensed to practice medicine, and have completed three years of specialty training after graduating from medical school. A certified psychiatrist has, in addition, practiced for at least two years and passed the examinations of the American Board of Psychiatry and Neurology. Psychiatrists can evaluate and diagnose all types of mental disorders, carry out biomedical treatments and psychotherapy, and work with psychological problems associated with medical disorders. Of the mental health professionals, only psychiatrists can prescribe drugs and medical therapies. Child psychiatrists specialize in working with children; geriatric psychiatrists concentrate on helping the elderly.

- **Psychologists** practice psychotherapy and work with individuals, groups, or families to resolve problems. Licensed psychologists have earned a doctoral degree from a program with specialized training and experience requirements; in addition, they have successfully completed an examination for a professional license from the state in which they practice. They work in many settings—mental health centers, hospitals and clinics, schools, employee assistance programs, and private practice.

- **Psychiatric nurses** are registered professional nurses who have advanced academic degrees at the master's degree level or above. They specialize in the prevention, treatment, and rehabilitation of mental health-related problems. These nurses conduct individual, family, and group therapy, and also work in mental health consultation, education, and administration.

- **Social workers** are trained to provide individual therapy, group therapy, diagnosis, referral, and consultation. Psychiatric social workers have master's degrees in social work and have completed field-placement programs designed to train them in basic psychiatric techniques.

- **Psychotherapists** are mental health professionals who offer a variety of counseling and therapy services. Some people who call themselves psychotherapists do not have adequate training. If you doubt the credentials of a therapist, check with one of the professional associations listed in the resource section of this book.

- **Mental health counselors** provide professional counseling services involving psychotherapy, human development, learning theory, and group dynamics to individuals, couples, and families. Their main goal is to promote and enhance healthy, satisfying lifestyles, whether their services are rendered in a mental health center, business, private practice, or other community agency. Clinical mental health counselors have earned at least a master's degree

Choosing Mental Health Services

and are required to have several years of clinical supervision before they are certified by the National Academy of Certified Clinical Mental Health Counselors.

- **Case managers and outreach workers** assist severely or chronically mentally ill individuals, including the homeless mentally ill, to obtain the services they need in order to live in the community. Most chronically mentally ill people need medical care, social services, and assistance from a variety of agencies, including those dealing with housing, Social Security, vocational rehabilitation, and mental health. Because such services are uncoordinated in many areas, case managers provide a critical service in monitoring a person's needs and ensuring that appropriate agencies get involved. In many instances, they also act as advocates for the client. Case managers can be nurses, social workers, or mental health workers and can be associated with mental health centers, rehabilitation programs, outpatient clinics, private and group practices, general hospitals, psychiatric hospitals, and prisons.

Choosing the Right Service

Locating the mental health services that best suit your needs can seem daunting. As well, how much you are helped by the service you choose depends on the "fit" between your personality and that of the person you turn to for help. To be sure you get the help you need, keep in mind a few simple suggestions:

- **Start with professionals you know.** Your family physician, priest, rabbi, minister, or a counselor with your employee assistance program are all excellent starting points. These people are trained in consultation and referral to local mental health resources.

- **Check the credentials** of the person you'll be seeing. Don't be afraid to ask about a therapist's education, certification, years of experience, professional philosophy, and areas of expertise. Ask for references if you feel you need to verify a person's approach to counseling.

- **Ensure confidentiality.** It goes without saying that every mental health professional is bound by a code of strict confidentiality. Professional association guidelines, as well as federal and state laws, underscore the importance of confidentiality in therapist-client relationships and govern the release of records. Some insurance companies require certain information from the therapist as a condition for payment, but that information can be released only if the patient gives written permission. The employee assistance program at your workplace is precluded from ever telling your employer that you are asking for advice or referral. If you hesitate to seek help because you are afraid that someone will find out, discuss your concerns up front.

- **Don't be afraid to switch.** If you feel dissatisfied or unaided by a particular mental health professional, seek help from someone else.

Resources

Your local medical bureau or local department of mental health listed in the telephone book. You also can check the Yellow Pages under "mental health," "health," or "social services."

For information on self-help organizations, contact the National Self-Help Clearinghouse at (212) 840-1259 or the Self-Help Center at (800) 553-4539.

National Mental Health Association (800) 969-6642

70

Alternative Medicine

The American medical system is complex in the range of services available. We get more tests, see more doctors, use more drugs, and spend more time in hospitals than any other people in the world. Our health care system also is expensive. In the last 20 years, medical costs have jumped from $75 billion to more than $600 billion each year.

Some people argue that our traditional, complex, and expensive system of modern medicine and technology is effective in curing illnesses and injuries that improve with drugs or surgery but that it falls short or is not as effective in dealing with conditions that are more related to lifestyle problems such as stress. They also feel that modern medicine does not address the connection between the mind, body, and spirit and the role all three play in a person's total health and well-being.

Based on this belief, and looking for less expensive alternatives to traditional medical care, some individuals are turning to non-traditional or "alternative" approaches to health care. If you choose to use an alternative therapy or care provider, it is important that you understand what type of care and results you can expect from the treatment. It is important to be a savvy health care consumer in order to get the best possible care. Here is some information you should know when considering alternative health care choices.

Some alternative therapies and alternative practitioners may be covered by your medical plan, but many are not. Be sure that you know what, if any, services your health plan will pay for before using this type of care if cost is an issue.

Alternative Treatments

- **Osteopaths** are doctors (Doctor of Osteopathy or "D.O." rather than Doctor of Medicine or "M.D.") whose training emphasizes disorders of the musculoskeletal system. They are trained in four-year programs in the basic medical, surgical, psychological, and pharmacological treatments; however, osteopathic training emphasizes a more holistic approach to healing. A major difference from traditional medical practice involves the use of the hands, or "manipulation," in diagnosis and treatment. If you choose an osteopath as your primary care provider, make sure his or her training has included a residency experience in addition to the medical curriculum and internship.

- **Chiropractors** have been awarded the degree of Doctor of Chiropractic ("D.C."). They have had two years of college-level training and four years of chiropractic training. This method of treatment is based on the belief that most diseases are caused by a misalignment of the bones. In particular, chiropractic holds that misalignment of individual vertebrae can affect the health of other parts of the body. X-rays can be used in making a diagnosis, but chiropractors cannot use prescription drugs or surgery to treat their patients. They can only manipulate the bones as treatment. Some individuals turn to chiropractors when standard medical treatment of back pain or headaches has not been effective. Chiropractors are licensed by their state with laws defining their scope of practice.

- **Acupuncture** is an ancient form of Chinese medicine based on the belief that energy circulating through the body controls health and that pain and disease result when this energy cycle is interrupted. The balance of energy can be restored by the insertion of long, thin needles at specific points in the body. Each point controls a different part of the body. The needles are rotated gently back and forth once they are inserted.

- **Acupressure** is based on the same general premise as acupuncture; however, pressure is applied (instead of needles) at specific energy points of the body.

- **Homeopathy** is a holistically based system of treatment based on the beliefs that: 1) like cures like, 2) treatment is always specific to the individual, and 3) less is more, lowering the dosage or diluting the treatment can increase effectiveness.

Alternative Medicine

Various animal, vegetable, or mineral substances are administered in small quantities to alleviate specific symptoms and complaints.

- **Herbal medicine** has become more popular with the increasing number of "health food stores." Herbology is the use of herbs obtained from sources such as trees, flowers, seaweed, and other plants to treat disease. Many traditional medications also are made from plants; however, herbalists believe that herbs work differently on the body than purified manufactured drugs, having fewer side effects and faster healing properties.

  Some plant extracts can have beneficial effects (e.g., garlic is believed to lower blood pressure and act as an antibiotic), but misuse or overuse could lead to serious reactions. Some producers do not monitor the purity or concentration of the extracts. Herbal remedies should be used with caution. If you do use them, be sure to only use the recommended amounts, don't mix herbal and prescription remedies, be on the lookout for allergic reactions to herbs, avoid herbal remedies when pregnant, and be sure to seek medical care if your symptoms get worse or continue.

- **Naturopathy** uses natural remedies such as sun, water, heat, and air as the treatment for disease. Examples of naturopathic treatments might include changes in diet (such as more fruits, no salt or caffeine), exercise, or steam baths.

- **Creative visualization** was first developed as a technique for treating cancer. Creative visualization or "imaging" uses positive thoughts and images to attain a certain result, such as being free of a disease.

Should You Use Alternative Services?

That decision is up to you. However, before you do, be sure to compare what the traditional medical system has to offer and what the alternative therapy claims. Check credentials and beware of any treatment or practitioner claiming to be the "only" effective treatment or approach.

Some physicians are willing to combine traditional and alternative treatments and may be a valuable resource for information on alternative treatments.

Finally, remember that you ultimately are responsible for your own health and well-being. Make educated health care decisions based on the information you obtain about the alternatives available to you.

Resources

Your doctor

Office of Alternative Medicine
National Institutes of Health
9000 Rockville Pike
Building 31, Room 5B-38
Bethesda, MD 20892
(800) 531-1794

Alternative Medicine, The Definitive Guide. Future Medicine Publishing, Inc.: Puyallup, Washington, 1994.

Avoiding Medical Quackery

No one wants to be sick. And, sometimes it seems like it will take a "miracle" to make us well again. Unfortunately, every year millions of individuals search for medical "miracles" that will never happen. It is estimated that more than 10 billion dollars a year are spent on medical quackery. These unproven goods and services cost consumers not only a lot of money; they also cost lives and health in terms of needless pain, worsening conditions, and, most of all, crushed hopes.

- **Quackery preys on people's fears.** Cancer patients and HIV-positive individuals fear that they will not survive and thus may be willing to embrace worthless and unproven treatments in the hope that they may be cured. The peddlers of false hopes tell people in these situations what they want to hear, whether it is totally true or not. Millions of people are taken in each year by health fraud. If that "cure" for baldness, smoking, or even cancer sounds too good to be true, it probably is. You may be just as likely to be harmed as helped by such products.

- **The snake oil salesman in a three-piece suit.** Medical quackery can use a variety of methods to get you to buy something you "can't afford to be without." Sometimes individuals go door-to-door selling consumers "cures," "supplements," or even equipment, such as hearing aids, to improve health or stop disease. These people are salesmen, not doctors. They are not qualified to advise you about your health. They also may make false and flagrant claims about their products since there usually are no witnesses in the privacy of your home. These products may be peddled at greatly inflated prices and have no proven effect.

- **Beware of group presentations.** The "health lecturer" can be another method used by medical quackery to sell you a product. They may rent a hall or hotel conference room and advertise a free lecture about a health topic or disease. There may just happen to be a line of "health foods" or "special equipment" that they are willing to sell to make or keep you free of disease.

- **Beware of "mail-order medicine."** How many catalogs have you received in the mail recently? The U.S. Chief Postal Inspector reports that mail-order fraud and quackery seem to be at an all-time high level. Nutritional cures, breast developers, and weight reduction devices are examples of common products sold through the mail, which appear to be overpriced and of unproven effectiveness. The U.S. Food and Drug Administration warns that exaggerated and deceptive claims are common in mail-order health literature.

- **Read health books carefully.** You also should critically read health books and printed materials that you receive or even purchase. Don't accept the printed word as absolute truth or be convinced that information is sound simply because you saw the author on a talk show or some infomercial. Although there are laws prohibiting publishing untrue statements about people, products, or events, clever wording can sometimes get around the law. Just because it is in print, don't automatically accept it as truth.

Ideas that Work

- **Be suspicious of miracle advertisements.** Avoid products advertised as "secret" remedies. Reliable organizations such as the American Cancer Society or the Arthritis Foundation and those listed in the resource section of this book keep track of unproven and ineffective treatments.

- **Get it in writing.** Ask for written explanations and materials describing what the treatment does. What are the side effects? What documented evidence exists that proves the treatment works? Testimonials from "users" do not count. Are there published articles in reliable medical journals that support the effectiveness and safety of this method of treatment?

- **Beware of payment up front requirements.** Quacks always want the money right away. Don't be anxious to part with your money. Insurance often doesn't pay for unproven therapy.

Avoiding Medical Quackery

- **Beware of new "cutting-edge tests" or medical procedures.** Beware of new diagnostic tests that sound unorthodox to you. Blood tests for food allergies and hair analysis are examples of unproven diagnostic tests that quacks sometimes use for prescribing questionable treatments. Also, beware of "advanced medical techniques" that the promoter claims are being suppressed by the medical establishment.

- **Talk to your medical doctor.** If in doubt, about ANY treatment, consult with your doctor. Don't discontinue any elements of your current treatment plan in favor of a new "cure" without your physician's knowledge and approval. While many doctors DO encourage and support alternative treatments such as relaxation and visualization and chiropractic for certain conditions such as back problems, they can be your reality check against potentially dangerous and outrageous claims made by medical quacks. Also, don't hesitate to share with your doctor written material that you hold suspect or for which you need clarification.

Resources

Your doctor

U.S. Food and Drug Administration
5600 Fishers Lane
Room 1675, HFE-88
Rockville, MD 20857
(800) 532-4440
(301) 443-9767 (fax)
Send a postcard, call, or fax to request free pamphlets on more than 12 quackery subjects (including "Quackery and the Elderly"), or visit the FDA web site at http://www.fda.gov (choose publications).

Fact-Finding: Locating Medical Resources

To become an informed consumer of health and medical services, it's important to have adequate information and resources concerning your health problem. Information enables you to ask your doctor the right questions about such topics as available treatment options and their relative risks, benefits, and costs.

Ideas that Work

Here are some suggestions for researching your medical or health problem:

- **Start with your primary care physician (PCP).** Sit down with your PCP and have him or her help you address the questions that are listed on the *INFORMED* Worksheets on pages 78-81. If your doctor doesn't have the time, ask if a staff member can help you. See if your PCP has any pamphlets, videos, or other educational material that describes your condition and is targeted to the layperson.

- **Get a second opinion.** If you question your doctor's recommendations, consult another doctor for a second opinion. In fact, your insurance plan may require it, especially in the case of elective surgery.

- **Telephone-based nurse service.** Your company or health plan may offer a telephone "nurse line" service that does the fact-finding for you. This type of service is not a diagnostic service, nor does it recommend treatment; rather, it helps coach you to ask your doctor the right questions regarding your health problem.

- **Telemedicine services.** Many local hospitals and HMOs provide educational services you can access through your telephone. An automated system allows you to select audiotapes that explain a health condition.

- **Go to a college or a medical school library.** If you live close to a medical school or college, try to access its library. A medical library is more comprehensive than a college library, and will give you more disease-specific information.

- **The World Wide Web (WWW).** The rapid growth of the WWW offers individuals access to a variety of health-related "home pages" sponsored by government agencies, universities, not-for-profit groups, pharmaceutical companies, managed care groups, and individuals. Many home pages provide interactive health quizzes, health information and resources, and electronic bulletin boards that allow individuals to post and respond to questions left within the network. Because the WWW has no quality control standards, it's best to be cautious when accessing health information, especially from groups who claim to have "the cure." See "Avoiding Medical Quackery" on page 73.

- **Support groups.** Many support groups (e.g., multiple sclerosis, AIDS, breast cancer) have their own resources you can access. Check with your local hospital, health department, not-for-profit agencies, and online services for support groups near you.

- **Government agencies.** The U.S. government, through such organizations as the National Institutes of Health (NIH), and your state health department have various publications and some hotlines (e.g., cancer, AIDS) that provide educational assistance to individuals. You also can contact NIH regarding any clinical trials of experimental treatments that may be in effect and find out what admission criteria is required to be part of these government-financed studies.

- **Not-for-profit groups.** Organizations such as the American Academy of Family Physicians, the American Cancer Society, the March of Dimes, the American Heart Association, the National Multiple Sclerosis Society, the Asthma Foundation, the American Diabetes Association, and the American Red Cross have their own educational materials and programs you can request.

Resources

Refer to pages 288-293 for organizations and other resources.

The INFORMED Medical
Decision-Making Process™

By using this section you will learn:

- How to use the INFORMED Medical Decision-Making Process.

- How to be an active partner with your doctor regarding treatment decisions.

- How to avoid hospitalization and reduce your medical costs.

- About your rights as a patient and what documents you can't live without.

The INFORMED Medical Decision-Making Process™

....

INFORMED is an eight-step process that allows you and your doctor to explore treatment options and their benefits and risks when faced with a major health decision (e.g., surgery, hospitalization, medical testing, and/or another treatment option).

The advantages of using this outline include:

• **Better communication:** INFORMED provides a standard outline that helps you and your doctor discuss key issues regarding your health problem.

• **Participation:** This eight-step process helps you become more active in the decisions involving your medical treatment.

• **Greater confidence, trust, and quality:** By learning more about your health problem and treatment options, you probably will have more confidence and trust in your treatment plan. Also, because you were active in the decision-making process, your satisfaction around your care will be greater.

THE INFORMED DECISION-MAKING PROCESS™

The primary goal of INFORMED is to help you become a more active participant in decisions regarding your medical care. You can help remember the INFORMED process by memorizing the decision-making sequence below:

Input: What is my problem? What are my doctor's recommendations: further medical tests, medications, surgery, hospitalization?

Need: Why do I need treatment? What happens if I do nothing? What do I expect from my doctor?

Fact-Finding: Aside from my attending physician, do I need further information and resources to make a better informed decision? Do I need to get a second opinion? (See page 68.) Fact-finding includes addressing the following areas:

Options: Do other options exist for my problem? What are they? Can they be ranked from least intensive (e.g., "do nothing") to most intensive (e.g., surgery)?

Risks/Benefits: For each option, what risks exist (e.g., infection, permanent disability, other complications, death)? Also, what are the benefits of each option (e.g., complete recovery, lower cost, avoiding surgery, avoiding hospitalization)? How do the benefits of each option meet my needs: e.g., complete cure vs. minor disability or discomfort?

Management: For each option, will there be a need to manage my problem after my primary treatment? For example, will I need to be on medication(s) for an extended period of time? Will I have to eliminate or reduce certain activities including my work? Will I need rehabilitation? What can I do to help prevent my problem from happening again?

Expense: What is the total cost of each option? Total cost includes: medical costs, time off from work, lost wages, emotional distress, loss of independence, disfigurement due to scarring, etc.

Decision: After weighing each available option with my doctor, which one seems the most appropriate for my situation?

INFORMED Questions

INPUT: The first step in learning about your health condition is understanding what your problem is and what is being recommended by your doctor such as more tests, special medications, hospitalization, and/or surgery.

Questions to Keep in Mind

1. Does your doctor know what your health problem is?
2. If yes, what is the problem (diagnosis)?
3. If your problem is not known, what could possibly be causing your symptoms?
4. What tests are recommended by your doctor?
5. What treatment is your doctor recommending?

NEED: Many times certain medical procedures are done that have no influence on the final outcome of the problem, so it's a good idea to discuss the need for a recommended procedure. Also, it's important to identify your own needs. What do you expect from your care? How realistic are those expectations in light of what your doctor has shared with you? For example, knee surgery may reduce your pain, but prevent you from getting back on the racquetball court.

Questions to Keep in Mind

1. Why do you need treatment? (Learn all you can about your problem.)
2. Why do you need a particular test(s)? How will it help your treatment?
3. What if you do nothing ("watchful waiting")?
4. What do you want (expect) from your treatment (e.g., a total cure, reduction in pain, independence, etc.)?
5. How realistic are your expectations?

FACT-FINDING: Information is power. The more you can learn about your problem the better able you'll be to ask the right questions, learn about possible treatment options, and ultimately have greater confidence in your treatment plan.

Questions to Keep in Mind

1. Are you satisfied with how your doctor has described your health problem? Do you understand what is being recommended? Do you need him or her to explain more?
2. Do you need a second opinion on your diagnosis or recommended treatment? (Check with your insurance carrier regarding second opinion guidelines.)
3. Besides your doctor, where else can you find out more about your problem? Refer to **Options**, below.

OPTIONS: When a medical procedure or test is recommended, it's important not to accept the recommendation on face value. It's recommended that you not only understand why a certain procedure is being recommended, but that you also question whether other options exist for your problem.

Questions to Keep in Mind

1. Why is your doctor recommending this course of action?
2. Do other options exist for your problem? What are they?
3. Can each treatment option be ranked by how "aggressive" it is? For example, "watchful waiting" is the least aggressive approach, whereas surgery may be the most aggressive approach.

RISKS/BENEFITS: Each treatment or test has its own risks and benefits. Surgery, for example, carries risks associated with anesthesia, infection, blood clots, scarring, and other problems. On the other hand, surgery can save a life-threatening situation (e.g., a tumor or clogged artery) or restore mobility and reduce pain by repairing a joint injury. It's important to discuss the potential consequences of any treatment option with your doctor.

INFORMED Questions

Questions to Keep in Mind

1. What are the potential risks (infection, disability, incontinence, impotence, death) associated with each option?
2. What are the potential benefits ("cure" potential, no surgery, no hospitalization, no scarring, reduced cost) of each option?
3. Can you and your doctor compare the risks and benefits of each option side-by-side on the INFORMED option chart?

MANAGEMENT: For each option, you will want to know about how to manage your problem after your primary treatment is over. For example, you may need to take certain medications, undergo therapy, and change your lifestyle practices in order to speed your recovery. In many cases, the management of your problem is a longer process that requires hard work and understanding. Therefore, it's important to understand the management process for each treatment option and its affect on your quality of life.

Questions to Keep in Mind

1. For each option, will any short-term and/or long-term management be required (i.e., medication, therapy, housing needs, nursing needs, nutritional needs, or activity or job restrictions)?
2. Will you have to eliminate or reduce certain activities, including those associated with your work?
3. What can you do to help prevent or further manage your problem?

EXPENSES: Needless to say medical care costs money, but there are other expenses that most people often overlook when they make a health-care decision. For example, there are the financial costs associated with time off from work and lost wages. On the other hand, there can be serious emotional costs due to the loss of independence or disfigurement and scarring due to surgery.

Finally, there are other quality of life issues that need to be considered. Prostate cancer surgery, for example, can lead to incontinence or impotence in many men. It's important, therefore, to consider the total costs of a suggested option before agreeing to start treatment.

Questions to Keep in Mind

1. What are the "ball park" expenses (those from your doctor, any specialists, hospitalization, surgery, medications, etc.) for each option?
2. What are the potential costs of the management of your problem (medications, rehabilitation, skilled nursing)?
3. Does your doctor accept what are considered "allowable charges"? "Allowable charges" are those amounts that insurance companies and government programs such as Medicare are willing to pay for a specific medical procedure or accommodation (e.g., semi-private room). It's important to check with your insurance carrier as to what is covered under your health plan before consenting to a medical procedure. Otherwise, you may be financially responsible for non-covered expenses.
4. Will you lose work because of your treatment? For how long?

DECISION: Upon completing the INFORMED option chart, sit down with your doctor and discuss your available options and their relative risks, benefits, and costs.

Questions to Keep in Mind

1. Have all your options been discussed?
2. Are there still issues that need further explanation by your doctor?
3. Are your expectations concerning your treatment realistic? Do these expectations coincide with what your doctor has explained to you?
4. Are you satisfied with your doctor's support in helping you understand and decide on your treatment option?

INFORMED Option Chart

	OPTION ONE	OPTION TWO	OPTION THREE
CHOICE	Do nothing (watchful waiting*)		
RISKS			
BENEFITS			
MANAGEMENT			
EXPENSE			
DECISION	❑	❑	❑

* "Doing nothing" involves no medical or surgical treatment. You continue observing (watchful waiting) your symptoms for improvement, worsening, or no change over a specified period of time. Based on your observations, future treatment may be advised by your doctor.

Hospitalization

Forty-four cents of every health care dollar is spent on hospitalization and its related tests and procedures. Because hospitalization is the most expensive part of health care, everyone is trying to reduce unnecessary hospital visits and find alternatives (e.g., home care, ambulatory surgical centers) that provide quality care at a lesser cost.

Avoiding the hospital should be a major goal of every person. Hospitalization has its own risks (e.g., infection, complications during surgery or medical testing, reactions to medications) even in the best institutions. Be sure to question the need for hospitalization when it's recommended and inquire about other options such as outpatient surgery. (See the *INFORMED* worksheet starting on page 79.)

Of course, there are many reasons why hospitalization is the right course of action (e.g., emergency trauma, complicated surgical or treatment procedures). However, even in these situations, you should be active in the decision-making process whenever possible.

The following are examples of key questions that you should discuss with your doctor when hospitalization is recommended.

Questions Regarding Hospitalization and Surgery

- **Outpatient vs. hospitalization?** If surgery or hospitalization is recommended, find out if there are any other options, like medication and outpatient surgery services, to treat your condition.

- **Explore all options whenever possible.** If options exist, ask your doctor about their benefits, risks, and costs.

- **Question the total cost.** Besides the monetary costs of a specific treatment, ask your doctor about the potential physical and emotional costs of a specific treatment plan (e.g., post-operative depression and disfigurement due to surgery).

- **Pre-plan your surgery and treatment plan.** When surgery or other intensive treatments (e.g., chemotherapy) are recommended, become aware of what to expect during the recovery or treatment phase.

Key questions:
- ❏ How much pain should I expect from my incision or procedure?
- ❏ How long does it normally take to completely recover from this kind of surgery?
- ❏ What are the risks of disability because of my surgery (e.g., nerve damage, limited mobility)?
- ❏ What will my treatment be after my surgery?
- ❏ What signs should I look for that indicate that the treatment is working?
- ❏ What are the possible complications of my treatment?
- ❏ What signs should I look for that indicate I may have a problem?
- ❏ What problems should I call you about?
- ❏ How long will I be out of work?
- ❏ Are there certain activities that I shouldn't participate in for a while? If yes, how long should I wait?

- **If a surgical specialist is recommended, don't be afraid to ask questions, such as:**
- ❏ Are you board certified?
- ❏ How many surgeries similar to mine have you done?
- ❏ What is your success rate?
- ❏ Who will assist you?
- ❏ What is his or her experience?
- ❏ Will he or she actually do the surgery while you assist?

Saving on Hospital Bills

It's estimated that up to 99 percent of all hospital bills have at least one error—usually an overcharge. The larger the bill and the longer the hospital stay, the greater the chance of billing errors. This does not mean that your health care provider is intentionally charging you for services not given. It simply means that mistakes happen, especially when many people are involved in your care, and your medical condition calls for more intensive treatment.

Ideas that Work

Here are some ways to reduce your hospital bills:

- **Allowable charges.** Before agreeing to a medical procedure, make sure your doctor will accept what your health plan will pay. This is called an allowable charge. If your doctor charges more, you will be stuck with the difference. When in doubt, always check with your health plan before undergoing an elective treatment.

- **Is pre-certification required?** For many elective procedures, your insurance carrier requires that you contact them before your treatment starts. Called pre-certification review, your carrier helps you decide if the treatment is needed or other options are available. Failure to use the pre-certification process can land you with the entire medical bill or a higher deductible. Read your health benefit material carefully.

- **Outpatient services?** Be sure to ask your doctor if a certain procedure (e.g., minor surgery) can be done on an outpatient basis. If hospitalization is required, avoid weekend admissions, since many diagnostic services are limited. Also, find out if any tests can be done on an outpatient basis before you're admitted.

- **Check your deductions and out-of-pocket maximums.** Errors can occur when your insurance company fails to calculate your deductible correctly or charges you beyond your out-of-pocket maximum. Make sure you understand your health benefit plan.

- **The meter is running.** Once you're admitted to the hospital, the charges begin. In reviewing your bill, make sure your admission and discharge dates are correct. As with hotels, you may be charged a fee for being discharged after a certain time of the day. Refuse this charge if the hospital delayed your departure.

- **Log it!** Keep a detailed record of what tests, drugs, supplies, and other services you receive on a day-to-day basis, or have a family member do it for you. Don't be shy about asking the medical staff what a certain dressing or drug is if you don't know.

- **Bring your own medications.** The $5 charge for an aspirin is normally a big shock to the first-time hospital patient. If hospital policy allows and your doctor agrees, bring your own medications (e.g., aspirin, ibuprofen) with you, as well as prescription drugs you currently use.

- **Itemize!** Always ask for an itemized list of all services performed instead of a cost summary. Compare the list to your log and identify any services that you believe were not given. Report these questionable charges to your health insurance plan.

- **Stick to your guns.** If you feel you have been overcharged and are getting nowhere with the hospital billing department, work with your health plan. Also, contact your state agency that regulates hospital finances: They may be able to help you in reducing your charges. Remember, to have documentation (e.g., a log) to support your case.

Resources

Your health plan

Your company benefit department

Your state regulatory agency for hospital financing

Patient Rights

To be an informed medical consumer, it's important for you to understand your rights and responsibilities, and to respect the fact that medical personnel must conform to their own professional code of ethics and practices. The American Hospital Association (AHA) has developed a document entitled "Your Rights as a Hospital Patient" to help patients become aware of their rights and the hospital's responsibilities in treatment. Although written for hospital patients, most of these principles are important for all patients—hospitalized or not.

According to the American Hospital Association:

- You have the right to considerate and respectful care.
- You have the right to be well-informed about your illness, possible treatments, and likely outcome, and to discuss this information with your doctor. You have the right to know the names and roles of people treating you.
- You have the right to consent to or refuse a treatment, as permitted by law, throughout your hospital stay. If you refuse a recommended treatment, you will receive other needed and available care.
- You have the right to have an advance directive, such as a living will or health care proxy. These documents express your choices about your future care or name someone to decide if you cannot speak for yourself. If you have a written advance directive, you should provide a copy to the hospital, your family, and your doctor.
- You have the right to privacy. The hospital, your doctor, and others caring for you will protect your privacy as much as possible.
- You have the right to expect that treatment records are confidential unless you have given permission to release information or reporting is required by law. When the hospital releases records to others, such as insurers, it emphasizes that the records are confidential.
- You have the right to review your medical records and to have the information explained, except when restricted by law.
- You have the right to expect that the hospital will give you necessary health services to the best of its ability. Treatment, referral, or transfer may be recommended. If transfer is recommended or requested, you will be informed of risks, benefits, and alternatives. You will not be transferred until the other institution agrees to accept you.
- You have the right to know if this hospital has relationships with outside parties that may influence your treatment and care. These relationships may be with educational institutions, other health care providers, or insurers.
- You have the right to consent or decline to take part in research affecting your care. If you choose not to take part, you will receive the most effective care the hospital otherwise provides.
- You have the right to be told of realistic care alternatives when hospital care is no longer appropriate.
- You have the right to know about hospital rules that affect you and your treatment and about charges and payment methods. You have the right to know about hospital resources, such as patient representatives or ethics committees, that can help you resolve problems and questions about your hospital stay and care.

Used with permission, the American Hospital Association.

84

Advance Directives

Although medical technology can keep patients alive indefinitely, many people do not want heroic measures to be taken if there is minimal chance of recovery. They don't wish to lead a life of such compromised quality, or to be an emotional or financial burden to their families. Yet many people are unable to communicate their wishes at the time when a decision must be made. Health care professionals, bound by a duty to protect life, often are caught in a dilemma.

To address this problem, health care advocacy groups have lobbied in most states for the right of citizens to specify their wishes in advance—through legal documents called "advance directives." This document is prepared before you are faced with a life-threatening condition or major medical procedure.

Ideas that Work

Most advance directives are either *a living will or a durable power of attorney for health care.*

- **Living will:** A formal document that is signed, dated, and witnessed by two people who are not involved in your health care and are not future heirs to your estate. A living will states what kind of life support and heroic measures you wish to receive if you're not able to make those decisions at the time and your condition has been listed as terminal. Living wills also can specify what other medical procedures can be performed. It's usually recommended that a lawyer review your document, though it's not required.
- **Durable power of attorney for health care:** A formal document that is signed, dated, and witnessed, naming another person to make medical decisions for you in the event you are unable to make decisions on your own. A lawyer is not required to write a durable power of attorney for health care.

Things to Keep in Mind:

- **Legality?** Most states legally recognize advance directive documents, but each state has its own requirements. Refer to "Resources" below.
- **Which one?** Depending on the state you live in, one document or both may be recommended. Advance directives usually can be combined, specifying not only life support limitations, but also the type of care you wish to receive if you're unable to make decisions on your own.
- **Let your doctor know.** Your doctor must be made aware of advance directives. You can generally assume that in extreme situations if no advance directives are known, all measures probably will be taken on your behalf.
- **Second thoughts?** *You can cancel or change your specifications at any time.* Also, you can tell your doctor that you want to change your orders. Declining heroic measures will not affect the overall quality of your care, or significantly change your doctor's decision-making process except in extreme situations.
- **No directives, what then?** If you have provided no advance directives and your illness prevents you from making any care decisions, your family, doctor, and hospital are responsible for your treatment plan. Sometimes a judge may be needed if there is disagreement about treatment options.

Resources

Choice in Dying
200 Varick St.
New York, NY 10014
(800) 989-WILL

Your local Area Agency on Aging. Call the Eldercare Locator Service at (800) 677-1116 for the Area Agency on Aging (AAA) nearest you.

Addressing Emergencies

By using this section you will learn:

- What medical conditions require emergency care.

- How to handle medical emergencies when you're away from home.

- How to respond to severe bleeding and shock.

- How to recognize and treat poisoning.

- About cardiopulmonary resuscitation.

- How to respond to a choking person.

- How to handle head injuries.

- How to respond to a drowning person.

Emergency Care

It's estimated that up to one third of Americans visit an emergency room every year. For the *majority of cases,* the emergency room is the *wrong treatment choice* because the medical problem doesn't require urgent care. Many conditions can be treated by your primary care physician or at home, resulting in less wasted time and emotional distress, and considerable cost savings.

Not only is the emergency room an expensive option, an overload of non-urgent cases also can slow down the response of medical staff to more serious problems.

It's important to be aware of conditions that do need emergency care. You should seek immediate medical attention for any of the following conditions by calling 911 (if available) or the operator (dial 0) for an ambulance or emergency response team:

- **Signs of a possible heart attack.** Signs may include severe pain in the middle of the chest, pain in the jaw or upper back, numbness (not alone), or pain that spreads to arms (especially left arm), shortness of breath, and cold sweats. You should take one aspirin and then seek emergency care.

- **Signs of a possible stroke.** Signs may include sudden fainting, dizziness, slurred speech, changes in vision, stupor, disorientation and/or marked weakness on one side of the face or one or more extremities on the same side of the body.

- **Signs of shock** in an ill or injured person may include pale, clammy skin; weak, rapid heartbeat with shallow, hurried breathing; lackluster eyes; cool extremities. The person, though conscious, may be confused and weak or sometimes anxious and excited. Until help arrives, have the person lie down, face up, with feet elevated (unless this causes pain or there is a suspected neck or back injury). Keep the person calm and still. See page 90.

- **Unconsciousness.** You are unable to awaken or arouse the person.

- **Extreme difficulty breathing.** This may indicate a severe allergic reaction or an asthma attack.

- **The person is not breathing or has no pulse.** If you are alone and a phone is nearby, call for help first, then apply CPR. If you're not alone, send one person to call for help immediately and apply CPR. See pages 92-93. If the person is choking, try the appropriate technique described on page 91. It is recommended that you learn CPR through your local chapter of the American Red Cross or American Heart Association.

- **Possible spinal cord injury.** The person should not move or be moved if there is an injury to the neck or back.

- **Severe bleeding.** Call for help if bleeding cannot be stopped after you have applied direct pressure for 10 minutes and you have no assistance. If you have assistance, drive the person to the closest urgent care center while your companion applies direct pressure to the wound. See page 90.

Other conditions that require urgent care (call the emergency room or your primary care physician first):

- **An infant less than 2 months of age has a fever of 100.4 degrees F or higher (rectal temperature).** This condition could indicate a serious infection and needs immediate attention.

- **Severe vomiting or diarrhea, especially in infants.**

- **Poisoning.** First, try to locate the toxic agent. Read the label and call your poison control center (find the number in the phone directory and keep it by all phones). Follow instructions carefully. See page 96, "Poisoning."

- **A serious injury, such as a possible broken bone(s), a head injury (without loss of consciousness), or serious burns.**

- **Severe pain.** Unexplained pain that doesn't go away or gets worse.

Medical Emergencies on the Road

Whether you're traveling in the United States or abroad, if you're really sick it's important to get medical attention right away. Your hotel may have a doctor on call. If you're in a foreign country, the nearest U.S. embassy will have a list of doctors in the area and will assist you in a medical emergency.

According to the American Medical Association, you may need immediate medical attention if you have any of the following symptoms:

- **Fever over 101 degrees F for two days or longer**
- **Chills with shaking**
- **Stiff neck**
- **Diarrhea, vomiting, and abdominal pain for more than two days**
- **Persistent heart palpitations or chest pains**
- **Coma or seizures**
- **Prolonged or severe weakness**
- **Prolonged asthma**
- **Extensive bleeding from the mouth, nose, ears, or rectum**
- **Poisoning**
- **Bite by a venomous animal such as a snake, bee, spider, or scorpion**
- **Bone fracture**

If your medical problem is very serious, don't take the time to contact the embassy to call a doctor. Call a taxi or an ambulance to take you to a hospital emergency room.

Ideas that Work

The following is a checklist for travelers who have medical conditions that may require attention away from home:

- **Consider a medical exam before leaving.** Be sure to have an examination if you plan to be out of the country for an extended period of time.
- **Are you covered?** Check with your employer or insurance carrier to make sure your health insurance will cover you at your destination.

- **Bring your medicine.** Carry enough medication to last the entire trip plus extra for unexpected delays returning home. Don't forget medication for headaches, colds, and allergies when appropriate. Do not mix your prescriptions in one container since they can be confiscated by customs. Therefore, carry all medications in their original containers. Keep them in your carry-on luggage to avoid losing them.
- **Medical records.** Take a copy of your personal medical records with you. Include a list of all medications, dosages, and their frequency. This list should be kept in a safe place other than where your medications are stored. Your doctor may be willing to provide you with a recent medical summary to alert others to your unique medical needs.
- **Identify yourself.** Wear a Medic Alert bracelet if you have a medical condition that warrants it.
- **See clearly.** Take extra glasses, contact lenses, and lens cleaning solution.
- **Make arrangements for your children.** If you are leaving children at home, make sure you sign an authorization for medical treatment and leave it with your children's caretakers before you leave.
- **Pay me now.** Many health providers require payment at the time of treatment for out-of-town patients. Therefore, be prepared to pay in cash or through a major credit card.

Resources

AirEvac
(800) 421-6111

International Association for
Medical Assistance to Travelers
(716) 754-4883

Medic Alert
(800) 432-5378

Bleeding/Shock

Uncontrolled bleeding is a serious emergency that requires prompt action. Blood loss can quickly put a person into a life-threatening condition called shock. Bleeding usually occurs in two general forms: an oozing wound that comes from cutting the skin and the disruption of veins, or a very bright red wound that comes from an artery with heavy bleeding and possible spurting.

Uncontrolled Bleeding

When faced with uncontrolled bleeding, follow these steps:

1. For serious bleeding and possible signs of shock (refer to next column), call 911 or your local emergency response team. However, don't delay treatment.

2. Apply direct pressure. Using a sterile dressing or a clean cloth, apply direct pressure over the wound for at least 10 minutes. If the dressing becomes soaked with blood, do not pull the  dressing from the wound—instead, place another clean dressing on top of the existing cloth.

3. Elevate the injured area if you don't suspect a broken bone. This helps slow down the bleeding.

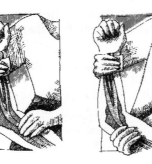

4. If bleeding doesn't stop, use pressure points. Maintain direct pressure over the wound and also apply pressure to a "pressure point" above the wound. (Refer to diagram at right.) For the arm, apply pressure to upper arm as shown. With a leg wound, apply pressure to the groin.

5. If you have assistance, drive the person to the closest urgent care center while your companion applies direct pressure to the wound.

Treating Shock

As discussed, shock is a serious life-threatening condition caused by lack of oxygen to vital organs. It's critical that blood loss be controlled as soon as possible and medical attention sought. The signs of shock include:
• rapid and weak pulse
• confusion, weakness, or unconsciousness
• pale and/or clammy skin
• shallow, rapid breathing

If the victim shows signs of shock, medical attention is needed immediately. Call 911 or your local emergency response team.

While you're waiting for help to arrive, quickly do the following:
• **Prop up the victim's feet higher than the head** (unless a leg has been injured).
• **Adjust for temperature.** If you are outside in hot weather, try to find a shaded area. If it's cold, use blankets to keep the victim warm. Loosen clothing and wait for help.
• **If there's uncontrolled bleeding, continue to apply the procedures listed above.**

Choking

Choking: Infant

The following rescue procedure is for infants under 1 year of age who are choking and cannot cry, cough, or breathe. If you are unsure of the infant's age, use this procedure unless the child is too long or too heavy to be held on your arm and hand, as shown in the figure to the right. If the child is too large, use the rescue procedure for a choking child.

Step 1: Deliver 5 back blows: Place the infant face down on your forearm, cupping his or her jaw with your hand. Using the heel of your other hand, strike the infant's back firmly 5 times between the shoulder blades.

Step 2: Turn infant over. Rotate the infant so that he or she is face up, with your arm supporting the back and your hand supporting the neck.

Step 3: Deliver 5 chest thrusts: Use your index finger and middle finger together to deliver 5 chest thrusts to the center of the breastbone (mid-chest, about 1/2-inch below the nipple line). Thrusts should compress chest downward about 1/2 inch to 1 inch.

Repeat steps 1, 2, and 3 until the infant coughs up the object, begins to breathe, or becomes unconscious. If the airway is clear, but the victim is not breathing, begin rescue breathing. (See page 92.)

Choking: Child or Adult

The following rescue procedure is for children and adults who are choking or turning blue and cannot breathe, talk, or cough. DO NOT use this procedure on a person who is not choking. Use it only on a person who cannot breathe or is turning blue, gray, or ashen.

Victim Standing or Sitting

Step 1: Wrap your arms around the victim from behind. Tip the victim slightly forward.

Step 2: Make a fist with one hand; grasp the fist with your other hand.

Step 3: Position your fist between the victim's navel and rib cage.

Step 4: Thrust your fist upward quickly and forcefully. Use an inward and upward motion, as if you are trying to lift the person off the ground.

Step 5: Repeat thrusts as necessary until object pops out and the airway is clear.

Victim on Floor

Step 1: Position the victim on his or her back, face up.

Step 2: Straddle the victim at mid-thigh (your knees should rest on the floor next to the victim's hips).

Step 3: Position your hands on the victim's mid-section: Put one hand on top of the other, with the heel of the bottom hand directly on the victim's stomach between the navel and ribcage.

Step 4: Deliver hard, quick thrusts at an inward and upward angle—as if you are trying to push something toward the back of the victim's neck.

Step 5: Repeat thrusts as necessary until the obstruction pops out and the airway is clear. If the airway is clear, but the victim is not breathing, begin rescue breathing. (See page 93.)

91

Rescue Breathing/CPR for Infants

Rescue Breathing

If an infant is not breathing, but has a pulse:

Step 1: Tilt the infant's head back slightly to open the airway.

Step 2: Seal your mouth tightly over the infant's nose and mouth.

Step 3: Give two slow gentle breaths. The infant's chest should rise and fall as you breathe into the nose and mouth. Do not blow too hard: Doing so can force air into the infant's stomach. If chest does not rise, reposition the infant's head and try two more breaths. If chest still does not rise, follow procedure for "Choking: Infant," on page 91, then try breaths again.

Step 4: Check for pulse: Place your first two fingers on the inside of the infant's upper arm. If you feel a pulse but the infant is not breathing, go to Step 5. **If you feel no pulse, begin infant CPR as shown in the right-hand column.**

Step 5: Give 1 slow breath every 3 seconds for 1 minute (about 20 breaths). Watch the chest as you give each breath to be sure air is getting into the lungs.

Step 6: Check pulse again and check for breathing. **If you feel a pulse but the infant is not breathing, call your local emergency number for help.** Then continue rescue breathing until the infant starts to breathe without your help, or until emergency help arrives. **Begin CPR if you fail to find a pulse.**

CPR

If an infant has no pulse and is not breathing, proceed with CPR. DO NOT do chest compressions on any person who has a pulse.

Step 1: Place fingers on center of infant's breastbone, 1/2 inch to 1-inch below nipple line.

Step 2: Compress chest 5 times in 3 seconds. Compressions should be about 1/2- 1-inch deep.

Step 3: Give 1 slow, gentle breath: Inhale, form a seal with your mouth over the infant's nose and mouth, then exhale slowly. Watch for infant's chest to rise as you exhale.

Step 4: Repeat cycle of 5 compressions and 1 breath for about one minute.

Step 5: Check for pulse and breathing.

Step 6: If there is no pulse, call your local emergency number for help. Continue cycle of 5 chest compressions and 1 slow breath, checking pulse and breathing every 3 minutes until the infant breathes without help, has a pulse, or until paramedics arrive.

Resources

It is strongly recommended that you take a CPR course from your local chapter of the American Red Cross or the American Heart Association.

Rescue Breathing/CPR for Children and Adults

Rescue Breathing

If a person is not breathing, but has a pulse:

Step 1: Tilt the victim's head back to open the airway.

Step 2: Check for breathing. Position your ear over the victim's mouth. Listen for breathing while looking at chest for rise and fall of breathing.

Step 3: Pinch the victim's nostrils closed and seal your mouth tightly over the victim's mouth.

Step 4: Give 2 slow breaths. The victim's chest should rise and fall as you breathe into the mouth. If it does not, reposition the victim's head and try 2 more slow breaths. If the chest still does not rise, follow the procedure for "Choking" on page 91, then try breaths again.

Step 5: Check for pulse: Press your first 2 fingers on the victim's carotid artery (on either side of the Adam's apple). If you feel a pulse but the victim is not breathing, go to Step 6. **If you feel no pulse, begin CPR.**

Step 6: Give 1 slow breath every 4 seconds for a child/every 5 seconds for an adult, for 1 minute (about 12–15 breaths). Take your mouth away between breaths. Watch the chest as you give each breath to be sure air is getting into the lungs.

Step 7: Check pulse again, and check for breathing. **If you feel a pulse but the victim is not breathing, call your local emergency number for help.**

Step 8: Continue rescue breathing until the victim breathes on his or her own or until help arrives; check for pulse every minute. **Begin CPR if you fail to find a pulse.**

CPR

If a person has no pulse and is not breathing, proceed with CPR. DO NOT do chest compressions on any person who has a pulse.

Step 1: Get on your knees next to the victim.

Step 2: *For an adult,* place one hand on top of the other, with *the heel* of the bottom hand on the victim's breastbone (locate the area where bottom ribs meet in the center of the chest, then move up 1 1/2 inches). *For a child,* place *the heel* of one hand on the breastbone.

Step 3: *For a child,* compress chest 5 times to a depth of 1 inch; *for an adult,* compress chest 15 times to a depth of 2 inches. Don't lift your hand(s) off chest between compressions. Lock elbow(s) during compressions and keep shoulders directly over hand(s).

Step 4: Lift and tilt victim's head, pinch the nose, and breathe into the mouth. *Give a child* 1 slow breath; *give an adult* 2 slow breaths: and watch for chest to rise.

Note: Use two hands for adult only; use one hand for child.

Step 5: Repeat cycle of compressions and breaths (15:2 for an adult; 5:1 for a child) for 1 minute. Recheck pulse and breathing. **If the victim is still not breathing and has no pulse, call the emergency number for help.**

Step 6: Continue giving CPR until victim has a pulse or until paramedics arrive.

Resources

It is strongly recommended that you learn CPR from your local chapter of the American Red Cross or the American Heart Association.

Drowning

Any near-drowning requires immediate action and prompt medical attention:

1. **Get the person out of the water,** summoning help if needed. This may be difficult in a large body of water. Depending on your own skills and the conditions, you may be able to swim to and retrieve the drowning person yourself. You could throw a rope or a buoyant object for the person to hold on to. Or, you could use a rowboat or canoe to get to the person. Once you reach the person, he or she can cling to the side while you row ashore; if you try to get the person in the boat, it may capsize.

2. **Begin resuscitation (see page 92 for an infant, page 93 for a child or adult) as soon as possible if the person is not breathing.** If possible, start the process while you are removing the person from water, for example, in the shallow area of a lake. Don't waste time trying to drain the lungs of water.

3. **Summon emergency medical assistance.** Any near-drowning can lead to complications, so prompt medical attention is necessary.

4. **If the person is breathing, lay him or her down in the recovery position** (stomach down, head turned to side) and keep him or her warm with blankets until medical help arrives.

F.Y.I BE WATER WARY FOR YOUR CHILD'S SAKE

- Never leave a child unattended—by an adult—near any body of water, even the small amount contained in a bucket.
- If you have a pool, install a child-proof fence around it.
- Teach your child to swim, if he or she is at least 3 years old, and to never go in the water without an adult.
- Put a life preserver on your child whenever he or she goes boating.
- Secure toilet seats with child-proof locks.

Head Injuries

The skull provides a lot of protection against many bumps and falls. So, the majority of head injuries are minor and do not require hospitalization. Minor head injuries typically require rest for a few days and acetaminophen for pain relief. Refer to "Abrasions" (page 152), "Bruises" (page 159), or "Cuts" (page 162), as appropriate.

It is important to observe the injured person closely in the hours and days following a head injury. This may mean waking him or her periodically during the first night following injury to be sure he or she can be awakened easily. **If there is any change in the level of consciousness (from slight confusion to loss of consciousness), the person's pulse becomes slow (below 70 beats per minute) or irregular, his or her pupils are of unequal size, or if any other troublesome symptoms arise, consult a doctor immediately.**

In the case of major head trauma, as may occur following a traffic accident or fall from a bike, seek emergency treatment. Keep the person lying down with the shoulders and head slightly elevated until help arrives. Do not move his or her neck.

Get Emergency Care if the Person:

- Is not breathing (see "Rescue Breathing," page 92 for an infant or page 93 for a child or adult).
- Has severe head or facial bleeding (see "Bleeding," page 90).
- Has a deformed skull, bruising behind an ear or around eyes, pupils of unequal size, or bloody or clear discharge from ears or nose.
- Is confused, lethargic, or vomits more than once or has a headache, speech difficulty, partial paralysis, partial memory loss, or convulsion either immediately following injury or in the hours or days following the trauma.

Poisoning

Nearly 1.7 million poisonings occur in the home each year. Most poisonings occur when someone swallows a poisonous substance, but they also may result from exposure to a gas or absorption of a substance through the skin. The best prevention against poisoning? Taking the time to poison-proof your home—especially if you have young children—and knowing what steps to take if you think someone in your household has been poisoned.

For Suspected Poisoning

If the person is unconscious:

1. Immediately call 911 or the emergency room (keep phone number by all phones). Apply emergency resuscitation if there's no breathing or pulse.

If the person is conscious:

1. Call the poison control center immediately (keep phone number by all phones), even if you're not sure a poisoning has occurred. *If you have the poison in hand, do not follow instructions on the label unless you're unable to reach the poison control center.*

2. Answer the questions from the poison control center as best you can (e.g., victim's age, the name of the poison, when it was taken, whether the person has vomited).

3. Follow the instructions that are given to you.

   –If the person has swallowed an acid, an alkali, or a petroleum product, do not induce vomiting: This can cause more harm. You'll probably be instructed to first have the person drink milk to dilute acid or alkali products. Water should be used for petroleum products.

   –If the above substances were not involved, you may be instructed to induce vomiting either by putting a finger to the back of the throat (this stimulates the gag reflex) or by giving syrup of ipecac. *Make sure you have syrup of ipecac in your home medicine cabinet. It can be purchased at your local pharmacy.*

4. Follow instructions on the package for further medical care.

F.Y.I   Poison-Proof Your Home

- Keep things out of sight, up high, and locked up. Take precautions with medicines, household cleaners, anything that contains alcohol, and house plants.
- Watch medications. Be aware that child-resistant caps are not childproof—they just slow kids down.
- Use original containers. Never place poisonous liquids in other containers; they can be mistaken later for something else.
- Keep your garage tidy. Gasoline, pesticides, paint products, and antifreeze should be kept beyond the reach of young children. Use as directed.
- Keep syrup of ipecac available if there are children in the home.

Using
Medications
Wisely

By using this section you will learn:

- How to use medications wisely.

- How to stock your home
  medicine chest.

- About common over-the-
  counter medications.

- About prescription medications.

Medication Use Guidelines

Medications, both over-the-counter and prescription, need to be used wisely. Treat these drugs with respect by following the recommendations listed below.

Ideas that Work

- **Use the following list and your "Medication Use Record," on page 287, when a drug is prescribed.** Ask your physician or pharmacist the following:
  - ❏ Why has this drug been prescribed?
  - ❏ What are its possible side effects?
  - ❏ Will it react with other drugs that I am taking?
  - ❏ How long will I need to take this drug?
  - ❏ What time of the day should I schedule my dose?
  - ❏ If side effects occur, what should I do?
  - ❏ Will this drug increase my sensitivity to sunlight?
  - ❏ What is the proper dosage?
  - ❏ Should I take it on an empty stomach?
  - ❏ Should I avoid alcohol or other foods or drinks?
  - ❏ How will I know if the drug is working?
  - ❏ Can this drug be substituted with a generic brand?
  - ❏ How should this drug be stored?
  - ❏ Are refills allowed?
- **Beware of overmedication, or interaction with other drugs you may be taking.** Keep your doctor and pharmacist informed of all drugs you take. Here are some examples of combinations to avoid:
  - – Seldane® (treats hay fever; has been removed from the market so check with your doctor before taking any you have) & Erythromycin® (treats a number of bacterial infections)
  - – Halcion® (treats insomnia) & Erythromycin®
  - – Mevacor® (lowers blood cholesterol levels) & Lopid® (treats patients with high serum triglyceride levels)
  - – Coumadin® (prevents and/or treats blood clots) & Tagamet® (treats stomach ulcers)
  - – Theo-Dur® (prevents or relieves asthma, chronic bronchitis, and emphysema symptoms) & Tagamet®
  - – Tagamet® & Dilantin® (prevents and controls seizures)
  - – Prozac® (treats major depression) & Dilantin®
  - – Calan® (treats angina, irregular heartbeat, high blood pressure, migraine headache, asthma, manic depression) & Duraquin® (treats irregular heartbeat)
  - – Calan® & Lanoxin® (treats congestive heart failure, irregular heartbeat, and other heart problems)
  - – Eldepryl® (treats Parkinson's disease) & Norpramin® (treats depression)
- **Order by mail.** You could save up to 50 percent on a drug(s) for a chronic condition. Contact your health plan to locate mail-order suppliers. The supplier should maintain individuals' medication files and have a toll-free number for questions.

F.Y.I   POINTERS FOR SAFE MEDICATION USE

- Know the name of the drug(s) you are taking.
- Know how to take a drug properly: e.g., with water, on an empty stomach, etc. Know how often you should take a prescribed or over-the-counter (OTC) medication and the proper dosage.
- Know what drugs (prescription and over-the-counter medications) you're currently taking that should not be taken with this medication. Check with your pharmacist.
- Understand the side effects of this drug(s).
- Don't share your prescription drugs with another person or borrow someone else's.
- Don't change your dosage without first consulting your doctor.
- If possible, have all your prescribed medications come from one pharmacy or chain so that one source will have a record of all your medications. This will help minimize potential adverse drug interactions.

Medication Use: Older Adults

More drugs are prescribed to people over age 65 than to any other group in America. Older adults consume one quarter of all drugs prescribed in the United States, and women take twice as many as men. The average older adult receives 13 prescriptions per year. Because the elderly are the largest single group of people using prescription drugs, they also are the group most likely to have problems with them.

One in five older adults has experienced undesirable reactions to prescription medications. There are a variety of age-related reasons that explain why seniors have twice as many adverse reactions to medications as do younger individuals. As individuals age, changes in the digestive and circulatory systems, kidneys, and body composition affect how the body is able to absorb, use, and eliminate medications. Decreases in the motility and gastric acid secretion in the digestive tract can slow a drug's passage through the stomach and intestines.

For some drugs, such as Digoxin® and Warfarin®, the change in the amount of drug absorbed because of this slowing can be critical to its effectiveness. As we age, the liver is less able to purify toxic substances from the body. If an older adult takes a drug that is filtered through the liver, the drug may have longer lasting and more severe effects than are normal.

Information about the types, benefits, and side effects of prescription drugs is seemingly endless. There are thousands and thousands of prescription drugs available, and the number increases each day. Remember that the best sources of information about your prescription medications are your doctor and your pharmacist. Take the time to understand what medication you will be taking, how much and when, as well as what adverse reactions you might expect. See "Medication Use Guidelines" (page 98) for more information on taking medications safely.

Although medications are prescribed to make us feel better, any drug can cause problems if taken incorrectly. Among older adults, there are a few specific categories of prescription drugs that cause the most serious problems. They are summarized in the following table.

99

PROBLEM DRUGS FOR OLDER ADULTS*

MEDICATION/BENEFITS	COMMON BRANDS	ADVERSE REACTIONS
Diuretics – lower blood pressure – eliminate excess fluid and salt in tissues	Lasix®, Hydromox®, Edecrin®, Diuril®, Hydrodiuril®, Aldactone®, Aldactazide®	–dehydration –low potassium –can worsen gout and diabetes
Anti-hypertensives – lower blood pressure	Inderal®, Apresoline®, Aldomet®, Serpasil®, Vasotec®, Lopressor®, Minipress®	–headaches –nausea –weakness/fainting –impotence –insomnia
Corticosteroids – decrease inflammation	Decadron®, Cortef®, Cyclocort®, Hydrocortone®, Medrol®	–fluid retention –osteoporosis and impaired healing of wounds with long-term use
Sedatives – sleeping aids – reduce anxiety – promote relaxation	Valium®, Librium®, Xanax®, Dalmane®, Restoril®, Seconal®, Nemabutal®, Deprol®, Equanil®, Miltown®	–memory loss –addiction –unsteadiness/falls –grogginess –agitation

*Do not stop taking any medication or change the dosage without your doctor's permission.

Your Medicine Chest

The following list is provided to assist you and your family in stocking your medicine chest. It includes basic items for the treatment and relief of common medical problems. Before you proceed, take note of these recommendations:

• Discard any over-the-counter or prescription medications that have passed their expiration date.

• Discard medications or supplies where packaging has been damaged (e.g., by water) or shows signs of tampering (e.g., safety lid is missing or loose).

• Never use another family member's prescription medication.

• Any drug can be harmful; read product information carefully and follow recommended dosages and schedules.

• Make sure all bottles are closed properly. Young children should be trained to stay out of the medicine cabinet—or better yet, lock the cabinet. Never leave any drug within the reach of small children.

Recommended Supply Checklist

❏ Thermometer. Include rectal thermometer if household has young children.

❏ Blood pressure cuff (sphygmomanometer) and stethoscope if someone in your household has blood pressure problems.

❏ Aspirin, acetaminophen, naproxen, or ibuprofen for fever, minor aches and pains, and headache. Aspirin, naproxen, or ibuprofen for reducing inflammation; ibuprofen or naproxen for menstrual cramps. **Because of the risk of Reye's syndrome, aspirin should not be given to or used by children or teenagers who have or are suspected of having flu or chicken pox. Use acetaminophen.**

❏ Antacid or sodium bicarbonate. For treating an upset stomach.

❏ Antibiotic cream (e.g., Neosporin®) for minor cuts.

❏ Antihistamines—oral and topical—e.g., Benadryl®. For treating minor allergies such as hay fever, cold symptoms, and some insect bites.

❏ Adhesive bandages, assorted sizes

❏ Gauze pads

❏ Disposable latex gloves

❏ Cotton balls and swabs

❏ Chemical ice pack

❏ Elastic bandage

❏ Scissors

❏ Tweezers

❏ Safety pins

❏ Toenail clippers

❏ Eye drops. To relieve dry or itchy eyes.

❏ Saline solution for eyes.

❏ Hydrocortisone. For the treatment of skin rashes and itching.

❏ Colloidal oatmeal soap (e.g., Aveeno®) for rashes and itching.

❏ Petroleum jelly. For diaper rash or "jock itch."

❏ Pectin substance (e.g., Kaopectate®). For controlling diarrhea.

❏ Syrup of ipecac. To induce vomiting upon poisoning. (Be sure you know when to use.)

❏ Anti-fungal powder or spray. To treat fungal infections such as athlete's foot.

❏ Sunblock or sunscreen (a minimum SPF of 15). To prevent sunburn.

❏ Water-soluble lubricant (e.g., K-Y Jelly®). For vaginal dryness.

❏ Zinc oxide preparation. To prevent sunburn.

❏ Dental floss. To prevent buildup of plaque on teeth.

Popular Over-the-Counter Medications

DRUG/BENEFITS	COMMON BRANDS	POSSIBLE RISKS/DRAWBACKS
Allergy Medications		
• **Oral Antihistamine/Decongestant Preparations** –Relieve and treat allergy symptoms –Relieve cold symptoms (e.g., congested nasal passages and runny nose – Antihistamines can help relieve itching from rashes and swelling from insect bites	Chlor-Trimeton®, Benadryl®, Allerest®, Sinutab®	• Antihistamine use can cause drowsiness and impaired functioning while operating machinery and driving. Also, it can complicate existing prostate problems and make contact lenses difficult to wear • Decongestants can cause agitation
• **Nose Drops/Sprays** –Relieve and treat allergy symptoms –Relieve congestion and runny nose	Afrin®, Contac®, Dristan®, Neo-Synephrine®	• After several days, symptoms can become worse because nasal lining becomes dry and irritated, causing even more swelling • Agitation and/or rapid heart rate • Addiction
Cold/Flu Medications • Relieve cold symptoms: fever, muscle aches, nasal congestion. Dry mucus	Contac®, Coricidan®, Dristan®, Triaminic®	• Drowsiness • Agitation • Possible upset stomach
Cough Preparations • Expectorant preparations loosen mucus • Suppressant preparations reduce the cough reflex	2/G®, Robitussin®, Romilar®, Cheracol-D®, Robitussin-DM®, Vicks Formula 44®	• Drowsiness • Constipation
Laxatives for Constipation • Increase bulk to stool by drawing in water	Effer-Syllium®, Metamucil®, Milk of Magnesia®, bulk laxatives that contain psyllium	• Diarrhea; dehydration with extreme cases of diarrhea • Tolerance to medications and constipation with prolonged use • Laxatives with phenolphthalein may present a cancer risk
Anti-Diarrheal Preparations • Thicken the stool or slow bowel • Relieve severe cramping	Kaopectate®, Metamucil®, Imodium A-D®, Pepto Bismol®	• No significant side effects • Nausea and sedation
Heartburn/Antacid Preparations • Neutralize stomach acid • Block the production of stomach acid	Tums®, Pepcid AC®, Tagament HC®	• Absorbable antacids generally are not recommended for people with hypertension or heart problems because they contain sodium.

Popular Over-the-Counter Medications

DRUG/BENEFITS	COMMON BRANDS	POSSIBLE RISKS/DRAWBACKS
Hydrocortisone Creams • Relieve itching and rashes from poison ivy, poison oak, and insect bites	Caldecort®, Cortaid®, Dermolate®, Bactine®, Lanacort®	• Long-term use (more than two weeks) can lead to skin damage • Short-term use on face and genitals is not recommended
PAIN/FEVER RELIEVERS **Aspirin** • Relieves mild to moderate muscle pain • Anti-inflammatory agent • Relieves tension headaches • Relieves arthritis pain • Reduces fever	Bayer®, Anacin®, Maximum Strength Anacin®, Maximum Strength Bayer®, Bufferin®, Alka-Seltzer®, Regular Strength Ecotrim®, Empirin®, Aspergum®	• Promotes bleeding and bruising • Stomach upset, stomach and duodenal ulcers, or gastrointestinal bleeding • Reye's syndrome in children and teens • Increased risk to woman or fetus in last trimester of pregnancy • Aspirin poisoning
Acetaminophen • Relieves mild to moderate muscle pain • Relieves headaches • Does not irritate stomach • Recommended for children and teens with fever because there is no risk of Reye's syndrome • For the pain of osteoarthritis	Regular and Extra Strength Tylenol®, Excedrin P.M.®, Liquiprin®, Anacin 3®, Datril®	• Liver damage in excessive amounts (greater than 5,000 mg) • Alcoholics at greater risk for liver damage • Does not reduce inflammation • No effect on some types of arthritis
Ibuprofen • Relieves muscle pain and soreness • Reduces menstrual pain • Relieves headaches • Useful in treating strains and sprains • Reduces fever • Relieves arthritis	Advil®, CoAdvil®, Medipren®, Motrin-IB®, Nuprin®, Pamprin-IB®, Alka-Seltzer Plus®	• Stomach upset, stomach and duodenal ulcers, or gastrointestinal bleeding • Potential kidney damage to people with kidney disease
Naproxen • Relieves fever, muscle pain and soreness • Reduces menstrual pain • Relieves headaches • Useful in treating strains and sprains • Night-time relief (i.e., 8 hours) • Relieves arthritis	Aleve®	• Should not be used by children, heavy drinkers, pregnant women, or people who have aspirin sensitivity, ulcers, or asthma

102

Common OTC Pain Relievers

The number of over-the-counter (OTC) pain relievers on store shelves is enough to give you a headache. What's best for everyday aches and pains? Can any over-the-counter tablet relieve really severe pain? Is there any pain reliever you shouldn't take under certain conditions? And what about generics—are they as potent as their brand-name siblings?

For occasional, ordinary pain, the "big four" pain relievers—aspirin (Bayer®, Bufferin®), acetaminophen (Tylenol®, Pamprin®), ibuprofen (Advil®, Nuprin®), and naproxen (Aleve®)—all work equally well in brand-name or generic forms, although acetaminophen has the fewest side effects. Keep in mind, however, that no over-the-counter preparation will be very helpful for severe pain. Once you take a certain dose of any of these drugs you experience a ceiling effect: More pills won't kill more pain. If you have the kind of persistent pain that can't be significantly reduced or eliminated by an over-the-counter pain medicine, it's time to see your doctor.

Ideas that Work

So what should you have on hand for your garden-variety backache, headache, arthritis, or menstrual cramps? Here's a rundown of your over-the-counter options for pain relief:

Aspirin: Reduces pain, fever, and inflammation. May cause stomach upset, heartburn, and indigestion. Do not take if you have ulcers, clotting problems, gastrointestinal problems, asthma, liver or kidney disease, or if you are pregnant or scheduled for surgery within five days. Do not give aspirin to children or teens. **Because of the risk of Reye's syndrome, aspirin should not be given to or used by children or teenagers who have or are suspected of having flu or chicken pox. Use acetaminophen.**

Acetaminophen: Reduces pain and fever; *does not reduce inflammation*. Will not cause stomach upset. Can cause liver damage with heavy dosing, extended use, or heavy alcohol consumption. Excellent choice for children and for anyone else who should not take aspirin.

Ibuprofen: Reduces pain, fever, and inflammation. May cause stomach upset, although it's not as irritating as aspirin. Good for menstrual cramps, inflammation, and dental pain. Do not take if you have heart disease, asthma, aspirin sensitivity, or if you are pregnant. Also, do not mix with naproxen—side effects can occur.

Naproxen: Reduces pain, fever, and inflammation. May cause less stomach upset than aspirin. Excellent for nighttime pain relief (a single dose lasts eight hours or more), menstrual cramps, and dental pain. Not recommended for children, pregnant women, heavy drinkers, or people with ulcers, aspirin sensitivity, or asthma.

Whatever pain reliever you choose, be sure to follow label instructions carefully (high dosages can be toxic). If one medicine gets to your pain faster and better than another, stick with it: Your body chemistry can have a significant impact on how a particular drug works for you.

Treating Common Medical Problems

By using this section you will learn:

- About the 145 common medical problems that account for most doctor visits.

- How to determine if a certain problem needs medical attention.

- How to apply HomeCare for medical problems that don't need a doctor's treatment.

- How to reduce your out-of-pocket medical expenses by reducing unnecessary doctor visits.

Introduction to Medical Self-Care

It's estimated that more than 80 percent of all common health problems—such as colds/flu, scrapes, and stomach upset—are treated by the individual, never requiring medical treatment by a doctor. This is not to say that you should never see your doctor for what you may think is a minor problem. In fact, a "bad" case of heartburn could be heart attack, or ongoing fatigue could indicate something serious.

An important self-care skill is having the "know how" to decide if a health problem is a medical emergency, needs medical advisement and a possible doctor's visit, or can be treated at home. Called medical self-care, it helps you make informed decisions about the need for medical or home treatment—through appropriate resources such as this book and, perhaps, a telephone "nurse line."

There are many benefits of having medical self-care skills. They include:

- **Greater knowledge.** The old saying, "Knowledge is power," also applies to medical self-care, since the more you know about your own health, the more likely you'll take care of your No. 1 asset: yourself.

- **Greater confidence.** Making health-related decisions can be very intimidating, after all, "that's what doctors are for." But, in fact, most doctors encourage their patients to develop self-care skills. By making decisions around common health complaints, you build confidence in addressing your own health and are better prepared to work with your doctor when medical treatment is needed.

- **Convenience.** Avoiding an unnecessary doctor visit when home treatment will do saves you time and the hassle of taking time from work or other commitments.

- **Saves money.** Reducing unneeded doctor visits can save you out-of-pocket expenses such as deductibles and co-pays. But, it also saves you other costs such as time from work and travel expenses.

- **Better partner with your doctor.** Medical self-care's goal is not to keep you away from your doctor. On the contrary, it encourages you to build an ongoing relationship with your primary care provider. By knowing when medical care is needed and being "in-tune" with your symptoms, you can help your doctor get to the root of your problem more quickly and develop a treatment plan that meets your needs.

Within this special section, more than 145 common symptoms or health complaints are reviewed to provide you with commonly accepted guidelines for deciding if your symptoms or health complaint need medical care or can be treated through home treatment (HomeCare). Pages 107-108 discuss in greater detail how to use this section.

Ideas that Work

- **Do you have a symptom or a health problem?** When you or a family member has a symptom (e.g., fever, sore throat) or health complaint (e.g., cut finger), go to the Table of Contents. You'll find your health complaint either listed in the "General Symptoms" section or under a general body category, such as "Conditions of the Head and Chest." Refer and turn to the corresponding page number. Also, the general index lists topics in alphabetical order.

- **Do not delay an emergency.** If you are told your problem requires immediate medical attention—DO NOT DELAY—seek emergency care.

- **When medical consultation is recommended.** Call your doctor's office to receive instructions on what to do next, for example, come immediately, make an appointment, watch symptom(s), continue HomeCare, etc.

- **When HomeCare is recommended.** Try recommendations that apply to your condition. If your symptom or problem is not identified, call your doctor for instructions.

This section is not a substitute for appropriate medical care. When in doubt, do not delay seeking medical attention.

How to Use the HomeCare Section

This section is designed to help you determine if your medical problem needs the attention of a doctor. When your medical problem does not require a doctor, you are referred to the HomeCare column on the right-hand side of the page. Each HomeCare column has special picture boxes (icons) that suggest a certain order of treatment. For example, rest, medication, and fluids may be recommended. Try the treatment in the order presented. *However, first be sure that your problem does not require medical attention by checking the section titled "Consult Your Doctor If."*

What Do the Self-Care Icons Mean?

 **Rest:** One of these icons will be followed by recommendations that you change or limit your overall activity level. Bed rest usually will not be necessary.

 Fluids: This icon will be followed by recommendations that you consume adequate levels of fluids to prevent dehydration, especially when a fever or diarrhea is present, or that you avoid certain drinks such as alcohol. Fluids also keep mucus more liquid and help you avoid secondary infections such as bronchitis. In most cases, water is the first choice, but it lacks needed minerals that may be depleted from your body because of illness. Therefore, fruit juices, electrolyte drinks (e.g., Gatorade®), or caffeine-free carbonated drinks may be recommended, also.

 Medication: When you see this icon, specific over-the-counter medications will be recommended. It is important to keep the following points in mind:

- Use the specified medication as directed by the manufacturer. Read the instructions on the side panel carefully.
- Do not overmedicate. Don't use more than the directed dosage and recommended schedule.
- If you have a pre-existing health problem, such as hypertension or prostate enlargement, refer to the warning message on the label. If your problem is identified, do not use the medication without consulting your physician.
- **Because of the risk of Reye's syndrome, do not use aspirin for children or teenagers who have symptoms of influenza (respiratory flu) or chicken pox. Use acetaminophen to treat fever and muscle aches.**

 Nutrition: When this icon is shown, the recommendations that follow will be for either special meals, depending on your problem, or a balanced diet. When you have a fever, it is important to consume enough calories to maintain your strength and make up for calories burned because of increased body temperature.

 Heat/Cold: This icon will be followed by recommendations that you apply either heat or cold to the injured area.

HEAT is used in therapy to bring blood and nutrients to an injured area. Hot compresses, heat packs, and whirlpool baths help relax muscles that are sore and tense. Heat is not recommended when there is swelling and inflammation of a joint, especially within the first 48 to 72 hours after injury. Heat treatment will increase the swelling, bleeding, and pain in the injured area.

COLD is used in cases of tissue swelling and inflammation. Cold temperatures constrict blood vessels, thereby slowing blood flow to the injured

How to Use the HomeCare Section

area, and reduce pain and discomfort. Commercial ice packs or ice cubes in a plastic bag are common ways to apply cold to an injured area. Another method is freezing Styrofoam® cups filled with water and peeling the top away as needed. Ice cups can be used when a joint such as an ankle or elbow needs to be massaged because of tendinitis. Ice therapy should be applied in intervals of 20 minutes on and 20 minutes off. *Be careful of frostbite: white skin and numbness.*

 Clean: This icon will be followed by recommended ways to clean an injury such as a cut or abrasion, or an area of the body exposed to chemicals or other external irritants such as poison ivy. In most cases, plain soap and water will be recommended over alcohol and other antiseptic preparations.

 Cover: When this icon is shown, you'll find recommended ways to bandage or cover a wound or injury.

 **Activity:** When one of these icons is shown, a recommendation will follow to either limit physical activity to allow proper healing or to do special exercises to speed recovery.

 **Note Well:** This icon represents the Latin term "nota bene" or "note well." When shown, it will be followed by additional methods for treating your problem at home.

 Prevention: When this icon is shown, the techniques that follow will help you prevent the problem from recurring.

Cough

Coughing is an automatic reaction to an irritation in the throat, breathing tubes, or lungs. The irritation can be caused by dry air, tobacco smoke, allergies, a piece of food stuck in the airway, or chemical fumes, or can be a reaction to a viral (e.g., colds and flu) or bacterial infection.

If you have a viral infection, you may cough up yellow or white mucus. Green or rust-colored mucus often indicates a bacterial infection. Viral infections need to run their course and usually don't need a doctor's attention. Bacterial infections, on the other hand, should be checked by your doctor, who usually will prescribe antibiotics as treatment. **Consult your doctor immediately if mucus is rust-colored, or is pink and frothy, and you have a fever of 102 degrees F or above. These symptoms may indicate pneumonia.**

Experts believe that you should not use cough suppressants if you have a *productive cough*, in other words, if you are coughing up mucus and other material. A productive cough is one way the body tries to rid itself of an infection.

With a nonproductive dry cough, you don't cough up any mucus. Throat lozenges, hard candies, or over-the-counter cough suppressants that contain dextromethorphan may reduce the discomfort of nonproductive coughs and coughs caused by irritation in the back of the throat from postnasal drip.

Consult Your Doctor If:

- **You cough up mucus that is rust-colored, or pink and frothy, and you have a fever of 102 degrees F or higher.**
- Your infant (under 3 months) has a cough.
- Your child has difficulty breathing, or is wheezing or breathing rapidly.
- You have a dry, nonproductive cough with no other symptoms, and it doesn't go away after one week.
- You cough up mucus that is thick and green.
- Your cough hasn't gone away after you've recovered from a cold or flu.

HOMECARE
If physician referral is not recommended at this time, try the following self-care procedures:

Fluids

- Drink plenty of fluids to help keep mucus more liquid and easier to cough up.
- Avoid caffeine drinks, e.g., coffee, soda, and tea, and alcohol, which increase urination.

Medication

- Use expectorants with care; try to loosen mucus through increased fluid intake first. Use expectorants as directed.
- If your cough is nonproductive, try a cough suppressant that contains *dextromethorphan*. Talk to your pharmacist.
- Try hard candy or throat lozenges to relieve an irritated throat.
- Antihistamines or decongestants may be tried to control postnasal drip. Use as directed.

Heat/Cold

- Try a vaporizer to increase the humidity in your home, especially your bedroom.
- A hot shower can help thin mucus.
- Fill your bathroom sink with hot water and place a towel over your head. Form a tent over the sink and breathe in the steam for 10 minutes. Repeat as needed.

Prevention

- If you smoke, try to quit.

* **Because of the risk of Reye's syndrome, aspirin should not be given to or used by children or teenagers who have or are suspected of having flu or chicken pox. Use acetaminophen.**

general symptoms

109

Diarrhea

iarrhea is a common sign of a gastrointestinal infection. Usually caused by a virus and sometimes by bacteria (e.g., food poisoning, poor drinking water), diarrhea is the body's way of clearing the infection from the intestine. Diarrhea usually is preceded by abdominal gas and cramping. When diarrhea is frequent or painful cramping occurs, an anti-motility compound such as Imodium A-D® is a useful over-the-counter preparation. Ask your doctor or pharmacist to recommend medication.

Other causes of diarrhea can be traced to medications such as antibiotics and drugs used to treat high blood pressure and arthritis. Nervous tension is another culprit that stimulates the digestive system.

Symptoms/Signs

- Loose or runny stools, usually preceded by abdominal gas and cramping

Consult Your Doctor If:

- Your diarrhea is black or bloody.
- You experience severe abdominal pain with diarrhea.
- You experience the signs of dehydration: increased thirst, dark yellow urine, limited urination, and skin that may be wrinkled and have no tone.
- Diarrhea continues for more than 48 hours after following HomeCare procedures.
- You experience diarrhea that comes and goes for more than one week.
- You have begun to take a new medication.
- Your infant has any diarrhea episodes, is feeding poorly, appears listless, and is less responsive to you.

HOMECARE
If physician referral is not recommended at this time, try the following self-care procedures:

Fluids

- To prevent dehydration, drink plenty of fluids such as water and preferably electrolyte solutions found in popular sports drinks. For breast-fed infants, feed as always, but offer extra water. For formula-fed infants, eliminate all but clear liquids (i.e., water or oral rehydration solutions: Pedialyte® and Rice-a-lyte®) for 24 hours.

Nutrition

- As tolerated, maintain a well-balanced diet from the major food groups including cereal, meats, cooked vegetables, and fruits.
- Greasy foods and milk products may make you uncomfortable.

Medication

- OTC preparations that contain pectin (e.g., Kaopectate®) solidify runny stools. Drink plenty of water with preparation.
- OTC preparations (anti-motility compounds) such as Imodium A-D® inhibit cramps and diarrhea.
- For children, the above OTC preparations are not considered safe or effective.

Prevention

- To prevent food-borne infections, be sure that food is properly prepared and stored.
- Wash hands with anti-bacterial soap and water before and after handling food.
- Clean all food preparation areas (e.g., countertops, cutting boards, sinks) with anti-bacterial cleaning agents.
- Never drink untreated stream or lake water.

Dizziness

A reduction in blood flow from the heart to the brain is a major cause of dizziness. Most often this is the result of postural hypotension, a pooling of blood in the legs. It can occur after vigorous exercise or when you stand up suddenly. This condition usually is harmless, unless episodes occur more often.

Recurring bouts of dizziness that come on suddenly are considered "spells." Alert your doctor as soon as possible to find and treat the underlying problem.

A more intense form of dizziness is vertigo, where a person has difficulty maintaining balance and/or the room seems to "spin." It may be accompanied by vomiting. Vertigo is difficult to diagnose; some cases may be caused by an inner ear infection and should be evaluated by your doctor.

Symptoms/Signs

- Lightheadedness, possible sensation of blacking out
- With a "spell," dizziness comes on suddenly and recurs
- In vertigo, difficulty maintaining balance and/or the room seems to spin, and, possibly, vomiting

Consult Your Doctor If:

- **You experience loss of consciousness or coordination, a rapid or irregular heartbeat, chest pain, trouble speaking, confusion, or shortness of breath. Seek emergency care.**
- You experience "spells."
- You experience vertigo: balance problems and/or the room seems to spin around.
- You suspect an inner ear infection. Refer to page 133.
- You're unable to participate in your normal activities because of your lightheadedness.
- You experience dizziness after using a new medication.

Rest

- Learn to manage your stress and tension.
- Learn a relaxation technique. Refer to pages 32-34.
- Avoid "jumping out" of a chair or bed if you have episodes of lightheadedness upon rising.

Activity

- After vigorous activity such as running, cool down slowly by walking around for two to three minutes.
- Don't hold your breath when lifting heavy loads. Breathe out when moving an object.

Medication

- Carefully follow directions for medication use (OTC and prescription). Be sure not to mix a new medication with other drugs or alcohol without your doctor's permission.

Prevention

- If you experience persistent "spells," make note of symptoms, time of day, and possible causes—such as medication use, eating habits, changes in activity, periods of stress—and share your log with your doctor.

general symptoms

111

Fatigue

F atigue, a lack of energy, and a general feeling of being tired can be linked to such physical causes as a viral infection, insomnia, sleep apnea, and "over-training syndrome" found among many endurance athletes. Fatigue also can be a result of emotional problems such as depression, anxiety, or stress. Low blood sugar (hypoglycemia) is rarely a cause for ongoing or chronic fatigue. Most of us have our bouts of tiredness and low energy, lasting a few days. This usually is in reaction to a minor infection, overwork, or playing too hard. It is especially important for people with changing work schedules or who "moonlight" to get adequate rest and practice appropriate self-care skills to avoid getting run down.

Recently, a lot of attention has been focused on Chronic Fatigue Syndrome (CFS), a mysterious ailment that leaves its victims with extreme fatigue and flu-like symptoms. Some people have had the illness for more than 10 years, limiting their ability to enjoy a normal life. Some cases have been linked to low blood pressure, which can only be detected through "tilt testing." In other cases, the cause is unknown and there's no standard treatment. However, many doctors now prescribe exercise, directing patients to start out slowly and build up activity levels.

Symptoms/Signs

- Feelings of being tired all the time or having no energy
- With Chronic Fatigue Syndrome: ongoing fatigue and other flu-like symptoms such as swollen glands, aching muscles, and low-grade fever

Consult Your Doctor If:

- Your fatigue is associated with a cold or flu and HomeCare doesn't reduce symptoms.
- Your fatigue doesn't go away after three weeks.
- You experience ongoing daytime fatigue and you are a heavy snorer. Refer to page 214.

HOMECARE
If physician referral is not recommended at this time, try the following self-care procedures:

Rest
- Get six to eight hours of sleep per night.
- Refer to "Insomnia" on page 208 or "Snoring" on page 214, as appropriate.

Activity
- Slow down! Modify your schedule if you are "burning the candle at both ends."
- Reduce your workouts for two weeks if you exercise heavily.

Fluids
- Avoid drinking too much alcohol.
- Reduce your ingestion of caffeine drinks.

Medications
- Do not rely on stimulants such as diet pills and amphetamines or illicit drugs such as cocaine to give you "energy."

Nutrition
- Eat balanced meals.
- Drink plenty of fluids, especially during hot, humid days and during strenuous exercise or other work.

Prevention
- Learn and practice relaxation and stress skills.
- Try to balance your work and play.
- Get enough sleep.

Fever

Contrary to general belief, an elevated body temperature is not necessarily an indication of illness. Your body temperature changes throughout the day and night in response to stress, physical activity, hormonal changes, and even as a reaction to spicy foods.

Most medical experts agree that "fever" is when body temperature measured with an oral (mouth) thermometer is higher than 99.5 degrees Fahrenheit. With a rectal thermometer (used for babies and small children), 100.4 or higher is a fever. Fever in itself is not a disease; it's the body's defense against infection. Many bacterial and viral infections are destroyed by an increase in body temperature.

Fever in older adults, especially the frail elderly, should be carefully watched since this is a sign of an underlying problem (e.g., infection) that could rapidly become more serious.

Symptoms/Signs

• Body temperature, as measured by an oral (mouth) thermometer, is higher than 99.5 degrees F. (A rectal reading will be about one degree higher than an oral reading.)

Consult Your Doctor If:

• **Fever is combined with a stiff neck (difficulty touching chin to chest), confusion, and lack of energy.**
• A child or adult has a fever of 103 degrees F or greater as measured by an oral thermometer.
• A child has a fever and shows signs of febrile seizures: Muscles throughout the entire body stiffen, eyes may roll, child's head may jerk, hands and/or feet may tap, and loss of bowel and urine control may occur. See "Seizure," page 241.
• A baby has a fever and is less than 3 months old.
• A child has a fever that returns after more than 24 hours of normal readings.
• A child has a fever and a history of febrile seizures.
• An adult has a fever of 101 degrees F that has not been reduced after three days of HomeCare.
• An adult has a low-grade fever that lasts more than several weeks.

Medication

• Aspirin, ibuprofen, or acetaminophen for reducing fever higher than 101 degrees F. Use as directed.*

Fluids

• It's important to maintain fluid balance. Drink plenty of water. Other caffeine-free drinks like fruit juices or ginger ale can be used.
• Avoid caffeine.

Heat/Cold

• Sponge the skin with lukewarm water (not cold water). Evaporation will have a cooling effect on skin and bring heat to surface.

Rest

• Limit activity. Bed rest may be advisable in cases of high fever and other symptoms such as diarrhea.
• Allow your child to rest as he or she desires.

Note Well

• Remove extra layers of clothing.

general symptoms

113

* Because of the risk of Reye's syndrome, aspirin should not be given to or used by children or teenagers who have or are suspected of having flu or chicken pox. Use acetaminophen.

Numbness

If you've ever had your foot "fall asleep," you know what numbness feels like. Most of the time, numbness is a harmless and temporary symptom associated with a minor injury, a pinched nerve, or arthritis. Sometimes, however, numbness is a sign of something more serious. Older people with diabetes can experience numbness as their disease affects the health of nerve fibers in the extremities, making them more prone to injury and infection. **When numbness comes on suddenly, it can indicate a stroke in progress—a life-and-death situation that requires emergency medical attention.**

Less commonly, numbness signals a toxicity of certain chemicals or medications (e.g., mercury, lead, solvents, insecticides, certain vitamins, etc.). Whatever the origin of the symptom, it's important for you to know when to seek medical help for numbness. A good rule of thumb is that you should see a doctor for any numbness that comes on suddenly or is not clearly attributable to some minor cause.

Symptoms/Signs

- Loss of feeling or sensation in any part of the body, sometimes accompanied by intermittent tingling or "pins and needles" sensation
- You experience numbness that is not associated with injury or another apparent cause

Consult Your Doctor If:

- **You experience sudden numbness in your face or in the arm or leg (or both) on one side of your body.**
- **Sudden numbness is accompanied by vision problems, speech problems, dizziness, lack of coordination, difficulty swallowing, or a sudden and severe headache.**
- Numbness is associated with injury to the neck or back, or weakness in any leg.

114

HOMECARE

If physician referral is not recommended at this time, try the following self-care procedures:

Note Well

- For numbness in the hands and feet due to exposure to cold, refer to "Cold Hands and Feet" on page 161.

Heat/Cold

- Keep areas of the body prone to poor circulation covered with warm, dry clothing.

Palpitations

It's not unusual for anyone to feel an occasional flutter in the chest or racing heart. Caffeine, alcohol, certain medications, tobacco, emotional excitement, anxiety, and stress all can cause palpitations in the healthiest of tickers.

It's when heart palpitations have no apparent cause or are accompanied by other symptoms that you should become concerned. A congenital defect, heart disease, respiratory problems, and other disorders can stress the heart muscle. In those cases, palpitations often are the only direct, early warning signal you'll have that there's something seriously wrong. A visit to your doctor is the surest way to tell whether irregular heart rhythms are benign "blips" on your cardiac screen or occasional wake-up calls that may save your life.

Symptoms/Signs

- Sensation that your heart is racing without cause, fluttering, missing a beat, or beating irregularly

Consult Your Doctor If:

- **Palpitations or chest pain are accompanied by nausea, vomiting, cold sweats, shortness of breath, lightheadedness, or faintness.**
- **You experience chest pain that spreads to the neck, back, shoulder, or arms.**
- You have questions about your palpitations.
- You experience palpitations after you start or stop taking any medication.
- You experience chest pressure or pain in the center of your chest that lasts for more than a few minutes or that comes and goes.
- You have a burning sensation that feels like severe heartburn or indigestion.
- You have unexplained pain in your lower jaw.
- Palpitations are associated with dizziness, lightheadedness, or passing out.

Medication
- Avoid diet pills or other stimulants.
- Avoid certain over-the-counter cold or allergy medicines (check with your doctor or pharmacist).

Activity
- Exercise moderately and regularly.
- Check with your doctor before beginning a new exercise program, especially if you've been sedentary for a while. Then start slowly and increase intensity gradually.

Rest
- Get plenty of sleep; fatigue can increase anxiety and the effects of stress, which can increase the frequency of palpitations.

Fluids
- Drink plenty of fluids (preferably water, six to eight glasses a day) to keep heart and chest muscles well hydrated.

Prevention
- Don't smoke. Avoid all tobacco products.
- Avoid alcohol and caffeine.
- Keep your weight in a healthy range; eat a balanced diet and exercise regularly.
- Practice stress-reduction techniques.
- Take medicines only as directed.
- Make sure that your doctor and pharmacist know about all the medications you're taking and whether you have any drug allergies.
- Do not use illicit drugs of any kind, especially "speed" and cocaine.

Runny Nose

The obvious source of a runny nose is a cold. Until your body rids itself of the virus that has invaded your respiratory system, your nose may leak copious amounts of mucus. Most of the time, the mucus is clear and watery. If it becomes thick and colored (yellow or green, for instance), you probably have a bacterial infection and need to see a doctor. Otherwise, gentle and frequent blowing will help keep nasal passages relatively clear.

If your nose runs but you don't have a cold, you probably have allergic rhinitis—allergies to certain plants, pollen, or dust. Therefore, avoiding offensive allergens should be your first plan of attack.

Finally, be careful using over-the-counter nasal sprays. Overuse (i.e., more than three days) can lead to a rebound effect, where the medication causes a runny or stuffy nose. Instead, try saline spray to wash away irritants, or to moisturize dry nasal passages. You can buy saline spray or make your own: Boil a mild saltwater solution of three tablespoons per eight ounces of water, let it cool, and then inhale the solution from your palm into your nose or through an aspirator.

Symptoms/Signs

- Intermittent or continuous drainage of mucus from the nose

Consult Your Doctor If:

- A runny nose and other cold symptoms are accompanied by a fever of 103 degrees F.
- Nasal mucus is discolored (e.g., yellow or green) or has a foul odor.
- You suspect your runny nose is a result of seasonal allergies.
- A runny nose is not accompanied by any other symptoms and lasts three weeks or longer.
- You experience wheezing, shortness of breath, or difficulty swallowing.
- Mucus is accompanied by severe facial pressure or pain unrelieved with OTC preparations.
- You have used over-the-counter nasal sprays for more than two weeks without relief.

Medication
- Try an over-the-counter anti-histamine or cold remedy.
- Use over-the-counter nasal spray medications for no more than three days, saline nasal spray as needed.

Heat/Cold
- Breathe steam to loosen mucus and clear out nasal passages. Take hot showers. Or fill a basin with boiling water, drape a towel over your head, bend over the basin, and breathe. Drinking hot beverages helps, too.

Nutrition
- Eat a well-balanced diet with plenty of fruits and vegetables rich in vitamins C, A, and E.
- Avoid dairy products, which can contribute to thicker and more profuse mucus.

Rest
- Get adequate rest to help re-energize your immune system.
- Limit activity in cold, dry weather.

Prevention
- If you have allergies, use your home and car air conditioner during allergy season. Keep windows closed. Consider using a portable air filter.
- Keep your home well humidified.

* Because of the risk of Reye's syndrome, aspirin should not be given to or used by children or teenagers who have or are suspected of having flu or chicken pox. Use acetaminophen.

Sore Throat

A sore throat can result from a number of factors, such as dry air, smoking (including passive smoking), allergies, air pollution, or a viral or bacterial infection. Mild throat irritation is common in people who sleep with their mouths open, which causes the throat to become dry and scratchy, or who have postnasal drip. Viral infections such as influenza and colds are common causes of sore throat. A more severe sore throat occurs with mononucleosis. "Mono" is a viral infection common among adolescents and young adults.

Sore throats also can be caused by bacteria, usually from the streptococcal strain. "Strep throat" symptoms usually are limited to pain and tenderness in the throat, and strep needs to be diagnosed by your doctor through a throat culture. Untreated, strep can lead to rheumatic fever (mostly in children) or inflammation of the kidneys. Antibiotics are the treatment of choice for strep.

A viral sore throat, on the other hand, usually has other associated symptoms such as a runny, congested nose, headache, and cough. These symptoms indicate a typical cold or influenza and rarely require a doctor's visit. It is important to remember that a viral sore throat *cannot* be treated with antibiotics.

Symptoms/Signs

- Symptoms of mononucleosis include sore throat, extreme fatigue and swollen glands
- "Strep throat" symptoms can be limited to pain and tenderness in the throat

Consult Your Doctor If:

- Throat is bright red, or pus or white spots are present on back of throat and symptoms are limited to the throat only.
- Sore throat is accompanied by fever of 102 degrees F or above and symptoms are limited to throat only.
- A mild sore throat lasts more than seven days.
- You have difficulty breathing or swallowing, or your child displays excessive drooling.

HOMECARE
If physician referral is not recommended at this time, try the following self-care procedures:

Rest
- Viral infections need to run their course. Bed rest usually is not needed.

Fluids
- Fluids will help relieve soreness. Try weak tea with honey and lemon to soothe the throat.

Medication
- Aspirin, ibuprofen, or acetaminophen for fever.*
- Decongestants with or without antihistamines for runny nose.
- Take cough drops to soothe a dry throat.

Note Well
- Salt water gargles may ease soreness.
- Try a humidifier in your home, especially in bedrooms.
- A vaporizer may help also.

Prevention
- If you smoke, quit. Smokers are more prone to upper respiratory infections.

117

* Because of the risk of Reye's syndrome, aspirin should not be given to or used by children or teenagers who have or are suspected of having flu or chicken pox. Use acetaminophen.

Swollen Glands

Most cases of swollen glands involve the lymph nodes, or with mumps, the salivary glands of the neck.

Lymph nodes are small glands that help your body fight infections such as colds, ear infections, and those in small cuts. They become swollen and hard when an infection occurs and may remain hard after the infection has passed. You can feel lymph nodes in your neck, armpits, and groin area. Swollen lymph glands usually are no reason for concern when they are present with minor infections. However, persistent swollen glands may indicate a more serious health problem requiring medical consultation.

Typically a childhood disease, mumps is caused by a virus and cannot be treated directly. Symptom relief, such as controlling fever and getting adequate rest, is the best action to take. Adults should be cautious if they haven't had the mumps: Complications such as sterility, although rare, can occur. See "Mumps" on page 240.

Symptoms/Signs

- Glands that are swollen or hard, and may be red and tender to the touch
- With mononucleosis: swollen glands (especially in the back of the neck) that are present with fever, sore throat, muscle aches, and fatigue
- With the mumps: one or both of the salivary glands (located below and forward of the ears) are swollen. Other symptoms include low fever, earache, headache, and/or fatigue

Consult Your Doctor If:

- The glands do not get smaller after three weeks.
- A single gland is getting progressively larger over several days.
- There is redness and inflammation in the skin above the gland.
- Swollen glands are accompanied by other symptoms such as fever and weight loss.
- You suspect the mumps.
- You suspect mononucleosis.

Note Well

- If lymph nodes are swollen—no treatment is required. Watch glands and other symptoms for three weeks.
- Evaluate and treat other symptoms as they occur, e.g. fever, sore throat, cough. Refer to other conditions within this book.
- If you have or suspect you have mononucleosis, avoid contact sports since the spleen may be enlarged and could rupture.

Heat/Cold

- Apply a warm washcloth or a cold compress, according to which seems to provide the best relief.

* **Because of the risk of Reye's syndrome, aspirin should not be given to or used by children or teenagers who have or are suspected of having flu or chicken pox. Use acetaminophen.**

Vomiting

V omiting usually is your body's reaction to something that doesn't belong in your system: a virus, bacteria, food you're allergic to, certain drugs, foreign objects, or poisons. As well, motion sickness, ear infections, emotional distress, pregnancy, or simply too much food or drink also can upset your stomach. Fortunately, most occasional vomiting can be prevented or alleviated with self-care remedies. But when vomiting is ongoing or severe, it could indicate a serious underlying medical problem such as heart attack, kidney or liver disorders, some types of cancer, or systemic infection. Whatever the cause, vomiting is a clear signal that something is wrong internally. Knowing when to treat it at home and when to seek medical care is crucial.

Symptoms/Signs

- With viral stomach flu or food poisoning: vomiting accompanied by fever, diarrhea, chills, headache, and extreme fatigue
- With viral gastroenteritis: vomiting or gagging as often as every five minutes; onset is usually sudden
- When a foreign body is lodged in the throat or intestine: vomiting accompanied by no other symptoms

Consult Your Doctor If:

- Vomiting is prolonged, lasting more than 12 hours in adults or four hours in small children without improvement.
- Vomiting is accompanied by severe abdominal pain, an earache, chest pains, or other unusual symptoms.
- Vomit appears black or bloody.
- Dehydration threatens. Symptoms may include intense thirst, dark yellow urine or lack of urination, lightheadedness, sunken eyes, cold and clammy skin with poor elasticity, and, in infants, less than three wet diapers in 24 hours.

Fluids

- To help prevent dehydration, drink plenty of clear fluids: Water, hot broth, sports drinks, or chew on crushed ice. For breast-fed infants, continue feeding as always, but offer extra water. For formula-fed infants, eliminate all but clear liquids (i.e., water or oral rehydration solutions: Pedialyte® and Rice-a-lyte®) for 24 hours.

Nutrition

- With acute gastroenteritis or stomach flu, it's wise to avoid food for 24 hours. After 24 hours, eat small quantities of bland foods such as clear soups, bananas, rice, applesauce, dry toast, mashed potatoes, or plain pasta.

Medication

- Take acetaminophen for accompanying fever and body aches. Avoid taking aspirin or ibuprofen, they can irritate the stomach.
- Try Emetrol®, an over-the-counter stomach-settling syrup (not recommended for diabetics).
- Use over-the-counter preparations to prevent vomiting associated with motion sickness.

Rest

- Get plenty of rest.

Prevention

- Make sure meats are properly stored and prepared.
- Avoid meat, seafood, poultry, prepared salads, dressings, and other foods that spoil if they've been left out for more than two hours.

general symptoms

119

Wheezing

Asthma, bronchitis, pneumonia, emphysema, allergies, smoking, or exposure to airborne irritants can cause airways in the lungs to become full of sticky mucus, white blood cells, and other debris. When that happens, the lining of the airways gets so severely irritated and swollen that mucus cannot move through the passages fast enough. The result: The air you breathe has a hard time getting through the clogged and constricted airways, so you hear a whistling sound (wheezing) from the chest.

Symptoms/Signs

- High-pitched or musical-sounding noise from the chest (not the throat) with every breath
- With asthma: shortness of breath; coughing that worsens at night or with exertion or cold air; tightness in the chest
- With bronchitis: cold symptoms; coughing that produces green, yellow, or gray mucus; mild chest pain or fever
- With smoking-related respiratory problems: shortness of breath; chronic coughing that produces thick mucus; limited lung capacity
- In children: suspect a foreign object has been inhaled if there is sudden wheezing and shortness of breath without previous history of asthma
- With a generalized allergic reaction: shortness of breath, tightness in the chest, or wheezing.

Consult Your Doctor If:

- **You become lightheaded or have difficulty breathing (seek emergency care).**
- **There may be a foreign body in the airway.**
- **You have symptoms of a generalized allergic reaction, including restricted breathing.**
- Mucus coughed up is streaked with blood.
- A cough persists for more than two weeks.
- Wheezing persists for more than two weeks or is accompanied by a persistent fever.

* Because of the risk of Reye's syndrome, aspirin should not be given to or used by children or teenagers who have or are suspected of having flu or chicken pox. Use acetaminophen.

120

Medication

- With bronchitis, allergies, or colds, try a decongestant containing pseudoephedrine to relieve congestion. (Non-viral bronchitis sometimes requires prescription antibiotics.)
- Avoid cough suppressants unless coughing interferes severely with sleep or work.
- Avoid aspirin or ibuprofen; take acetaminophen instead.*

Fluids

- Drink lots of fluids to keep mucus thin.

Activity

- With asthma, consult your doctor about how to remain active without triggering an attack. Otherwise, exercise normally unless exertion makes wheezing worse.
- With bronchitis, limit your activity.

Nutrition

- Avoid food triggers that may cause an allergic reaction.

Prevention

- Avoid respiratory irritants and allergens.
- Avoid foods or drugs that you have had an allergic reaction to.
- Treat colds and the flu quickly and effectively.
- Reduce and manage stress.
- Humidify and/or use a portable air filter in your bedroom for bronchitis.

Asthma

A sthma is an upper respiratory condition caused by a tightening of the muscles and swelling of the lining in the small breathing tubes (bronchioles) of the lungs. This tightening, called *bronchospasm,* causes labored breathing as the airways become narrowed and restrict air flow. Also, the breathing tubes become inflamed and swollen and produce excess mucus, which further inhibits breathing. Asthma is more common in children than adults; about 30 percent of children outgrow this problem before reaching adulthood.

Other respiratory ailments, such as allergies (e.g., to pollens, molds, dust mites, animal dander, and certain foods), colds, and influenza, can trigger asthma attacks. Other factors such as cold air, tobacco smoke, strenuous exercise, air pollution from industrial and auto emissions, pesticides, chemical fumes, and stress can cause asthma attacks or make the condition worse.

If you're asthmatic, it's important to be aware of which agents trigger your attacks and avoid or minimize exposure. Treatment of asthma usually requires an initial medical visit and evaluation. Medication administered through an inhaler may be prescribed to relax bronchospasms during acute attacks or help prevent future attacks by reducing inflammation and swelling.

Symptoms/Signs

- Typical symptoms of an asthma attack include labored breathing (wheezing), shortness of breath, tightness in the chest, and coughing

Consult Your Doctor If:

- **You have an acute asthma attack and HomeCare is not successful in reducing symptoms.**
- You or your child experience asthma symptoms for the first time.
- Your child has episodes of wheezing.
- You cough up green, yellow, or bloody sputum.

HOMECARE
If physician referral is not recommended at this time, try the following self-care procedures:

Rest

- Reduce your activity when an asthma attack occurs.
- Try to remain calm. Stress can increase symptoms.

Medication

- Use any prescribed medication only as directed by your doctor.
- Avoid using antihistamines during an asthmatic attack, which may further restrict your airways.

Fluids

- Drink plenty of clear fluids to help thin and loosen mucus.
- Coffee has been shown to help relieve attacks in some people.

Activity

- Stay physically active. Monitor your activity (e.g., exercise intensity) if you have experienced exercise-induced asthma attacks.

Prevention

- Know what factors (e.g., pollens, smoke, dust, fumes, cold weather, certain foods such as milk and eggs) cause your attacks.
- Avoid these agents or minimize your exposure by keeping your home dust-free. Wash bedding weekly and remove carpeting, if possible.
- If you smoke, try to quit. Avoid smoke-filled areas.
- Try to reduce the stress in your life. Learn a relaxation technique. See pages 32-34.
- Install an air conditioner in your home and possibly an air filtration system.

Bad Breath

Occasional bad breath (halitosis) is as natural as breathing itself. Indeed, you'd be hard pressed to find someone who has good breath all of the time—especially first thing in the morning. It's when breath is so offensive or chronically foul that there's cause for concern beyond the effect it has on your social life. The most obvious causes of bad breath—bad dental hygiene, smoking, poor diet—are easily treatable and should be attended to without delay, since they eventually can cause more serious medical problems. But other problems such as liver disease, lung disease, respiratory infections, digestive disorders, and kidney failure can all cause bad breath as well.

If your halitosis is particularly strong and won't go away no matter what self-care remedies you try, it's important to see your doctor to determine whether some underlying medical condition is to blame.

Symptoms/Signs

- Foul mouth odor

Consult Your Doctor If:

- Your breath ever smells like urine or feces.
- Your breath has an unusually fishy or fruity odor.
- Your bad breath does not go away regardless of the home care procedures you try.

HOMECARE

If physician referral is not recommended at this time, try the following self-care procedures:

Clean

- Brush and floss teeth two or three times daily, especially after meals. Don't forget to brush your tongue.
- If you can't brush or floss after a meal, rinse with water or mouthwash, or chew sugar-free gum.
- Have your teeth professionally cleaned and examined.

Medication

- Rinse mouth often with a medicated or antiseptic mouthwash.
- For temporary relief, try over-the-counter breath sprays or breath-freshening drops (remember, that such products only cover up bad breath for about 15 or 20 minutes).

Nutrition

- Chew on parsley, cloves, or fennel seeds after meals to freshen breath.
- Eat a balanced diet.
- Don't compound bad breath by eating pungent foods that linger on your breath: garlic, onions, hot peppers, certain deli meats, and cheeses will leave an offending air for 24 hours after you eat them.

Fluids

- Drink plenty of water to keep mouth moist (dry mouth is a leading cause of bad breath).
- Avoid coffee or other drinks that leave breath smelling foul.

Prevention

- Regularly follow all of the above recommendations for treating bad breath. Most important: Practice excellent oral hygiene and visit your dentist twice a year.
- Don't smoke or use tobacco products.

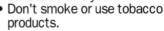

Bleeding Gums

Bleeding gums are never a good sign—unless blood on your toothbrush spurs you to start taking care of your teeth, before gum disease (gingivitis) sets in. Left untreated, bleeding gums can slowly deteriorate into gums that become filled with pus pockets, pull away from teeth, and eventually stop doing their part to keep your teeth where they belong.

Dental disease is 100 percent preventable if you follow your dentist's advice about brushing, flossing, rinsing, and keeping appointments for regular checkups. Your average time investment for lifelong dental health is about 10 minutes a day. That may not seem like a lot of time, but it's about nine more minutes than most people spend on daily dental hygiene.

Symptoms/Signs

- "Pink" toothbrush bristles after brushing
- Blood stains on dental floss or toothpick
- Bleeding during or after dental cleaning

Consult Your Dentist If:

- You notice pus near the gumline.
- Gums are swollen or bleed at times other than during brushing or flossing.
- Your gum recedes or pulls away from tooth.
- Your teeth become loose or fall out.
- Bridgework or partials begin to fit differently, or your bite feels out of alignment.

Medication

- Rinse mouth with mouthwash after brushing and flossing. A mouthwash such as Listerine® or those containing cetylpridinium chloride or domiphen bromide have been proven effective.
- Always brush with a toothpaste containing fluoride.

Clean

- Brush and floss teeth two or three times daily, especially after you eat. Ask your dentist to show you proper brushing and flossing techniques.
- If you can't brush or floss after a meal, rinse mouth with water or mouthwash, or chew sugarless gum to remove food particles and acids from teeth and gum surfaces.
- Along with regular brushing and flossing, try making a paste of baking soda and water to rub or gently brush on teeth and gums. Baking soda helps neutralize mouth acids.
- Have your teeth cleaned professionally every six months.

Nutrition

- Eat a well-balanced diet high in vitamins A and C (found in yellow fruits and vegetables, as well as green, leafy vegetables).
- Avoid sugary foods.
- Avoid sugary beverages, alcohol, and excessive amounts of fruit juices (choose fresh or unsweetened juices whenever possible).

Prevention

- Don't smoke or use tobacco.
- To prevent bleeding gums and gum disease, regularly follow all of the above recommendations for treating bleeding gums.

head and chest

123

Bronchitis

It usually happens after the onset of the initial symptoms of a cold: Your cough gets worse, and the mucus you cough up—instead of being clear—is yellow, green, or gray. While your body was preoccupied with fighting that cold, bronchitis set up shop in your lungs, clogging airways with mucus and wracking your body with a rattling cough. Fortunately, such "acute" bronchitis will go away within a week or so. But when symptoms linger for weeks or months, the diagnosis is usually chronic bronchitis.

Smoking, allergies, exposure to chemical irritants in the air, or just breathing in too much dust can cause both chronic and acute bronchitis. In either case, it's important that you not ignore your symptoms, since repeated or prolonged bouts of bronchitis can cause irreversible lung damage or pneumonia, or contribute to heart problems.

Symptoms/Signs

- With acute bronchitis: tightness in the chest; deep, heavy cough from the chest (not the throat) that brings up yellow or grayish mucus; slight fever; associated with severe colds; clears up within five to seven days without treatment
- With chronic bronchitis: persistent mucus-producing cough (most days of the month, three months out of the year, for two consecutive years); no underlying condition or disease to explain the cough; symptoms worse in the morning and in damp, cold weather

Consult Your Doctor If:

- **A high fever, chest pain, shaking chills, shortness of breath, or night sweats accompany your symptoms of bronchitis.**
- You have repeated bouts of acute bronchitis or your cough does not improve after a week.
- You cough up blood or mucus tinged with blood.

* Because of the risk of Reye's syndrome, aspirin should not be given to or used by children or teenagers who have or are suspected of having flu or chicken pox. Use acetaminophen.

HOMECARE
If physician referral is not recommended at this time, try the following self-care procedures:

Medication

- As long as your cough produces mucus, don't use cough suppressants; coughing removes secretions that harbor infection.
- Ask your doctor whether an over-the-counter or prescription bronchodilator (inhaler or tablet) would help relieve your symptoms.
- Take a cough expectorant if your cough is nonproductive. (No mucus is coughed up.)

Heat/Cold

- Breathe in warm, moist air (from a hot shower, a sink filled with boiling water, or a vaporizer) to loosen mucus and open airways.

Fluids

- Drink extra fluids to keep mucus thin and moving freely.
- Avoid alcohol and caffeine, which promote dehydration.

NB

Note Well

- Quit smoking.
- Whenever possible, lie with your head lower than your chest to help clear your lungs of mucus. A good position to try: For 10 or 15 minutes at a time, lie on your bed, face down, with your waist bent over the edge of the mattress and your head supported by your arms or pillows on the floor.

Prevention

- Avoid contact with people who have colds, flu, or respiratory infections.
- Avoid secondhand smoke, dust, and other air pollutants.
- Exercise regularly, but avoid exercise fatigue.

Canker Sores

Of all the types of mouth sores you can have, the only good thing about canker sores is that other people usually can't see them. These painful ulcers can crop up—singularly or in clusters—on your gums, tongue, soft palate, or on the inside of your cheek or lip. Most canker sores disappear within five to 10 days, but while they're active, they can make your mouth miserable. You may have trouble eating, especially if you enjoy salty, spicy, or acidic foods. Sometimes the sores can even interfere with talking or sleeping.

Doctors aren't sure what causes canker sores, but most agree that mouth trauma, food allergies, hormone imbalances, or emotional stress seem to be predisposing factors among people who have canker sores. Since they're not caused by viruses or bacteria, canker sores don't spread through person-to-person contact. And, in most cases, canker sores can be treated through self-care.

Symptoms/Signs

- Early stage: tingling or burning sensation on the tongue, soft palate, gums, or on the inside of the cheek or lip
- Middle stage: small, round, reddish, swollen area(s) where tingling or burning occurs
- Eruptive stage: painful rupture(s) on swollen area(s) covered by a white or yellow membrane with a red rim or "halo"

Consult Your Doctor If:

- Any mouth sore does not heal within two weeks.
- You have accompanying inflammation of the eyes or experience similar sores on your genitals.
- You have white spots in your mouth that are not canker sores.
- Canker sores significantly interfere with your ability to eat, speak, or sleep.

HOMECARE
If physician referral is not recommended at this time, try the following self-care procedures:

Medication

- Try sucking medicated lozenges or antacid tablets occasionally to decrease the acidity of your mouth.
- Use an over-the-counter medication containing carabamide peroxide (Gly-oxide®, Amosan® or Cankaid®, for example) to speed healing.
- Gargle with an antiseptic mouthwash to temporarily relieve pain.
- For chronic problems, ask your doctor about using a prescription dental paste (such as triamcinolone) or antibiotic mouthwashes to help reduce inflammation and pain.
- Apply Zalictan®, an over-the-counter preparation, to protect area from saliva acids and bacteria, and to keep prescription medicines from being washed away.

Nutrition

- Avoid chocolate, nuts, and foods that are spicy, salty, or acidic (tomatoes, citrus fruits, etc.).

Note Well

- Avoid scraping or biting mouth sores.

Prevention

- Avoid abrasive or irritating substances (tobacco, jalapeño peppers, very hot or steaming foods, hard pretzels, etc.).
- Use only a soft toothbrush to brush your teeth.
- Practice stress-reduction techniques.

125

Chemicals in the Eye

Exposure of the eyes to chemicals is a serious risk for employees who work with solvents and other substances. Home products such as cleaning products, paints, and fertilizers pose their own risks to both adults and children. **Immediate action is required when a chemical agent is accidentally splashed into the eye.**

The best way to prevent exposure is to wear proper eye protection (shatterproof glasses or goggles) and to follow procedures in handling caustic agents.

Symptoms/Signs

- Burning or irritation to the eyes due to exposure to chemicals

Seek Medical Attention If:

- You have been exposed to a strong chemical agent such as an acid (e.g., sulfuric acid) or a corroding agent (e.g., lye). **Flush the eye with water immediately and continue for at least 15 minutes. Go to the nearest treatment center.**

- You experience symptoms such as continued burning or irritation in the eye, blurred or poor vision, extreme redness or whiteness, watering or discharge.

- HomeCare procedures fail to give relief and eye continues to hurt after 30 minutes of treatment.

Clean

- Flush eye immediately with water. Don't flush with head back. Keep head down: either immerse in sink or splash water up into eye. Flush under lids.

Prevention

- Wear glasses or goggles.
- For chemicals, follow safety guidelines as specified by manufacturer. Read labels.

Chest Pain

Chest pain is a symptom that should never be ignored, especially for people who have a family history of heart disease or have significant risk factors such as high blood pressure, high cholesterol, tobacco use, low physical activity, and excess body weight.

Chest pain also can be traced to a number of other causes such as heartburn, an ulcer, a hiatal hernia (part of the upper stomach pokes up through the diaphragm), pleurisy (lung infection), blood clots in the lung's blood vessels, acute bronchitis, gallbladder problems, a pulled muscle, or a broken rib. A common cause of chest pain is a strained or pulled muscle, usually between the ribs. A sign of this kind of injury: You stick your finger on the site of pain and the pain increases or the site is sensitive to the touch.

Symptoms/Signs

The following are classic signs of a heart attack:

- pressure or pain in the middle of your chest that lasts more than a few minutes, or goes away and comes back
- pain that spreads to the shoulders, neck, or arms
- chest pain with lightheadedness, fainting, sweating, nausea, or shortness of breath

If you're a woman, you may have one or some of these less common signs:

- unusual chest, stomach, or belly pain
- nausea or dizziness
- shortness of breath or trouble breathing
- unexplained anxiety, weakness, or fatigue
- fast and rapid heartbeat, cold sweat, or paleness

Seek Immediate Medical Attention If:

- **You have one or more of the symptoms listed above. Take one aspirin and seek emergency medical care.**
- **Your chest pain occurs after you have been bedridden due to surgery, illness, or injury. You may have a blood clot in your lung. (It often is accompanied by shortness of breath.)**
- Your chest pain is due to a blow to the chest from a fall or other accident, and you have difficulty breathing or your ribs are sore to touch.

HOMECARE
If physician referral is not recommended at this time, try the following self-care procedures:

Note Well

- **If heart attack or another serious condition has been ruled out by your doctor,** the following HomeCare tips can be tried for chest wall pain due to a muscle strain. Refer to page 137 for "Heartburn," as appropriate.

Activity

- Avoid activities that require bending, twisting, and lifting until pain is reduced.
- Try to breathe with diaphragm (e.g., belly breathing) only.

Medication

- For chest wall pain due to a pulled muscle: aspirin, ibuprofen, or acetaminophen may be tried. Rub-on salves such as Ben-Gay® also may help.

Heat/Cold

- A heating pad over the injured area may help.

Note Well

- Avoid wrapping the chest with elastic bandages; it may lead to pneumonia.
- Take a deep breath every hour to fully inflate lungs and help prevent pneumonia. This is especially important if you're a smoker.

Colds and Flu

Colds and influenza (respiratory "flu") probably are the No. 1 reason why people see their doctor. However, they are two illnesses that can't be cured by medical treatments; both conditions need to "run their course." Because both are viral infections, they cannot be treated by antibiotics. As the chart below shows, there's little difference between the symptoms of a cold and flu. A person can have all the symptoms of both conditions with either a cold or the flu. Severe symptoms are more likely with flu. The best course of action, except for complications such as pneumonia or ear infections, is to treat the symptoms and reduce the discomfort.

Symptoms/Signs

COLDS	FLU
• Runny nose	• Runny nose
• Sneezing	• Sneezing
• Sore throat, coughing	• Coughing
• Headache	• Headache
• Low-grade fever	• Fever
• Red, itchy eyes	• Fatigue, muscle aches
• Congested ears	

Consult Your Doctor If:

- You have severe ear pain or trouble breathing or swallowing.
- Cough is severe or lasts more than 10 days.
- Mucus or sputum is thick, smelly, or green or rust-colored.
- Fever stays at 102 degrees F for three days.
- You have a history of severe heart or lung disease.

128

* Because of the risk of Reye's syndrome, aspirin should not be given to or used by children or teenagers who have or are suspected of having flu or chicken pox. Use acetaminophen.

Fluids

- Drink plenty of fluids such as water, fruit juices, and caffeine-free drinks and teas.

Medication

- Aspirin, ibuprofen, or acetaminophen for fever.*
- Antihistamines or decongestants to help clear nasal congestion.

Rest

- Reduce your activity.
- Bed rest may be needed depending on your symptoms.

Heat/Cold

- Stay warm.
- A vaporizer or humidifier can help keep mucous membranes moist.

Nutrition

- Hot broths such as chicken soup can help clear nasal congestion and soothe the throat.
- Try to eat balanced meals.

Prevention

- Influenza shots prior to flu season are recommended for adults over age 65 and those under age 65 who suffer from heart or respiratory ailments.
- Wash your hands often, especially if a family member has a cold or flu.

Cold Sores

Cold sores (also called fever blisters) are caused by the herpes simplex virus (HSV1), which, once you have it, stays with you for life. Experts estimate that HSV1 infects between 50 percent and 80 percent of all people and usually is spread through direct contact with the cold sores or saliva of an infected person. Fortunately, only about 10 percent of HSV1 carriers ever experience a cold sore.

If you are infected with HSV1 and suffer through a primary or first cold sore episode, factors such as sunlight, hormones, stress, fever, and injury can cause future blister eruptions—usually on your lips, for everyone to see. The good news is that, with a little preventive care and some home treatment, the frequency and severity of cold sore outbreaks can be significantly reduced. Also, it should be noted that HSV1 is not the same virus that causes genital herpes (HSV2), although you can spread HSV1 to your genital area.

Symptoms/Signs

- Tingling, itching, burning, sensitivity, swelling, or redness at blister site (before blister begins to form)
- Painful, fluid-filled blisters appearing on the lips or in the mouth accompanied by a fever (usually only with first occurrence)

Consult Your Doctor If:

- You experience eye pain, sensitivity to light, or discharge from your eye.
- Any mouth lesion or blister does not heal after two weeks of home treatment.
- Your cold sore attacks are especially frequent or severe.

HOMECARE

If physician referral is not recommended at this time, try the following self-care procedures:

Medication

- Over-the-counter cold sore medications (usually topical lip balms containing phenol or camphor) may reduce cracking, alleviate pain, and speed healing.
- Acyclovir ointment (prescription only) may speed healing; ask your doctor.

Heat/Cold

- Apply ice to affected area when you first notice tingling under the skin to help reduce inflammation and the severity of an outbreak.

Clean

- After a blister has broken, regularly dab alcohol or witch hazel on the open sore (use a clean cotton ball or cotton swab each time).
- Wash your hands with soap before and after any contact with a blister.

Nutrition

- Eat more potatoes, dairy products, and brewer's yeast; the lysine in these foods has been shown to reduce the frequency of cold sores. Before taking any lysine supplements, however, check with your doctor. Pregnant or nursing women should avoid excess lysine, as it can interfere with fetal and infant growth.

Note Well

- Avoid sharing eating utensils with or kissing anyone with a cold sore.
- Reduce stress in your life.
- If you have active blisters, avoid handling newborn or infant children.
- Wear a sunblock (SPF 15 or greater) on your lips when you go outdoors.
- Don't squeeze, pinch, or pick at any blister.

Conjunctivitis

lso known as "pinkeye," conjunctivitis occurs when the mucous membrane of the eyelid and white part of the eye become inflamed. Most often, the cause is a bacteria or virus that takes up residence in the eye, although allergies can produce many of the same symptoms as conjunctivitis (with allergies, however, there is almost always severe itching around the eyes, which usually is relieved with antihistamines). If the conjunctivitis is bacterial, your doctor can prescribe antibiotic ointment to help clear up the condition. If a virus is the culprit, antibiotics won't help at all. But most of the time, conjunctivitis will clear up on its own within a few days and without the use of prescription ointments or even a trip to the doctor.

Symptoms/Signs

(in one or both eyes)
- Red, bloodshot appearance
- Feeling of sand or dirt in the eye
- Burning sensation
- Excessive tearing
- Crust around edges of eyelids, especially upon waking
- Some sensitivity to light

- You experience eye pain.
- Vision is impaired.
- Sensitivity to light is extreme.
- Your condition fails to improve after three days of HomeCare.

130

HOMECARE
If physician referral is not recommended at this time, try the following self-care procedures:

Heat/Cold

- Apply warm compresses for 5 to 10 minutes, once or twice an hour.

Note Well

- Children should stay home from school and away from other children until symptoms have disappeared.
- Adults should stay home from work only if eye pain is severe or if there is excessive pus.

Clean

- Use a cotton-tipped applicator moistened with water to clean the eyelid edges.
- For adults: Use a solution of one part baby shampoo and 10 parts warm water to remove crust from around the eyelids.

Medication

- Prescription antibiotic ointment placed on the eyes at night can help prevent crusting.

Prevention

- Keep hands clean and away from eyes.
- In order to avoid spreading the infection, do not reuse any cloths used to clean the eye.
- If you're prone to conjunctivitis, always wear goggles when you swim.
- Remove contact lenses during outbreaks. Clean them well and wear glasses until symptoms go away.
- Sterilize contact lens case if symptoms persist.

Contact Lens Irritation

If you've ever worn glasses, you know what a nuisance they can be: Lenses with strong prescriptions can be heavy and distort peripheral vision. Sweaty workouts are maddening if you're wearing frames that keep slipping down your nose. And eyeglasses can change your appearance in ways you may not necessarily find attractive. Contact lenses can alleviate all of that forever—but only if you take special care to clean, store, and wear your lenses properly. Otherwise, you place your eyes at risk for corneal abrasion, keratitis (inflammation of the cornea), corneal ulcers, and eye infections that can make your life miserable or even threaten your vision permanently.

Depending on the visual correction you need, you can choose from a variety of lenses designed to suit your work and your lifestyle. Your doctor can help you choose the type that is best for you, but it's up to you to make a commitment to wear them in good health—and to take care of minor irritations before they become major problems.

Symptoms/Signs

- Red, irritated, burning, or dry eyes
- Feeling that a foreign object is in your eye
- Blurred vision or sudden changes in vision
- Secretions from either eye

Consult Your Doctor If:

- **You experience an eye injury while wearing contacts (seek care immediately).**
- You develop irritation, redness, or burning that is not alleviated quickly with HomeCare treatment.
- You develop any unusual or severe symptoms, such as excessive eye secretions, pronounced changes in vision, etc.

Medication

- If your eyes are mildly dry or red, try an over-the-counter lubricating drop as recommended by your doctor.
- If your eyes are irritated due to abrasion or infection, your doctor may prescribe antibiotic drops.

Clean

- If eyes become irritated, try cleaning lenses. If cleaning does not solve the problem, proceed with enzymatic disinfection.
- Always wash your hands before handling your contacts. However, be sure to avoid soaps containing moisturizers, which can leave a residue on fingers that can be transferred to your lenses.
- Disinfect contact lenses each time you take them out for any length of time. Never skip cleaning steps.
- Use fresh cleaning and disinfecting solutions; never store contacts in water or use saliva to wet your lenses. Throw out any solutions that have passed their expiration date.

Prevention

- Use enzymatic cleaners regularly, as directed by your doctor.
- Never wear dirty or damaged contact lenses.
- Sterilize your contact lens case once a week by boiling it in a pot of water on the stove for 10 or 15 minutes.
- Extended-wear lenses should be worn no longer than seven days.
- Don't wear your contacts when sleeping.

head and chest

131

Dental Problems

Dental problems such as tooth decay and gum disease are caused by a buildup of plaque and bacteria around the teeth and gums. The main culprits are infrequent brushing, failure to floss regularly, not using toothpaste that contains fluoride, and not seeing your dentist every 6 to 12 months for regular cleaning and inspection.

Bacterial buildup creates a film on your teeth called plaque. Plaque attracts sugars that in turn produce acids that can slowly decay the enamel tooth covering. Dental plaque also causes gum disease through the production of acid that inflames the gums or degrades the supporting bone.

Toothache usually is caused by a cavity that has worn through the tooth enamel and has irritated the nerve. A more serious condition is called an abscess. An abscess is a local infection that may include fever, soreness, swelling in the jaw, and redness around the infected tooth. **Your dentist should be notified immediately if you think you have an abscess.**

Bleeding gums are an indication of periodontal disease, which affects the stability of the teeth and jaw. Signs of periodontal disease include reddened, swollen gums; loose teeth; and bleeding when brushing. Though poor oral hygiene is the main cause, pregnancy, medications, or diabetes also may increase the risk.

Consult Your Dentist If:

- You have signs of an abscess: soreness, swelling in jaw, reddened gums, and fever.
- You have a toothache and you can see or feel a cavity.
- Your gums are bleeding or inflamed, or a tooth is loose.
- Your tooth has been knocked out.

132

HOMECARE

If physician referral is not recommended at this time, try the following self-care procedures:

Medication

- To reduce toothache pain, aspirin, ibuprofen, or acetaminophen can be used. Use as directed.

Fluids

- Avoid cold beverages when a cavity is present.

Nutrition

- Avoid sugary foods and hard candies.
- Moderate your consumption of foods and beverages that contain sugar.
- Eat green and yellow fruits and vegetables.

Note Well

- Fluoride treatment or sealants may be recommended by your dentist.

Prevention

- Brush between meals with fluoride toothpaste.
- Floss every day.
- Limit your consumption of sugary foods.
- Visit your dentist every 6 to 12 months for preventive checkups.

Earache

Earache is a common problem, usually occurring in people who have allergies or suffer from a cold. When the eustachian tube, which equalizes air pressure from the middle ear to the throat, swells shut, fluid builds up behind the eardrum, causing pressure and pain. The fluid then can become infected. Indications of ear infections include fever and localized pain. Usually, antibiotics are prescribed by your doctor if a bacterial infection is discovered.

Children are especially prone to earaches because their eustachian tubes are smaller and swell shut more easily from upper respiratory problems. Also, bottle-feeding in bed increases the chances of ear infection.

Many earaches occur in the outer ear, as in the case of so-called "swimmer's ear" (the pain is worse when the earlobe is pulled). See page 143.

Symptoms/Signs

- Local pain and pressure in the ear with accompanying fever
- In children, suspect an ear infection if your child has fever and pain and complains of "fullness in the head" and partial hearing loss in the affected ear
- In infants, irritability, crying, and rubbing and pulling the ears are possible indications of infection
- Swimmer's ear: Pain in the outer ear, especially when the earlobe is pulled

Consult Your Doctor If:

- Your infant shows signs of an ear infection: rubbing or pulling the ears, crying, irritability and inability to sleep.
- You or an older child experience severe ear pain that is unrelieved by HomeCare. This may indicate a ruptured eardrum.

HOMECARE

If physician referral is not recommended at this time, try the following self-care procedures:

Heat/Cold
- To help loosen nasal mucus, take a hot shower or use a vaporizer.
- To relieve pain, place a warm washcloth or heating pad (carefully) to the ear. Occasionally shake head and swallow.

Medication
- In adults: aspirin, ibuprofen, or acetaminophen to reduce pain and possible fever. Use as directed.*
- Antihistamines or decongestants may help relieve stuffiness and nasal secretions.

Fluids
- Drink plenty of water or juices.

Activity
- Reduce your activity.

Prevention
- Don't give a baby a bottle while he or she is lying down.
- If you're prone to ear infections, use ear plugs when you swim; insert a cotton ball or piece of lamb's wool loosely into the outer ear canal when you shower, wash your hair, or use hair spray.

133

* Because of the risk of Reye's syndrome, aspirin should not be given to or used by children or teenagers who have or are suspected of having flu or chicken pox. Use acetaminophen.

Ear Wax

Whoever said "Never stick anything smaller than your elbow in your ear" knew the value of ear wax, the body's remarkable ear-cleaning and protection system. All along the external ear canal, thick skin containing oil glands and modified sweat glands grows ever outward, excreting ear wax along the way. Dust, dirt, dead skin, and anything else that gets in your ear is trapped in the wax and transported to the outer ear, where it eventually falls out on its own.

Unfortunately, many people, thinking that ear wax is dirty and socially unacceptable, go to great lengths to remove the wax from sight. Using everything from cotton swabs to paper clips, they end up pushing dirt back into the ear canal, compacting the wax against the eardrum and risking injury to the skin that the wax protects against infection. If you must remove wax from your outer ear canal, use only a wet washcloth wrapped around your index finger and use a gentle, circular motion to clear out only the wax that has made its way to the outermost regions of your ear. If your ear's natural cleaning system seems not to be working properly, see your doctor.

Symptoms/Signs

- Wax that varies in color over time and appears at the mouth of the ear canal, or hard, brownish or amber wax that partially or fully blocks the ear canal

Consult Your Doctor If:

- There is persistent itching or pain in your ear canal.
- Any fluids or pus drain from your ear.
- A painful, swollen, red bump appears in your ear canal.
- You experience any hearing loss or hear ringing in your ears.
- You know or suspect that an insect or foreign body is lodged in your ear.

Medication

- Avoid using over-the-counter ear drops to soften or remove ear wax unless recommended to do so by your doctor. Putting any liquid in your ear when you have even a tiny hole in your eardrum can cause infection.
- If an insect becomes trapped in your ear canal, put a few drops of mineral oil in your ear canal to immobilize the creature until your doctor can remove it.

Clean

- Use only your middle finger wrapped in a wet washcloth to clean your outer ear canal. Never use cotton swabs or any other device to remove ear wax.

Note Well

- Never try to remove a foreign body lodged in your ear. Doing so may push the object farther into the ear canal and risk injury to the eardrum. Consult your physician.

Prevention

- Never insert any object other than your washcloth-wrapped finger into your ear canal.

head and chest

Eye Injury

Injury to the eyes is a major risk in certain jobs such as manufacturing, carpentry, yard maintenance, and mining. Work around the house and recreational activities can increase the risk of dirt and other small objects getting into the eye. The use of shatterproof glasses or goggles is your first line of defense.

When the eye is affected by a foreign object, it's wise to take the problem seriously. First, try to locate the object in the eye. If the object is located in the corner or close to the lower lid, moisten the twisted tip of a tissue and gently dab the object. This should lift the object from the eye.

Gently wash the eye out with water, saline solution used for contact lenses, or a commercial eye wash solution. Using your thumb and forefinger, carefully and gently grasp the eyelid above the eyelash and repeatedly lift it away from the eye. This allows the natural fluids to wash the eye or help move an object toward the edges.

You should never rub the eye. This may cause the cornea to be scratched and increase the chances of infection. If you have difficulty locating or removing the object, see your doctor immediately.

Symptoms/Signs

- An object that penetrates the eye such as a sharp object
- A "floating" object such as dirt, an insect, or sawdust that irritates the eye

Consult Your Doctor If:

- Your eye is bloody or torn.
- The object appears to be stuck in the eye.
- HomeCare procedures have failed to remove the object.
- You have vision problems or pain and discomfort 24 hours after removing the object.

HOMECARE

If physician referral is not recommended at this time, try the following self-care procedures:

Note Well
- Use a moistened, twisted tip of a tissue to remove object in the corner of the eye or close to lower lid. Gently dab and lift object from eye.

Clean
- Gently wash the eye with water, contact lens solution, or a commercial eye wash solution. Repeat lifting eyelid from eye to promote eye fluids. Keep eye wash in your medicine cabinet.

Cover
- In cases where there is still *minor* discomfort after the object has been removed and the eye cleaned, cover the eye with a gauze patch for 24 hours.

Prevention
- Wear shatterproof safety glasses or goggles in jobs or tasks that expose you to dirt, wood splinters/sawdust, or metal particles.

head and chest

135

Hearing Loss

One in 10 Americans has hearing loss that interferes with his or her ability to understand normal speech. And the No. 1 reason for such hearing loss is, simply, too much exposure to loud noises. It's easy to think nothing of mowing the yard every week or going to an occasional rock concert without wearing ear protection for either activity. That's because the damage you do to your hearing during those relatively brief periods is hardly noticeable. You might experience a "muffled" sensation shortly after exposure to loud noises, but the feeling usually goes away and you assume that you've suffered no ill effects. Years down the road, however, you may start to notice that it's harder and harder to understand what people are saying at parties or in a crowded restaurant. The real tragedy is that such hearing problems are almost always entirely preventable.

Symptoms/Signs

- Ringing, humming, buzzing, roaring, or squealing noises that either come and go or are continuous, in one or both ears
- Difficulty hearing high-pitched voices or understanding certain words in speech, especially those that contain S, F, SH, CH, H, or soft C sounds, or understanding words in a conversation when there's a lot of background noise

Consult Your Doctor If:

- You experience any sudden hearing loss.
- You notice signs of hearing loss in an infant or young child.
- You hear ringing or other sounds that either come and go or are continuous, in one or both ears.
- Any ear noises are accompanied by ear pain, dizziness, vertigo, nausea, or vomiting.

136

Clean

- Avoid cleaning your outer ear canal with anything other than your middle finger wrapped in a damp washcloth. Never stick any object—even a cotton swab—into your ear.
- If you need to have impacted ear wax removed from your ear canal, consult your doctor.

Nutrition

- Reduce salt intake.
- Avoid alcohol and caffeine.

Prevention

- Avoid loud noises, or wear adequate ear protection when you're exposed to them. The noise from a lawn mower or personal stereo can be loud enough to damage hearing permanently.
- For ear protection, never rely on cotton stuffed into the ear canal. Use high-quality ear plugs, regulation ear muffs, or a combination of both for maximum protection.
- Control your cholesterol and blood pressure levels.
- Exercise regularly to improve blood flow and normalize blood pressure, which can affect your hearing.

Heartburn

A s part of the digestive process, the stomach produces hydrochloric acid. Heartburn is caused when the stomach acid irritates the stomach lining or backs up into the esophagus. Common contributors to heartburn are overeating, alcohol, caffeine, aspirin, ibuprofen, tobacco, and emotional stress.

If heartburn is a problem for you, eating smaller portions and more times a day can help reduce it. Usually, heartburn doesn't require medical attention unless it lasts more than three days. Prolonged discomfort may suggest a medical condition such as a hernia or ulcer, which should be evaluated by a doctor.

People having a heart attack may sometimes think they have heartburn. Take one aspirin and get medical help right away if you have:
- **pressure or pain in the middle of your chest that lasts more than a few minutes, or goes away and comes back**
- **pain that spreads to the shoulders, neck, or arms**
- **chest pain with lightheadedness, fainting, sweating, nausea, or shortness of breath**

Women sometimes have less common signs:
- **unusual chest, stomach, or belly pain**
- **nausea or dizziness**
- **shortness of breath or trouble breathing**
- **anxiety, weakness, or fatigue for no reason**
- **fast and rapid heartbeat, cold sweat, or paleness**

See "Chest Pain" on page 127.

Symptoms/Signs

- Burning sensation and discomfort just below the breastbone

Consult Your Doctor If:

- **"Heartburn" is combined with shortness of breath, or pain in your jaw, radiating down your arm or in your back. Get emergency care.**
- Heartburn lasts more than three days.
- You vomit black or bloody material.
- Your stools are black and tar-like.

Nutrition
- Avoid vinegar, chocolate, oranges, lemons, grapefruits, pickles, and tomatoes.
- Avoid fatty foods and peppermint.
- Avoid alcohol and caffeine.

Activity
- Stay mildly active for two hours after eating. An after-dinner walk may aid digestion.

Rest
- Wait one to two hours after eating before lying down. If you need to lie down, lie on your left side.
- If you need to rest, keep your shoulders one to two feet above hips.

Medication
- For chronic heartburn, two OTC medications, Pepcid® and Tagamet®, reduce the production of stomach acid. Use as directed.
- Antacids in liquid or tablet form can relieve gastric discomfort.
- Avoid using aspirin or ibuprofen, which can further irritate the stomach.

Prevention
- Avoid overeating.
- Try to manage your level of stress.
- Don't smoke.
- Avoid tight-fitting clothing and belts that squeeze the abdomen or stomach.

137

Hoarseness

Think of your vocal cords like strings on a violin: When they're in tune, you sound normal or "on key." But when the cords become over stressed or obstructed in some way, the sound you create is altered or silenced altogether. There are a host of reasons people become hoarse. Some, such as shouting at a sporting event or giving a long lecture, can dry out mucous membranes and cause vocal cords to become irritated. Other problems—infection associated with a cold or the flu, polyps, allergies, chemical fumes, and tumors, to name a few—also can affect vocal cords or throat muscles so that the sounds they produce are distorted.

In any case, most hoarseness is temporary and easily remedied with a few days of voice rest and some self-care procedures. Be sure, however, that you see your doctor if any voice change is prolonged or recurring, or if you have other symptoms that could point to something more serious than simple "voice overload."

Symptoms/Signs

- A breathy, raspy, or whisper-like voice
- Changes in voice volume (loudness) or pitch (how high or low the voice is)
- Throat may feel tight, dry, scratchy, or obstructed

Consult Your Doctor If:

- Hoarseness lasts longer than two weeks or has no obvious cause.
- You have throat pain not associated with a cold or the flu.
- You cough up blood.
- You have difficulty swallowing.
- You notice a lump in your neck.
- There is a complete loss or pronounced change in your voice that lasts longer than a few days.

HOMECARE

If physician referral is not recommended at this time, try the following self-care procedures:

Medication

- Use medicated throat lozenges or an over-the-counter throat spray.

Fluids

- Gargle with warm salt water or drink hot liquids.
- Drink plenty of water.

Nutrition

- Avoid spicy foods, caffeine, and alcohol.

Note Well

- Use a humidifier in your home, especially in your bedroom.
- Avoid speaking whenever possible until hoarseness disappears. Some cases require complete voice rest.

Prevention

- Avoid shouting, speaking in smoke-filled rooms, or talking a lot with a cold or flu.
- Don't smoke and avoid second-hand smoke.
- Avoid excessive alcohol consumption.

Migraine Headache

It's estimated that 18 million people suffer from migraine headaches. Women are three times more likely to have migraines. Migraine and the more painful cluster headache are called vascular headaches, because experts believe that they are caused by the blood vessels (vasculature) in the head contracting, then expanding (dilating)—causing pain to the nerve endings of the head.

All vascular headaches can be precipitated by a variety of factors such as stress, certain foods (e.g., processed meats with nitrates, chocolate, aged cheese, and foods prepared with monosodium glutamate), alcohol (especially red wine), menstrual periods, irregular or excessive sleeping patterns, excessive use of pain killers, tobacco, a number of prescription drugs (e.g., oral contraceptives), and withdrawal from caffeine and other drugs.

Symptoms/Signs

- "Classic" migraines are characterized by throbbing pain, usually on one side of the head; other symptoms include nausea, vomiting, or dizziness. Some people experience an aura prior to onset of the headache: they see "stars," flashes of light, or blind spots. Common or "simple" migraine headaches usually cause pain throughout the head and are not accompanied by an aura

- Cluster headaches produce excruciating pain around one eye and recur repetitively over days, weeks, or months, then disappear for a period of time, only to occur again

Consult Your Doctor If:

- **Your headache is associated with slurred speech, dizziness, or weakness in your arms and legs. Seek emergency care.**
- You suffer from migraine or cluster headaches. Professional assessment and treatment usually is recommended, with medication and other treatment options weighed.
- A common vascular headache continues after HomeCare has been tried for more than a week.

HOMECARE
If physician referral is not recommended at this time, try the following self-care procedures:

Medication
- An over-the-counter analgesic medication (e.g., Excedrin Migraine®) may provide relief for mild to moderate attacks.
- Follow directions carefully when using medications.
- Consider discontinuing oral contraceptives.

Rest
- Get adequate levels of sleep and rest. However, avoid oversleeping.
- When headache occurs, go to a quiet, darkened room; lie down and relax your body. Refer to page 33.

Nutrition
- Avoid chocolate, aged cheese, red wine, and food additives such as nitrates and monosodium glutamate, which may increase symptoms. Keep a log to track possible foods or agents that trigger attacks.

Fluids
- Drink plenty of water. Avoid alcohol and caffeine drinks.

Note Well
- Try to stay physically active.
- Learn relaxation techniques that may reduce the number of headache episodes.

Prevention
- For all vascular headaches: Get plenty of sleep and relaxation and eat right.
- Be sensitive to and avoid your headache triggers such as alcohol, special foods, additives, or perfumes that cause symptoms.

Nosebleeds

osebleeds can be pretty scary: The amount of blood you seem to lose from one nosebleed can be quite profuse, although not ordinarily dangerous. Because the septum (the cartilage wall that divides your two nostrils) contains many fragile blood vessels that are close to the surface, any physical blow to the nose can cause blood to flow out. As well, some medical conditions such as hardening of the arteries, high blood pressure, sinus infection, or the common cold can cause minor nosebleeds, all of which usually can be stopped within 10 minutes or so. Long-term use of antihistamines also can cause minor bleeding—usually when blowing your nose—because of excessive drying of the nasal passages.

If your nose bleeds only in the winter, make sure your house is well humidified and not too warm. Also, keeping nasal linings moist with petroleum jelly can keep your nose from bleeding in cold, dry weather. Otherwise, take care not to blow your nose too hard, and use the procedure outlined in the HomeCare section to staunch the flow of blood if you do get a nosebleed.

Symptoms/Signs

- Bleeding from one or both nostrils

Consult Your Doctor If:

- You cannot stop the flow of blood from your nose after 30 minutes of home treatment.
- You have nosebleeds often but don't know why.
- Your nosebleed is a result of being hit in the nose and is accompanied by a deformity in the shape or outline of your nose.

HOMECARE
If physician referral is not recommended at this time, try the following self-care procedures:

Note Well

- To stop a nosebleed, remain in a sitting or standing position and do not tilt your head back. Blow your nose once to remove any blood clots that may be keeping tiny blood vessels open. Pack the bleeding nostril with gauze or cotton coated with petroleum jelly, then pinch your nose closed. Continue pinching for at least 10 minutes without letting go. If nose is still bleeding after 10 minutes, repack your nose with fresh cotton or gauze and apply pressure for another 10 minutes.

Heat/Cold

- Although many people apply ice packs to a bleeding nose, ice usually does nothing to slow blood flow from the septum.

Rest

- Avoid lying down when you have a nosebleed: sitting or standing will help slow the flow of blood to the nose.

Prevention

- Discourage children from picking their noses.
- In dry weather, use a humidifier to add moisture to the air.
- Avoid taking aspirin, since it thins the blood, making bleeding harder to stop.
- Avoid blowing your nose too hard; avoid blowing your nose at all for several hours after a nosebleed.
- Control your blood pressure (people with hypertension are more likely to have nosebleeds).
- Don't smoke, since smoking dries out nasal cavities.
- Avoid the chronic use of antihistamines.

Ringing in the Ears

If you hear noises in your head, chances are you're not crazy—you're just suffering from tinnitus. For approximately 36 million Americans, ear noises are an occasional bother. But for seven million people nationwide, loud and constant "ringing" in the ears is severe enough to interfere with normal living.

Nearly all tinnitus sufferers have some degree of either temporary or permanent hearing loss. Often, if hearing can be restored or improved, tinnitus will either go away or decrease in intensity. If you have sudden, occasional or temporary tinnitus, check with your doctor to see if the cause (exposure to loud noises, impacted ear wax, allergies, infection or medications, for example) can be eliminated. If your tinnitus is constant or permanent, your doctor may be able to pinpoint the cause and recommend treatments that can at least make ear noises more tolerable.

Symptoms/Signs

- Ringing, humming, buzzing, roaring, or squealing noises that either come and go or are continuous, in one or both ears
- Hearing impairment or loss

Consult Your Doctor If:

- You have symptoms of tinnitus.
- You experience any sudden hearing loss.
- Ear noises are accompanied by ear pain or pressure, vertigo (loss of balance), or nausea and vomiting.
- You suspect a particular medication is causing your tinnitus.

Medication

- Avoid aspirin; taking too much or taking related compounds can cause tinnitus. Use acetaminophen instead.

Clean

- Avoid cleaning your outer ear canal with anything other than your middle finger wrapped in a damp washcloth. Never stick an object—even a cotton swab—into your ear.
- If you need to have impacted ear wax removed from your ear canal, consult your doctor.

Nutrition

- Reduce salt intake.
- Avoid alcohol and caffeine.

Note Well

- Surround yourself with noises that mask tinnitus sounds. A ticking clock, low-volume music or radio static, "white noise" machines, and ceiling fans often are quite effective.
- Ask your doctor about purchasing an electronic tinnitus masker or hearing aid to reduce your awareness of head noises.

Prevention

- Avoid loud noises, or wear adequate ear protection when you're exposed to them. The noise from a lawn mower or personal stereo can be loud enough to damage hearing permanently.
- For ear protection, never rely on cotton stuffed into the ear canal. Use high-quality ear plugs, regulation ear muffs, or a combination of both for maximum protection.
- Control your cholesterol and blood pressure levels.

141

Sinusitis

Every year, more than 31 million Americans spend more than $1.5 billion on medicine to alleviate the discomfort of sinus infection, or sinusitis. Usually, sinusitis develops when a cold, allergies, or other respiratory irritation causes nasal membranes to become so swollen that they can no longer keep mucus flowing freely. Pressure increases, mucus builds up, and blocked sinus cavities become a breeding ground for bacteria. Once an infection sets in, antibiotics usually are the only way to completely rid sinuses of infection. Sometimes, however, chronic or severe sinusitis requires surgery to drain sinus cavities, or to repair bone or tissue abnormalities that keep infections coming back.

Symptoms/Signs

- Prolonged pressure or pain in the forehead or cheeks, between and behind the eyes, or near the upper teeth
- Yellow or green nasal mucus that may develop a bad odor or taste
- Puffy eyelids
- Coughing or difficulty breathing
- Fever

Consult Your Doctor If:

- You develop thick, yellow, or greenish nasal discharge or if cold symptoms do not improve after more than one week.
- You have pain over the eyebrow, or below the eye, or in the upper teeth—usually on one side of your face.
- You have a severe headache that is not relieved by aspirin or acetaminophen.
- Swelling of the face increases.
- Fever is over 101 degrees F.
- Your nose bleeds.
- Vision changes or becomes blurred.
- There is no improvement after three days of home treatment.

HOMECARE

If physician referral is not recommended at this time, try the following self-care procedures:

Medication

- Use over-the-counter nasal decongestant sprays for no more than three days.
- Try an oral decongestant containing pseudoephedrine to help clear nasal passages.
- Take acetaminophen or ibuprofen as needed for pain (aspirin may promote congestion).
- Avoid antihistamines unless you have allergies that contribute to sinus inflammation.
- Nasal saline sprays may be tried.

Heat/Cold

- Apply warm compresses over eyes and cheeks periodically to relieve pain.
- Take a hot shower twice a day, or breathe deeply over a pan of steaming water (drape a towel over your head to trap the steam).

Note Well

- Avoid air travel, swimming, diving, and high-altitude sports when symptoms are present.
- Garlic, horseradish, and spicy foods may help drain sinuses.

Fluids

- Drink plenty of liquids, especially hot ones.
- Avoid alcohol and caffeine drinks.

Prevention

- Avoid airborne irritants. Control allergens such as dust mites.
- Blow nose gently to avoid forcing mucus into sinuses or inner ears.
- Keep your nose lubricated with saline sprays or petroleum jelly.
- Use an air filter in your bedroom.

Swimmer's Ear

You don't have to go swimming to end up with the itchy infection called otitis externa, or "swimmer's ear." Water that splashes into the ear canal during a shower or a shampoo can get trapped in the dark, warm environment near the eardrum, creating a perfect breeding ground for bacteria. As the bacteria burrow into the skin, the skin inside the ear begins to itch. Many people, unaware that an infection is beginning to set in, scratch the ear canal with a finger or cotton swab, which removes the protective layer of bacteria-fighting ear wax. As a result, the bacteria have access to more skin surfaces and continue to multiply, creating a full-blown infection that may have to be treated with antibiotics. There are measures you can take, however, to stop the infection in its earliest stages, or to keep bacteria from taking up residence in the first place.

Symptoms/Signs

- Persistent itching or tickling in the ear canal (early stages)
- Pain in the ear canal
- Watery fluid draining from the ear
- Feeling of fullness inside the ear
- Crusting in the ear canal
- Hearing impairment due to pus buildup and inflammation (advanced stages)

Consult Your Doctor If:

- You experience persistent pain inside the ear canal.
- You have fluid draining from the ear.
- You have crusting in the ear canal.
- You notice any hearing loss or impairment.
- You experience pain upon applying over-the-counter drops into your ear: This may indicate a perforated eardrum.
- You have swelling of the external ear.

Medication

- Use over-the-counter ear drops that combat bacterial growth if your only symptom is ear itchiness.
- Take acetaminophen for ear pain only until you can get in to see your doctor.

Heat/Cold

- Apply heat (use a heating pad set on low or a covered hot water bottle) to reduce pain until you can get in to see your doctor.

Clean

- Clean your outer ear area daily, using your middle finger wrapped in a soft cloth.
- Never use any instrument to remove wax from the ear canal: Ear wax protects the ear from infection.

Note Well

- Don't scratch an itchy ear, since scratching can remove protective wax, irritate skin, and worsen an infection.

Prevention

- If you are prone to ear infection, use ear plugs whenever you swim or shower.
- Following a shower or a swim, apply a mixture of 50 percent rubbing alcohol and 50 percent white vinegar into the ear canal (using a dropper) as you hold your head at a right angle to the floor, ear facing the ceiling. Wiggle the outer ear gently to work the solution into the bottom of the ear canal, then turn your ear toward the floor, allowing the solution to run out. This will help keep ears dry and kill germs.
- Swim only in clean swimming pools. Avoid lakes and ponds.

143

Tension Headaches

Most headaches are caused by muscular tension in the scalp and surrounding muscles of the jaw, neck, shoulders, and back. For most people, tension headaches are a physical/emotional reaction to outside stressors such as personal or work problems, working in one position for an extended period (such as word processing), and being exposed to excessive noise. Headaches also are a common symptom of viral infections such as a cold or flu or bacterial infections such as sinusitis, and can be triggered by outside agents such as perfumes, mold, and noise.

Except for headaches caused by infections, headache pain is best treated by reducing the pressure in your life and avoiding headache triggers. Periodic tension headaches rarely are an indication of other health problems, such as a brain tumor or hypertension. Brain tumors usually are accompanied by other symptoms such as paralysis and personality changes.

Symptoms/Signs

- Muscular tension in the scalp and muscles of the face, neck, and shoulders

Consult Your Doctor If:

- Your headache is associated with fever and stiffness in the neck. This may indicate meningitis.
- Your headache is associated with slurred speech, dizziness, or weakness in your arms and legs.
- Your headache is accompanied by vision problems.
- Your headaches become much worse and more frequent.

HOMECARE
If physician referral is not recommended at this time, try the following self-care procedures:

Rest

- Learn a deep muscle relaxation technique. Refer to page 33.
- Get adequate sleep.

Fluids

- Drink alcohol in moderation or not at all.
- Avoid drinking too much caffeine.

Medication

- Take aspirin, ibuprofen, or acetaminophen to relieve headache pain. Use as directed.*

Heat/Cold

- Apply a heating pad or warm washcloth to the back of the neck.
- A long, hot shower or bath, followed by a self-massage to the back of the neck, temples, and forehead may help.

Activity

- Exercise regularly. Regular physical activity has been shown to reduce stress and muscular tension.

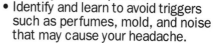
Prevention

- Massage the neck muscles.
- Check your work posture.
- Identify and learn to avoid triggers such as perfumes, mold, and noise that may cause your headache.

* Because of the risk of Reye's syndrome, aspirin should not be given to or used by children or teenagers who have or are suspected of having flu or chicken pox. Use acetaminophen.

Toothache

If you bite down and it hurts, chances are you have a decayed or abscessed tooth. Both conditions arise as a result of bacteria that has invaded the pulp (soft inner tissue) of the tooth, either through an injury to the tooth or from poor dental hygiene. Usually, warning signs (e.g., an increasing sensitivity to temperature or certain types of food; bad breath; red, swollen gums) precede an actual toothache to let you know that if you don't start taking care of your pearly whites, tooth troubles are just around the corner.

Sometimes, though, tooth pain is a symptom of non-dental disorders such as sinusitis or neuralgia. Sinusitis (inflammation of the sinuses) usually is short-lived and responds quite well to home treatment. (Refer to page 142.) Neuralgia, on the other hand, is difficult to treat with self-care measures, often requires drug therapy, and in some cases necessitates surgery to relieve the pressure of blood vessels that may be pressing on a nerve. Unlike a decayed or abscessed tooth, teeth bothered by neuralgia or sinusitis are not likely to require dental work.

Symptoms/Signs

- Tooth sensitivity to hot and cold and certain foods
- A dull to throbbing pain at the tooth site that is made worse by chewing, shaving, or brushing teeth
- Tooth pain that occurs only when you bite down on dense foods (bagels, pizza crust, etc.)

Consult Your Dentist If:

- You experience tooth pain that is not alleviated after a week of self-care measures.
- Tooth pain is accompanied by fever; swelling in the face or neck; bloody nasal discharge; or pain, redness or swelling of an eye.

Medication

- Non-prescription pain relievers (e.g., acetaminophen, ibuprofen, aspirin) may temporarily reduce or eliminate tooth pain until you're examined by your dentist. For severe pain or infection, your dentist may prescribe stronger medications.

Note Well

- Keep affected tooth clean but avoid too-brisk brushing of gums. Rinse mouth often with warm salt water.
- If your tooth falls out, rinse and wrap in clean tissue paper and take it to your dentist.

Prevention

- Practice excellent oral hygiene; brush after meals with a fluoride toothpaste, floss daily, and see your dentist twice a year for a checkup.
- Avoid excessive amounts of starchy or sugary foods.
- Don't smoke or use tobacco products.
- Have broken or chipped teeth attended to immediately; have loose or missing fillings and crowns fixed promptly.
- Avoid chewing on the affected tooth.
- Make sure that partial dentures are well fitted.

head and chest

145

Vision Problems

Most vision problems are either temporary or completely treatable, but there are some conditions that can partially or completely rob us of our ability to see, sometimes within a short period.

Since many eye disorders don't have noticeable symptoms until it is too late to reverse or stop loss of vision, have your eyes examined regularly by an eye care professional. Also, any changes to your vision should be discussed with your doctor.

Symptoms/Signs

- **With narrow-angle glaucoma (medical emergency): severe eye pain, nausea, redness in the eye, blurred vision**
- **With hemorrhage or retinal detachment (medical emergency): seeing brown or red spots, a shower of star-like spots or bright flashes of light; sensation that a curtain is moving across the visual field; loss of vision**
- With cataracts: hazy, fuzzy, or blurred vision; occasional double vision; frequent changes in eyeglass prescriptions; a filmy feeling over the eye(s); changes in pupil color from black to gray, yellow, or white; problems with light (distortion, sensitivity, etc.)
- With age-related macular degeneration: difficulty in reading and close work due to a "dimming" effect; blank spots in visual field; straight lines appear wavy
- With glaucoma: progressive narrowing of the visual field (tunnel vision)
- With congenital (infant) glaucoma: cloudy eyes, light sensitivity, excessive tearing
- With nearsightedness or farsightedness: problems focusing close up or far away

Consult Your Doctor If:

- You injure your eye. See page 135.
- You notice any symptoms described above.
- You have persistent eye pain.
- You notice a sudden change in your vision.
- Your peripheral (side) vision diminishes.
- The color of your iris changes.
- You have red, encrusted, or swollen eyelids.

146

HOMECARE

If physician referral is not recommended at this time, try the following self-care procedures:

Medication

- Avoid over-the-counter eye drops unless your doctor recommends them.
- For glaucoma, your doctor will prescribe eye drops to relieve pressure in the eye.

Cover

- Don't cover your eye unless instructed to do so by your doctor.

Activity

- When vision problems occur suddenly, proceed cautiously with physical activity, since impaired vision may cause you to lose your balance or misjudge distances.

NB

Note Well

- If you wear contact lenses, clean them regularly and according to your doctor's instructions.
- Have your eyes checked periodically by an eye care professional—**at least once a year if you have diabetes.**
- Wear sunglasses in sunlight or high-glare situations.

Constipation

A general misconception about regularity is that daily bowel movements are an indication of well-being. The fact of the matter is that being "regular" is different for each person.

Constipation is defined as difficulty in passing stools, rather than not being able to "go" to the bathroom. Most constipation problems can be fixed by increasing your fluid intake and increasing your consumption of fiber, found in fruits, vegetables, cereals, and whole-grain breads.

An added benefit of changing your dietary habits is that you will reduce your risk of colon cancer, diverticulosis, polyps, and hemorrhoids.

Symptoms/Signs

• Difficulty in having a bowel movement

Consult Your Doctor If:

• Your constipation happens with weight loss, abdominal pain or swelling, or the passage of stools that are pencil-thin or have dark blood, or are black and tar-like.

• Your constipation continues after you have tried HomeCare procedures for more than one week.

HOMECARE
If physician referral is not recommended at this time, try the following self-care procedures:

Fluids

• Increase your intake of fluids such as water and fruit juices.

Nutrition

• Increase your intake of fruits, whole-grain cereals and breads, and vegetables.

Activity

• Increase your physical activity. Brisk walking, aerobic dance, and jogging have been shown to stimulate bowel movements.

Medication

• Avoid the frequent use of laxatives. If a laxative is used, try a bulk product that contains fiber. Don't use a laxative that contains phenolphthalein. See page 101, "Popular Over-the-Counter Medications."

Prevention

• The best way to avoid constipation is to follow dietary recommendations, drink plenty of water, and be physically active.
• If constipation continues to be a problem despite increasing fluids and fiber in your diet, consider adding bulk agents containing psyllium (e.g., Metamucil®) or stool softeners (e.g., Colace®). Talk to your doctor or pharmacist.

Hemorrhoids

Hemorrhoids, or "piles," occur when the veins that surround the anus become enlarged and eventually bleed because of increased pressure. Certain conditions increase the risk of hemorrhoids, including being overweight, being constipated, continually straining when trying to defecate, excessive coughing or sneezing, and being pregnant. People in occupations that require long bouts of sitting, such as truck drivers, have a higher incidence of hemorrhoids.

Typical symptoms of hemorrhoids are rectal pain, itching, and bleeding. Rectal bleeding can be a cause for concern, as it may suggest a more serious condition such as an ulcer or cancer. The blood from hemorrhoids is bright red and may be present on the outside of the stool or on the toilet paper. **You should consult your doctor immediately if there's rectal bleeding that makes your stools look black and tar-like. This may be a sign of significant blood loss from higher up in the bowel.**

Symptoms/Signs

- Rectal pain, itching, and bleeding. Blood from hemorrhoids is bright red on toilet paper and on outside of stool.

Consult Your Doctor If:

- Minor hemorrhoidal bleeding doesn't stop after three weeks of HomeCare.
- Stools are black or tar-like.
- Your child complains of rectal pain or itching, especially at night. This may indicate pinworms.
- Onset of hemorrhoids is associated with a significant change in bowel habits.

HOMECARE

If physician referral is not recommended at this time, try the following self-care procedures:

Fluids

- Drink plenty of fluids—six to eight glasses of water per day.

Nutrition

- Eat more fiber, found in fruits, vegetables, and whole-grain cereals.

Note Well

- Use toilet paper gently. Use only white non-perfumed paper that is super soft. Wetting the paper with warm water before use may help as well.

Medication

- Of the scores of hemorrhoid medications, none has proved to be more effective than any other. Ask your pharmacist. Consider trying more than one product and see which one gives you the best relief.
- If constipation continues to be a problem despite increasing fluids and fiber in your diet, consider adding bulk agents containing psyllium (e.g., Metamucil®) or stool softeners (e.g., Colace®). Talk to your doctor or pharmacist.

Stomach Cramps

It could be something you ate. Or it could be a virus you picked up from someone at work. Whatever the cause, stomach cramps almost never make their debut alone. Accompanied by any number of symptoms—from diarrhea and nausea to fever and abdominal swelling—stomach cramps usually are a sign that your body has been invaded by something it doesn't like.

For the most part, stomach cramps that are a result of food poisoning, a stomach virus, or diarrhea are treatable at home. When stomach cramps are accompanied by diarrhea (and they almost always are), take care to drink plenty of fluids, especially if you're very young, very old, or have a chronic condition that has compromised your body's ability to fight infection. Beverages with sugar, potassium, and other minerals (Gatorade® is a good choice) can help replace fluid as well as the substances your body needs to stay healthy.

Symptoms/Signs

- Mild to severe abdominal pain that is episodic, intermittent, or rhythmic (as opposed to continuous and acute)

Consult Your Doctor If:

- Stomach cramps are accompanied by sudden, severe diarrhea, bloody diarrhea, or fever over 102 degrees F.
- Stomach cramps are localized in the lower-right abdomen.
- Intermittent stomach cramps are accompanied by two or more of the following symptoms: vomiting, progressively painful abdominal swelling, progressive constipation (or total inability to move bowels or pass gas), weakness, dizziness, bloody/black stools, foul breath, or low-grade fever.
- Stomach cramps are not relieved by self-care measures within three days.

Medication

- When accompanied by diarrhea, try not to take any medication for the first two or three hours, since the diarrhea may be flushing infection or irritating substances out of your body. After that time, try a bismuth preparation (e.g., Pepto-Bismol®) or an over-the-counter anti-diarrheal medication (e.g., Imodium A-D®).

Nutrition

- Avoid heavy or greasy foods, dairy products, or foods rich in fiber while you have cramps and during recovery.

Fluids

- Stay well hydrated when stomach cramps are accompanied by diarrhea: Try to drink one pint of water, clear broth or a drink such as Gatorade® to replace fluids and minerals you've lost.

Note Well

- Monitor body temperature.
- Get plenty of rest as you recover.

Prevention

- Never eat undercooked meat or fish, mushrooms that you've picked yourself, or prepared salads or meats that have been unrefrigerated for more than an hour.
- Always wash your hands well with anti-bacterial soap before and after handling food.
- Throw away any leftovers or canned foods that you suspect may be contaminated or spoiled.
- Avoid eating foods you know you're sensitive to.
- Manage stress in your life.

digestive

149

Stomach Flu

Stomach flu (gastroenteritis) usually is a sudden viral infection that brings on stomach cramps, vomiting, nausea, and diarrhea. It also can be caused by bacteria found in untreated drinking water (dysentery) or food poisoning (salmonella). The symptoms of gastroenteritis are the body's attempt to cleanse itself of noxious agents such as certain bacteria. Symptoms generally last only one or two days.

Stomach flu can be especially dangerous to infants, small children and the frail elderly because of rapid dehydration caused by vomiting and diarrhea. Excessive vomiting or diarrhea should be carefully watched.

Symptoms/Signs

- Stomach cramps, vomiting, nausea, and diarrhea that usually last less than two days

Consult Your Doctor If:

- **Excessive vomiting or diarrhea occurs in infants, small children, the frail elderly, or people with other health problems.**
- **There are signs of dehydration: increased thirst, dark yellow urine, limited urination, and skin that may be wrinkled and have no tone.**
- Nausea, loss of appetite, and general abdominal pain is followed by pain in the lower right part of the abdomen.
- You have a fever of 102 degrees F or higher.
- After only liquids are used, diarrhea continues for more than two days.
- Diarrhea is bloody or black.
- Vomiting continues on and off for more than 12 hours in an adult or 8-12 hours in a small child without significant improvement.

150

* Because of the risk of Reye's syndrome, aspirin should not be given to or used by children or teenagers who have or are suspected of having flu or chicken pox. Use acetaminophen.

HOMECARE

If physician referral is not recommended at this time, try the following self-care procedures:

Fluids

- Choose crushed ice and sips of water for the first few hours.
- Drink clear liquids for the next 24 hours.
- For breast-fed infants, continue feeding, but offer oral rehydration fluids first. For formula-fed infants, eliminate all but clear liquids (e.g., water or oral rehydration solutions) for 24 hours.

Nutrition

- No foods for the first 24 hours.
- Slowly introduce bananas, rice, applesauce, and toast (BRAT) diet on Day 2.

Medication

- Aspirin, ibuprofen, or acetaminophen for fever. Do not use aspirin or ibuprofen if you are already vomiting: This will further upset your stomach.*
- Do not give your child anti-diarrheal drugs, unless recommended by his or her doctor.

Rest

- Reduce your activity. Bed rest may be needed.

Prevention

- Make sure meats are properly stored and prepared.
- Avoid dressings, prepared salads, shellfish (especially raw oysters), poultry, and other meats left out more than two hours.
- Wash your hands before and after handling food.

Ulcers

For decades, most people (including doctors) believed that diet and stress caused peptic ulcers, irritations in the stomach and small intestine. However, researchers have discovered that a bacteria (Helicobactor pylori) causes more than 70 percent of all such ulcers. Antibiotics can quickly eradicate the bacteria and liberate millions of people who have suffered through years of abdominal pain and bland diets.

For patients whose ulcers are not linked to H. pylori bacteria, staying away from aspirin or non-steroidal anti-inflammatory drugs (NSAIDs) such as ibuprofen can speed relief and healing to irritated gastrointestinal linings. In any case, you need a doctor's diagnosis to determine the exact cause of any burning or abdominal discomfort. This is especially true for people who may have the symptoms of an ulcer but really have an underlying, more serious disease or abnormality.

Symptoms/Signs

- Gnawing or burning in the upper abdomen, usually worse on an empty stomach (pain may last minutes or hours)
- Upper abdominal pain that is made worse by drinking alcohol or eating spicy, heavy, or fibrous foods
- Possible bloating, nausea, vomiting, excessive belching, indigestion, heartburn, weight loss, black or tarry stools, or feeling of fullness after eating small amounts of foods

Consult Your Doctor If:

- **You have symptoms of heartburn accompanied by shortness of breath, pain in your chest or jaw, or pain that radiates down your arm or to your back. Seek emergency care.**
- You suspect you have an ulcer.
- Heartburn lasts more than three days.
- Your bowel movements are black and tar-like.
- You vomit black or bloody material.
- You have periods of unusual weakness or dizziness, or you pass out.

Medication

- Avoid aspirin and anti-inflammatory drugs (NSAIDs) such as ibuprofen.
- Ask your doctor if antibiotics will alleviate or cure your ulcer.
- Try adding a regimen of bismuth medication (Pepto-Bismol®, for example) if you're on antibiotics to treat your ulcer (check with your doctor first).
- Use antacids (as directed) to neutralize stomach acids.

Nutrition

- Avoid high-fat, overly fibrous, or very spicy foods until your ulcer is healed.
- Eat six small meals a day instead of three large ones.
- Avoid taking iron supplements unless advised to do so by your doctor.

Activity

- Exercise moderately to reduce stress.

Fluids

- Drink lots of water to dilute stomach acids.
- Avoid drinking too much milk: It may soothe stomach acids temporarily, but it'll also cause your stomach to secrete more acid later.

Note Well

- Don't smoke.
- Restrict use of alcohol.
- Eat a well-balanced diet.
- Reduce stress whenever possible.

digestive

151

Abrasions

Skin abrasions are surface wounds in which layers of the skin are scraped or torn. The primary cause of abrasions is falls; the hands, elbows, knees, and hips are the major sites of injury. Team sports such as football, basketball, and softball, and activities such as skateboarding, cycling, and in-line skating are most frequently associated with abrasion injuries. You should wear gloves and protective knee and elbow pads when engaged in activities for which falls are common. People who work in areas that are slippery (e.g., wet floors, icy walkways) or who climb uneven terrain should be especially careful.

Symptoms/Signs

- Torn or scraped skin with bleeding

Consult Your Doctor If:

- There are signs of infection: increasing pain or tenderness, swelling and redness, red streaks coming from the injury, presence of pus, a fever of 101 degrees F or higher without other causes, such as a cold or flu.
- Date of last tetanus shot is unknown, or wound is not small and clean and your last tetanus shot was more than five years ago.

HOMECARE
If physician referral is not recommended at this time, try the following self-care procedures:

Clean
- Rinse the wound with cool water.
- Wash around the wound with soap and water. Avoid getting soap in the wound.
- Use tweezers cleaned in alcohol to remove dirt, glass, or gravel that remains in wound.

Cover
- If wound covers a large area, oozes blood, or is exposed to clothing or dirt, cover with an *occlusive* or *semiocclusive* bandage (see your pharmacist). This dressing keeps the wound moist—reducing scarring and speeding healing.

Medication
- Aspirin, ibuprofen, or acetaminophen for pain. Use as directed.

Heat/Cold
- An ice pack or cool compresses can be tried to help reduce pain.

Prevention
- Wear gloves and protective pads on knees and elbows when appropriate.
- Beware of slippery or uneven surfaces.
- A tetanus booster shot every 10 years is recommended. See page 44.

Acne

Nearly eight out of 10 teens will develop acne, but, as all too many adults know, pimples can continue to crop up for decades after you enter adulthood. Most experts agree that acne is linked to heredity and hormone levels. Hormones stimulate oil production in the glands around hair follicles, the ducts surrounding these follicles become clogged, and a whitehead or blackhead results. It's when one of these skin clogs becomes inflamed that you get a raised, red pimple.

Most of the time, occasional bouts of whiteheads, blackheads, or pimples can be cleared up rather quickly and painlessly with simple home treatment. For an unfortunate minority, however, acne can cause extremely painful, cyst-like lesions that leave deep scars. Such severe cases usually require medical treatment by a dermatologist.

Contrary to popular belief, diet plays a relatively minor role in acne frequency or severity. But certain drugs, stress, industrial chemicals, and some bacteria can trigger acne episodes. Avoiding such triggers can be a first step toward minimizing or eliminating skin eruptions altogether.

Symptoms/Signs

- Blackheads, whiteheads or red, swollen bumps on the skin (usually the face, neck, chest, shoulders, or back)
- Bumps that come to a head, erupt, drain clear, yellowish, or pus-like fluid, and then crust over
- A large (up to an inch in diameter) cyst or pustule accompanied by pain and red/purple inflammation; may or may not erupt

Consult Your Doctor If:

- You suspect a cyst or pimple has become infected or inflamed (red or purple, swollen, painful, or does not get better with home treatment).
- Persistent acne is severe and leaves scars.

HOMECARE
If physician referral is not recommended at this time, try the following self-care procedures:

Clean

- Keep all acne-prone areas very clean, using soap and lots of water to rinse. Pat areas dry—don't rub or scrub skin.
- Try over-the-counter soaps or astringents designed to dry the skin.
- Avoid washing acne-prone areas with either very hot or very cold water. Lukewarm or tepid water is best for not aggravating skin conditions.

Medication

- Try over-the-counter acne medications, especially those containing benzoyl peroxide, that facilitate skin peeling within the follicles of your skin.
- For severe or recurrent problems, ask your doctor about prescription acne medications such as Accutane® or Retin-A® *(use only as directed by your doctor, and never take Accutane if you are pregnant or could possibly become pregnant).*
- If your doctor prescribes Retin-A® for your acne, stay out of the sun as much as possible.
- Don't mix over-the-counter and prescription acne medications.

Cover

- Don't cover acne outbreaks with bandages or tight-fitting clothing.

Note Well

- Keep skin clean.
- Reduce stress and anxiety.
- Avoid acne "triggers," such as certain makeups, drugs, and moisturizers.
- Use non-comedogenic or acne-free facial preparations.

Animal/Human Bites

Contrary to what many people think, household pets—not wild animals or stray pets—are the culprits in most cases of animal bites. Although less common, human bites should be taken as seriously as animal bites. Even if the surface tear doesn't look bad, there could be damage beneath to the tendons and joints. In addition, the human mouth is home to many bacteria and viruses.

Any bite that breaks the skin is serious and should be attended to immediately by a health care professional. Also, an animal care or control professional will need to catch and observe a wild animal or stray to determine if it is infected with rabies.

Aside from the threat of rabies (from animal bites), other diseases and bacterial infections can set in quickly from either an animal or human bite. People without current tetanus immunizations are particularly vulnerable; tetanus can lead to death, so hospitalization is required to treat it. (Signs and symptoms of tetanus include stiffness and/or spasms of the jaw, neck, and other muscles; irritability; painful convulsions.) Also, the hepatitis B virus can be transmitted by a human bite. Refer to page 44 for the recommended schedule of immunizations.

If a bite does not break the skin, treat the injury at home as a minor wound. After you've treated the bite, watch for signs of infection.

For wounds that bleed excessively, apply pressure (see "Bleeding," page 90) to the bite area until you can get emergency medical treatment.

Consult Your Doctor If:

- You show signs of infection: swelling, red streaks coming from the wound, excessive soreness, fever, or pus draining from the wound.
- An animal or human bite breaks the skin.
- A bite is from a non-pet.
- You are bitten and have not had a tetanus shot within the past five years.
- You develop tingling or increased sensitivity in the bite area three to seven weeks after a bite.

HOMECARE
If physician referral is not recommended at this time, try the following self-care procedures:

Clean

- Immediately clean a minor bite thoroughly with soap and water for five minutes, then apply an antiseptic such as hydrogen peroxide or alcohol. For serious bites, control bleeding first by applying pressure; do not clean a wound that is actively bleeding.

Medication

- If you are not current with your tetanus immunizations, the doctor will give you a tetanus shot immediately.
- If the biting animal has rabies or is suspected of having rabies, your doctor will prescribe a series of shots to prevent the disease.
- After cleansing a minor bite thoroughly, apply an antibiotic ointment.
- Your doctor may prescribe oral antibiotics to prevent infection.

Cover

- Cover minor bites (after cleansing) with a non-stick bandage.

Prevention

- Avoid contact with wild animals.
- Be careful around pets you don't know. Even an animal that seems friendly can become aggressive quickly.
- Make sure your pets have complete and up-to-date immunizations.
- Be sure you are up-to-date on your tetanus shots. See page 44.

Athlete's Foot

You don't have to play tennis all day or run marathons to suffer painful bouts of athlete's foot. Anyone whose feet are damp regularly from perspiration is the perfect host for the fungus that causes skin between toes and on the sides and soles of feet to crack, peel, itch, blister, and flake.

Once you've got it, athlete's foot takes about four weeks of aggressive home treatment to disappear completely. After it's gone, an equally aggressive course of prevention often is necessary to keep the organism at bay. Sweaty footwear, damp socks, and less-than-clean showering areas are all dank enough to harbor athlete's foot fungus. Avoiding those infection sites and becoming an otherwise ferocious fungus fighter usually is the only way you can avoid future flare-ups.

Symptoms/Signs

- Itchy, cracked, peeling, red, flaky skin on or between toes (or, sometimes, between fingers and on the palms of the hand)
- Itchy, blister-like bumps on the sides or soles of feet

Consult Your Doctor If:

- Your foot is swollen, sore, blistered, red or has pus in sores or blisters.
- Symptoms do not improve after treatment with anti-fungal preparations.
- You have diabetes or poor circulation in your feet and develop symptoms of athlete's foot.
- Inflammation of the skin makes it difficult for you to walk.
- Your legs swell and you have a fever.

Medication

- Apply over-the-counter, anti-fungal preparations designed to combat athlete's foot fungus (Tinactin®, Micatin®, Desenex®, Aftate®, etc.), two or three times a day, until you have no symptoms for at least two weeks.

Clean

- Keep feet scrupulously clean and dry.
- Remove dead skin from feet by scrubbing affected areas with a nail brush; pay special attention to the skin between each toe. Rinse and dry well, then apply anti-fungal powder.
- Keep shoes clean. Wipe the insides of athletic shoes with a damp cloth dipped in an antibacterial solution such as Lysol®, or spray Lysol® disinfectant inside shoes. Allow shoes to dry completely.
- Keep your shower or bathtub clean; spray or wipe down bathing areas with antibacterial cleansers regularly.

Note Well

- Avoid wearing shoes that fit too tightly or aren't breathable, especially those made from waterproof materials. Also, try to alternate shoes from day to day to give each pair time to dry out completely.
- Wear all-cotton or wool socks and change them two or three times throughout the day, if possible. Avoid synthetic fabrics that trap perspiration.
- Wear thongs or other foot protection when you're in public showers, spas, or pool areas.
- Follow all of the above recommendations for keeping feet clean, dry, and protected from infection.

skin conditions

155

Bed Sores

Although nearly three-quarters of the people suffering from bed sores are over 70 years old, anyone can develop bed sores simply from being confined to a chair or bed as a result of illness or injury. And while "bed sores" sound like a minor irritation or side effect, the truth is that more than 60,000 people die from bed-sore complications each year.

Left untreated, bed sores (also known as decubitis ulcers or pressure ulcers) can eat away at skin and muscle tissue, eventually exposing bones and joints. For patients who already have compromised physical health or weakened immune systems, infection from advanced-stage bed sores can be deadly. Fortunately, simple preventive techniques can keep the physical pressure of incapacitation from damaging skin and underlying tissue.

Symptoms/Signs

- Reddened patch of skin that becomes a crater-like sore or ulcer; usually found where a bone is close to the skin (hips, shoulder blades, elbows, etc.) or where skin is pressed against a bed or chair for long periods

Consult Your Doctor If:

- Any skin reddening resulting from pressure does not disappear when pressure is removed.

156

Prevention

All suspected or existing bed sores should be treated by a medical professional. Some of the following suggestions for preventing bed sores are intended for people who take care of bedridden or immobilized patients:

- Inspect skin daily for signs that a bed sore may be developing.
- Keep skin and bedding clean. Use lotions, creams, or gels to keep skin from drying out. Use cornstarch on skin to reduce friction from sheets or clothing.
- Change position every two hours (for people confined to bed) or every hour (for people confined to a chair). People confined to a chair who can shift their own weight should change position at least every 15 minutes. Remember to lift rather than drag anyone you're repositioning.
- Invest in a special mattress or cushion designed to prevent bed sores (such products usually contain air, foam, water, gel, or a combination of materials).
- For people confined to bed: Place pillows under legs from midcalf to ankle to keep heels off the mattress (however, never position pillows only behind the knees). Use pillows or cushions to keep knees or ankles from touching each other.
- Incontinent patients should wear absorbent pads/briefs with a quick-drying surface. Use a protective ointment to keep urine and bowel movements from irritating skin.
- Avoid using donut-shaped (ring) cushions.
- Avoid raising the head of the bed.
- Proper nutrition and plenty of fluids are essential.

Blisters

"I walked so far, my blisters had blisters" isn't necessarily a testament to the speaker's stamina or courage. Indeed, blisters usually are a sign that you're doing something you're not used to doing, or you're doing something the wrong way. Shoveling snow, knitting, wearing new shoes around the office, or running a marathon can give you blisters. In fact, any time you apply unusual amounts of friction to skin anywhere on your body, you're likely to get a blister.

Although they look innocent enough and may not cause too much discomfort (as long as you stop doing whatever it was that gave you the blister in the first place), blisters can escalate into nasty infections that may have to be treated by your doctor. So do what you can to prevent blisters, and, failing that, do what you can to keep existing blisters from becoming more than just temporary nuisances.

Symptoms/Signs

- Reddish, painful, swollen area of skin with a fluid-filled bubble of skin near the center (blister has opened and fluid has drained if skin bubble is torn away)

Consult Your Doctor If:

- Redness, swelling, or pain increases.
- Fluid from a blister has an odor or is thick or colored (normal blister fluid looks like water).

HOMECARE
If physician referral is not recommended at this time, try the following self-care procedures:

Clean
- Clean open blisters gently with soap and water.

Medication
- Apply Neosporin® or Bacitracin® ointment to an open blister that you've cleaned, before you put a bandage on it.

Cover
- Cover an unopened blister to protect it from further irritation. A moleskin "donut" can be used around the blister.
- Cover an open blister (after you've cleaned it) with a non-stick bandage. Change bandage twice daily or as needed.

Activity
- Avoid any activity that further irritates a blister.

Note Well
- Generally, avoid opening a blister.
- If you cannot protect an unopened blister from further irritation, you may want to drain it: Sterilize a needle (using a flame or alcohol) and stick it into the side of the blister. Gently squeeze out all fluid, leaving all skin intact. Coat blister with antibiotic ointment and cover with a non-stick bandage.

Prevention
- Buy shoes that fit.
- Wear soft, breathable socks. Wear work gloves when needed.
- Apply cornstarch or talcum powder before putting on socks or work gloves.

Boils

Sounding more like a biblical plague than a modern medical condition, boils (also called furuncles, carbuncles, and styes) are relatively common and usually pose no serious health threat. They can erupt around an inflamed hair follicle, usually on the face, scalp, underarm, thigh, or buttocks. Often, small boils arise and subside within a week or two. Deeper boils or boil sites with multiple pus-filled, pimple-like heads are probably caused by a staph infection and can recur in cycles or erratically for years after the first eruption.

Most boils respond well to a relatively simple regimen of very warm compresses and careful cleansing procedures. Sometimes, however, boils fail to drain properly, or they become very painful and inflamed. In such cases, a visit to the doctor to have the area drained usually is necessary, and a 10-to-14-day cycle of oral antibiotics may be prescribed.

Symptoms/Signs

- Red, painful, pus-filled abscess beneath the skin's surface
- Minor swelling around boil area
- Appearance of a pimple-like head or multiple heads in center of swollen area(s) that sometimes erupt and drain fluid, pus, or both

Consult Your Doctor If:

- You have a boil on or near your lip, nose, armpit, groin, breast, or between buttocks.
- A boil is very large or causes significant inflammation of surrounding areas.
- You have boils accompanied by a fever.

HOMECARE

If physician referral is not recommended at this time, try the following self-care procedures:

Heat/Cold

- At the first sign of a boil, apply very warm, wet compresses to the area for 20 minutes, three to four times a day for a week or until the boil comes to a head and breaks.
- Sit in a hot bath for 20 minutes daily until boil erupts.

Clean

- After a boil erupts, clean the area and apply an antibacterial cream (e.g., Neosporin® or Bacitracin®).

Cover

- Cover erupted or draining boils with a bandage to keep fluid from spreading infection or staining clothes. Change bandage often—three or four times a day.

Note Well

- Do not pinch or squeeze boils that are not fully drained. You may cause a deeper infection.

Prevention

- Bathe daily.
- Keep boil area or boil-prone areas very clean; wipe skin with a clean cotton ball soaked in alcohol or Betadine antiseptic solution to keep infection from spreading.
- For boils on the face: Before shaving, wash your face with an antibacterial soap. After shaving, apply alcohol to affected areas. Immerse razors in alcohol between shaves, and don't share your razor.
- When you have a boil, use clean towels, washcloths, bed linens, and clothing daily; use hot water to launder all items that come in contact with a boil.

Bruises

You can be fancy and call them "contusions," but bruises—the most common skin injury—are just discolorations that you sometimes get from bumping into something (or having something bump into you). The actual injury you receive is to the deeper tissues beneath your skin; a bruise appears when blood from injured tissue accumulates near your skin's surface. The bruised area may be tender or downright painful for a day or two, but the pain usually goes away as a bruise's color fades.

Every once in a while, athletes or people who overwork their bodies during exercise will notice an unexplained bruise a day or two after a hard workout. Those bruises result from tiny tears in the blood vessels under the skin and are no more serious than blunt-trauma bruises.

Symptoms/Signs

- Discoloration of unbroken skin at site of blunt trauma (fresh bruises may be reddish at first, turning dark purple or blue within a few hours, then turning yellow or green after a few days as bruise heals)

Consult Your Doctor If:

- You have a bruise that swells or is extremely painful, especially if you take blood-thinning medication.
- A bruise to a toe or finger results in a hemorrhage (collection of blood) under a toenail or fingernail.
- You notice that you're bruising easily or for no apparent reason.
- A bruise does not fade significantly within 10 days or fails to fade completely after three weeks.

Heat/Cold
- Apply cold compresses to bruised area as soon as possible to reduce swelling and speed healing. Reapply for 15 minutes, once an hour for the first day or two if bruising is widespread or severe.
- After 48 hours, apply heat to increase blood flow to bruised area.

Note Well
- If you have a large bruise on your leg or foot, elevate your leg as much as possible for the first 24 hours after the injury.

Medication
- Avoid taking aspirin to relieve pain, since aspirin inhibits blood clotting. Take acetaminophen instead.

Activity
- With large bruises to the limbs, activity may need to be restricted for the first 24 to 48 hours.

Prevention
- Avoid placing furniture by doorways or common walkways within your home.
- Be sure that carpeting is secure and slip resistant.
- Be sure that all electrical cords are not in open areas where you may trip.
- Keep floors dry and clear of clutter.

skin conditions

159

Burns

HOMECARE
If physician referral is not recommended at this time, try the following self-care procedures:

Burns are classified in three categories according to their severity, with third-degree burns being the most serious:

First-Degree: Limited to the skin's surface, first-degree burns (such as a typical sunburn, see page 180) are red and painful. They usually do not require medical attention.

Second-Degree: Splitting or blistering of skin is evident, indicating that deeper skin layers have been damaged.

Third-Degree: Severe tissue damage is evident involving the skin, fatty tissue, nerves, and other tissues deep below the surface. **Indications of third-degree burns include swelling, skin that is charred or white, and limited pain because nerves have been damaged or destroyed.**

Consult Your Doctor If:

- Third-degree burns are evident.
- There are extensive second-degree burns or any second-degree burns on the face, hands, or feet.
- Pain continues for more than two days.
- There are signs of infection:
  - Increasing pain, redness or tenderness.
  - Fever of 101 degrees F or greater.
  - Area becomes increasingly swollen.

Beware of Sunburn

- Exposure to ultraviolet radiation increases your risk of skin cancer. The American Cancer Society urges people to minimize their sun exposure and to use sunscreen with a minimum SPF of 15.
- Examine your skin every three months: Look for birthmarks, moles, or brown spots that have changed color, size, or texture; have an irregular outline; are bigger than a pencil eraser; or continue to itch, scab, or bleed. Consult your doctor if you discover any of the above changes.

Heat/Cold

- Apply cool compress or cool water to burn area for 5-10 minutes. Continue until pain is reduced.
- **Beware:** Applying ice compress may further damage tissue.

Medication

- Aspirin, ibuprofen, or acetaminophen to reduce pain. Use as directed.
- *Antibiotic creams have questionable value.*
- Aloe may be tried to help soothe the pain and discomfort.

Cover

- Do not cover burn with gauze dressing or bandage, unless area is irritated by clothing or other objects.

Fluids

- Drink plenty of water.

Note Well

- Avoid breaking blisters. Do not remove skin.

Prevention

- Avoid excessive sun exposure.
- Use sunscreen with a sun protection factor (SPF) of at least 15.
- Practice fire prevention. Assume pots and skillets are hot.
- Keep children out of the kitchen while cooking. If possible, try to use rear burners of your stove.

skin conditions

160

Cold Hands and Feet

"Cold hands, warm heart" isn't just what people with cold hands say to apologize for their chilling touch: It's actually true. When your body needs to maintain an adequate core temperature in cool weather, it simply reduces blood flow to your hands and feet to keep heat loss to a minimum. For people who smoke, take certain medications, or have an iron deficiency, diabetes, or heart disease, chilled extremities can even be a problem in relatively mild temperatures.

Simple self-care and prevention usually is enough to keep most people's hands and feet from turning icy. If you have Raynaud's syndrome (your fingers or toes turn blue and sting with pain upon exposure to cold) or acrocyanosis (your hands and feet are always cold and usually very wet with perspiration), self-care and prevention measures usually work, but your doctor may need to be consulted.

Symptoms/Signs

- Cool or cold skin on hands and feet, sometimes accompanied by clamminess, perspiration, or mild numbness
- With Raynaud's syndrome: fingers and toes suddenly turn pale upon exposure to cold, sometimes turning blue or red and often accompanied by stinging pain
- With acrocyanosis: constant chill to hands and feet, even in mild temperatures, usually accompanied by profuse perspiration
- With circulatory disease: occasionally chilled hands and feet, even in mild temperatures, sometimes accompanied by numbness

Consult Your Doctor If:

- You lose feeling in any extremity.
- Your (cool) hands or feet ache with use or when elevated.
- Your hands or feet have poorly or non-healing sores.
- Self-care measures fail to keep the hands or feet warm.

Medication
- Use absorbent foot powders to keep feet dry.
- Avoid over-the-counter cold remedies and diet pills.

Heat/Cold
- Avoid putting hands or feet in cold water.
- Use warm—not hot—water to warm chilled extremities slowly.

Nutrition
- Eat a meal (preferably a hot one) before going outdoors in cool weather.
- Eat iron-rich foods or talk to your doctor about taking iron supplements if you're anemic.

Note Well
- Wear gloves and moisture-wicking socks.
- Swing your arms in large circles or your legs in half-circles to move blood to your extremities.

Fluids
- Drink plenty of fluids throughout the day.
- Avoid caffeine and alcohol.
- Drink hot cider, broth, or decaffeinated tea to warm hands and feet quickly.

skin conditions

161

Cuts

Once a skin cut (laceration) occurs, it's important to determine if the wound requires medical attention because of one of the following conditions: uncontrolled bleeding; a jagged wound; potential damage to muscles, nerves, and other soft tissues; possible infection. Infection usually becomes evident 24 hours after injury. You also should consider seeing your doctor if the cut is too large or deep for you to keep the edges together. Keeping the edges of the wound together helps keep the dirt out and decreases scarring. Stitches provide the best insurance for holding the edges together, but they can cause scarring also. Because of this, your doctor may suggest using butterfly bandages.

You can easily learn to look for signs of infection and the healing process. Ask your doctor. Also, you can learn to remove stitches yourself.

Symptoms/Signs

• Depending on the severity of the cut, minor to uncontrolled bleeding

Consult Your Doctor If:

• **The wound cannot be closed and bleeding cannot be stopped,** the edges won't come together, or the wound is very irregular and there are flaps of tissue.

• Date of last tetanus shot is unknown, or wound is not small and clean and your last tetanus shot was more than five years ago.

• The wound is very dirty or contains foreign material that is not easily washed away.

• There is weakness or numbness below the injury.

• There is a long or deep cut to the face, chest, fingers, back, stomach, or palm of the hand, or over a joint.

• There are signs of infection such as increasing pain or tenderness, swelling and redness, red streaks coming away from the injury, pus, or a fever of 100 degrees F or higher without another cause, such as cold or flu.

HOMECARE

If physician referral is not recommended at this time, try the following self-care procedures:

Clean

• Rinse the cut with cool water.
• Wash around the wound with soap and water. Avoid getting soap in the wound.
• Use tweezers cleaned in alcohol to remove dirt, glass, or gravel that remains in wound.

Cover

• Apply pressure directly to wound with clean gauze pad until bleeding has stopped.
• Apply an antibiotic ointment and bandage to help prevent scarring and promote healing.
• Apply "butterfly" bandage to a deeper cut after bleeding has stopped or slowed.
• Do not pick at the scab.

Medication

• Antiseptics such as hydrogen peroxide are not recommended. They can irritate the wound and cause further discomfort.
• Take aspirin, ibuprofen, or acetaminophen for pain. Use as directed.

Note Well

• A tetanus booster shot is recommended every 10 years. See page 44.

Dandruff

If you avoid wearing dark colors because of your dandruff, you're not alone. Nearly everyone has dandruff—some obviously more than others. To cure it, you'd have to stop new cell growth on your scalp, which just isn't possible. But you can control the flaking and even slow down the rate at which old scalp cells fall away as they are replaced by new ones.

The first line of defense against the white stuff is shampooing daily and using an over-the-counter dandruff shampoo. If you notice no improvement after three or four weeks of home treatment, you could be dealing with a condition such as seborrheic dermatitis, which flakes like dandruff but has accompanying scalp inflammation that can weep or crust over. Seborrheic dermatitis can sometimes be helped by dandruff shampoos but often requires a prescription of a hydrocortisone-containing cream or lotion to make a real difference.

Symptoms/Signs

- Itchy scalp
- White or gray flakes that are obvious on hair and clothing

Consult Your Doctor If:

- Heavy dandruff does not improve after a few weeks of home treatment.
- You have very stubborn dandruff accompanied by scaly patches of skin on the sides of your nose, in your eyebrows, or on your chest.

Clean

- Try different over-the-counter dandruff shampoos until you find one that works for you, then use as needed. Preparations containing selenium sulfide or zinc pyrithione work quickly and slow down the flaking process. Those with salicylic acid and sulfur loosen flakes so they can be washed away more easily. Coal-tar shampoos retard cell growth (but see warning, below).
- Don't use dandruff-treatment products containing coal tar for prolonged periods without consulting your doctor. Be aware that coal-tar products make your scalp more sensitive to the sun and may tint light-colored hair light-brown or orange.
- Shampoo every day if possible, or at least five times per week. Use a mild, non-medicated shampoo to control scalp oil without irritating your scalp. If you don't see results, switch to an anti-dandruff shampoo. Use a conditioner to keep hair from drying out. Always rinse hair well.

Medication

- If you're using a prescription scalp lotion or shampoo, or if you are using an over-the-counter coal-tar preparation, wear a hat to protect your scalp.
- For heavy, stubborn dandruff, ask your doctor to recommend a prescription dandruff shampoo.

s k i n   c o n d i t i o n s

163

Eczema

Like dry skin, the itchy rash of eczema can flare up for any number of reasons: contact with harsh detergents, rough fabrics, or cosmetics, as well as poor sleep habits, emotional distress, allergies (about 3 percent of the time), poor circulation in the legs (i.e., statis dermatitis), or a compromised immune system. Most of the time, bouts of eczema come and go, but during dry winter months eczema can linger for weeks and can be almost impossible to soothe. As a result, eczema sufferers have to look beyond typical dry-skin treatments in order to start healing broken skin and restoring moisture to affected areas.

Symptoms/Signs

- Mild to severe itching
- Red, raised skin lesions
- Cracked, dry, or scaly skin
- Peeling skin
- Swollen legs in some cases
- Oozing and crusting (in severe cases)

Consult Your Doctor If:

- Oozing or bleeding rash does not respond to HomeCare.
- Itching is not satisfactorily controlled by, or conditions are worsened by, over-the-counter hydrocortisone creams.
- You suspect childhood eczema is caused by an allergy.
- A scaly rash appears on your face and is accompanied by unusual joint pain and coughing.

skin conditions

164

HOMECARE

If physician referral is not recommended at this time, try the following self-care procedures:

Medication
- Over-the-counter hydrocortisone creams and antihistamines to relieve eczema's itch.
- Calamine lotion for "weeping" eczema to help stop the oozing.

Nutrition
- In children, eggs, milk, and orange juice may cause skin rash; check with your doctor before eliminating foods from your child's diet.

Heat/Cold
- Apply cold, wet dressings to itchy areas. Ice-cold milk is most soothing, but cold water will do.
- Avoid hot water whenever possible, especially at bath time.

Clean
- Keep skin moist and well lubricated. Apply a therapeutic lotion (Eucerin®, Keri®, Lubriderm®) or baby oil immediately after contact with water, before skin has had a chance to dry.
- Use soap sparingly, and choose "non-soap" or superfatted bath bars rich in lanolin, cocoa butter, or cleansing cream.

Note Well
- Avoid scratching, which could cause a secondary bacterial infection, the affected area.
- Invest in a humidifier that ties into your home heating system.
- Avoid false fingernails: Acrylic and fingernail glue can aggravate eczema.
- Wear cotton or non-itchy fabrics that don't irritate skin.
- Wear rubber gloves (avoid latex products if you have a latex allergy) when cleaning or doing dishes.

Frostbite

You don't have to go mountaineering in the dead of winter to get frostbite. Just shoveling snow or changing a tire on a cold day can freeze skin to the point where, even after careful rewarming, there is permanent tissue damage.

Simple common sense prevents frostbite: Don't venture outside in sub-freezing temperatures. If you have to go out, dress appropriately. That means wearing mittens, warm socks, and a hat that covers your ears. Also, know the signs of frostbite and what to do if they appear on your skin or someone else's. Sometimes, for example, the method you use in an attempt to rewarm frostbitten skin can do more damage to tissues than the frostbite itself would do. It's also important to know that hypothermia—a dangerous drop in the body's core temperature—often accompanies frostbite and must be treated first, before you try to rewarm frostbitten skin. See page 167 for information on how to recognize and treat hypothermia.

Symptoms/Signs

- Skin that is somewhat numb and white; may blister or peel when rewarmed (mild frostbite)
- Skin that is cold, hard, white, or grayish and numb; may turn blue or purple, or swell and blister when rewarmed (severe frostbite)

Consult Your Doctor If:

- Symptoms of severe frostbite develop.
- Skin remains numb during and after rewarming.

Note Well

- Find a warm area quickly.
- Never rub frostbitten skin.

Heat/Cold

- Use very warm water (100 to 105 degrees F) to rewarm frostbitten skin quickly: Immerse in a tub or basin or apply compresses. Rewarming can be painful.
- Remove clothing from frostbitten areas and cover with blankets.
- Frostbitten skin burns easily so do not rewarm too close to dry heat or a campfire, or with a heating pad.

Note Well

- If you can't get to a warm area immediately, use your body to rewarm: Put frostbitten hands under armpits. Rewarm frostbitten toes with warm hands. Cover face with hands to warm nose and cheeks.

Fluids

- Drink warm liquids (coffee, tea, broth, cocoa).
- Do not drink alcoholic beverages, which promote heat loss.

Rest

- Do not walk on feet that have been frostbitten and recently rewarmed.
- Rest with frostbitten areas elevated to minimize swelling of rewarmed tissue.

Prevention

- Dress appropriately outdoors (mittens or gloves, hat, etc.).
- Go in at the first sign of over-chill.
- Don't drink alcohol in cold weather.
- Have your home heating unit checked annually.

skin conditions

165

Hyperthermia

You get hot, you sweat, and the sweat evaporates, taking heat away from your skin and keeping your core temperature on an even keel. But when you overload your "air conditioner," hyperthermia—over-exposure to heat—begins to set in. And if you don't take measures to properly cool your body back down, you could end up with a heat-related illness such as heat fatigue, heat exhaustion, or often-fatal heat stroke.

It doesn't even have to be extremely hot outside for you to notice the first signs of hyperthermia. A moderate air temperature combined with humidity decreases your skin's ability to "throw-off" body heat. Also, a chronic medical condition, such as high blood pressure, or taking certain medications (e.g., diuretics and antihistamines) can quickly cause hyperthermia without much exertion or time in the sun. But with sound preventive action, and prompt self-care, most cases of hyperthermia can be avoided or quickly treated.

Symptoms/Signs

- Heat exhaustion: increased thirst, weakness, mental or physical disorientation, nausea, profuse sweating, cold or clammy skin, visual disturbances
- Heat stroke: confusion, bizarre behavior, strong and rapid pulse, extreme fatigue, rapid heartbeat, loss of consciousness, body temperature over 104 degrees F, lack of sweating with dry, red skin (young people who are very young or very fit may continue sweating, however)

Consult Your Doctor If:

- **You or someone you are with has trouble remaining conscious or has other symptoms of heat stroke (seek emergency care immediately).**
- You or someone you are with experiences symptoms of heat exhaustion and does not respond to self-care measures within 30 minutes.

Rest
- As soon as you notice any symptoms of hyperthermia, rest in a cool, shaded area with feet elevated. Remove excess clothing.
- Stop all activity at the first signs of hyperthermia.

Heat/Cold
- Splash skin with cool or tepid water, or apply cool towels or sheets to skin.
- If possible, move to an air-conditioned setting.

Fluids
- Drink lots of cool water, fruit juices, or sports drinks such as Gatorade®.
- Avoid alcohol and caffeine altogether.

Note Well
- In hot/dry or warm/humid weather, dress in light-colored, loose-fitting clothes, wear a hat, drink plenty of fluids, stay out of the sun, and avoid strenuous activity.
- Use your air conditioner whenever possible or visit air-conditioned places such as shopping malls, movie theaters, and libraries during the hottest part of the day.
- Don't go shirtless, and change perspiration-soaked clothes often.

Prevention
- Increased alcohol consumption and overeating in hot weather increase the risk of heat stroke. Use sound judgment.

Hypothermia

The thermometer outside your front door doesn't have to register below freezing for winter weather to threaten your health. Temperatures up to 50 degrees F can be deadly, particularly when accompanied by rain, wind, or your own physical exhaustion. As well, the elderly or the very young are especially vulnerable to cool temperatures, even indoors.

Hypothermia—a mild to severe drop in the body's core temperature—can easily be prevented. Just knowing the weather forecast and preparing for the cold by dressing appropriately can literally mean the difference between life and death. Severe hypothermia requires emergency medical intervention. However, any amount of body cooling needs to be taken seriously and treated with caution and care. Be aware of your body's first warning signals that it's getting too cold: It's an important first step toward eliminating a potentially dangerous threat to your health.

Symptoms/Signs

- Shivering
- Numbness in hands and feet
- Confusion, sleepiness, physical exhaustion, slurred speech, memory lapses
- Slow and shallow breathing; slow and weak heartbeat
- Cool, pale skin; fingers, toes, and lips may be slightly blue
- Cessation of shivering with diminished alertness or loss of consciousness, slow pulse, and breathing (severe hypothermia)

Consult Your Doctor If:

- Anyone with symptoms of hypothermia suffers from diminished alertness, mental confusion, or loses consciousness.
- Self-care measures don't relieve hypothermia symptoms within 30 minutes, or if symptoms get progressively worse despite self-care.

HOMECARE
If physician referral is not recommended at this time, try the following self-care procedures:

Heat/Cold

- Move to a warm, sheltered area.
- Use blankets or skin-to-skin contact (i.e., torso to torso) to raise body temperature or to keep warm.
- In cases of very mild hypothermia, a warm bath can help restore body temperature.
- Remove any wet clothes and replace with dry clothes or blankets. Keep the head covered.

Fluids

- Drink hot tea, broth, or water.
- Avoid alcohol altogether.

NB

Note Well

- Know weather conditions and forecast before spending time outdoors.

Prevention

- Always dress appropriately in cold weather: Wear layers of breathable clothing next to the skin, under wind-blocking or woolen outer layers. Always wear a hat and gloves.
- Never sleep outdoors in clothing you've worn earlier in the day.
- Keep clothes dry in cool weather; change from wet to dry clothes as soon as possible.

167

Ingrown Toenail

Every step you take when you have an ingrown toenail feels like one step too many. The soft skin that the nail has penetrated throbs, swells, turns red, and—if you don't do something about the situation pretty quickly—becomes infected. Many people can live a lifetime without ever having a toenail dig in where it's not supposed to, but people with unusually curved toenails or who constantly suffer toe trauma (construction workers or ballerinas, for example) are at increased risk and know from experience that prevention is the key to pain-free feet.

It's easy to ignore your feet until they give you a problem. Pay attention to how you trim your toenails and how you choose your shoes, and you'll probably never have to "outgrow" an ingrown—or end up at your doctor's door with an infected toe.

Symptoms/Signs

- Toenail (usually on the big toe) growing into soft tissue next to the nail, near the tip of the toe, causing pain and discomfort

Consult Your Doctor If:

- You have severe pain and pus at the site where the toenail is ingrown.
- Any toenail becomes discolored and has crumbling edges.
- You have diabetes or poor circulation and have any pain, swelling, or redness in your toes or feet.

168

Medication

- If you suspect that your ingrown toenail is becoming infected (swelling, redness, pus, etc.), soak your foot in iodine solution. Apply an antibiotic cream (Neosporin®, Bacitracin®, Polysporin®) and cover with a non-stick bandage.
- Try an over-the-counter product made to soften the ingrown nail and the skin around it for easier trimming. Do not use if you have poor circulation or diabetes.

Clean

- Soak feet in very warm water for 15 or 20 minutes to soften nail for easier trimming.
- Keep area around ingrown nail very clean: Use alcohol, hydrogen peroxide, or anti-bacterial soap.

Cover

- Cover an ingrown toenail with a non-stick bandage only if you suspect that it is infected, you have applied antibiotic ointment, and you are waiting to see your doctor.
- Do not cover non-infected ingrown toenails; if you must wear socks, wear only clean, white cotton socks with wide-toe, breathable shoes.

Prevention

- Trim toenails regularly (about once a month). Be sure that nail is trimmed all the way to its edge and if possible, round-off sharp corners.
- Keep feet and area under toenails clean.
- Avoid using any so-called nail care products.
- Wear shoes that fit and are not too tight or pointed excessively at the toe. Also, avoid wearing high heels.
- Avoid tight socks and pantyhose whenever possible.
- If you're diabetic, practice good foot care.

Jock Itch

Like athlete's foot, jock itch is caused by a fungus that thrives in warm, dark, moist places. Athlete or couch potato, male or female, anyone can get jock itch—characterized by severe itching in the groin, thigh or anal area, as well as a raised, red rash with blisters that may ooze liquid or pus.

"Clean and dry" are the watchwords for both prevention and treatment of jock itch—for skin, clothes, athletic supporters, underwear, sheets, towels, or anything else that comes into contact with your genital area. For most people, such basic personal hygiene practices are routine. But remember: Even very meticulous individuals can forget to bring fresh gear to the gym every once in a while. And wearing yesterday's tennis shorts for today's midday match can be enough to incite an infection.

Symptoms/Signs

- Severe itching on upper thighs, buttocks, genitals, or groin (males and females)
- Raised, red rash in above areas (may be accompanied by blisters that weep or ooze)

Consult Your Doctor If:

- Jock itch symptoms do not get better with home treatment.

Medication

- Apply over-the-counter anti-fungal preparations designed to combat jock itch fungus (e.g., Tinactin®, Desenex®, Aftate®), two or three times a day, until you have no symptoms for at least two weeks.

Clean

- Bathe daily. Wash affected area well, dry completely with a fresh, clean towel, then apply anti-fungal powder or cornstarch to reduce irritation and prevent reinfection.

Note Well

- Avoid wearing too-tight underwear, and choose undergarments made from 100 percent cotton.
- Don't wear pantyhose, Spandex shorts, or tights.

Activity

- During severe flare-ups, avoid activities that make you sweat profusely.

Prevention

- Never share a towel with anyone.
- Never wear underwear, workout clothes, or an athletic supporter that hasn't been laundered since it was last worn.
- Regularly follow all of the above recommendations for keeping areas prone to jock itch clean, dry, and protected from infection.

skin conditions

169

Puncture Wounds

Unlike scrapes and cuts, which usually are on the skin's surface, puncture wounds can be deep and pose a greater risk of infection. Unfortunately, they're often neglected because of their small surface size.

Puncture wounds are common to the fingers, hands, and the bottom of the feet, and are caused by sharp, pointed objects such as nails, pins, needles, staples, and wire. Puncture wounds are common in occupations such as construction, carpentry, medicine (needle sticks), and textile manufacturing.

It is important to thoroughly clean the wound in order to avoid infection, especially with wounds of the hand, head, chest, back, or abdomen.

Deep puncture wounds can damage underlying blood vessels, nerves, and organs. **Indications of additional injury, such as loss of movement, numbness, profuse bleeding (spurting indicates that an artery has been injured), or signs of shock, require immediate medical attention.**

Symptoms/Signs

- Superficial to deep penetration of the skin with a sharp object. Bleeding can be minimal (e.g., pin prick) to major.

Consult Your Doctor If:

- **There are signs of shock: pale, sweating skin; dizziness; rapid, weak pulse.**
- **You cannot stop the bleeding.**
- You suspect internal injury to nerves, organs, or blood vessels.
- There are signs of infection: increasing pain or tenderness, swelling and redness, red lines coming away from the injury, presence of pus, or a fever of 101 degrees F or higher without another reason, such as cold or flu.
- Object remains in wound.
- Wound is in hand, head, chest, back, or abdomen.
- It has been more than five years since your last tetanus shot or date of last tetanus shot is not known.

170

Clean

- Rinse the wound with cool water.
- Wash around the wound with soap and water. Avoid getting soap in the wound.
- Encourage the wound to bleed, unless serious. Bleeding helps bring material to the surface.

Heat/Cold

- To help draw foreign matter and bacteria from wound, soak in warm water three times a day for two to four days.

Cover

- Apply an antibiotic ointment and bandage to help prevent scarring and promote healing.

Medication

- Aspirin, ibuprofen, or acetaminophen for pain. Use as directed.
- Antiseptics such as hydrogen peroxide are not recommended. They can irritate the wound and cause further discomfort.

Prevention

- A tetanus booster shot every 10 years is recommended. See page 44.
- Store sharp objects carefully.
- Follow procedures when handling syringes and needles.

* Because of the risk of hepatitis and AIDS through needle sticks, medical personnel should follow infectious disease control measures for the handling of needles and syringes.

Rashes

∙∙∙

Luckily, most rashes aren't serious, lasting only a few days to a week. But some rashes—especially the ones that occur as reactions to something you eat, medicine you're taking, or an insect sting—are a signal from your body that something is seriously wrong. When a rash is the result of an allergy, it's important to avoid the offending substance in the future, since subsequent contact can result in more severe reactions, some requiring emergency medical treatment. But when a mild, localized rash crops up because you've used an irritating laundry soap, brushed up against a poison ivy plant, or gotten a little too close to someone with the chicken pox, a little time and self-care can treat most cases of rash.

Symptoms/Signs

- Raised, red patches of skin that itch, burn, tingle, or are sore or numb
- Rash from contact dermatitis: itchy, red skin that can be flaky or blistered. Refer to page 182.
- Rash from hives or extreme cold or heat: very itchy large, red welts in exposed areas. Refer to page 185.
- Rash from a virus (e.g., chicken pox or measles): itchy, red spots or blisters all over the body. Refer to page 176.
- Rash from bacteria (e.g., impetigo): small red bumps on the arms, legs, chest, or buttocks; may appear yellow as crust forms
- Rash from tick bite: raised, red, ring-shaped or "bull's eye" rash at site of tick bite. Refer to page 172.

Consult Your Doctor If:

- Your rash has a distinct ring-shaped or "bull's eye" appearance.
- Your rash is accompanied by a fever.
- Large areas of skin are affected.
- You feel warm and flushed, or experience dizziness, disorientation, or **difficulty breathing (seek emergency medical care).**
- Progressive swelling happens with the rash.

HOMECARE
If physician referral is not recommended at this time, try the following self-care procedures:

Medication
- Apply calamine lotion or an over-the-counter hydrocortisone cream to soothe prolonged itching. Try a diaper rash ointment if the skin feels sore rather than itchy.
- For hives, try an over-the-counter oral antihistamine for relief from itching and inflammation.

Heat/Cold
- Avoid applying heat to affected area.
- Apply cold compresses to soothe itching and reduce inflammation.

Clean
- Wash affected area with soap and water or alcohol, then quickly pat area dry. Apply cornstarch-based body powder before dressing.

Cover
- Don't cover a rash; wear loose, natural-fiber clothing so that air can circulate freely around affected area.

Activity
- Avoid activities that cause you to sweat profusely or get overheated.
- Don't go swimming when you have a rash.

171

Rashes, Adult

Rash	Symptoms	Cause
Psoriasis	Dry, red patches of skin with a top layer of thick, silvery scales or small, scaly spots; cracked skin, itching, some bleeding or joint pain may accompany rash	Hereditary
Seborrhea	Scaly, itchy, oily patches of skin on the scalp, face, neck, or chest. May be red or yellow and crusty. Profuse, itchy dandruff	May be hereditary
Shingles	Pain or tingling followed by a red skin rash that contains small blisters filled with clear fluid. Blisters cloud and crust over after a few days; crust disappears within two or three weeks of first symptoms, but pain or skin sensitivity can linger	Virus; affects people who have had chicken pox
Athlete's Foot	Itchy, cracked, peeling, red, flaky skin on or between toes; sometimes appears between fingers and on the palms of the hand, or as itchy, blister-like bumps on the sides or soles of feet	Fungus, usually picked up in less-than-clean showering areas
Jock Itch	In males or females: raised red rash on the groin, thigh, buttocks, or genital or anal area, accompanied by severe itching and red blisters that may ooze liquid or pus	Fungus
Lyme Disease Rash	Red, "bull's eye" rash radiating from site of tick bite, accompanied by chills, fever, muscle aches, fatigue, swelling of the joints	Bacterial infection transmitted by bite from deer tick (Ixodes)

When to See Your Doctor

If large areas of your skin are affected

If severe dandruff does not respond to regular use of dandruff shampoo, or if affected areas become infected (swollen and red with pus or radiating red lines present)

If pain from shingles is severe, you experience shingles symptoms accompanied by any eye pain, or you experience chronic pain long after a shingles rash has disappeared

If your foot is swollen, sore, blistered, red, or has pus in sores or blisters; if symptoms do not improve after home treatment; if you have diabetes or poor circulation in your feet and develop symptoms of athlete's foot; or if your legs swell and you have a fever

If symptoms do not improve with home treatment

If you suspect you have Lyme disease

HomeCare

Psoriasis cannot be cured. Exposure to sunlight (without burning) and use of over-the-counter shampoos and other preparations for psoriasis can minimize symptoms. Avoid picking or scratching scales. Reduce stress and anxiety, which may worsen condition.

Shampoo hair often with dandruff shampoo; rinse hair thoroughly. Apply over-the-counter hydrocortisone cream to relieve itching in areas other than the scalp. Ask your doctor about a prescription shampoo or topical medication to treat your condition.

Take an over-the-counter analgesic for pain. Apply an antibiotic ointment to blisters. Ask your doctor about a prescription for acyclovir (also known as Zovirax®). Do not use the over-the-counter shingles remedy Zostrix® until blisters have disappeared. Apply cool, wet compresses to affected areas to relieve pain. Keep blisters clean (use alcohol) and covered until they crust over.

Apply over-the-counter, anti-fungal preparations designed to combat athlete's foot fungus (e.g., Tinactin®, Micatin®, Desenex®, Aftate®, etc.), two or three times a day, until you have no symptoms for at least two weeks. Apply cool, wet compresses to ease pain and inflammation. Keep feet clean and dry. Remove shoes and socks whenever you can.

Apply over-the-counter anti-fungal preparations (e.g., Tinactin®, Desenex®, Aftate®, etc.) two or three times a day, until you have no symptoms for at least two weeks. Keep area as cool as possible. Bathe daily. Avoid wearing too-tight underwear, pantyhose, Spandex shorts or tights. Avoid sharing a towel with anyone else. Avoid wearing underwear, workout clothes, or an athletic supporter that hasn't been laundered since it was last worn.

Call your doctor. Lyme disease when detected early can be treated with antibiotic therapy.

Rashes, Allergy

Rash	Symptoms	Cause
Contact Dermatitis	Red, itchy patches that may blister, drain, then crust over; limited to area on the body where contact with irritating substance occurred	Contact with a substance that causes allergic reaction and inflammation (e.g., poisonous plants, harsh soaps, jewelry, lotions, cosmetics, etc.)
Eczema (Atopic Dermatitis)	Reddish rash, cracked, scaly, or peeling skin that may bleed or ooze, mild to severe itching, a "pulled-tight" feeling to skin	Wide-ranging: may be hereditary, associated with respiratory allergies or asthma, could result from emotional upset or contact with harsh detergents and rough fabrics
Poison Ivy/ Poison Oak	Raised, red patches or streaks on the skin with blistering and minor swelling, moderate to severe itching, watery liquid seeping from blisters	Contact with any part of poison ivy or poison oak plants
Drug Rash	All-over itching, hives, red, raised patches on skin not limited to one area, blisters, swelling	Reaction to over-the-counter or prescription drug. Symptoms usually occur after first dose and get worse with subsequent doses.
Food Allergy Rash	Itching, swelling, hives, blisters	Reaction to consuming food you're allergic to

When to See Your Doctor

If rash becomes infected, has radiating red streaks, is accompanied by fever, or does not improve with home care after two weeks

If severe eczema does not respond to home care, or if itching is not satisfactorily controlled by over-the-counter hydrocortisone creams

If you have a reaction involving your eyes, face, or genitals; if very large areas of skin are affected; if the rash is accompanied by fever or swollen lymph nodes

Seek emergency care if you have difficulty breathing, become dizzy or confused, or experience swelling in the face, throat, or tongue.

Seek emergency care if rash is accompanied by swelling of the face, neck, tongue, or throat; severe abdominal pain or vomiting; fainting, wheezing, or difficulty breathing.

HomeCare

Avoid the irritating substance. Keep rash clean, but avoid soap; use alcohol instead. Take oatmeal baths or apply hydrocortisone cream for itch relief. Use plain calamine lotion to dry up weeping blisters.

Apply cold, wet compresses or over-the-counter hydrocortisone cream to relieve itch. Use plain calamine lotion to stop the oozing. Avoid hot water, especially at bath time. Use moisturizing cream or lotion on non-weeping eczema to keep area from drying and cracking. Avoid harsh soaps.

Apply plain calamine lotion to soothe itch and dry blisters. Apply cold, wet compresses or over-the-counter hydrocortisone cream to relieve moderate itching. Use alcohol or soap and water to clean rash after blisters have broken. Don't cover affected areas (except with loose, breathable clothing). Try an oral antihistamine (e.g., Benadryl®) for itching.

Stop taking over-the-counter medication you suspect caused reaction; call your doctor before discontinuing prescription medication. To relieve itch, apply cool compresses or hydrocortisone cream to affected areas. Try an oral antihistamine that contains diphenhydramine (e.g., Benadryl®) for excessive itching or inflammation.

Avoid food you suspect caused reaction.

Rashes, Childhood

Rash	Symptoms	Cause
Cradle Cap	Thick patches of dry skin on infant's scalp, hairline, eyebrows, eyelids, nose; some patches may appear crusty or yellow	Unknown
Diaper Rash	Irritated, red skin of buttocks and thighs	Irritation from urine, bowel movements, or laundry detergents; in some cases, a fungal or bacterial infection is to blame (rash will have a scalloped border)
Chicken Pox	Red rash that develops blisters that ooze and scab over, accompanied by mild to severe itching and fever	Virus
Ringworm	Red "rings" that progress from a center point on the skin or scalp. On the scalp, ringworm may cause bald spots	Fungus, usually contracted from sharing hats, brushes, and combs, or from handling pets with ringworm
Roseola	Sudden high fever, swollen lymph nodes; red rash appears on trunk and neck as fever decreases	Virus
Rubella (German Measles)	Mild, all-over rash that disappears within three to four days, low-grade fever, swollen lymph nodes, itching	Virus
Rubeola (Regular Measles)	All-over rash, fever, dry cough, red or swollen eyes, sore throat, runny nose, sensitivity to light, white spots on inside of cheek	Virus
Prickly Heat	Tiny, white, "pin head" bumps surrounded by red skin. Intense itching accompanied by tingling or prickly sensation. Common in infants and adults.	Excessive or prolonged perspiration
Scarlet Fever	Sandpaper-like rash on neck, chest, armpits, and groin accompanied by fever, sore throat and vomiting. Sometimes, tongue is swollen.	Bacteria

When to See Your Child's Doctor

If condition does not improve with HomeCare treatment

If rash does not respond to home treatment, becomes bright red, crusty, or blistered, or if you suspect a fungal or bacterial infection

If fever over 102 degrees F lasts for more than two days, skin appears bruised from no apparent cause, sores develop in the eyes, symptoms are accompanied by vomiting, extreme fatigue, and severe headache, or signs of infection (red streaks from site of blister, pus, increasing pain or tenderness) appear

If ringworm spreads despite home treatment, or if the scalp is affected

If high fever causes convulsions

If symptoms worsen daily, fever exceeds 102 degrees F, severe headache is present, extreme fatigue sets in, or convulsions are present

If fever rises to 101 degrees F or higher for more than three days, or if child has sore throat, earache, discolored fingernails, discolored nasal mucus, convulsions, or difficulty breathing

If rash becomes infected or does not improve after one week of home treatment

If you suspect scarlet fever

HomeCare

Shampoo scalp daily; try mild dandruff shampoo or use a soft brush to remove excess scales and crust. Apply baby oil to scalp after shampooing.

Change child's diaper as soon as it is wet or soiled; wash diaper area at every change and dry skin thoroughly. Expose affected areas to air as much as possible. Apply petroleum jelly or diaper ointment (e.g., A&D®, Desitin®) to protect skin that will be exposed to a soiled diaper for prolonged periods (at night, for example).

Use acetaminophen to relieve fever (**never** give aspirin to children with chicken pox). Give tepid oatmeal or baking soda baths or apply cool, wet compresses or calamine lotion to relieve itching.

Use over-the-counter, anti-fungal preparations such as Tinactin® or Desenex®, or try iodine-based soaps or solutions (e.g., Betadine®).

Use acetaminophen and cool, wet compresses (or tepid baths) to reduce fever.

Use acetaminophen to relieve fever (do not use aspirin). Apply cool, wet compresses to relieve itching.

Use acetaminophen (not aspirin) to reduce fever. Try a cough medicine and plenty of liquids to relieve cough.

Keep affected areas cool and dry. Keep your child from activities that cause excessive perspiration. Seek out an air-conditioned environment for your child. Apply plain calamine lotion or corn starch to affected areas.

Use acetaminophen (not aspirin) to reduce fever, offer plenty of liquids, be sure your child gets plenty of rest, and see your child's doctor for prescription antibiotics.

Shingles

A nyone who has had chicken pox is a prime candidate for developing its sister disease, shingles. That's because you never actually "get rid" of chicken pox once you've had it: The blisters may disappear, but remnants of the virus remain in your body for the rest of your life, waiting for an opportunity (when you're stressed or your immune system is suppressed) to reappear as shingles. Therefore, people who have AIDS also are susceptible to shingles.

Unlike chicken pox, the discomfort you experience with shingles may not go away when your blisters disappear. Indeed, almost half the people over age 60 who experience a bout of shingles develop chronic neuralgia, a lingering soft-tissue pain that results from inflamed nerve endings. Because the medications to treat shingles (acyclovir and valacyclovir) work best in the disease's early stages, it's a good idea to see your doctor as soon as you suspect you have shingles.

Symptoms/Signs

- Pain or tingling (usually limited to one side of your body or face), followed by a red skin rash (often running in a "belt" from spine to chest) that contains small blisters filled with clear fluid that cloud and crust over after a few days. Occasionally, early-stage symptoms are preceded by flu-like symptoms—four or five days of fever, fatigue, headache, chills, or an upset stomach.

Consult Your Doctor If:

- Pain from shingles is severe.
- You suspect shingles within 48 hours of the onset of a rash.
- You experience shingles symptoms accompanied by any eye pain or involvement of the nose.
- You experience chronic pain long after a shingles rash has disappeared.

178

HOMECARE
If physician referral is not recommended at this time, try the following self-care procedures:

Medication

- Take an over-the-counter analgesic (aspirin, acetaminophen, ibuprofen, or naproxen) for pain.
- Apply an antibiotic ointment to blisters to keep infection at bay. (Polysporin® is a good choice.)
- In the first 48 hours, ask your doctor about getting a prescription for valacyclovir or acyclovir to speed recovery time.
- Do not use the over-the-counter shingles remedy Zostrix® until blisters have disappeared. Zostrix® is intended for late-stage shingles pain only and can cause great discomfort if applied to blistered skin.

Heat/Cold

- Apply cool, wet compresses to affected areas to relieve pain.
- Avoid heat and direct sunlight.

Cover

- Keep blisters covered until they crust over to avoid spreading the shingles virus to someone else.

Prevention

- If you've never had chicken pox, ask your doctor about receiving a chicken pox immunization.

Spots and Moles

Everybody has skin spots—moles, freckles, birthmarks, age spots, etc. Such discolorations are almost always harmless; some even come and go over the course of a lifetime. Still, it's important to pay close attention to all of your spots or moles, since a sudden or marked change in them can mean trouble.

Because unusual spots and moles sometimes pose a serious threat to your health, home treatment is not recommended when you notice an abnormality. Don't delay seeing your doctor under such circumstances: Many forms of skin cancer spread rapidly to underlying tissue and can be deadly if not diagnosed and treated early. Chances are, however, that your doctor will congratulate you for your quick response and tell you that your condition is either benign or easily treatable.

Symptoms/Signs

- Moles that are larger than a pencil eraser, asymmetrical, irregularly shaped, or contain shades of red, blue, white, or black
- Skin tags (small skin "stalks" or flap-like growths usually on the neck, armpits, upper trunk, and body folds) that become red and inflamed
- Yellow, brown, or black growths on face, chest, shoulders, and back that are slightly raised, waxy, or gritty, and may be more than an inch in diameter

Consult Your Doctor If:

- Your spots or moles exhibit any of the above symptoms.
- Any spot or mole suddenly changes in size, height, shape, or color.
- Any spot or mole bleeds, itches, or becomes painful.
- A skin tag becomes irritated or infected.
- See your doctor if a mole meets any criteria of the ABCD test:
  - **Asymmetry:** one half does not match the other half
  - **Border:** border is not well defined or is blurred
  - **Color:** has any red, white, blue, or black color to it
  - **Diameter:** is larger than six millimeters—the size of a pencil eraser—or grows in size

Prevention

- Avoid getting sunburned: Wear sunscreen daily and avoid direct sunlight between 11 a.m. and 3 p.m. daylight saving time.
- If you are swimming or sweating profusely outdoors, choose waterproof sunscreen and reapply it every hour or so.
- If you're going to be out in the sun, wear loose-fitting clothes that offer the greatest coverage to exposed skin; also, wear a broad-brimmed hat.
- Eat a well-balanced diet rich in vitamins C and E, and beta carotene.
- Check your body every month or so for unusual spots or moles, or changes in either. Use a hand mirror to look closely at your back, the back of your neck and thighs, and the tops of your ears.

skin conditions

Sunburn

It's no secret that the sun's ultraviolet rays damage your skin, causing it to age prematurely and increasing your risk of skin cancer. Still, millions of people every year suffer sunburns that kill off healthy skin cells and injure blood vessels close to the skin's surface. And anyone who experiences one or more blistering sunburns in a lifetime doubles his or her chances of melanoma, the deadliest form of skin cancer that kills nearly 7,000 Americans every year.

The best way to avoid the damaging effects of the sun is to avoid sun exposure whenever possible—which, for most active people, isn't always practical. The good news is that adequate sunscreen and protective clothing can act as an effective shield to keep skin healthy and young looking. Remember, too, that a tan is no protection against the ill effects of the sun: It's simply another form of damage to delicate tissues that you're better off avoiding altogether.

Symptoms/Signs

- Skin is reddened and warm to the touch
- Minor swelling and itching in affected areas
- Blistering in more serious burns

Consult Your Doctor If:

- You have nausea, fever, chills, or lightheadedness.
- Blistering is extensive and severe.
- You develop a rash or notice patches of purple discoloration.
- Your sunburn seems to worsen or spread 24 hours after exposure.

HOMECARE

If physician referral is not recommended at this time, try the following self-care procedures:

Medication
- Take aspirin, acetaminophen, or ibuprofen to reduce swelling and relieve pain.
- Use over-the-counter hydrocortisone cream to relieve inflammation and itch.
- Apply a topical analgesic containing benzocaine, lidocaine, camphor, phenol, or menthol to temporarily soothe mild pain.

Heat/Cold
- Apply cold compresses (use ice-cold water, vinegar, skim milk, or witch hazel) several times a day, or soak in a cool bath with one cup of baking soda added to bath water.

Clean
- Avoid soap or use only a mild soap to wash burned areas; rinse well.

Note Well
- Apply aloe vera gel or moisturizer to burned areas immediately after bathing.
- Never peel areas of skin where blisters have broken or dried.

Prevention
- Apply sunscreen with a sun-protection factor (SPF) of at least 15 whenever you're outdoors. Reapply often if you swim or sweat. Replace your sunscreen every summer.
- Never apply sunscreen to infants under 6 months old: Simply keep them out of the sun altogether.
- Wear protective clothing—a hat, long sleeves, etc.
- Avoid exposure when the sun is most intense (between about 11 a.m. and 3 p.m. daylight saving time).
- A wet cotton T-shirt does not provide adequate protection.

Warts

Warts are caused by a common virus (and certainly not by contact with toads as legend has it) that anyone can contract through an open cut, usually on the hand or foot. Left untreated, almost any wart will go away on its own. The problem: It can take two years for that to happen.

Most people don't want to wait that long, so they try over-the-counter wart preparation or folk remedies. With a little hit-and-miss home treatment, common warts can disappear within a few weeks or a couple of months. More aggressive cures include freezing, burning, or cutting warts off, all of which have to be performed by your doctor. Whatever course you choose, just be absolutely sure that what you're treating is a wart and not some other, more serious skin condition that wart preparations could actually make worse.

Symptoms/Signs

- Raised, flesh-colored growths that feel hard or rough on the surface, have dark dots or specks in the center, and are not covered by a smooth or continuous layer of skin
- Usually small and granular
- May appear in clusters
- Not painful, except in the case of plantar (foot) and genital warts

Consult Your Doctor If:

- You have warts or granular growths in your genital or anal area.
- A wart drains fluid or becomes irritated, painful, or inflamed.
- A wart appears on your face or neck.
- You have any doubt that the growth is a wart (it is dangerous to use home treatment methods on many skin growths that are not warts).
- Any wart fails to respond to home treatment within two weeks.

Medication

- Apply an over-the-counter wart treatment (typically they contain salicylic acid as the active ingredient). Follow directions carefully to avoid irritating or ulcerating healthy skin surrounding wart; do not use if you have diabetes or impaired circulation.
- For plantar (foot) warts, apply Zeasorb® powder as needed to keep feet as dry as possible.

Cover

- For some home treatment preparations, use an adhesive bandage to keep medication from becoming washed or rubbed away.
- For plantar warts, use a pad (made from foam rubber, designed to pad calluses or corns) to relieve pressure and reduce discomfort.

Note Well

- Apply vitamin E oil, vitamin A oil (fish liver oil), castor oil, vitamin C paste (made from crushed vitamin C tablets and water), or Vergo® vitamin cream to wart daily; cover with adhesive bandage.
- If wart bleeds, apply pressure to area until bleeding stops.

Prevention

- Wear shoes or rubber thongs around pool, spa, or locker-room areas.
- Promptly treat any cut or skin abrasion (especially those near your fingernail or toenail cuticles): Wash thoroughly with soap and water or alcohol, then apply anti-bacterial ointment and a bandage until cut is healed.
- Try not to touch warts (yours or other people's) directly.

skin conditions

181

Contact Dermatitis

Contact dermatitis is an allergic skin rash caused by an external chemical agent that comes in contact with the skin. Common sources of dermatitis are poison ivy, poison oak, and poison sumac; insecticides; solvents; caustic industrial chemicals; cosmetics; jewelry; and synthetic fibers. With dermatitis, the rash often takes the outline of the offending agent, such as the elastic bands from undergarments, or is localized on one part of the body. If a localized rash appears, it's important to identify the possible cause:

- Have you been close to poison ivy, poison sumac, or poison oak?
- Have you changed laundry detergents, soaps, deodorants, shampoos, or cosmetics?
- Have you been exposed to insecticides or other chemicals (e.g., dry cleaning solvents)?
- Have you purchased new clothing or jewelry?

Symptoms/Signs

- Localized rash that often takes the shape of the allergic agent or is limited to one part of the body
- Skin reaction (e.g., rash, blisters) due to an allergic reaction to chemicals or plant oils, such as poison ivy, that can spread to other parts of the body. Refer to "Poison Ivy," page 187.

Consult Your Doctor If:

- The rash does not improve after one week.
- The rash becomes bright red, seeps pus, or has red streaks that come away from the infected area.
- You become feverish.
- Itching is severe and does not respond to HomeCare procedures.
- Rash is near your eyes, especially if the eyes are reddened or lids are severely swollen.

Clean

- Immediately after known contact, use soap and water to remove chemicals or other agents. A non-lipid cleaning solution such as Cetaphil® is better than soap. For oily substances, use rubbing alcohol, then use soap and water.
- Follow manufacturer's guidelines for exposure to chemicals or insecticides.

Medication

- Apply cool compresses of Burrow's solution (see your pharmacist) for cases of poison ivy, oak, or sumac. Use as directed.
- Antihistamines to reduce itching. Use as directed.

Cover

- If practical, do not cover. Expose rash to air. Don't scratch it for relief. Scratching can spread the rash and cause infection.

Note Well

- Use cosmetics that are hypoallergenic.

Prevention

- Avoid areas that are infested with poison ivy, sumac, or oak.
- Handle chemicals with care.
- NEVER burn poison ivy, oak, or sumac.

Food Allergy

....

Food allergies can affect all age groups but are most frequent among children. Food allergies in children have been linked to a number of foods such as peanuts (the worst), strawberries, citrus fruit, seafood, wheat, eggs, nuts, beef, and cow's milk. There is some evidence that suggests that breast-feeding helps protect infants from future allergies, and that early exposure to cow's milk may increase the chances of asthma later in life. However, a family history of allergies is perhaps the best predictor of future allergy problems.

As with any allergy, avoiding contact with the allergen is the best self-care procedure. If you suspect you or a family member has a food allergy, it's important to try to identify the food agent that causes the reaction. As with most allergy problems, a process of trial and error may be the best way to identify the culprit.

Symptoms/Signs

- Wheezing
- Swelling of the lips, tongue, or throat
- Skin rash or fainting
- Itching of the palms, soles of the feet, or other parts of the body
- Runny nose
- Gastrointestinal distress such as cramping, vomiting, or diarrhea

Consult Your Doctor If:

- **You have an acute allergic reaction that produces severe breathing problems; wheezing; dizziness; shock; choking or difficulty swallowing; swelling of the lips, tongue, or throat; tightness in the chest; hives; or fainting.**
- You experience a rash, without the symptoms described in the previously bulleted list.

Medication
- Antihistamines may be used for mild to moderate reactions.
- Treat symptoms as indicated in other sections.

Note Well
- Use tissue or handkerchief to gently blow mucus from nose. Do not blow hard: An ear infection or bloody nose could result.

Activity
- Reduce your activity when an allergic reaction happens.

Rest
- You may need to rest after an allergic reaction.

Nutrition
- Soybean milk substitute may be tried if infant shows intolerance to cow's milk.
- Avoid foods that may cause a reaction: Track down possible offenders.

Prevention
- Breast-feeding may build resistance to some allergies in infants.
- If known, avoid foods that may cause allergic reactions.
- Avoid foods more likely to cause allergies when starting infants on solids.

allergies

183

Hay Fever

Millions of Americans go through pollen season and "just grin and sneeze with it." Allergic rhinitis (hay fever) is the most common respiratory allergy: It is a response to outside substances called allergens. Among adults, dust (especially dust mites), animal dander, molds, feathers, and pollen are the most common allergens; among infants, food, animal dander, and dust are the most common.

For most victims, allergy season is a period of moderate discomfort. But for others, pollen or dust can cause significant physical problems and be a year-round challenge.

In cases of severe allergy, professional medical consultation is recommended to determine the actual substances that cause the allergic reaction. Skin or blood tests may be recommended to determine the specific allergen. People who have severe allergies may go through "hyposensitization" techniques that help them become less sensitive to the allergen through a series of injections.

Most people who have mild to moderate hay fever can follow the HomeCare procedures listed. Whenever possible, avoiding the known allergens is the best course of action.

Symptoms/Signs

- Runny nose, sneezing
- Watery, itchy eyes
- Wheezing
- Stuffy head, clogged sinuses, headache
- Ticklish throat, from postnasal drip

Consult Your Doctor If:

- You have difficulty breathing or severe wheezing.
- Nasal discharge is green or yellow.
- Your life has become miserable due to the symptoms.
- The symptoms have become much worse.

184

HOMECARE

If physician referral is not recommended at this time, try the following self-care procedures:

Medication

- Antihistamines to help relieve symptoms. *Use with caution; read labels.*
- Nasal decongestants for stuffy head.
- Cough drops for postnasal drip.

Note Well

- Use tissue or handkerchief to gently blow mucus from nose. Do not blow hard: An ear infection or bloody nose could result.
- Cover nose and mouth with a mask when doing household chores that have worsened symptoms in the past, such as cutting the lawn or dusting.
- If you're allergic to molds, consider using an air conditioner with an electrostatic filter during the summer.

Rest

- You may need more rest when an allergic reaction strikes.

Prevention

- If possible, avoid contact with allergens such as flowers, grasses, specific foods, and dust.
- Keep house pets out of bedrooms. Try to keep your pet clean and groomed.
- Dust allergy can be reduced by wrapping your pillows and mattresses in special covers and washing sheets weekly in hot water.
- Consider using a portable air filter in your bedroom.

Hives

Anytime you have hives, you can bet that your body is trying to send you a warning about something you've eaten or something that's bitten you. When an allergy-causing substance invades your system, your cells release chemicals called histamines, which in turn cause blood vessels to leak fluid into skin layers. The result is itchy, blotchy discomfort that can last for a few hours or a few days.

Hives by themselves generally are harmless and almost always respond to home treatment. **But when hives are accompanied by other, more frightening symptoms—tightness in the throat, wheezing, and shortness of breath—the allergic reaction is an emergency and requires prompt medical attention.** The best treatment for all allergic reactions, of course, is prevention. Staying away from substances you know you're allergic to will keep hives at bay.

Symptoms/Signs

- Raised, red, randomly distributed welts on the skin
- Moderate to intense itching

Consult Your Doctor If:

- **You have hives all over your body, accompanied by difficulty swallowing and shortness of breath or wheezing (seek emergency medical care).**
- **You have hives in your mouth or throat (seek emergency medical care).**
- You have chronic hives (a minimal outbreak that lasts more than six weeks).
- You have a severe case of hives that does not respond to home treatment.

HOMECARE
If physician referral is not recommended at this time, try the following self-care procedures:

Medication

- An over-the-counter antihistamine such as Benadryl® can quickly alleviate itching.
- Apply calamine lotion to soothe itching.
- Hydrocortisone cream (1 percent) may relieve itching on a small area of the skin.
- If you're severely allergic to certain substances, ask your doctor if you should carry an allergy kit that contains injectable epinephrine to head off severe and potentially life-threatening reactions that usually begin with hives and shortness of breath.

Clean

- A lukewarm or tepid bath containing colloidal oatmeal (e.g., Aveeno®) can relieve itching temporarily.

Heat/Cold

- Cold compresses can help relieve itching.

Prevention

- If you are eating when an outbreak of hives occurs, stop. Chances are, it's some substance in the food that's causing the reaction.
- Stay away from the substances that you've had an allergic reaction to in the past. Insect venom, shellfish, nuts, certain berries, eggs, milk, antibiotics, and aspirin are common offenders.

allergies

185

Insect Bites and Stings

People react differently to insect bites or stings. In most cases an insect bite or sting is not serious, with discomfort limited to the area of the injury. However, some people may experience an extreme allergic reaction that requires immediate medical attention. This response can be caused by an individual's sensitivity to certain agents (e.g., bee venom) or by the toxicity of the agent that causes a severe reaction in all victims.

Generally, there are two types of allergic reactions: a localized reaction and a generalized allergic reaction.

Symptoms/Signs: Localized

- Swelling, itching, and redness that is limited to the site of the bite

Symptoms/Signs: Generalized

- **A generalized (systemic) reaction is life-threatening. Symptoms can include hives covering the body, wheezing, tightness in the throat, shortness of breath, swollen eyes, and possible abdominal pain. It is important to seek medical emergency assistance as soon as possible.**

Consult Your Doctor If:

- You suffer a generalized reaction as described above.
- A localized reaction does not improve within 72 hours.
- There are signs of infection after a localized reaction subsides (usually after 24 hours): fever, redness and swelling, and the presence of pus.

Note Well

- If stung by a bee, get the stinger out as fast as possible to minimize the amount of venom it releases. Use tweezers, credit card, knife blade, fingernail, or fingers.
- Carry a kit containing epinephrine if you suffer generalized reactions and you regularly work or play outdoors. Instruct family and co-workers on its use, in case you're incapacitated. Talk to your doctor.

Heat/Cold

- Apply ice or cold packs immediately following bite or sting.

Activity

- Reduce your activity immediately if you begin experiencing a generalized reaction.

Medication

- To relieve itching, an antihistamine can be used as directed. Don't scratch the area to relieve itching. This can cause infection.
- Baking soda paste also can be applied to bite area.

Prevention

- Avoid places where insect bites and stings are more likely to happen.
- Use insect repellents that contain diethyltoluamide (DEET).
- Avoid brightly colored clothes, as they may attract bees.
- Avoid using perfumes and perfumed soaps and shampoos when in grassy and wooded areas. These products attract insects.

allergies

186

Poison Ivy and Poison Oak

Skin rash that develops as a result of contact with poisonous plants can range from mildly irritating to downright painful. Poison ivy and poison oak are the two most common offenders in the United States, probably because about 85 percent of the population is sensitive to the urushiol resin present on the external parts of each plant. Skin that comes in contact with the resin becomes red and develops blisters that itch, usually within 24 to 48 hours after exposure. Neither fluid from broken blisters nor scratching will spread the rash, but scratching can spread bacterial infection, which could lead to scarring. Severe cases or those involving the face, eyes, or genitals may require medical treatment. Most of the time, however, rashes clear up on their own within two or three weeks. The best medicine: Learn to recognize and avoid poison ivy and poison oak altogether (see illustrations below). A general rule of thumb to remember is: "Leaves of three, let them be."

Symptoms/Signs

- Raised, red patches or streaks on the skin
- Blistering and minor swelling in affected areas
- Moderate to severe itching at rash site
- Watery liquid seeping from blisters

Consult Your Doctor If:

- You have a reaction involving your eyes, face, or genitals or that covers a large area.
- The rash is accompanied by fever or swollen lymph nodes, indicating an infection has set in.

Poison Ivy

Poison Oak

H O M E C A R E
If physician referral is not recommended at this time, try the following self-care procedures:

Clean

- If possible, thoroughly wash (within five to 10 minutes) any skin that has come in contact with a poisonous plant. Use generous amounts of soap and water or isopropyl alcohol.
- Soap and water or alcohol can help keep the area free from infection after blisters have broken.
- *Never* clean skin with bleach or gasoline or other household chemicals.

Medication

- Plain calamine lotion (without antihistamines) may soothe the itch and act as a drying agent.

Heat/Cold

- Cold, wet compresses applied as needed will reduce itching and inflammation, especially after blisters have broken.

Cover

- Don't cover affected areas (except with loose, breathable clothing).

Prevention

- Remove poisonous plants from your property. Wear protective clothing, goggles, gloves, and a dust mask.
- Never burn poisonous plants, as the smoke they produce carries urushiol resin dust.
- Avoid handling pets, clothing, or other objects that may have come in contact with poisonous plants.
- Try the OTC barrier lotion Ivy Block® that contains bentoquatam and can protect for up to four hours. Use as directed.

allergies

187

Achilles Injuries

Injuries to the Achilles tendon—which connects the calf muscle to the heel bone—are common among recreational and competitive athletes, especially those active in racket sports and long-distance running. The degree of injury and its accompanying pain ranges from tendinitis or bursitis to complete rupture of the tendon.

The causes of Achilles tendon pain have been associated with over-training and poor training techniques, insufficient blood flow to and within the tendon, mini-tears within the tendon, and over-pronation (rolling inward) of the foot.

Achilles tendon tenderness or pain should be taken seriously since complete rupture of the tendon is possible if one tries to "play through the pain." Pain management of mild to moderate tendinitis and bursitis usually includes curtailment of athletic activity, the use of nonsteroidal anti-inflammatory drugs such as naproxen, strengthening and stretching exercises, and the use of heel lifts. Treatment for severe Achilles tendinitis involves reducing the inflammation first through the use of medication and ice baths, and taking weight off the foot.

Symptoms/Signs

- Pain in the Achilles tendon (about two to three inches above heel), especially when running or jumping

Consult Your Doctor If:

- Self-care for mild to moderate tendinitis or bursitis fails to relieve discomfort and improve mobility.
- You experience a sudden, sharp pain in the Achilles tendon. A loud snapping or popping sound may be heard.
- Pain within the Achilles tendon prevents you from putting some or all of your weight on the injured foot.

188

Heat/Cold

- Apply ice packs for 20 minutes several times a day during the first two days, or for as long as the area is warm to the touch.
- Try applying heat packs to the injured area after inflammation has subsided.

Medication

- Take aspirin, naproxen, or ibuprofen for pain and inflammation. Use as directed.

Activity

- Decrease athletic activity by 50 percent.
- Once inflammation has subsided, perform strengthening (such as stationary biking, rowing, or stair-climbing) and stretching (careful, no force) exercises.

Note Well

- Add a 3/8-inch heel lift to shoes during the recovery period.

Prevention

- Do ongoing conditioning exercises that include strengthening and stretching of all leg muscles.
- Warm up and cool down properly when exercising.
- Wear proper footwear that avoids over-pronation of the foot. Consult a podiatrist if you have ongoing foot problems.
- Avoid over-training and learn proper technique for your sport.

Ankle Injuries

The ankle is a hinge joint that connects the lower leg bones with the foot through many tough fiber cords called ligaments. Because of these ligament "bridges," the ankle is quite strong and able to handle a lot of force and movement.

If you twist your ankle, it often can result in an injury to these ligaments. An ankle **strain** occurs when the ligaments are stretched beyond their normal limit. An ankle **sprain** occurs when the ligaments are partially or completely torn.

You can twist your ankle by stopping suddenly or just putting your foot down the wrong way (e.g., turning it in). People in occupations such as construction, ground maintenance, and surveying are prone to twisted ankles, as are "weekend warriors" who engage in softball, basketball, and racquet sports.

If you've had a severe ankle injury, your first concern is to determine if a fracture has occurred. Indications of a possible fracture include: swelling, discoloration (black and blue), and a joint that is deformed or bent in an odd way. If a fracture is suspected, keep the ankle immobilized, apply ice to the injured area and seek medical attention immediately.

Most ankle injuries are not fractures or severe sprains, and can be treated using the self-care procedures listed under HomeCare.

Symptoms/Signs

- Swelling and pain in the ankle
- General stiffness in the joint
- The above with discoloration and/or a deformity in the joint. Suspect a fracture.

Consult Your Doctor If:

- You suspect a fracture. See above.
- Pain prevents you from placing weight on the ankle 24 hours after the injury occurred.
- You are unable to bear weight on the ankle or pain continues after 72 hours.

H O M E C A R E
If physician referral is not recommended at this time, try the following self-care procedures:

Heat/Cold

- Apply ice pack to ankle to minimize swelling: Ice area for 20 minutes, rest for 20 minutes. Continue for two to three hours or until swelling is reduced.

Cover

- Wrap ankle firmly in elastic bandage if injury has significant swelling. Do not wrap too tightly. It should provide comfort, not increase the pain. Keep on for 24 to 48 hours.

Rest

- Rest ankle for 12 to 24 hours; avoid putting weight on it.
- Keep ankle elevated if swelling occurs.
- Expect limited range of motion for two weeks or longer.

Medication

- Aspirin, naproxen, or ibuprofen can be used to reduce pain and inflammation. Use as directed.

Activity

- Once pain and swelling have subsided, slowly rotate, flex, and extend ankle three times a day to prevent adhesions.

Prevention

- Wear appropriate foot gear with adequate ankle support.
- Beware of rough terrain that could cause a twisted ankle.

musculoskeletal

189

Arthritis

Arthritis is a painful condition of the joints. Common symptoms include inflammation, heat and redness in the affected area, and stiffness and difficulty in moving the joint(s) through the full range of motion. There are more than 100 kinds of arthritis. However, most arthritis cases fall within four general categories:

- **Osteoarthritis.** A degeneration of the smooth cartilage that forms the surface of a joint, e.g., knee or shoulder. Osteoarthritis is the most common form of arthritis. It can result from an injury to the joint, or from repeated force that places an unnatural load on the joint. *There is no evidence that moderate exercise such as walking, jogging, or cycling increases the risk of arthritis if the activity is practiced with proper technique and equipment.*
- **Rheumatoid arthritis.** Inflammation and deterioration of the joint membrane (usually in the fingers and toes). Rheumatoid arthritis is called an autoimmune condition because the body's immune system destroys its own tissue. Other body organs such as the heart, kidneys, lungs, skin, and eyes can be damaged.
- **Gout.** Acute, severe pain and swelling in one joint (e.g., big toe) that is caused by a buildup of uric acid crystals in the fluid that bathes the joint.
- **Ankylosing spondylitis.** A degeneration of the joints that support and are part of the spinal column.

Symptoms/Signs

- Inflammation, heat and redness in the affected area, and stiffness and difficulty in moving the joint(s) through the full range of motion

Consult Your Doctor If:

- You experience an inflamed joint(s) with fever.
- You experience joint pain with flu-like symptoms (especially if you suspect a tick bite; see page 172).
- Pain prevents you from moving the joint through its range of motion without extreme discomfort.
- You have a new, sudden onset of pain and swelling in a joint.

HOMECARE
If physician referral is not recommended at this time, try the following self-care procedures:

Rest
- Rest affected area when you experience flare-ups of inflammation.

Heat/Cold
- Apply heating pads or hot towels to affected area for 20 minutes.

Medication
- Aspirin, naproxen, or ibuprofen can help arthritis pain. They also help with the swelling of rheumatoid arthritis. Acetaminophen can help arthritis pain, but not swelling.

Activity
- Gently move stiff joints through their range of motion, three times a day, 10 to 20 times per set.
- Water exercises are excellent for many arthritic conditions. Consult your doctor if you're inactive.

NB
Note Well
- Try to keep body weight within recommended range. Excess body weight can place added stress on already weak joints.
- If affected person has difficulty with everyday activities (e.g., opening jars, holding utensils), consider buying user-friendly home aids.

Prevention
- Try to avoid heavy, repetitive strain on joints.
- Use the proper equipment and techniques in work and play. Practice proper work posture.
- Avoid tick-infested areas that may expose you to Lyme disease.

Back Pain

Back pain is very common. It's estimated that 70 to 80 percent of all adults have had at least one episode of back pain. The good news is that the majority of all back pain episodes will go away within a few days, regardless of the treatment. However, back pain is still a major problem. For some people, pain management is an ongoing concern.

Most lower back pain is due to the spasm of the muscles that support the spinal column. Very few back problems are due to a "slipped disc," where the disc bulges out and irritates the nerve roots.

Back problems can be traced to trauma, poor posture, poor lifting techniques, repetitive twisting movements, sitting for extended periods, vibration from vehicles and machinery, poor physical conditioning, and stress. Refer to pages 251-255 for more information on back pain and back care.

Symptoms/Signs

- Pain and stiffness in the back
- Pain is related to other symptoms such as pain and numbness in leg or foot, frequent urination, menstrual pain, etc.

Consult Your Doctor If:

- **Injury is due to a fall or being hit in the back and prevents the victim from moving legs. Keep person still and call for emergency care.**
- Pain or numbness moves into the leg or foot.
- Pain is severe even though you can still move.
- Low back pain happens with other physical symptoms such as painful or frequent urination, menstrual pain, flu, gastrointestinal distress, or abdominal pain.
- Low back pain is associated with loss of control of bladder or bowels.
- HomeCare procedures fail to provide relief after 72 hours.
- Low back pain is associated with weakness of any muscles in the leg or foot.

Rest

- Reduce your activity.
- For severe back pain, rest on a firm mattress or the floor with your back flat for the first 24 to 48 hours. Placing a pillow under the knees or lying on the ground with your feet on a chair in a sitting position will reduce symptoms.
- Sleep on your side with your hips flexed 90 degrees and a pillow between your knees to prevent twisting of the spine.
- Please note that recent studies have shown that prolonged bed rest aggravates back problems. Generally the sooner you can get up and about, the sooner you recover.
- Do flexibility exercises while resting.

Heat/Cold

- If you experience an acute injury, apply ice packs for 20 minutes every hour, for first 24 to 48 hours.
- Heating pads are not recommended for the first 48 hours for acute injuries. Heat can be used for mild pain and discomfort.

Medication

- Aspirin, ibuprofen, or naproxen may help reduce pain and inflammation.

Prevention

- Practice proper lifting techniques. See pages 253-254.
- Keep back, leg, and abdominal muscles conditioned. See page 255.
- Use proper work posture.
- Do flexibility exercises. See pages 10-12.
- Maintain proper aerobic conditioning and avoid weight gain.
- Avoid sleeping on your stomach.

musculoskeletal

191

Broken Bones

HOMECARE
If physician referral is not
recommended at this time,
try the following
self-care procedures:

Broken bones are classified in two categories: (1) simple fractures, where the broken bone does not penetrate the skin, and (2) compound fractures, where the bone is forced through the skin, with external injury and bleeding present.

You should consult your doctor if you suspect a bone fracture. However, every suspected fracture does not require immediate medical attention. Medical attention for simple fractures, such as those to the fingers, can be delayed for 24 hours if the affected area is immobilized with a splint. For example, you can tape the injured finger to the healthy finger next to it. Swelling can be treated with ice packs; pain can be reduced with aspirin or ibuprofen.

Immediate medical care should be taken for shock, which is a serious and life-threatening reaction to injury. Signs of shock include skin that is cold, pale, and clammy; rapid, weak pulse rate; increased thirst and dizziness; or fainting. Follow these first-aid procedures:

Lay the victim flat, elevate feet 4 inches from ground (unless injury is to head or chest). If bleeding is present, slow or stop bleeding through direct pressure to wound. Call 911 or seek medical assistance.

Rest

- If fracture is questionable and no serious medical conditions are present, rest and immobilize area for 24 to 48 hours. See doctor if condition doesn't improve.

Heat/Cold

- Ice packs can be used in the first 24 to 48 hours if you're not sure whether there is a fracture.

Medication

- Aspirin, naproxen, or ibuprofen to reduce pain and inflammation.

Symptoms/Signs

- Limb or joint area may be deformed, sensitive to the touch or painful to move, have acute swelling, be discolored or cold, or have no feeling
- With a compound fracture, the bone pierces the skin with related bleeding

Consult Your Doctor If:

- **There are signs of shock. See above.**
- **A compound fracture is evident: The bone is sticking through the skin.**
- The injury is deformed, sensitive to the touch, painful to move, shows acute swelling, is discolored or cold, or has no feeling.
- The injury is to the neck or back and the victim is unable to move.

Bursitis

You don't have to be an athlete or have a physically demanding job to suffer from bursitis, a condition characterized by a chronic, dull ache that gets worse when you move. It can affect any one of the body's 150 bursae—tiny sacs of fluid that protect muscles and tendons from irritation resulting from contact with adjacent bones. When you exercise too strenuously or too often, or when your work requires repetitive physical exertion, the friction from your movements can cause these sacs to become inflamed. The resulting pain usually goes away within a week or so with proper treatment, but recurrent flare-ups are common and frustrating.

Symptoms/Signs

- Localized dull ache or stiffness, especially in joint areas
- Pain is worse with movement
- Affected area feels swollen or is warm or hot to the touch

Consult Your Doctor If:

- Bursitis pain is disabling or doesn't subside after 10 days of home treatment.
- You notice excessive swelling, bruising, or a rash in the affected area.
- Pain is sharp or shooting, especially when you exercise or exert yourself.

HOMECARE
If physician referral is not recommended at this time, try the following self-care procedures:

Medication

- Take aspirin, naproxen, or ibuprofen for pain and inflammation. Use as directed.

Heat/Cold

- Apply ice packs for 20 minutes several times a day during the first two days, or for as long as joint area is warm to the touch.
- After joint is no longer warm, apply heat to stimulate blood flow.

Activity

- Stop any activity that you suspect has caused the pain or that makes the pain worse.
- Use various stretching exercises to speed recovery and to restore full range of motion.

NB
Note Well

If the joint is swollen:
- Wrap the injured area during waking hours with an elastic bandage.
- Elevate the injured joint above your heart to help reduce swelling.
- Do not massage the affected area.

P
Prevention

- Warm-up and stretch before physical activity.
- If your work is physically strenuous, pace yourself and take breaks often.
- Avoid resting your elbow on hard surfaces (e.g., your desk).
- Use knee pads or a cushion when you kneel.
- Avoid shoes that don't fit or that have worn-down heels.
- Don't sit for long periods of time. Get up and move about.

Elbow Pain

Elbow pain can be traced to a number of causes: (1) bursitis, an inflammation of the fluid-filled bursa sac at the tip of the elbow; (2) "tennis elbow," an irritation of the tendon that slides over the elbow joint; (3) pain from a fall in which the arm is hyperextended (e.g., sticking the arm out to break a fall); or (4) direct trauma, such as chipping a bone or tearing the soft tissues around the joint.

In most cases, elbow pain results from repetitive movements that place strain on tendons, the bursa, and soft tissues that support the elbow. Tennis elbow usually is caused by repeated twisting or rolling of the forearm, wrist, and hands. Tennis elbow is common in sports such as tennis or baseball (pitching), and in jobs that require twisting movements such as assembly and carpentry (e.g., using a screwdriver) or meat packing (e.g., cutting).

Symptoms/Signs

- **Disfigurement and severe pain of the elbow joint due to a fall or collision. Requires immediate medical attention.**
- Severe pain at rest or during movement
- Swelling and redness in the joint. May be accompanied by fever
- Abrasion of elbow with bleeding and torn skin. See page 152, "Abrasions."

Consult Your Doctor If:

- **You suspect a fracture or dislocation of elbow due to fall or direct injury.**
- You cannot move your elbow (elbow seems locked).
- There are signs of infection: fever, redness, heat, and swelling in the elbow.
- There is numbness or weakness in the hand.
- Pain is not reduced after two weeks of HomeCare.

194

Medication
- Aspirin, naproxen, or ibuprofen may help reduce inflammation and discomfort. Use as directed.

Heat/Cold
- For first 48 hours, apply ice packs to elbow for 20 minutes at several times during the day.
- Heating pads are not recommended if swelling is present.

Rest
- Rest the elbow for one to two days; a sling may help.
- Avoid repetitive movements and stress on elbow joint.

Activity
- After 48 hours, move elbow through full range of movement every hour.
- Strengthen and stretch forearm and shoulder muscles once pain has subsided and before activity.

Prevention
- Use equipment that fits properly (e.g., a screwdriver handle that fits the hand or a tennis racquet with a grip and weight appropriate for you).
- Keep your forearm muscles strong.
- Take regular stretch breaks, especially if you do repetitive tasks.
- Maintain a proper posture. Also, use proper technique when performing tasks that require repetitive movements.

Finger Pain

Almost all finger pain is related to arthritis—usually osteoarthritis, also called degenerative joint disease. Nearly everyone develops some symptoms of osteoarthritis by the time they're 60 years old: It's just a by-product of aging. Rheumatoid arthritis, on the other hand, is not a result of wear and tear on the joints. Indeed, most cases occur between the ages of 20 and 50. Although the direct cause is not known, researchers suspect that a virus triggers a response by the immune system that causes inflammation in the joints. Pain in the fingers usually is a first sign of both types of arthritis.

Occasionally, sore fingers are not associated with arthritis. Mothers sometimes have sore fingers after their child is born; the pain can last up to a year, but usually diminishes over time. Gout, although most often associated with pain in the big toe, can affect any joint with sudden, intense pain, swelling, and redness.

Carpal tunnel syndrome, a nerve problem in the wrist, is a cause of numbness and tingling in the fingers and can seriously limit use. Whatever the cause, finger pain can be frustrating, since it can interfere greatly with day-to-day activities.

Symptoms/Signs

- Pain and swelling of finger joints
- Overall achiness or stiffness of finger joints
- Pain or numbness in fingers after use or exertion

Consult Your Doctor If:

- Home treatment does nothing to relieve discomfort after six weeks.
- You experience sudden or unexplained swelling and pain in finger joints.
- You have finger pain accompanied by fever.
- You cannot use your finger(s) as a result of pain or swelling.
- There's numbness in the fingers, except the little and ring fingers; and tingling in the fingers when the wrist is tapped. This indicates carpal tunnel syndrome. See page 205.

HOMECARE
If physician referral is not recommended at this time, try the following self-care procedures:

Medication

- Use an over-the-counter analgesic (aspirin, acetaminophen, ibuprofen, naproxen) to relieve pain.
- Finger pain without inflammation is better treated with acetaminophen.
- Over-the-counter lotions and creams containing capsaicin, camphor, or menthol may relieve minor joint pain of osteoarthritis.
- For severe and chronic pain, your doctor may prescribe corticosteroid injections or other drug therapies.

Heat/Cold

- Apply ice for 20 minutes several times a day if swelling is present.
- Apply warm compresses as needed to relieve stiffness.
- Keep hands warm and covered in cold weather.

Note Well

- Avoid overusing your hands and fingers whenever possible.

Rest

- Rest your hand as much as possible for the first 24-48 hours.
- Get plenty of rest. If you have rheumatoid arthritis, you may need about 10 hours of sleep in a 24-hour period.

Prevention

- Avoid repetitive activities that overuse the joints in the fingers.
- Use assistive devices such as faucet turners, openers for jars, and extended handles for grooming aids if you have trouble grasping objects.

musculoskeletal

Foot Pain

Of the many reasons for foot pain in the general population, the causes of foot pain in the elderly are the most serious. Gout, peripheral nerve degeneration caused by diabetes or rheumatoid arthritis, and vascular disease can all place a great deal of stress on the joints, muscles, and circulation within the feet. Unfortunately, in the advanced stages of some diseases, it is difficult to feel "warning" pain in the feet due to extensive nerve damage and accompanying numbness. As a result, people with such diseases are at significantly increased risk for open sores on their feet and circulatory problems that, if left untreated, can lead to tissue death, gangrene, and amputation.

If you have foot pain from arthritis or any disease (such as diabetes or cardiovascular disease) that could quickly compromise the health of your feet, take special care to avoid cuts, blisters, sprains, or fractures. Inspect your feet often for redness, swelling, discolorations, or sores. And do whatever you can to improve your health so that your feet aren't as vulnerable to damage from infection or poor circulation.

Symptoms/Signs

- Pain, inflammation, swelling, or redness in one or more toe joints
- Generalized muscle pain or sensitivity in the feet
- Generalized foot pain that is preceded by tingling or numbness

Consult Your Doctor If:

- You have severe pain, swelling, stiffness, and redness in any toe joint.
- Foot pain from arthritis makes it difficult for you to perform daily tasks.
- You repeatedly experience pain in the arch of your foot, either while walking or at rest.
- Moderate to severe foot pain is preceded by tingling and numbness in the foot, and is accompanied by loss of bladder or bowel control, weakness, or partial paralysis.

HOMECARE

If physician referral is not recommended at this time, try the following self-care procedures:

Medication
- Non-steroidal anti-inflammatory drugs (e.g., ibuprofen, naproxen) are choices for treating the symptoms of gout and osteoarthritis, or relieving foot pain in general.
- Foot pain associated with peripheral vascular disease or rheumatoid arthritis may require prescription medication.

Heat/Cold
- Hot or cold compresses may relieve pain associated with rheumatoid arthritis.

Clean
- Keep feet scrupulously clean. Clean and treat any open sore or wound on the foot immediately, especially if you're diabetic.

Note Well
- Wear socks or support stockings and well-fitting, supportive shoes.
- Rest inflamed joints, especially during severe episodes.

Prevention
- Don't smoke.
- Keep in shape, exercise regularly, eat a well-balanced diet, and practice stress reduction.
- Climb stairs with your stronger leg (foot) first and with your weaker leg when descending.

Foot Pain (Fasciitis)

A common foot injury among active individuals, such as runners and dancers, is plantar fasciitis. The plantar fascia is a thick, fibrous band of tissue that runs along the bottom of the foot from the base of the toes to the heel. The fascia can become inflamed when excess stress is placed on this area and causes the tissue to tear. Over time, scar tissue forms over the tears and makes the fascia stiff and less flexible to movements of the foot. Another complication of plantar fasciitis is the risk of bone spurs, which can form when the fascia begins to tear from the heel bone.

The causes of plantar fasciitis can be traced to a number of factors such as high arches or flat feet that over-pronate (the foot rolls inward too much when the foot is planted), rigid soles that cause the fascia to stretch, or worn-out footwear that doesn't provide enough support from over-pronation.

HomeCare can treat most cases of plantar fasciitis. If you have heel pain related to fasciitis or a bruised heel, commercial heel pads can be just as effective as specially fitted orthotics. However, persistent pain may require medical consultation. If you are an athlete, you may consider consulting with a podiatrist who usually is very familiar with this kind of overuse injury. Treatment may include ultrasound, friction massage, and, perhaps, special shoe inserts (orthotics) that place the foot in a "neutral" position, thus preventing over-pronation. In severe cases the last resort is surgery.

Symptoms/Signs

• Pain on the bottom of the foot in the mid-heel area

Consult Your Doctor If:

• HomeCare measures do not improve your condition after four weeks.

Heat/Cold

• Apply ice packs for 20 minutes several times a day during the first two days, or for as long as the area is warm to the touch.
• Try warm whirlpool baths after pain and inflammation have subsided.

Medication

• Take aspirin, naproxen, or ibuprofen for pain and inflammation. Use as directed.

Activity

• Decrease athletic activity by 50 percent.
• Once inflammation has subsided: Sit on the edge of a chair with a towel laid out on the floor in front of you. In your bare feet, crimp your toes and grab the towel with them. Repeat this five to 10 times for a session. Do two sessions per day.
• Stretch the front of your shin and calf muscles. Refer to page 12.

Note Well

• Take pressure off of the spur: Cut a circle to fit your heel out of foam that has adhesive backing on one side. Then, cut a hole out of the middle.
• Commercial heel pads can be as effective as specially-fitted orthotics in relieving heel pain.

Prevention

• Wear footwear that prevents over-pronation and provides adequate support.
• Avoid running on crowned roads.
• Strengthen the front of your shin and your calf muscles.
• Warm up and cool down properly when exercising.
• Avoid exercising on hard surfaces.

musculoskeletal

197

Knee Pain

The primary function of the knee is to support weight and movement in a forward direction. Actions that twist or put excessive force on the inside or outside of the knee joint can easily stretch or tear the ligaments and wear away or tear cartilage that support and protect the knee. In many cases, surgery is done as a last resort.

Knee pain can be caused by a repeated force placed on the knee, such as during prolonged kneeling ("housemaid's knee"). Over time, the bursae (protective fluid sacs) of the knee can become inflamed and cause pain. Knee pads are recommended for jobs that require kneeling.

Another cause of knee pain is so-called "runner's knee," which is a gradual wearing of the cartilage behind the kneecap. Runner's knee usually is traced to weak thigh muscles, running on crowned roads (roads that slope from middle to edge), and an excessive inside rolling of the foot (pronation) when it makes contact with the ground. Strength training, changing to a flat running surface, and anti-pronation running shoes or special inserts (orthotics) help prevent the problem.

Osteoarthritis is another cause of knee pain that usually is a long-term artifact left by a previous injury. Exercise usually is the preferred treatment to better stabilize the knee joint and reduce deterioration. When other conservative treatments fail, surgery or complete knee replacement is sometimes recommended.

198

Consult Your Doctor If:

- You have an injury that prevents you from walking or putting full weight on the injured leg, or your knee cannot be straightened or wobbles from side to side.
- Your knee has rapid, extensive swelling, with or without injury.
- Knee pain is accompanied by fever.
- You have dull pain or discomfort related to jogging, cycling, or prolonged kneeling, that's behind or around the kneecap and doesn't go away after four weeks of HomeCare.
- You have pain or swelling in your calf muscle, below the back of your knee.

HOMECARE
If physician referral is not recommended at this time, try the following self-care procedures:

Rest
- Avoid taking part in activities that may place stress on the knee.
- To prevent your knee from "locking," don't sleep with pillow under knee.
- A cane or crutches may help to take weight off the injured knee.

Medication
- Aspirin, naproxen, or ibuprofen may help to reduce pain and inflammation. Use as directed.

Heat/Cold
- Apply an ice pack for the first 24-48 hours after injury: 20 minutes on, 20 minutes off.
- Hot bath or whirlpool may help thereafter.

Activity
- Avoid keeping knee in a fixed position for extended periods of time. Every hour, gently straighten and flex the injured leg.
- Once healed, strengthen the front and back thigh muscles. Refer to page 15. Consider consulting a sports trainer. Walking or doing pool exercises are excellent options.

Prevention
- Wear knee pads if your job requires prolonged kneeling.
- If you jog or run, wear the proper shoes; avoid uneven surfaces.

Leg Pain

M ost leg pain or cramps usually are temporary and can be attributed to injuries resulting from sudden trauma, overuse, improper footwear, or poor technique during sports activities. In most cases, occasional leg pain or cramps can be treated through self-care. However, leg pain can flare up suddenly (as anyone who has suffered through nighttime leg cramps can tell you) for no apparent reason. Phlebitis, an inflammation of a vein in the leg is a life-threatening condition since blood clots can form and break away and become lodged in the lungs.

Symptoms/Signs

- With phlebitis the leg is painful, swollen, hot, and feels heavy. **Shortness of breath or chest pain with or without these symptoms requires immediate medical care.**
- With leg cramps: calf muscle becomes tightly and painfully contracted (balled up), often during sleep
- With shin splints: shooting or stabbing pain along the shins with each step. Refer to page 202.
- With mild strains: extreme muscle tenderness. Refer to page 200.
- With sprains: shooting pain, severe swelling, and bruising of the injured joint
- With tendinitis: tenderness, warmth, swelling and/or pain in knees or ankles; pain diminishes as you continue, and is sharp once you've stopped. Refer to page 204.

Consult Your Doctor If:

- **You experience shortness of breath or chest pain with or without the symptoms of phlebitis. Seek emergency medical care.**
- Any injury to your leg is accompanied by tingling, prolonged numbness, radiating pain, swelling or bruising that worsens after home treatment, or an inability to put weight on the injury after 24 hours.
- You experience lingering leg muscle or joint pain that has no apparent cause.
- You experience swelling or numbness in any part of the leg and have not sustained an injury.

HOMECARE
If physician referral is not recommended at this time, try the following self-care procedures:

Rest
- Unless an injury is severe, rest no more than 48 hours, since mild to moderate exercise will increase blood flow and encourage healing.

Heat/Cold
- Apply ice to affected areas after exercise.
- Apply ice immediately to any injured area.
- Before exercising, apply warm compresses or minimal heat to affected areas.

Cover
- Use a flexible brace or wrap only during and shortly after periods of activity.
- With an injury, compress affected area between icings to reduce swelling.

Medication
- Take over-the-counter anti-inflammatory medications such as aspirin, naproxen, or ibuprofen.

Prevention
- Warm up before and cool down after exercise. Stretch leg muscles; refer to page 12.
- Drink plenty of fluids.
- Vary your activities to avoid overuse.
- Get into shape gradually. Moderate, daily exercise is safer than the strain of occasional strenuous activity.
- Use proper equipment and technique for every sport or activity.
- Choose your exercise surface carefully: jog on a running track instead of asphalt; opt for wood floors instead of concrete for basketball or aerobics workouts.

Muscle Strains

Your weekend softball game ends suddenly when, rounding first base, you feel acute pain in the back of your thigh. Or you're playing catch with the kids when you suddenly feel a pull in your shoulder. These injuries are examples of muscle strains, often called muscle pulls.

Strains are tears or stretches in the muscle fibers or the tendons that connect muscles to bones. Strains can range from relatively mild injuries, with some muscle fibers being torn, to large muscle tears with swelling and bleeding present. Causes of muscle strain include:

- **muscular imbalance,** where one side of the joint is stronger than the other, or the opposite muscle doesn't relax while the other contracts. This can be traced in most cases to either a lack of conditioning or overtraining one muscle group vs. an opposing muscle group, e.g., front of the thigh (quadriceps) vs. the back of the thighs (hamstrings).

- **muscle fatigue,** which places additional stress on the muscle and connective tissue.

The more active you are, the greater your risk of injury. Poorly conditioned people also are at risk when they suddenly engage in strenuous activity without proper pre-conditioning.

It's therefore important for the "weekend warrior" and the serious marathoner alike to take the time to adequately prepare for your activity. Listen to your body. If something hurts, your body is telling you something is not right. Ease up or stop.

Remember: Properly warm up and cool down, and ease into your activity. Take the time to get in shape before you plunge into your activity.

Symptoms/Signs

- Pain, swelling, and tenderness in a muscle group or joint

Consult Your Doctor If:

- There's excessive swelling, bruising, and/or tenderness in the injured area.
- Pain prevents you from moving.

HOMECARE

If physician referral is not recommended at this time, try the following self-care procedures:

Rest

- Reduce your activity. Avoid movements that place stress on injured area.

Heat/Cold

- Apply cold pack or ice massage: 20 minutes on, 20 minutes off for two hours. Continue for 24 to 48 hours after injury.
- Heating pads, whirlpools, or analgesic balms may be tried on third day if swelling is gone.

Cover

- Apply elastic bandage to injured area.

Note Well

- Elevate injured area for 24 to 48 hours depending on severity of injury.

Medication

- Aspirin, naproxen, or ibuprofen may help to reduce pain and inflammation. Use as directed.

Activity

- Try slow, gentle stretches with a mild strain. Avoid stretching for a few days if injury is moderate or severe; do general movements (e.g., slow walking, gentle arm circles) that promote circulation.
- Properly condition for your activity.
- Use weight training to achieve adequate levels of strength in major muscle groups.

Neck Pain

The most common reason for neck pain is poor posture at work or at home. At work, sitting for prolonged periods of time in a fixed position can lead to occasional stiffness or cramping. This is especially common among people who do word processing or data entry. At home, a poor sleeping position is a major culprit. Sleeping on a firmer mattress or changing to a thinner pillow will usually correct the problem.

Many people respond to emotional stress by tensing the neck muscles. Over time this can lead to both neck pain and headaches.

Neck pain also can be caused by blows to the head and neck, as in the case of falls and motor vehicle accidents. Sudden twisting or snapping of the head can lead to muscle strain and ligament damage. A pinched nerve also can be a consequence of neck injury or arthritis.

In most cases of occasional neck pain, self-care, modifying your work posture, and taking periodic rest breaks usually will correct the problem and prevent reoccurrences.

Symptoms/Signs

- **A serious, life-threatening situation that demands immediate medical attention is the suspicion of meningitis. Symptoms of meningitis include fever, headache, and a stiff neck that prevents a person from touching the chin to the chest.**
- Stiffness and/or pain in the neck
- Pain that radiates down the arm or tingling in the hands

Consult Your Doctor If:

- **Neck pain is related to an acute injury or blow to the head.**
- **You have a fever, headache, and a stiff neck that prevents you from touching your chin to your chest.**
- Pain radiates down one arm or you experience tingling in your hands.
- Pain does not lessen after seven days.

HOMECARE
If physician referral is not recommended at this time, try the following self-care procedures:

Medication
- Aspirin, naproxen, or ibuprofen to relieve pain and inflammation. Use as directed. Avoid giving aspirin to children or teenagers if neck pain is related to flu or chicken pox because of the risk of Reye's syndrome.

Heat/Cold
- Try hot showers, hot compresses, or a heating pad. Besides relaxing tense muscles, stretching is easier after muscles are warmed.

Note Well
- Take a bath towel, fold lengthwise to form a four-inch band. Wrap around neck before bedtime.

Activity
- Stay physically active.
- Stretch: Gently drop your head to your chest and from one side to the other. Do not tip head back.

Prevention
- Sleep on a firm mattress.
- If you have pain in the morning, use a thinner pillow or none at all.
- Practice proper posture when doing repeated work tasks such as word processing and lifting. Take rest breaks every hour.
- Do exercises that stretch the muscles of the neck and shoulders. See pages 10-11.
- Learn a general relaxation technique. See pages 33-34.
- Massage your neck muscles.

Shin Pain

One of the most common exercise injuries, shin splints are the result of pounding on too hard a surface for too long, especially when your legs aren't properly conditioned. Dancers, basketball players, runners—even race walkers—who change their routine or get back into the exercise game after a long break are most susceptible.

When you perform a weight-bearing exercise, your leg muscles swell slightly and press against the bones in your lower leg. Too much exercise causes these muscles (as well as the surrounding ligaments, tendons, and bones) to become irritated and inflamed. When that happens, you have shin splints; when you really overdo it, you risk going beyond shin splints to a stress fracture. Fortunately, shin splints aren't serious and almost never require medical attention. The best course of action is to take it easy for two or three weeks to allow your muscles to heal and to try the HomeCare recommendations to the right.

Symptoms/Signs

- Dull ache (at rest) or shooting pain (when bearing weight) on the shin, the long bone that runs along the front of the leg from knee to ankle

Consult Your Doctor If:

- Home treatment does not relieve shin splints within three weeks.
- You have a small area (about the size of a nickel) of stabbing pain on a bony area of your lower leg.

HOMECARE
If physician referral is not recommended at this time, try the following self-care procedures:

Rest

- Rest your legs by avoiding moderate- or high-impact activity for two to three weeks after onset of pain.
- After pain of shin splints has subsided, resume regular exercise and activity slowly and at a reduced intensity. Never exercise "through the pain." Choose non-impact activities such as bicycling or swimming until pain is completely gone.

Heat/Cold

- Apply ice to affected areas for first 24 to 48 hours to reduce swelling and inflammation.
- Apply warm compresses or minimal heat to affected areas to reduce discomfort and speed healing.

Medication

- Aspirin, naproxen, or ibuprofen may help to reduce pain and inflammation. Use as directed.

Cover

- For comfort and support, use a flexible brace or wrap (e.g., an ace bandage) only during and shortly after periods of activity.

Prevention

- Wear properly cushioned and well-fitting footwear with good arch support. Replace worn shoes.
- Choose your exercise surface carefully: jog on a running track, grass, or dirt trail instead of asphalt or concrete; opt for wood floors instead of concrete for basketball or aerobics workouts.
- Stretch all muscle groups daily.
- Warm up before and cool down after each workout.
- Get into shape gradually.

Swollen Ankles

Most people associate swollen ankles with pregnancy, and, indeed, swelling is common in pregnancy because fluid increases and accumulates in the body's tissues, especially in the lower legs and hands. Once a baby is delivered, the fluid levels will return to normal and the mother's swelling will rapidly diminish. Swelling during pregnancy is not a danger to the fetus or the mother, unless it is accompanied by elevated blood pressure, elevated urine protein levels, severe headaches, and swelling in the face, especially around the eyes. **This combination of symptoms may point to toxemia, a serious condition that requires immediate medical attention.**

Swelling of the ankles in people who are not pregnant can have a number of causes. Liver problems, kidney malfunction, acute premenstrual symptoms, and circulatory diseases can cause fluid to pool in the ankles. Your doctor will provide you with a plan to help reduce swelling such as taking diuretic medication. Still, if you notice sudden, unusual, or rapid swelling of your ankles or any other part of your body, and the swelling is not associated with an injury, it's a good idea to call your doctor right away.

Symptoms/Signs

- Swelling in ankles, feet, or lower legs
- "Pulled-tight" feeling on skin around ankles

Consult Your Doctor If:

- **You are unable to lie flat at night due to shortness of breath.**
- You are pregnant and ankle swelling is accompanied by swelling in the face, especially around the eyes.
- Your ankle swells, becomes tender, and skin appears red or purple.
- You have a chronic disease and notice any sudden or unusual swelling.
- Swelling is associated with pain in the back of the leg.

HOMECARE

If physician referral is not recommended at this time, try the following self-care procedures:

Rest
- Whenever possible, relax with your feet elevated to reduce swelling.
- If your swelling is pregnancy-related, rest often on your left side.

Heat/Cold
- Seek out air-conditioned environments; getting overheated will make swelling worse.

Nutrition
- Reduce sodium intake. Beware of processed foods and juices that may have a high sodium content.
- Use the salt shaker sparingly.

Activity
- Avoid any physical exertion in hot weather.

Fluids
- Drink plenty of water throughout the day.
- Avoid alcohol and caffeine.

Note Well
- If your swelling is pregnancy-related and you work on your feet, take frequent breaks and elevate your feet. If you work at a desk, use a footrest to raise your feet as high as possible. Avoid crossing your legs.

musculoskeletal

203

Tendinitis

A nytime you overuse or misuse a muscle, you risk injuring the fibrous bands of tissue—called tendons—which connect that muscle to a bone. The resulting tendinitis (microscopic tears and an inflammation of the tendon), although quite painful and physically limiting, usually clears up if you give the damaged tissue time to heal. But when you attempt to play or work through the pain and have not had adequate rest, you risk damage that can require a long rehabilitation, cortisone shots, or surgery to correct. As well, people with chronic tendinitis often never regain full use of the affected joint area, even after surgery. The key to recovery is fast action: As soon as you notice pain or inflammation, ice down the sore area, give it a few days of rest, then slowly start exercising again to get blood moving and speed healing to the tendon. Smart prevention and early home treatment can effectively treat most bouts of tendinitis.

Symptoms/Signs

- Tenderness, warmth, swelling, and/or pain in joint areas (especially knees, wrists, shoulders, and ankles)
- Joint-area pain that is intense when you begin an activity, diminishes as you continue, and is sharp once you've stopped

Consult Your Doctor If:

- You have severe, radiating, or persistent muscle pain.
- You experience numbness or tingling.
- Pain worsens over time or persists for more than 10 days despite self-care measures.
- You experience sudden pain with a snapping sound such as in your Achilles tendon below the calf.

HOMECARE
If physician referral is not recommended at this time, try the following self-care procedures:

Rest

- Rest injured area for 48 hours or until swelling and pain has subsided. (Unless tendinitis is severe, rest no more than 48 hours, since exercise will increase blood flow.) Avoid placing stress and repetitive strain on injured area.

Heat/Cold

- Apply ice to injured area for 20 minutes on, 20 minutes off for first 48 hours after injury.
- Try warm compresses or minimal heat to injured area after swelling and pain have subsided.

Cover

- If injury is severe, wrap with an elastic bandage or wear a brace such as around the elbow.

Medication

- To reduce pain and inflammation, take aspirin, naproxen, or ibuprofen as directed.

Activity

- Return to your activity slowly. Don't play or work through the pain.
- Stretch all muscle groups daily.
- Vary your activities to increase flexibility and avoid overuse.
- Use proper equipment and technique for every sport or activity.

musculoskeletal

204

Wrist Pain

The wrist consists of eight bones forming a stable platform that allows the hand to move freely. When the hand is bent back or dropped down, it places stress on the tendons and nerves that pass through the wrist. If the wrist is locked in either position for extended periods, damage and pain can occur. Therefore, the best hand position for word processing or data entry keeps the hands in a flat position.

A serious wrist condition called carpal tunnel syndrome (CTS) has become one of the fastest growing occupational injuries. CTS commonly occurs among people whose work requires them to do repetitive movements with their hands. Pregnancy also increases the risk of CTS.

Other causes of wrist pain include rheumatoid arthritis, osteoarthritis, and injuries due to falls or trauma.

Symptoms/Signs

- Symptoms of CTS include pain in wrist and forearm; weakness and loss of mobility in the hand; numbness in the fingers, except the little and ring fingers; and tingling in the fingers when the wrist is tapped
- Severe pain, swelling, and discoloring after trauma (e.g., falling on your wrist, hitting your hand) to the wrist

Consult Your Doctor If:

- You have fever, swelling, or severe pain even at rest.
- There is weakness, numbness, or tingling in your fingers that doesn't go away after 48 hours of following HomeCare suggestions.
- Your wrist is deformed, discolored, swollen, or sore to the touch after an accident.

Rest

- Chronic wrist pain requires rest from the activity that caused the problem; one to two weeks is usually adequate.

Medication

- Aspirin, naproxen, or ibuprofen may help inflammation. Use as directed.

Note Well

- A splint from a drugstore or medical supply house could be tried for a few days and then at night for three weeks.

Prevention

- Strengthen forearm muscles. Squeeze tennis ball 20 times, three times per day.
- Stretch fingers and wrists every hour. Do not do these exercises if you experience pain in your wrists or hands.
- Use appropriate posture and technique during repetitive tasks.

musculoskeletal

205

Computer Tips

- Maintain good posture, with proper support for your lower back.
- Keep your wrists in a straight position.
- Rest your feet comfortably on the floor or a footrest with 90-degree angles at the knee and ankle joints.

Anxiety

H O M E C A R E
If physician referral is not
recommended at this time,
try the following
self-care procedures:

When it spurs you to action or makes you more alert in uncertain situations, an occasional bout with anxiety is natural and usually beneficial. But when general feelings of anxiety begin to interfere with daily activities, serious health problems—both physical and mental—can result.

However, once anxiety is determined to be at the root of ongoing physical or emotional problems, there are a variety of treatment options available, including psychotherapy or medication.

Symptoms/Signs

- Episodes of accelerated, pounding, or irregular heart-beat
- Sleep problems, e.g., sleeplessness
- Increased sweating or chills
- Tightness or pain in the chest, shortness of breath, feelings of choking
- Headaches, dizziness, diarrhea, or nausea
- Trembling, twitching, restlessness, or feeling "keyed up"
- Avoidance of fear-arousing situations
- Ongoing fatigue
- Feelings of helplessness or unreality

Consult Your Doctor If:

- **You experience chest pain, dizziness, shortness of breath, or ongoing stomach problems; although anxiety may be the cause, you need to rule out other serious health problems first.**
- Anxiety interferes with your ability to function normally (e.g., you stay home more, avoid certain everyday situations, etc.)
- Your anxiety is not limited to occasional and typical anxiety-producing events (e.g., final exams, public speaking, competition).
- Anxiety is associated with depression. See pages 207 and 264-265.

Activity

- Exercise every day to relieve tension and activate body chemicals that relieve anxiety, make you feel more calm, and improve sleep.

Rest

- Learn and practice relaxation techniques such as progressive muscle relaxation and breathing exercises to control anxiety symptoms. See page 33.

Note Well

- Talk it out: Family, friends, your worksite employee assistance program, or someone in your church may be able to help you deal with feelings of anxiety.

Prevention

- Avoid caffeine, decongestants, antihistamines, diet pills, or other drugs that can worsen the symptoms of anxiety.
- Avoid alcohol.

Depression

Everyone has their ups and downs. But if you find that you are frequently down, or when you are down, that it seriously interferes with your usual activities, depression may be a likely diagnosis. In some cases, depression is a reaction to a major life event, such as the death of a loved one, divorce, loss of a job, or a health problem. (Twelve to 36 percent of patients with medical disorders develop depression.) It also can be caused by an underlying medical disorder or interactions between various drugs. Chronic drinking of alcohol, even in moderate amounts, can cause or worsen depression. Also, any stimulant (including caffeine) can cause depression during withdrawal.

Depression can be mild to severe. If you suspect that you or a loved one is clinically depressed, it's best to see your doctor for a professional evaluation. An estimated 80 percent of depressed individuals can be treated, with most feeling better within weeks. See pages 264-265 for more information on depression.

Symptoms/Signs

Signs include the following every day, all day, for at least two weeks:

- feeling sad
- losing interest in activities you used to enjoy
- losing or gaining weight
- feeling very tired all the time
- not being able to concentrate or make decisions
- feeling guilty or worthless
- trouble sleeping (sleeping too much or too little)
- being slowed down or restless when doing things or talking, so much that others can observe
- thinking about killing yourself

Seek Professional Help If

- **You have any thoughts of suicide. Call a suicide prevention hotline, found in the local white pages, or seek professional help through your doctor, local mental health clinic, or clergy.**
- You recognize the signs of depression in yourself or a loved one.

HOMECARE
If physician referral is not recommended at this time, try the following self-care procedures:

Note Well

- Have a confidant. Talk it out with a friend or family member. Don't be afraid to share your feelings with someone you trust.
- Don't be afraid to seek professional help through your local mental health agency, employee assistance program, clergy, or personal physician.
- Avoid the use of alcohol in coping with your problems.

Medication

- Avoid mood-altering drugs, especially illicit drugs such as marijuana or cocaine.
- Use prescription drugs only as directed.

Rest

- Use a relaxation technique to help reduce tension. See pages 33-34.

Activity

- Exercise can boost your energy level and your sense of well-being. In particular, moderate exercise, such as walking, may help prevent depression or lessen its severity.

Nutrition

- Eat well-balanced meals to keep your energy level up.
- Avoid overeating, a common problem with depression.

Insomnia

Approximately nine percent of adults suffer from chronic sleeplessness and another 27 percent experience occasional episodes of insomnia. Yet, rarely do people take their sleep problems seriously let alone talk about their sleep difficulties with their doctor.

The consequences of sleeplessness—such as fatigue, low energy, and poor concentration—are a significant reason for reduced work performance and increased accidents. Sleeplessness is rarely caused by a physical problem. Rather, habits such as using caffeine, exercising close to bedtime, napping during the day, or feeling stressed or excited all can disrupt sleep patterns. Also the "rebound" that can occur a few hours after drinking alcohol may make getting to sleep difficult or cause awakening shortly after getting to sleep.

A disorder linked to insomnia is restless leg syndrome. With this, the legs (or feet or arms) feel uncomfortable at rest and symptoms—an unpleasant but not painful creeping or crawling sensation—begin shortly after going to bed. Walking around for 10 minutes and flexing or massaging muscles before going to bed may head off symptoms.

Perhaps the greatest health risk resulting from sleep problems is the chronic use of sleep aids such as antihistamines or sleeping pills. Reliance on sleep aids can create dependency and increased tolerance. This can produce a cycle of unnatural sleep patterns and more fatigue. If a sleep aid is prescribed by your doctor, it should be short-term and "integrated" with behavioral techniques such as stress management and self-care methods outlined in the HomeCare section.

In some cases, chronic insomnia may require an evaluation by a sleep specialist.

Symptoms/Signs

- Inability to fall asleep or stay asleep, or waking up too early
- Daytime fatigue, poor concentration, or irritability
- Abnormal snoring

Consult Your Doctor If:

- The HomeCare recommendations do not improve your sleep pattern after four weeks.

HOMECARE
If physician referral is not recommended at this time, try the following self-care procedures:

Fluids

- Avoid drinking alcohol and caffeine-containing drinks such as coffee, tea, and colas.
- Don't use alcohol as a sleep aid.

Rest

- Associate your bed and bedroom with sleeping only.
- Practice a relaxation exercise. See pages 33-34.
- Have a fixed bedtime and wake-up time.
- Have a set bedtime routine that begins one-half hour before you go to bed.
- Do not watch TV in bed.

Heat/Cold

- A hot bath or warm shower promotes muscle relaxation.

Nutrition

- Eating starches such as pasta can help promote relaxation and drowsiness. However, don't overdo it.
- Warm milk also can help you become drowsy.

Activity

- Avoid heavy exercise in the late evening. Exercise earlier in the day.

Note Well

- If you can't sleep, get up and read in a chair until you feel drowsy.
- Avoid using sleep aids such as sedatives and antihistamines. Talk to your doctor.

Jet Lag

J et lag is that feeling of disorientation, fatigue, and sleeplessness that causes you to be staring at the walls of your hotel room at 3 a.m. when you should be getting a good night's rest. Jet lag is caused by an upset of the body's biological clock resulting from moving at rapid speeds across time zones. As the global marketplace expands, more people will be required to travel transcontinentally.

Recently, the natural hormone melatonin has been promoted as a "natural sleep" aid. Sold as a nutritional supplement, individuals should be cautious in its use since its long-term effects have not yet been established and quality control among manufacturers can vary.

Symptoms/Signs

- Inability to fall asleep or stay asleep, or waking up too early
- Daytime fatigue, poor concentration, disorientation, or irritability

Consult Your Doctor If:

- Physician referral is not recommended. However, if you travel extensively (especially internationally), the short-term use of sleep aids may be effective in helping you sleep while you adjust to a new time zone. Talk to your doctor if self-care doesn't work.

Rest

- Get plenty of rest before your trip. Try to alter your sleep patterns to be more in sync with your destination time zone. Even a change of one or two hours can make a positive difference.

Nutrition

- Eat right. Try eating high-protein meals when you want to be alert and high-carbohydrate meals when you want to sleep.

Fluids

- Avoid alcohol in flight. The effect of alcohol can be twice as great at high altitude. Drink plenty of water to prevent dehydration and headaches.

Prevention

- Set your watch to your destination time. While in flight, try to match your sleeping and eating schedule with that of your destination.
- Move around. Don't remain seated for the entire flight as long as conditions are safe.
- Acclimate on arrival. Try not to schedule meetings immediately upon arrival; take time to relax, and, if possible, go to bed at your usual hour or the regular time in the new time zone.
- Get a little sun. Sunlight may help to reset your internal clock. Try to spend some time outside during the first few days at your destination.

209

Memory Problems

Whether your age is 18 or 80, you can suffer from a poor memory. Alcohol, marijuana, some prescription drugs, depression, and thyroid problems can all make you more forgetful. You may forget certain things because they're not important—or because you didn't make the effort to store the information properly in the first place. As well, people have more memory troubles as they grow older. After age 20, the ability to recognize faces or find one's car at the airport starts to decline; after age 35, it's more difficult to retrieve names. If you think your memory is failing, try some memory-enhancing strategies before you assume that getting older is hindering your recall.

Real memory problems, however, usually are associated with conditions far more serious than poor storage techniques or diminished neural pathways. One of the hallmarks of Alzheimer's disease, for example, is increasing forgetfulness and inability to name familiar objects or people. Memory loss resulting from a stroke, on the other hand, occurs suddenly and is accompanied by other serious physical symptoms.

Symptoms/Signs

- Inability to remember things or categories of things you've had no trouble remembering in the past
- Increasing forgetfulness or short-term memory losses
- Sudden memory impairment

Consult Your Doctor If:

- You notice a sudden and extreme change in memory.
- You have trouble remembering very recent events (e.g., a wedding you attended last week or a visit from an out-of-town relative).
- You have trouble performing familiar tasks (e.g., driving to the grocery store or cooking a meal).
- You suspect a drug or drug dosage your doctor has prescribed is causing memory loss.
- You have symptoms of depression. See pages 207 and 264-265.

Medication

- If you suspect that your memory problems are caused by a prescription you are taking, check with your doctor before discontinuing its use or changing its dosage.

Note Well

- Use memory cues and employ better storage techniques to improve your memory. Use calendars or notebooks to write down important information, make lists, create routines (e.g., always put your car keys in the same place when you come home). Make a conscious effort to notice more details or be a more active listener, especially when being introduced to someone.

Prevention

- Although there is currently no way to prevent memory-robbing conditions such as Alzheimer's disease, you can work to keep your memory skills sharp by playing memory games, using memory aids, and making "remembering" a priority.
- If you drink alcohol, do so in moderation only. Get help if you have an alcohol problem. Refer to pages 39-42.

Mental Confusion

Mental confusion is a symptom most often associated with illnesses or conditions of older people. Indeed, individuals with diabetes, Alzheimer's disease, cirrhosis, and hypertension are all at risk for bouts of mental confusion when their diseases are not controlled as they should be. Additionally, mental confusion is a sign of serious events such as stroke, septic shock, transient ischemic attack (a temporary blockage in the artery supplying the brain), and interacting medications, all of which are more common in older individuals.

Because people with this symptom often are unaware of their diminished mental acuity as the condition worsens, it's important to identify the cause quickly. Pay close attention to changes in how you feel physically. Are you unusually tired or thirsty? Does a new prescription make you feel anxious or drowsy? Ask a friend or family member to check on you often, especially if you live alone; they are better able to notice any unusual symptoms or changes in your condition.

Seek emergency care if you are diabetic and mental confusion is accompanied by weakness, extreme thirst, abdominal pain, dry mouth, or labored breathing.

Symptoms/Signs

- Physical disorientation
- Impaired judgment
- Inability to concentrate despite efforts to do so
- Diminished ability to communicate with or understand others

Consult Your Doctor If:

- **Mental confusion is accompanied by a severe headache, high fever, or impaired speech or vision.**
- Mental confusion is accompanied by excessive thirst, frequent urination, unexplained weight loss, or numbness/tingling of the hands and feet.
- You suspect mental confusion is a side effect of medication.
- Mental confusion is accompanied by increasing lapses in memory and distinct personality changes.

Medication
- Be sure you are taking medications as prescribed. Call your doctor or pharmacist if you are unsure about dosage or have questions about drug interactions or allergies.
- If you are on insulin for diabetes, be sure to follow your doctor's instructions concerning dosage, etc.

Activity
- Do not drive a car or operate machinery during episodes of mental confusion.

Rest
- Get plenty of rest, since fatigue can worsen symptoms of mental confusion.

Fluids
- Drink plenty of fluids; dehydration can contribute to increased confusion, disorientation, and agitation.
- Don't drink alcohol, or do so in moderation only.

Prevention
- Take all medications only as prescribed.

stress / sleep

211

Shift Work

The human body is geared for sleep at night and activity during the day, and is primarily influenced by the effect of sunlight on the brain. When the body's natural clock (called circadian rhythms) and sleep patterns are changed, sleep problems can occur. It's hardest on night shift workers, whose sleep time averages two to four hours less than day workers. Also, night shift workers report waking up feeling tired more often than day workers. If you have trouble sleeping while on shift work, the guidelines in the HomeCare column to the right may help.

Symptoms/Signs

• Inability to fall asleep or stay asleep, or waking up too early
• Fatigue, poor concentration, disorientation, or irritability during waking hours

Consult Your Doctor If:

• Physician referral normally is not needed. However, talk to your doctor if self-care doesn't work or the above symptoms affect your productivity and safety.

Prevention

• Stick to one shift—if you can. Rotating shifts disrupts the normal sleep cycle. If you have a choice, try to stay on one shift. If you need to rotate, one week is the minimum time recommended by experts to allow your body to adjust. Also, try to rotate in a clockwise direction (e.g., nights to days, and days to evenings). This "forward" rotation has been found to be easier to adapt to than a counter-clockwise rotation.
• Light up your night. Bright lighting has been found to "trick" the brain into believing that it's daytime and helps adjust your internal body clock.
• In the morning light, wear sunglasses on your drive home. By decreasing the amount of sunlight to your eyes, your internal clock is fooled into believing that it's getting close to bedtime. However, if you feel sleepy while driving, keep your sunglasses off.
• Set a definite sleep time. Avoid lingering around the house or doing chores that eat into your sleep time. Establish a regular "lights out" and try to stick to it.
• Keep out the light and noise. If you sleep during the day, hang some room-darkening shades or a quilt over the window, or try wearing "eye shades." The hum of a fan can help cover up outside noises. Make sure to get a commitment from family members to respect your sleep time.

Sleep Problems—Children

If misery loves company, then take solace in knowing that you're not alone in dealing with a baby or child who won't go to sleep or won't stay asleep when he or she "should." Sleep problems in children are a common parental complaint.

In a baby, time will resolve the problem. By 3 to 4 months of age, most babies sleep for a six- to eight-hour stretch at night. By 7 to 12 months of age, most infants sleep through the entire night consistently.

If your child is not a baby and is not exhibiting other signs of illness, you may need to break some bad sleep habits. Your child may have become dependent on you to get to sleep, but must learn to sleep on his or her own. A regular schedule and a bedtime ritual of quiet activities give your child cues that it's time to settle down. Once asleep, don't reinforce waking behavior by giving your child a snack, etc. Above all, consistency is key.

A dramatic sleep disturbance is "night terrors." These usually occur at 3 to 4 years of age and may persist for several years. Typically, they occur during the first two hours of sleep, as contrasted with nightmares, which occur later in the night. In a night terror, the child appears to be awake (may even be sleepwalking) and very afraid, but still seems to be experiencing a frightening dream. It may be difficult to talk with or calm the child. The episode may last several minutes to a half hour and will not be remembered the next day.

Symptoms/Signs

- Inability to fall asleep or stay asleep, or waking up too early
- Frequent, frightening dreams, or terrors

Consult Your Doctor If Your Child:

- Has night terrors that are frequent, severe, or could be associated with an emotional or physical trauma the child is experiencing during the day.
- Has sleep problems that are not improved by HomeCare and that are disrupting family life.

HOMECARE
If physician referral is not recommended at this time, try the following self-care procedures:

Note Well

- Keep bedtimes regular and bedtime rituals quiet and brief.
- Be gentle but firm about bedtimes and remaining in bed. A security object, such as a blanket or stuffed animal, may ease the separation from you.
- If your child awakens, briefly console him or her in his or her own bed.
- If your child suffers a night terror, calm him or her in a dimly lit room until he or she responds to you.
- Add a warm bath to the bedtime ritual to promote muscle relaxation.

Rest

- Don't let your child nap too long or too late in the day.

Activity

- Avoid stimulating activity in the late evening. Read a book to your child before bedtime.

Medication

- Many antihistamines and decongestants can interfere with sleep. Consult with your pharmacist or doctor for an alternative.

Prevention

- If night terrors occur at the same time every night, awaken your child 15 to 30 minutes prior to that time to prevent another night terror.

stress/sleep

213

Snoring

. . . .

Snoring can disturb sleeping patterns to the point where you are less alert or productive during the day. Almost all snoring is caused by: flabby throat muscles, large tonsils, nasal obstructions, obesity, allergies, pregnancy, smoking, or alcohol use. Most snoring is easily remedied by some simple self-care methods.

On the other hand, obstructive sleep apnea is considered the most serious sleep disorder since it may produce fatal pulmonary and cardiovascular events. Classic symptoms include loud snoring and breathing irregularities where the person literally stops breathing because the airway closes after inhaling. Then, as oxygen levels are reduced, the person unconsciously wakes up and "catches his breath." This pattern is repeated hundreds of times, interrupting the person's sleep throughout the night. Because of these sleep disruptions, the victim usually feels tired throughout the day. Sleep apnea is more common in men than women.

Obstructive sleep apnea needs to be assessed by a physician who is trained in this area. Depending on the severity of the condition, treatment may involve the use of a continuous positive airway pressure (CPAP) device or the surgical removal of tissues in the nose and throat that are creating the obstruction.

Symptoms/Signs

- Gurgling, snorting, or loud throat noises during sleep
- With sleep apnea: loud snoring and breathing irregularities that cause the person to literally stop breathing and then suddenly catch his or her breath

Consult Your Doctor If:

- You or your bed partner notice that you experience cycles of snoring, breathing cessation, and violent jerking or snorting as breathing restarts during sleep.
- You experience extreme fatigue, daytime sleepiness, or poor concentration despite having had what you think is a good night's sleep.
- You experience no relief from snoring-induced sleep problems no matter what self-care measures you try.

214

Medication
- Avoid sedatives and antihistamines before bedtime.

Nutrition
- Avoid heavy meals within three hours of going to bed.
- Eat a well-balanced diet designed to keep your weight within a healthy range for your height, age, and body type.

Activity
- If you're overweight, begin an exercise program designed to help you tone muscles and lose body fat.

Fluids
- Avoid alcoholic drinks three hours before bedtime.

Note Well
- If you suffer from allergies, reduce bedroom allergens (dust, pet dander, mold, etc.) to alleviate nasal stuffiness.
- Don't sleep with windows open: Use the air conditioner instead.

Prevention
- Establish regular sleeping patterns and avoid getting overtired.
- Keep your allergies in check.
- Sleep on your side.
- Use a humidifier in your bedroom if your bedroom is too dry.
- For severe apnea, talk to your doctor about the continuous positive airway pressure (CPAP) mask.

Incontinence

For about 12 million people, bladder control is a daily problem that can rob life of all spontaneity. The causes of urinary incontinence vary: Hormonal imbalances, chronic cough, excess weight, childbirth, frequent constipation, neurologic disorders, the effects of certain medications, hyperactive bladder muscles, or an enlarged prostate can be at the root of the problem.

Fecal incontinence, the inability to control bowel movements, can be especially disheartening. For some, a mere sneeze or cough can cause leakage of soft stool. Exercising regularly and eating a diet rich in fruits and vegetables, whole grains, and plenty of fluids will help keep you regular. Avoid the chronic use of laxatives; instead, increase fiber intake or add a bulk formula to your diet (e.g. Metamucil®).

The good news is that most cases of incontinence can be treated with behavior modification, medication, medical devices, and, in some instances, with surgery.

Symptoms/Signs

- With urinary incontinence: Leaking urine as soon as you feel a strong need to urinate or when you sneeze, cough, laugh, walk, exercise, get up from a chair, or get out of bed
- With fecal incontinence: Any amount of stool, liquid or solid, that leaks out or is excreted when you are not trying to have a bowel movement

Consult Your Doctor If:

- You have any symptoms of incontinence for more than a week.
- You experience burning, pain, or bladder spasm upon urination.
- You have pain in the lower back or left abdomen, fever, nausea, or vomiting with symptoms of incontinence.
- Your urine contains blood.
- Your bladder is full but you can't release any urine.
- You have chronically impacted bowels and cannot correct the problem through self-care.
- Your stools are black and tarry or contain blood.
- You notice any sudden, major changes in normal bowel habits.

HOMECARE
If physician referral is not recommended at this time, try the following self-care procedures:

Cover

- For chronic incontinence, use adult absorbent undergarments (e.g., Depends®).

Nutrition

- Avoid spicy or greasy foods and products that contain artificial sweeteners, all of which can irritate the bladder.
- Increase whole grains and fresh fruits and vegetables in your diet to improve regularity.

Fluids

- Drink plenty of liquids, especially water—about one to two quarts throughout the day, tapering off intake close to bedtime.
- Avoid caffeinated and carbonated drinks, alcohol, and citrus juices, all of which can irritate the bladder.

Note Well

- Do Kegel exercises that strengthen the muscles surrounding the bladder: To isolate these pelvic floor muscles, stop the flow of urine midstream several times when you urinate. Once you know how, you can Kegel anywhere, but don't do these exercises when you urinate. Aim for 20-30 times a session, doing several sessions a day.
- Sit on the toilet at the same time every day for 15 minutes to encourage regularity and maintain continence during the rest of the day.
- Go to the bathroom on a set schedule. Gradually increase the time between visits until urination can be controlled for several hours.
- If you smoke, quit: Smoker's cough can damage pelvic muscles, and nicotine can interfere with bladder function.
- Lose excess weight.

Urinary Problems (Men)

Almost all male urinary problems have one of two sources: prostate problems and sexually transmitted diseases. When it's the prostate that's the problem (as it is for more than a third of men over age 50), chances are it's prostatitis, or inflammation of the prostate gland. As the prostate swells, it presses on the urethra, causing difficult, frequent, or painful urination. Less commonly (but increasing in frequency as the population ages and men are living longer), urinary problems are caused by prostate cancer. Fortunately, early detection makes prostate cancer highly treatable. For more information, refer to "Prostate Problems," on pages 279-280.

When urinary problems are not the result of prostate abnormalities, you may have an infection, most likely of the sexually transmitted variety. Genital herpes and gonorrhea, for example, can both cause pain on urination. Inflammation of the urethra and of the prostate also can be caused by bacteria introduced into the penis during intercourse.

Symptoms/Signs

- Pain or burning on urination
- Increased urinary frequency

Consult Your Doctor If:

- You have difficulty emptying your bladder or are unable to urinate.
- You experience painful or unusually frequent urination.
- You have blood in your urine or semen.
- Any of the above symptoms are accompanied by pain in the pelvis or lower back or during ejaculation.

216

HOMECARE
If physician referral is not recommended at this time, try the following self-care procedures:

Fluids

- Drink cranberry juice from the first sign of a urinary problem to increase the acidity of your urine and flush out bacteria.
- Drink plenty of water—about 12 ounces an hour.
- Avoid alcohol, caffeine, and sweetened or artificially sweetened drinks.

Medication

- If you have difficulty urinating, avoid taking antihistamines.

Prevention

- Have your doctor give you a yearly digital rectal exam and prostate-specific antigen (PSA) test.
- Practice safe sex: Use a condom to reduce your risk of sexually transmitted diseases.
- Drink at least eight glasses of water a day.
- If you're susceptible to urinary tract infections, avoid excessive caffeine, alcohol, and high-sugar drinks.

Urinary Problems (Women)

Bladder infections are the most common urinary problem among women. The female anatomy allows normally harmless bacteria from the anal area to easily reach the urinary tract. In addition, sexual activity can introduce unwanted bacteria into the urethra. If the bacteria gain a foothold in the urinary tract, a bladder infection or kidney infection can result.

Less common but potentially serious causes of urinary problems in women include benign uterine fibroids and a host of sexually transmitted diseases: pelvic inflammatory disease, chlamydia, candidiasis, genital herpes, vaginitis. Whether you experience painful urination, increased urine frequency or difficult urination, take care not to let urinary problems go untreated. You may risk damage to your bladder, your kidneys, and your health in general.

Symptoms/Signs

- Painful, difficult, or unusually frequent urination
- Urine that contains pus or blood, or is unusually dark or discolored

Consult Your Doctor If:

- If you have painful, burning, or frequent urination accompanied by low-grade fever, lower back pain (dull or acute), fatigue, nausea, a yellowish discharge, or painful sexual intercourse.
- If you notice blood in your urine.

Fluids

- Drink cranberry juice from the first sign of a urinary problem in order to increase the acidity of your urine and flush out bacteria.
- Drink plenty of water—at least 12 ounces an hour.
- Avoid alcohol, caffeine, and sweetened or artificially sweetened drinks.

Clean

- Keep vaginal and anal area clean. Wipe from front to back after using the toilet.
- Do not douche unless advised to do so by your doctor.

Activity

- Abstain from sexual intercourse if it is painful or increases urinary discomfort.

Prevention

- Practice safe sex: Use a condom if you are unsure whether your partner may infect you with a sexually transmitted disease.
- Practice good hygiene: Wipe from front to back after using the toilet.
- Drink at least eight glasses of water a day.
- If you're susceptible to urinary tract infections, avoid excessive caffeine, alcohol, and high-sugar drinks.
- Drink a glass of water before intercourse, and urinate within 15 minutes after intercourse.
- Take showers instead of baths.
- Don't "hold" your urine: Urinate as soon as you feel the urge.

217

Balding/Hair Loss

Two out of every three men will eventually experience some form of balding, while an even higher percentage of both men and women will face some type of hair loss in their lives. Unless it's hereditary—and most balding is—hair loss from other causes (hormonal imbalances, acute illness, certain drugs, severe emotional stress, poor diet—even certain hair styles) can be alarming, but it's usually not permanent.

If you have slowly thinning hair or a receding hairline, there are hundreds of expensive, usually useless and sometimes dangerous products and procedures you can try in your fight to save your hair. Even minoxidil (Rogaine®), which is one of the only drugs to have proven its ability to grow hair in bald areas, produces "satisfactory" results in only 10 percent of the people who try it. Non-drug options such as hair transplantation offer more permanent solutions to hereditary hair loss, but their cost and relative risks are high enough to keep most people from venturing further than an initial consultation.

Symptoms/Signs

- General thinning of scalp hair
- Isolated bald patches on scalp (smooth, or accompanied by irritation or scaling)
- Generalized loss of body hair

Consult Your Doctor If:

- You have unexplained bald patches.
- You notice unusual and excessive shedding after combing or brushing.
- You experience sudden hair loss on any part of the body.
- You have ring-like bald patches that are red, scaly, and itchy.
- You are taking minoxidil (Rogaine®) and experience severe itching, headaches, dizzy spells, or heartbeat irregularities.

218

HOMECARE
If physician referral is not recommended at this time, try the following self-care procedures:

Medication

- Don't use minoxidil (Rogaine®), which is available over-the-counter, if you have a heart condition.

Heat/Cold

- Avoid high-heat hair dryers or other styling appliances that can dry and damage hair.

Clean

- Keep hair clean, but avoid excessive shampooing, which can cause hair breakage.

Nutrition

- Eat a well-balanced diet with adequate protein and iron intake.
- Avoid high doses of vitamin A.

NB

Note Well

- Avoid wearing tight-fitting hats or wigs for extended periods.
- Avoid wearing "pulled-tight" hairstyles (ponytails, braids, etc.) for extended periods.
- Avoid brushing or combing hair excessively.
- Blot wet hair with a towel; avoid vigorous towel drying.
- Learn to control stress and tension. See pages 28-34.
- Beware of certain hair products (e.g., perms) and treatments (e.g., hair straightening) that may damage hair.

Hernia

H ernia is a general term for any protrusion of organ tissue outside the area it normally occupies. But two of the most common types of hernias occur almost exclusively in men and involve part of the intestine pushing through a weakened internal opening into the groin (direct inguinal hernia) or scrotum (indirect inguinal hernia). Inguinal hernias usually result from physical overexertion or straining during lifting. They can either be very painful or go completely unnoticed until a routine physical exam uncovers the characteristic hernia "bulge."

Often, your doctor will be able to push a hernia bulge back into place with relative ease, but this is only temporary. However, when the hernia does not respond to physical manipulation, it is probably trapped or strangulated and may require surgery. Strangulated hernias that are not treated can result in the death of the trapped tissue, which can become infected and require emergency, life-saving surgery.

Symptoms/Signs

- Unusual pressure in the groin
- Abdominal or groin discomfort when lifting or bending at the waist
- Painful lump or bulge in the groin or scrotum
- Moderate to severe pain in the scrotum. See page 221.
- Swelling of the scrotum

Consult Your Doctor If:

- You experience any symptoms of a hernia.
- You have unexplained pain in the lower abdominal/groin area for longer than a week.
- You experience swelling or pain in the scrotum due to trauma to the groin.

Nutrition

- Eat a diet high in fiber to avoid straining during bowel movements.

Activity

- Avoid heavy lifting or any physical exertion that strains your abdominal muscles.
- If your job or exercise routine places a strain on your lower back or abdomen, use a back support belt.

Prevention

- Keep physically fit and maintain a weight that is within a healthy range for your age and frame.
- Avoid heavy lifting without proper back support.
- Avoid straining during bowel movements.
- Learn proper lifting techniques. See page 254.

men's health

Impotence

It's not at all unusual for men to experience occasional bouts of impotence. Too much alcohol, stress, fatigue, and some medications can put a damper on an ordinarily strong sexual response. Fortunately, most episodes of impotence are short-lived and can be easily "cured" with a little self-care.

But repeated or chronic impotence can become a major stumbling block to intimacy or can even signal that there is something wrong physically. High blood pressure, heart disease, hardening of the arteries, diabetes, hormone imbalances, and substance abuse frequently interfere with the ability of the penis to achieve or maintain an erection.

In any case, it's a good idea to try to deal with psychological or emotional causes for impotence before seeking medical help. Learning how to relax, going slowly during sex, and talking to your partner about all aspects of intimacy often can be all the "remedy" you need.

If your problem does turn out to be physical, your doctor can offer a number of effective treatments. For example, your doctor may prescribe a pill (e.g., Viagra®) that you can take one hour before sexual activity.

Symptoms/Signs

• Inability to achieve or maintain an erection

Consult Your Doctor If:

• You suspect that medication or a physical ailment may be causing your impotence.
• After a few months of home treatment, you are not able to achieve or maintain an erection.

Medication

• Ask your doctor to recommend another medication (e.g., hypertension medication) if one you are taking seems to be causing your impotence.

Note Well

• Avoid using recreational drugs; some of the most widely used drugs (marijuana, amphetamines, opiates, etc.) are associated with increased impotence.
• Don't smoke.
• Find ways to relax, reduce stress, and eliminate anxiety from your life.
• Work with your partner to minimize or relieve any psychological or emotional stress that affects your intimacy.
• Don't associate erection and ejaculation with sexual "success;" find other ways to give and receive pleasure—options that don't always lead to intercourse. Slow down your lovemaking and become reacquainted with your body (and your partner's).

Activity

• Exercise aerobically three or four times a week (but avoid excessive exercise, which can interfere with sexual performance).

Prevention

• Reduce your risk of atherosclerosis (hardening of the arteries) by controlling your intake of fat and cholesterol, managing your weight, not smoking, exercising regularly, and controlling your blood pressure.
• If you drink alcohol, do so in moderation only.

Testicular Pain

Testicular pain is one of the most intense pains a man can experience—so much so that the pain itself often causes nausea and profuse sweating. Most often, pain in the testicles is a result of blunt trauma, which is why it's important to wear a protective cup every time you participate in contact sports. Fortunately, permanent damage to the testicles due to injury is quite rare.

Other reasons men experience testicular pain include testicular torsion (wherein the spermatic cord attached to the testicle becomes twisted), epididymitis (inflammation of the epididymis, a tube that transports sperm), varicocele (a mass of varicose veins in the scrotum), hernia, kidney stones, cysts, and (rarely) tumors.

You should always take unexplained testicular pain seriously and see your doctor as soon as possible. **If you experience sudden and excruciating testicular pain that is not caused by injury, seek emergency medical care. Likewise, if an injury to the testicles includes puncture by a sharp object, you should seek immediate treatment to avoid complications such as blood clots, infertility, or loss of a testicle.**

Symptoms/Signs

- Pain or tenderness in one or both testicles

Consult Your Doctor If:

- **You experience sudden and severe pain in either testicle.**
- You experience pain in the scrotum that develops gradually but does not subside.
- Testicular pain is accompanied by the elevation of one testicle in the scrotum, nausea, fever, or testicular swelling.
- Blunt trauma to the testicles results in pain, bruising, or swelling that does not subside within an hour.
- You notice a lump or any swelling in the scrotum that may or may not be painful or tender.

HOMECARE
If physician referral is not recommended at this time, try the following self-care procedures:

Medication

- If your doctor determines that you have epididymitis, he or she may prescribe an antibiotic to kill the infection. You can take an over-the-counter pain reliever to ease the pain and inflammation.

Heat/Cold

- If your doctor determines that you have epididymitis, you can relieve some of the pain and swelling by applying ice packs to the scrotum periodically. Check with your doctor.

Activity

- If physical activity increases testicular pain, cease the activity.

Prevention

- Do a monthly self-examination. See page 45.
- Wear an athletic cup or supporter when participating in contact sports or those that have the risk of injury to the testicles, such as baseball or softball.

men's health

221

Breast Lumps

Whether it's a cyst, a swollen gland, some fibrous tissue, or an unusual lump you've never noticed before, any abnormality you feel in your breast tissue can send you into a panic. Fortunately, eight out of 10 lumps that women find are not cancerous, and of those that are cancerous, more than 90 percent are curable if they're found early.

That's why it's important for every woman to become intimately familiar with what her normal breast tissue feels like so that any unusual lumps or dense areas can be recognized and checked by a doctor. The keys to detection and prevention are breast self-examination, regular breast exams by a medical professional, and periodic mammograms for women over 50. If you don't know how to do a breast self-examination, ask your doctor to demonstrate. Then examine your breasts every month without fail. Keep in mind that about 11 percent of all women will develop breast cancer in a lifetime—and those who survive usually are the ones who detected a lump early, through self-examination and regular mammography.

Symptoms/Signs

- A lump or hardness in the breast or armpit, a discharge from the nipple, and/or unusual changes to breast tissue

Consult Your Doctor If:

- You find any lump or feel any unusually dense or fibrous tissue in your breast you haven't had checked by a doctor before.
- You notice wrinkling, puckering, or dimpling of the skin on your breast.
- Your nipple retracts (pulls inward).
- You have a red, scaly rash or sore on your nipple.
- You notice any discharge from your nipple.
- There is a sudden and unusual increase in the size of one breast, or if one breast appears unusually lower than the other.
- You are breast-feeding and experience flu-like symptoms, fever, and painfully swollen breasts.

HOMECARE
If physician referral is not recommended at this time, try the following self-care procedures:

Prevention

- Do a breast self-examination every month. See page 45.
- Have your doctor check your breasts during your regular checkup.
- Have regular mammograms if you're over 50. If you have a family history of breast cancer, consult your doctor for a screening schedule. Refer to page 43.
- Exercise regularly.

Fluids

- If you have a history of fibrocystic cysts, avoid caffeine. Drink plenty of fluids.

Nutrition

- Eat a well-balanced diet low in fat.

Heat/Cold

- For abscesses, swollen glands, or clogged milk ducts, warm compresses can help reduce swelling.

Menopause

Not that long ago, the "change of life" was a time many women dreaded. Hot flashes, mood swings, depression, and many other symptoms of menopause often were assumed to be an inevitable package of misery that women had to endure at mid-life. More and more, however, women are finding that the cessation of their menstrual cycle can offer a new-found freedom—no more worrying about birth control, monthly menstrual discomfort, or medical conditions such as endometriosis. As well, fully 75 percent of all women are either symptomless (except for the gradual cessation of menstruation) or experience only slight symptoms during this phase in their lives.

Whether it happens to you at age 40 or age 55, menopause is a natural stage of womanhood that can bring out positive aspects of your personality you may not have been aware of before. If you do have some discomfort or more symptoms than you bargained for, try some home-care remedies or talk to your doctor about hormone replacement therapy. And don't hesitate to pamper yourself a little now and then: You've earned it.

Finally, always consult with your doctor at the onset of menopause to discuss your risk of osteoporosis and its prevention.

Symptoms/Signs

- Hot flashes (flushed face and a sudden, all-over warmth)
- Vaginal dryness
- Uncomfortable or painful intercourse
- Irregular menstrual periods
- Mood swings, mild depression, listlessness, or insomnia

Consult Your Doctor If:

- You experience unusual or prolonged vaginal bleeding.

Nutrition

- Eat a well-balanced diet rich in calcium. Try to eat five or six small meals a day instead of three big ones in order to keep your metabolism and body temperature on an even keel.

Note Well

- Keep cool: Use the air conditioner at home and in your car; invest in a small fan for your desk at work—anything that keeps hot flashes at bay.
- Wear loose-fitting, layered clothing. Remove a layer when you are hot.
- Use over-the-counter, water-soluble lubricants such as K-Y Jelly® to replace vaginal moisture during intercourse. Avoid petroleum-based lubricants.

Fluids

- Drink plenty of water.

Activity

- Find an exercise routine you enjoy and stick to it. Four or five sessions of aerobic activity each week can keep bones strong, regulate hormones, and help cure insomnia.

Prevention

- There is nothing you can do to prevent menopause—nor should you want to. Menopause is a natural and often liberating part of your life's cycle. Approach this time of change with a positive attitude, paying attention to the self-care regimen outlined above, and you may find that menopause is a time you enjoy and appreciate.

women's health

223

Menstrual Cramps

Cramping in the lower abdomen is a common problem during a woman's menstrual period. Menstrual cramps are caused by natural substances called prostaglandins that are found in higher concentrations during the menstrual period, and can lead to severe cramping for some women. In many cases, cramping can be reduced through HomeCare.

Symptoms/Signs

- Cramping in the lower abdomen
- Headache, backache, thigh pain, diarrhea, constipation, dizziness, and nausea also are common

Consult Your Doctor If:

- Cramping does not stop when your period is over.
- You have a fever, diarrhea, or a rash during your period.
- Menstrual bleeding has been unusually heavy for several months.
- After experiencing "normal periods," you suddenly have painful cramping.
- Cramping occurs with signs of major intestinal problems such as black, tarry stools, or blood in the stools themselves.

Preventing Toxic Shock Syndrome

Toxic Shock Syndrome (TSS) is a potentially fatal bacterial infection that is linked with superabsorbent tampons and diaphragms. **Symptoms of TSS include a sudden high fever, headache, vomiting, diarrhea, weakness, and redness of the skin, mouth, and vagina. Immediate medical attention is required.**

HOMECARE

If physician referral is not recommended at this time, try the following self-care procedures:

Medication
- Ibuprofen is a very effective treatment for menstrual cramps. Aspirin also can be used. Use as directed.

Heat/Cold
- Take a hot bath; try to relax.
- Apply heating pads or hot water bottles to relax muscles and reduce cramping.

Nutrition
- Reduce your intake of salt and sodium products, especially the week prior to the start of your period.
- Increasing your magnesium and calcium intake can help reduce cramping.

Activity
- Physical activity has been shown to help reduce cramping for some women.
- Lie on your back with legs up on the wall. Lie still for 15 minutes and try to relax.

Fluids
- To help relax, try herbal teas (e.g., chamomile).
- Avoid caffeinated foods (e.g., chocolate) and drinks, which may increase tension and irritability.

Prevention
- Try sanitary napkins instead of tampons. Change them often.
- Regular physical activity may help reduce cramping episodes.
- To help prevent TSS: Use tampons with the lowest absorbency and that contain natural fibers, rather than "polyester-like" materials. Change every four to six hours.
- Do not keep diaphragms in longer than 24 hours. Use as directed.

PMS

Premenstrual syndrome (PMS), which is the result of hormonal changes in the body prior to menstruation, is an unwelcome part of the menstrual cycle for many women. PMS can be mild for some, severe for others. The physical and emotional changes associated with PMS usually take place seven to 10 days prior to menstruation and may disappear just before or at the start of menstruation.

Symptoms/Signs

- Weight gain, headaches, acne, bloating, breast tenderness, diarrhea or constipation, dizziness, and fatigue
- Emotional symptoms include mood swings, increased tension and anger, irritability, sadness, and unexplained crying

Consult Your Doctor If:

- Your symptoms are severe for several months and do not improve with HomeCare measures.

Nutrition

- Decrease sugar and sodium intake; increase your protein intake.
- Talk to your doctor about taking vitamin B_6 and vitamin E supplements.
- Increasing your magnesium and calcium intake can help reduce cramping.

Medication

- For menstrual cramps, try ibuprofen or naproxen. Aspirin may also be used, but the above medications usually are more effective. Use as directed.

Note Well

- Discuss your PMS problems with your partner. Try to work together to deal with emotional and physical changes.
- To reduce ankle swelling, keep legs elevated.

Fluids

- Limit your intake of caffeine found in coffee, tea, chocolate, and cola drinks. Caffeine can increase irritability and breast tenderness.
- Avoid alcohol, especially if depression is one of your symptoms.

Prevention

- Try to get extra sleep a few days before you usually experience symptoms.
- Learn a relaxation technique to use when feeling tense. See pages 33-34.
- Soak in a warm bathtub to help relax aching muscles.
- Stay physically active.

women's health

225

Prenatal Risk Assessment

The chart below is designed to help women who are planning to have a baby understand the potential risks of certain behaviors and the potential effects on the health of the baby and the mother. **The more high-risk behaviors that you plan to continue during your pregnancy, the greater your chances of preterm labor or other serious problems.**

If you have any of the risk factors described below, discuss them with your doctor before conception. If you find out that you're pregnant and have any of these risk factors, see your doctor as soon as possible to discuss your care plan. The right-hand column ("Ideas that Work") provides you with additional assistance. *However, these ideas are not a substitute for appropriate medical supervision.*

Risk Factors	Consequences of Continuing or Not Controlling Risk Factors	Ideas that Work
Smoking ❑ Smoking while pregnant ❑ Continued exposure to smoke-filled rooms	**For You:** • Miscarriage • Preterm delivery **For Your Baby:** • Low birthweight • SIDS (Sudden Infant Death Syndrome)	• Stop smoking before you're pregnant. • Enroll in a stop-smoking program. • Avoid smoke-filled areas. • Refer to "Resources."
Alcohol ❑ Drinking 3-5 or more drinks a day before conception ❑ Drinking alcohol while pregnant	**For You:** • Miscarriage • Preterm delivery • Liver problems • Accidents (e.g., drunken driving) • Alcoholism **For Your Baby:** • FAS (Fetal Alcohol Syndrome), leading to emotional and learning problems • Birth defects, mental retardation • Low birthweight • Increased death rate	• Don't drink while you're trying to get pregnant. • Don't drink alcohol during pregnancy or while nursing your baby. • If you have a drinking problem, seek help. See "Alcohol Use," page 39.
Drug Use ❑ Using illegal drugs (crack, cocaine, LSD, heroin, marijuana) ❑ Using prescription or over-the-counter drugs during pregnancy without physician's approval	**For You:** • Miscarriage • Conception problems (cocaine and marijuana) • AIDS or hepatitis from IV drug use • Preterm delivery **For Your Baby:** • Low birthweight • Birth defects, mental retardation • Addiction • AIDS or hepatitis virus from mother	• Abstain from all illegal drugs. • If you have a drug problem, get help *before* you become pregnant. • If you use any prescription or over-the-counter drugs (e.g., antihistamines), make sure your doctor approves their use. • Refer to "Drug Abuse," page 35. • If you have HIV, notify your obstetrician. The risk of transferring HIV to a newborn can be greatly reduced with medications.

Prenatal Risk Assessment

Risk Factors	Consequences of Continuing or Not Controlling Risk Factors	Ideas that Work
Obesity ❑ Being 20 percent or more over ideal weight	**For You:** • High blood pressure • Diabetes • Slow healing of incisions **For Your Baby:** • Delivery problems from heavier-than-average baby	• Achieve an acceptable weight before you become pregnant. • Follow your doctor's recommendations on proper nutrition and exercise. • Keep your weight gain within 35 pounds during your pregnancy.
Eating Disorders ❑ Always on a diet ❑ Binge eating, followed by forced vomiting (bulimia) ❑ Never feel thin enough ❑ Extremely concerned about weight gain during pregnancy	**For You:** • Preterm delivery • Anemia **For Your Baby:** • Impaired growth and development • Low birthweight • Birth defects • Increased death rate	• Expect to gain between 25 to 35 pounds during your pregnancy. • Eat balanced meals. • Don't try to lose weight during pregnancy. • Don't take diet pills. • If you have an eating disorder (e.g., bulimia or anorexia). seek assistance. • Refer to "Resources."
Sexually Transmitted Diseases (STDs) ❑ Have already or may have been exposed to herpes, gonorrhea, syphilis, chlamydia, HIV (AIDS virus), or hepatitis	**For You:** • Miscarriage • Preterm delivery • Complications during delivery • AIDS **For Your Baby:** • Birth defects • Increased risk of getting STD from mother (e.g., AIDS) • Eye infections (e.g., from herpes) • Pneumonia (e.g., chlamydia)	• If you think you already have or have been exposed to any STD, see your doctor *before* getting pregnant. • Avoid high-risk groups. Refer to page 50. • If you have HIV, notify your obstetrician. The risk of transferring HIV to newborn children can be greatly reduced with medications. • Use condoms.
Age ❑ Are you age 35 or older or under age 18?	**For You:** • Miscarriage • Labor complications **For Your Baby:** • Increased risk for some birth defects (e.g., Down's syndrome) if you're over age 35. • Pneumonia (e.g., chlamydia)	• If you have high blood pressure, diabetes or heart disease, see your doctor before becoming pregnant. • Get early and continued medical supervision. • Refer to "Resources."
Other ❑ You **are not** taking a daily supplement of folic acid.	**For Your Baby:** • Increased risk of neural tube defects (e.g., Spina bifida)	• For three months before and during pregnancy, women should take a daily supplement of folate: 0.4 mg.

Preventing Preterm Labor

When a woman goes into labor three or more weeks before her baby is due, it is described as a preterm labor. A preterm baby has an increased chance of having health problems because its body is not well enough developed to live outside the mother's womb.

Ideas that Work

- **You are at a greater risk** for preterm delivery if you:
  - Suffer trauma (e.g., an automobile accident)
  - Are pregnant with more than one child.
  - Become pregnant within less than two years of your last pregnancy.
  - Had a preterm baby previously.
  - Smoke, drink alcohol, and/or misuse drugs.
  - Are a DES daughter.
  - Are younger than 18 or older than 40.
  - Are under a lot of stress and personal pressure.
  - Are bleeding from the vagina.
  - Have had two or more second-trimester abortions or miscarriages.
  - Have had three or more urinary tract infections during this pregnancy.
  - Have a vaginal or cervical infection.
  - Are being abused by your partner.

  If you have any of these conditions or other problems, discuss them with your doctor.

- **You can reduce the chance of a preterm delivery:**
  - Review your risk factors before you try to conceive. See pages 226-227.
  - See a doctor as soon as you find out you're pregnant, and on a regular basis thereafter.
  - Stop smoking, drinking alcohol, and/or using drugs. Check with your doctor before taking any medication.
  - Eat a well-balanced diet and gain the weight your doctor recommends.
  - Get enough rest.
  - Drink three quarts of water in a 24-hour period.
  - Find support from friends and other people who can help when you are stressed or feel down.
  - Take advantage of prenatal educational services that your health plan, employer, or local hospital may sponsor.
  - Know the signs of labor and what to do when experiencing preterm labor.

- **Signs (can be subtle) of preterm labor include:**
  - Five or more contractions in one hour
  - Menstrual-like cramps that come and go or don't go away
  - Pelvic pressure: a feeling that the baby's head is pushing down; it may come and go
  - A low, dull backache (more than usual) that comes and goes or doesn't go away
  - Abdominal cramps with or without diarrhea
  - Leakage or bleeding from the vagina
  - Feeling of pressure in lower back, abdomen, or thighs
  - Change in vaginal discharge. It may be more watery, have more mucus, or be blood-tinged
  - The baby is not moving as much as usual

- **If you show signs of preterm labor:**
  - **Lie down on your left side for an hour.**
  - **Drink two to three glasses of water.**

  If the signs do not go away in one hour, or you have fluid leaking from your vagina, call your doctor or clinic immediately. Early intervention is critical to prevent preterm delivery.

Resources

Your health care provider or local chapter of the March of Dimes.

228

Vaginal Bleeding

It's not uncommon for a woman to have unusual vaginal bleeding during her child-bearing years. Changing hormone levels, weight gain or loss, heavy exercise, infections, difficulties with birth control methods (especially IUDs), certain drugs—even stress—can cause spotting or bleeding at times other than menstrual periods or can cause the periods to be too heavy or lengthy.

But vaginal bleeding also can alert you to something that is not quite right with your reproductive system. Endometriosis (an overgrowth of tissue that lines the uterus), uterine fibroids and polyps, ectopic pregnancies, miscarriages, certain types of cancer, and thyroid disease can all trigger vaginal bleeding. So, report any unusual vaginal bleeding to your doctor.

Symptoms/Signs

- Vaginal bleeding not associated with regular menstrual cycle or medical procedure (pelvic examination, abortion, surgery, etc.)

Consult Your Doctor If:

- You experience unusual or severe pelvic pain, especially during menstruation.
- Menstruation becomes increasingly painful month after month, your flow lasts for more than eight days, or your flow is too heavy (blood gushes, contains large clots, or cannot be contained with standard "heavy flow" sanitary products).
- Your menstrual cycles shorten to less than 21 days.
- You experience sharp pain deep in your pelvis during intercourse.
- You become weak, pale, and lightheaded while standing.
- You have any vaginal bleeding when you are past menopause and not taking hormones.
- You have difficulty urinating, or you urinate frequently and do not have a urinary tract infection.
- You experience unusual spotting or bleeding between menstrual periods, especially if bleeding lasts for more than three days or occurs for more than three months in a row.
- You are pregnant and have any bleeding or spotting.

HOMECARE
If physician referral is not recommended at this time, try the following self-care procedures:

Medication
- Avoid taking aspirin during any episode of vaginal bleeding. Take acetaminophen or ibuprofen instead.

Nutrition
- Eat a well-balanced diet that contains plenty of sources of iron.

Cover
- Use tampons or sanitary pads to protect clothing and gauge your bleeding so that you can accurately report blood flow to your doctor.

Activity
- Avoid any activity that increases abnormal bleeding.

women's health

229

Vaginal Dryness

The female reproductive system and its functioning is maintained by the body's delicate balance of hormones. When hormone levels change—either because you're pregnant, breast-feeding, going through menopause or taking hormones as part of a doctor-recommended therapy—you'll probably notice many changes in your body. One such change, associated with a decrease in the hormone estrogen, is vaginal dryness.

Aside from interfering with lovemaking, vaginal dryness is not serious unless it is accompanied by other symptoms (see below). There are many products on the market designed to replace vaginal moisture, but the ones that most closely mimic normal vaginal secretions are water-based (Lubifax® or K-Y Jelly®). Some women prefer oil-based lotions or creams, or plain petroleum jelly. These are good choices, too—unless you are using a diaphragm or condom: Oil-based lubricants can quickly destroy any contraceptive device made from latex.

Most of the time, vaginal dryness disappears when breast-feeding women wean their infants or when menopausal women opt for hormone replacement therapy.

Symptoms/Signs
- Decrease in or lack of normal vaginal secretion, causing pain or discomfort during intercourse

Consult Your Doctor If:
- Vaginal dryness is accompanied by vaginal itching or redness.
- You experience any abnormal vaginal discharge or bleeding.
- You notice any blisters, lesions, or changes in vaginal skin texture.

Medication

- If you are going through or have gone through menopause, ask your doctor about estrogen replacement therapy.

Note Well

- Avoid non-lubricated intercourse, which can cause vaginal irritation or abrasion.
- Use a non-irritating lubricant during intercourse.
- If you use condoms during intercourse, buy the lubricated variety.
- Avoid using any petroleum-based lubricant with any condom or diaphragm; use water-based lubricants instead.

women's health

230

Vaginitis

Vaginitis (inflammation of the vagina) usually results in one or more of the following symptoms: abnormal discharge, itching, and pain (especially during intercourse). Infection is the most common cause of vaginitis.

When the vagina is irritated due to an infection, friction caused by intercourse usually makes the condition worse. Therefore, intercourse is not recommended until the infection has been treated. Vaginal dryness also can cause pain and irritation during intercourse. A lubricant such as K-Y Jelly® or Replens® can help reduce vaginal dryness.

Infections of the vagina can be caused by yeast (also called monilia or candida), trichomonas, chlamydia, gonorrhea, and herpes. Although yeast infections are rarely spread during sex, the other four infections are sexually transmitted.

Yeast infections usually cause itching and a discharge that is not foul smelling (it may smell like baking bread) and looks a bit like cottage cheese. You are at a greater risk for yeast infections if you have diabetes, use birth control pills, are on hormone replacement therapy, or are taking antibiotics. Medications (which have a very good cure rate) are now available over the counter for treating yeast infections.

Symptoms/Signs

- Abnormal discharge, itching, and pain within the vagina

Consult Your Doctor If:

- The problem is vaginal dryness and vaginal symptoms and discomfort don't go away after one month of stopping tampon use and using lubrication (e.g., K-Y Jelly®).
- You or your sexual partner have symptoms that suggest a sexually transmitted disease (e.g., painful discharge, pain on urination).
- It's the first vaginal infection you have ever had.
- You have tried over-the-counter medication for one episode of a possible yeast infection with no success.

HOMECARE
If physician referral is not recommended at this time, try the following self-care procedures:

Nutrition

- Reduce your intake of sugar. If you have diabetes, be sure to watch your blood sugar levels.

Medication

- Consider using an over-the-counter vaginal medication (e.g., Monistat®) for one episode if you have typical symptoms of a yeast infection (monilia vaginitis): itching, a cheesy discharge that may smell like baking bread, no pain, and no fever. Use as directed and see your doctor if symptoms persist.

Prevention

- Use tampons only during times of heavy menstrual flow, if at all. See page 224.
- For vaginal dryness and friction, use a lubricant during sexual intercourse. Do not use petroleum jelly with condoms; use a water-based lubricant such as K-Y Jelly® instead.
- Use only water when washing around the vagina. Soaps, bubble baths, and shampoos can strip natural oils from the membranes that protect the vaginal walls.
- Use a condom when there is risk of a sexually transmitted disease.
- Wear underwear that's made from cotton rather than polyester. Cotton breathes more and allows the vagina to stay dry and cool.
- Sleep without underwear to allow adequate ventilation.
- Try using a less absorbent tampon or pads if vaginal dryness is a problem.

231

Infant Feeding: Breast or Bottle?

Before your baby's birth, you should explore the breast- vs. bottle-feeding issue with your health care provider.

Breast-feeding is strongly endorsed by health professionals. Breast milk:

- Is rich in antibodies to protect the baby from disease, resulting in fewer and milder illnesses and illnesses of a shorter duration.
- Is more easily digested by the baby, resulting in less colic and intestinal problems such as diarrhea and constipation.
- Aids in tissue development and physical maturation. The hormones in breast milk may promote the growth of the gastrointestinal tract and regulate digestive function.
- Adjusts to meet the baby's needs. The level of fat, protein, minerals, and lactose in the milk change to meet the growing baby's nutritional needs.
- Is less expensive than formula.

Breast-feeding does take a little time to "learn," but actually takes less time when you factor in time to buy and prepare formula and bottles. Many nursing moms enjoy the intimate nature of breast-feeding and obtain a great deal of emotional satisfaction from the experience. However, it may require a bit of a lifestyle adjustment until you get used to it. Lactation consultants can provide support.

After you've explored the breast vs. bottle issue, tell your health care provider about your decision before the baby is born. Also, let the hospital staff know your decision when you arrive.

Ideas that Work

- **Breast-feeding:** The "learning period" for breastfeeding can be three to six weeks and varies from woman to woman. Don't get discouraged with this process. If you are getting frustrated or the baby is having difficulty latching on, get immediate, hands-on help from your pediatrician, nurse-midwife, or a lactation nurse.

When you nurse, choose a quiet place so you and your baby can relax and enjoy this time together. Nurse your baby as often as he or she is hungry, usually every two to three hours during the first two to three weeks. Breastfed babies usually eat more frequently than bottle-fed infants because breast milk is digested more quickly than formula. Drink plenty of liquids and eat a well-balanced diet to keep up your supply of milk and to keep yourself healthy.

The most common cause of painful nipples in the first few days of breastfeeding is positioning. Be sure to have the entire nipple and as much of the areola as possible in the baby's mouth. If a breast becomes painful and hot and if you have a fever, you may have a blocked milk duct or a breast infection. Contact your health care provider to treat the problem right away.

- **Bottle-feeding:** Be sure to prepare the formula exactly according to directions. Do not dilute ready-to-feed formula. Keep bottles refrigerated until you're ready to use them so the formula doesn't spoil and make your baby sick. Throw away formula left in the bottle after your baby is done feeding. Don't microwave bottles to warm the formula; they can explode or burn your baby's mouth or esophagus. Test the temperature of the warmed formula on the inside of your wrist to make sure it isn't too hot before you feed it to the baby.

Resources

National Institute of Child Health and Human Development
Building 31, Room 2A32
Bethesda, MD 20892
(301) 496-5133

National Maternal and Child Health Clearinghouse
2070 Chain Bridge Road, Suite 450
Vienna, VA 22182
(703) 821-8955

LaLeche League (breast-feeding information and support): (800) LALECHE

Infant Feeding: Breast or Bottle?

F.Y.I

Breast-feeding and Returning to Work

In recognition of the growing numbers of working mothers who choose to continue nursing their babies after they return to the workplace, some employers designate a room for pumping, provide breast pumps, and have a refrigerator for nursing moms. If your company provides this support, take advantage! Even if your company is not able to offer these benefits, you can still successfully pump at work. The following tips may help:

- **Buy or rent a good breast pump.** Make sure the pump works well for you. Nurse specialists at the hospital in which you delivered or a lactation consultant can make suggestions.

- **Find a quiet, private place to pump at work.** Express your milk during your morning and afternoon breaks.

- **Store your milk.** Bring a small cooler with reusable ice packs to store your milk, or store the milk in a refrigerator in the company lunch room. Breast milk can be refrigerated for up to five days and frozen for up to four months.

- **Wear appropriate clothing.** Shirts and blouses with front openings and a nursing bra will cut down the time it takes to pump your breasts at work. Keep a spare top at work in case your breasts do leak.

- **Maximize your feeding time with your baby.** Breast-feed right before you leave your baby and immediately after getting home.

Resource

Breast-feeding Success for Working Mothers by Marilyn Grams, M.D. Carson City, Nev.: Achievement Press, 1985.

Bed-Wetting

Bed-wetting tends to run in families and it usually is caused by a bladder that has not yet learned to relax, but instead wants to empty itself more quickly. By age 5, 90 percent of children are dry at night. Bed-wetting is considered abnormal if it occurs in girls older than 5 and boys older than 6, or if your child has been dry for at least three to six months.

Unless your child has other physical symptoms or there has been a major change in your child's life, the best thing you can do is be patient and reassure your child that he or she will grow out of this problem. Get him or her involved in the treatment. Do not become angry or punish your child; he or she needs your support to overcome what is probably for him or her an embarrassing occurrence.

Symptoms/Signs

- Involuntary urination at night at least twice a month

Consult Your Doctor If Your Child:

- Was previously dry at night and has other symptoms, such as fever, abdominal pain, increased frequency of urination, painful urination, or blood in urine. He or she may have an infection.
- Has symptoms of diabetes, such as excessive thirst and hunger along with frequent urination.
- Was dry for three to six months before the bed-wetting episode began and HomeCare procedures have not helped.
- Is still wetting the bed and she is older than 5 or he is older than 6, especially if wetting is occurring during the day as well.
- Also has constipation or soils his or her underpants with stool.
- Has a neurological disorder or delay in development (e.g., in walking, talking, or toilet training).
- Is wetting his or her bed due to heavy stress. Psychotherapy may be needed.

Fluids

- Before your child goes to bed, limit the amount of fluids he or she drinks. Encourage intake earlier in the day and evening.
- Don't give your child drinks with caffeine.

Note Well

- Be sure your child urinates before bedtime.
- Don't get your child up at night to go to the bathroom.
- You may try a reward system, for example, a gold star on a calendar for a dry night. However, never punish for an accident.
- If you suspect stress is the cause, encourage your child to talk about what's troubling him or her.
- If your child is over 2 years old, allow him or her to wear training pants instead of diapers. This shows confidence.

Nutrition

- Try eliminating foods that might irritate your child's bladder, such as chocolate, carbonated drinks, juices, and milk.

Colic

Colic is a common problem among infants from about 2 weeks to 3 months of age. A colicky baby's crying spells may last for several hours and tend to occur in late afternoon or evening. Though no one is certain of the cause, colic seems to be associated with abdominal pain. Stomach discomfort can result from swallowing too much air during feeding, an allergic reaction to milk, a sugar intolerance, or from overheated milk.

If you have a colicky baby, all of the people in your household suffer as well. Lost sleep, frustration, and the added stress can make matters much worse. The added tension in your family can even cause your infant to become more irritable. Keeping the household on an even keel may reduce the worst effects of colic. You may get some relief by trying the suggestions outlined in the HomeCare column. Remember, whatever you do, the problem probably will go away within a few months.

Symptoms/Signs

- Extended, recurring episodes of crying in an infant. The baby may draw legs up toward abdomen.

Consult Your Doctor If Your Child:

- Has crying episodes that are accompanied by diarrhea (see page 110) or vomiting (see page 119).
- Has an earache. See page 133.
- Creates stress in your household that becomes overwhelming.
- Has a crying episode that lasts longer than four hours.
- Is more than 4 months old and attacks aren't diminishing.

Nutrition

- Check to see that your baby is being fed enough.
- If you are breast-feeding your baby, avoid highly spiced foods and alcohol.
- Do not rush the feeding of your baby.
- Change the brand of formula or substitute soy milk for cow's milk formula if you suspect your baby is allergic to cow's milk.

Note Well

- Check to see that the nipple hole on your baby's bottle isn't too small. Milk should drip at a rate of one drop per second.
- Rocking, walking, or driving may soothe baby.
- No medications have been proven safe and effective for colic.

Heat/Cold

- Don't overheat your baby's formula. Heat it to body temperature.
- Lay your baby over a hot (not too hot) water bottle on your lap.

Prevention

- Burp your baby after each ounce of milk is taken.

children's health

235

Croup

Croup—an infection of the voice box, windpipe, and bronchial tubes—usually affects children between the ages of 3 months and 5 years. Most of the time, the child has a cold in the days preceding the onset of croup symptoms. Croup usually resolves itself with home treatment within five to seven days. However, symptoms can quickly worsen, so continue home treatment until you're sure your child is rid of the infection and has no symptoms.

Symptoms/Signs

- Loud, seal-like, barking cough
- Increased effort required to breathe
- Wheezing upon breathing in
- Fever
- Hoarseness
- Symptoms worse at night

Get Emergency Medical Care If Your Child:

- Has increasingly labored breathing, a high-pitched whistling or wheezing noise upon inhalation, or breathing that causes the area between the ribs to heave excessively or draw inward during inhalation.
- Gasps for air or breathes with his or her mouth open and chin jutting out.
- Drools excessively or has difficulty swallowing.
- Cannot bend his or her neck forward.
- Has blue lips or skin.
- Has a heart rate exceeding 160 beats per minute.
- Becomes unconscious.
- Shows signs of pneumonia: a fever of 102 degrees F and mucus that is rust-colored or pink and frothy.

Consult Your Doctor If Your Child:

- Is less than 3 months old and has croup symptoms.
- Has a fever of 102 degrees F or higher.
- Becomes very restless or agitated and cannot be calmed.

HOMECARE

If physician referral is not recommended at this time, try the following self-care procedures:

Heat/Cold

- Use a cold steam vaporizer or have child breathe cool night air.
- If this is not effective, turn on a hot shower, close the bathroom door for 10 minutes, then bring your child into the bathroom; remain in the steam for 10 to 20 minutes.

Medication

- Use acetaminophen to reduce fever and discomfort.*
- For certain types of infection, your child's doctor may prescribe antibiotics.

Fluids

- Have your child drink clear, warm liquids to loosen mucus.

Rest

- Help your child sleep in an upright or semi-reclined position, if lying down appears to make breathing more difficult. For infants, use a safety seat or swing, or hold your child while he or she sleeps.

Note Well

- Do your best to remain calm; your child will be very frightened and agitated and needs your reassurance that he or she will be OK.
- Don't allow anyone to smoke in the same house as a child with croup.
- Sleep in the same room with your child until croup symptoms are gone; symptoms can quickly worsen and require immediate medical attention.

* Because of the risk of Reye's syndrome, aspirin should not be given to or used by children or teenagers who have or are suspected of having flu or chicken pox. Use acetaminophen.

Crying

....

Crying is an expression of displeasure. Just as adults vary in their tendency to cry, each child responds differently in various situations. Crying can be a healthy and necessary way to resolve inner upsets.

Infants have no other way to communicate when things aren't going well for them. Most often, the issue is something as simple as hunger, dirty diapers, or a loud noise. Correcting the problem usually stops the crying.

A special type of crying occurs during the "fussy period." This is most common during the first three or four months of life, often beginning by 2 weeks of age. Typically, an otherwise happy baby will have daily (usually around the same time of day) episodes of crying. These episodes can last several minutes to several hours. Because many of these babies seem to get tense abdomens and appear to double up in pain, the affliction is commonly called "colic." Over time, these episodes will lessen. Refer to "Colic," on page 235, for more on this fussiness.

"Temper tantrums" bring on a great deal of crying in toddlers and preschoolers. The tantrum usually is an expression of anger or frustration over a general lack of control over things. Depending on the parent's reaction to this type of behavior, it may become an effective, but unhealthy, method for a child to "get his or her way" when conflict arises. Typically, the best response is to ignore the tantrum and let it run its course, unless you need to physically restrain your child from hurting himself or herself or others. Do not reward and encourage this behavior by indulging the child. Teach your child to express feelings verbally rather than physically.

Consult Your Doctor If Your Child:

- Has symptoms other than crying that require medical care. (Refer to those symptoms in this book for evaluation and treatment.)
- Has an unusually persistent crying spell.
- Has severe, persistent tantrums.

HOMECARE
If physician referral is not recommended at this time, try the following self-care procedures:

Note Well

- Check for obvious sources of pain: an open diaper pin, clothing that's too tight, areas of injury to the body, a red eye (children can scratch their corneas or eyeballs easily), a small hair tightly wrapped around a finger or toe.
- Try feeding, burping, rocking, comforting. If cramping seems to be the problem, try laying the child on his or her stomach, across a warm (not hot) pad on your lap.
- Remain calm. A baby or a child in the midst of a tantrum may become even more upset if the parents are very upset and anxious.
- If this is a recurring fussy period or a tantrum, all underlying causes have been eliminated, and the treatment recommended above is unsuccessful, place the child in his or her bed. Keep the room and house quiet. Allow the child to "wind down" alone.

Medication

- If the child has had very hard stools recently or has not had a stool for a day or two, an infant-size glycerin suppository can be safely inserted into the rectum to induce a bowel movement.

Nutrition

- If you are breast-feeding, try a bland diet and avoid foods that often cause gas. Avoid all alcohol and caffeine.
- For your bottle-fed baby, try a soy-based formula for four to five days.

Prevention

- Try to maintain a regular feeding and sleeping schedule. Hungry, tired children are fussier and more apt to throw tantrums.

Diaper Rash

Nearly every baby will get diaper rash now and then. Combine an infant's sensitive skin and the irritating nature of urine and feces and you have the perfect recipe for a sore, red bottom. Given the usual cause—not changing diapers often or quickly enough after wetting or soiling—most of the treatment and preventive measures you can take are pretty self-evident: Do what you can to keep your baby dry.

Sometimes there is a little more to a rash in the diaper area. Yeast infections, harsh detergents used for washing diapers, and other irritants also can cause a rash. If you try basic care for diaper rash and don't notice improvement, consider another course of action. Change detergents, try a barrier cream (avoid powders, which can be a health hazard when inhaled by your baby) with every diaper change for two weeks, or—probably best of all—leave your baby's bottom uncovered for a while each day, whenever it's convenient for you.

Symptoms/Signs

- Red, blotchy (sometimes raised) patches on buttocks, thighs, and genitals

Consult Your Doctor If Your Child:

- Has diaper rash that contains blisters or crusty areas.
- Has a diaper rash with bright red spots that together form a solid red area with a scalloped border.
- Has a diaper rash that shows no improvement after two days of home treatment.

Clean

- Change diaper frequently.
- During each diaper change, use plain water or mild soapy water and a soft cotton cloth or cotton balls to clean baby's bottom. Pat dry with a soft cloth. Avoid disposable baby wipes that contain alcohol.

Cover

- Avoid bulky diapers that can create a "hot-house" effect next to baby's skin.
- Try to give your baby a good deal of diaper-free time each day. Fresh air works wonders on diaper rash.

Medication

- Though it may slow healing, you can try an over-the-counter diaper rash cream or ointment with zinc oxide.

Prevention

- Change diapers as soon as you know they are wet or soiled.
- Use a mild detergent to wash diapers. Double rinse if child already has a rash.
- If you use cloth diapers, opt for more breathable diaper covers than plastic or rubber pants.
- Be sure that diaper does not fit your baby too snugly; a baby's bottom needs room to breathe.
- If your baby is especially prone to diaper rash, use a barrier cream (e.g., A&D Ointment®, Balmex®, Desitin®) with each diaper change to keep moisture away from skin.

Head Lice

No matter how clean you keep your child and your child's surroundings, it's almost inevitable that you'll have to fight at least one battle with head lice. Children are most susceptible because they spend so much time in close proximity to one another, and they're more likely than adults to share combs, brushes, hats, and clothing. Getting rid of lice on your child and in your home requires quick recognition of the problem and immediate, full-scale treatment of everything the lice could have come in contact with.

First, make a diagnosis. Head lice are small (1/8 to 1/4 inch), yellow-gray bugs with six legs. They are easiest to spot at the nape of the neck or near the ears. Female lice lay tiny, round, white eggs (called "nits") on individual hairs, which are very difficult to remove. Eggs hatch in about 10 days and the lice live by sucking blood from your child's scalp; it's the bugs' saliva that causes the intense itching. Sometimes, a scaly rash forms on the scalp. At the first sign of itching, inspect for lice and eggs.

If you find evidence of lice, immediately begin home treatment. Any type of lice infestation may require more than one round of home treatment; be persistent for 10 days after you think you've licked the problem.

Symptoms/Signs

• Intense itching of the scalp
• Tiny, red bite marks
• Lice on scalp, clothing, hats, or bedding
• Nits on hair shafts

Consult Your Doctor If Your Child:

• Still has lice after HomeCare procedures are followed.

Medication

• Use over-the-counter shampoos or lotions, such as NIX® or RID®, to kill lice and nits. Follow directions very carefully. Repeat as needed.
• Ask your doctor about a prescription for Kwell® head lice shampoo if over-the-counter preparations are not working well.

Note Well

• Use tweezers or a fine-toothed comb (usually provided with over-the-counter shampoos) to remove lice and nits from your child's hair shaft. If this doesn't work well, try soaking hair in a solution of equal amounts of water and vinegar. Follow this with a shower and shampoo.

Clean

• Wash all clothing, towels, hats, scarves, bedding, combs, and brushes that have been used since the infestation. Use hot water and a disinfecting detergent. Repeat as needed.

Activity

• Keep your child at home until at least one treatment with medicated shampoo has been completed.

Prevention

• Don't let your child use other children's combs or brushes, or wear their hats or jackets.
• Check your child's hair and scalp regularly for signs of lice and their eggs, especially during peak season (August–November).

children's health

239

Mumps

The mumps, a common childhood disease before widespread immunization against it, causes the salivary glands below the ear to swell. If you can't feel your child's jawbone, he or she probably has the mumps. Occurring most often in children ages 2 to 12, the symptoms rarely last more than two weeks. If your child does have the mumps, concentrate on symptom relief; the virus has to run its course. Your child will be contagious for about one week prior to and two weeks after the appearance of symptoms. *Adolescent and adult males who have not had the mumps and have not been immunized against it should avoid a child with mumps due to the risk of complications such as sterility.*

Symptoms/Signs

- One or both of the salivary glands (located below and in front of the ears) are swollen. Other symptoms include low-grade fever, loss of appetite, muscle aches, headache, pain behind ear upon chewing or swallowing, and/or fatigue.

Consult Your Doctor If Your Child:

- Has headache, stiff neck, lethargy, convulsions, or aversion to light after developing mumps.
- Has upper abdominal pain, nausea, or vomiting after developing mumps.

HOMECARE
If physician referral is not recommended at this time, try the following self-care procedures:

Fluids

- Provide your child with plenty of fluids to prevent dehydration and soothe sore glands.

Rest

- Your child should rest in bed while he or she has a fever.

Heat/Cold

- Provide ice packs or a heating pad for swollen glands.

Medication

- Give your child acetaminophen to relieve fever and discomfort, if needed.*

Activity

- Keep your child home, away from others, while he or she is contagious.

Prevention

- Have your child vaccinated against mumps. See page 44.
- If your child is exposed to someone with the mumps and does not have immunities against it, see his or her doctor within 24 hours for a vaccine.

* Because of the risk of Reye's syndrome, aspirin should not be given to or used by children or teenagers who have or are suspected of having flu or chicken pox. Use acetaminophen.

Seizure/Convulsion

A seizure (convulsion) can be extremely frightening for any parent, but it can be especially troubling when a child has one for the first time. A seizure in a child who has never had one before typically is the result of a spiking fever. Overheating causes misfiring of electrical impulses in the brain. These febrile seizures usually occur in children 6 months to 5 years old, often before parents are even aware that a child is ill, are short-lived (less than five minutes in duration), and leave no lasting effect. Susceptibility to seizure tends to run in families.

If a convulsion does occur, your primary goal is to prevent your child from injuring himself or herself and inhaling vomit. **If poisoning (see page 96) or an infection could be the cause, seek emergency help.**

As soon as your child has recovered fully from a convulsion and is alert, do what you can to keep the fever down (if present, refer to page 113) and keep him or her comfortable. He or she probably will be very sleepy. Write down the details of the convulsion—duration, physical movements, body temperature, etc.—and report them to your physician.

Symptoms/Signs

- Rigid body, clenched fists and jaw, twitching in limbs or face
- Eyes rolling back in head
- Excessive salivation
- Possibly, unconsciousness

Consult Your Doctor Immediately If Your Child:

- Has never had a seizure before.
- Has a seizure that lasts for more than a few minutes.
- Is less than 6 months old or is more than 5 years old and has a seizure.
- Has a seizure that is not associated with a fever.
- Has a fever of 102 degrees F or higher that you cannot reduce.
- Has a seizure after taking a prescribed medicine.

HOMECARE
If physician referral is not recommended at this time, try the following self-care procedures:

Note Well

During a seizure, do the following:
- Lay child on a soft/padded surface to avoid self-injury. Do not restrain.
- If your child vomits, turn his or her head to the side to prevent choking.
- Keep your child's mouth clear of all objects. There's no danger he or she will "swallow" his or her tongue.
- **After** a seizure, begin resuscitation (page 92 or 93) if breathing and pulse do not resume.

Medication

- Use acetaminophen to reduce and control fever.

Heat/Cold

- Use cool (not cold) compresses or a tepid sponge bath to cool your child slowly. Never put your child in a bathtub during a convulsion.
- Do not use ice baths or packs; body temperature will fall too quickly.

Cover

- As you try to bring the fever down, remove your child's clothes. After the fever is under control, dress the child lightly.

- After the convulsion is over and your child is alert, give clear, cool (not ice-cold) fluids.

Fluids

Prevention

- Reduce fevers of 102 degrees F and higher: Use acetaminophen or children's ibuprofen and tepid baths.

Tonsillitis

Just a generation ago, doctors regularly removed tonsils from children who had occasional bouts of tonsillitis because they thought tonsils served no real function. More recently, research has shown that tonsils really are infection catchers—the first line of defense against more serious respiratory infection, that is. Quite simply, tonsillitis is the inflammation of the tonsils due to infection. If the tonsils weren't there, the infection would settle in elsewhere.

Most common in children aged 5 to 15, tonsillitis usually goes away within five to seven days of the first symptoms. HomeCare can alleviate many of the symptoms, which can be easily mistaken for those of flu or a cold-flu combination. But often, a bacterial infection such as strep is the culprit, warranting treatment with antibiotics to keep the infection from spreading to other areas. Only in recurrent cases, where a child experiences multiple (three or more), severe infections within a 12-month period, will a doctor consider a tonsillectomy (removal of the tonsils).

Symptoms/Signs

- Severe sore throat, often with difficulty swallowing
- Fever, possibly accompanied by chills
- Headache
- Fatigue or lethargy
- Swollen, tender glands of the jaw and throat
- Dark red and swollen tonsils, possibly with white specks, streaks, or spots

Consult Your Doctor If Your Child:

- Has difficulty breathing.
- Has symptoms of tonsillitis that do not improve after 48 hours, especially if accompanied by a high fever (see fever guidelines on page 113).
- Has symptoms of tonsillitis and a history of recurrent tonsillitis.
- Has a sore throat that worsens, especially on one side, despite the use of antibiotics.

H O M E C A R E
If physician referral is not recommended at this time, try the following self-care procedures:

Medication

- If your child has tonsillitis resulting from a streptococcal infection, his or her doctor probably will prescribe antibiotics that are to be taken for at least 10 days.
- Use acetaminophen to reduce fever and relieve discomfort.*

Fluids

- Have your child drink plenty of clear, warm liquids to relieve throat pain.

Rest

- Your child should get plenty of bed rest to help his or her body fight infection. He or she should remain home from school until fever is gone and symptoms are improving.

Note Well

- If your child is old enough, have him or her gargle often with warm salt water.

Prevention

- Teach your child to wash his or her hands with soap and water after direct contact with others, especially during cold and flu season.
- Keep your child away from others with colds and sore throats.

* Because of the risk of Reye's syndrome, aspirin should not be given to or used by children or teenagers who have or are suspected of having flu or chicken pox. Use acetaminophen.

Special Health Issues

By using this section you will learn:

- About treatment options for specific health conditions.

- How to manage common health problems through appropriate treatment options.

- About key questions you should consider when talking to your doctor.

Alzheimer's Disease

Alzheimer's disease currently affects more than four million Americans. It is a costly disease both in terms of personal functioning and medical services. The average duration of Alzheimer's disease is eight years. More than 70 percent of individuals with less severe symptoms are cared for at home at an estimated cost of more than $12,000 per year. The cost for nursing home care is double this amount, and most individuals end up spending some time in a nursing home.

Q. What is Alzheimer's disease?

A. Alzheimer's disease is a condition that damages the brain cells responsible for intellectual functioning in the brain, including memory, intelligence, judgment, and speech.

Q. What causes Alzheimer's disease?

A. Alzheimer's is a neurological disease caused by a loss of brain cells as well as changes in the cerebral cortex (the outer layer of the brain) where an accumulation of tangled fibers and/or plaques around nerves forms. Why these abnormalities develop in the brain has not been determined. It is not thought to be caused by hardening of the arteries, nor is there any evidence that it is contagious. There do appear to be different genetic and non-genetic causes. For example, some genes cause the disease to appear early in life while other genes predispose a person to the disease but require a trigger such as stroke, head trauma, or clogged arteries. Research techniques in the areas of histology, virology, immunology, toxicology, and biochemistry are being used by researchers to determine the actual cause of Alzheimer's disease.

In the meantime, research continues to provide hope. For example, anti-inflammatory drugs such as ibuprofen appear to reduce the risk of Alzheimer's disease. (However, chronic use of these drugs can lead to such serious side effects as peptic ulcers and impaired kidney function, so clinical trials are needed.) High doses of vitamin E also appear to delay the progression of the disease.

Q. What are the risks to my health if I get Alzheimer's disease?

A. This disease can cause individuals to have trouble concentrating and making decisions. They may feel disoriented and lose the ability to recall words or form sentences. Later, there may be paranoia and extreme depression. There may be risks to personal safety as these intellectual and personality changes may cause individuals to wander away from home and get lost. In the disease's final stages, the Alzheimer's patient may become completely dependent upon others for all aspects of daily living.

Q. What are the common symptoms?

A. Alzheimer's disease develops slowly. At first the individual has only minor memory loss and occasional disorientation. Gradually, the person becomes more forgetful, especially about recent events. Things may be misplaced. The water faucet may be left on. The individual may ask previously answered questions. As memory loss increases, confusion, irritability, restlessness, and agitation appear. Speech, judgment, and orientation may be affected.

Depression is common, especially in the early stages of the disease, and may be brought on by the diagnosis of Alzheimer's, the social isolation, the awareness of the loss of physical or mental abilities, or changes in brain chemistry. Unfortunately, depression can make mental challenges more difficult and can increase the patient's sense of isolation. See "Depression," pages 264-265.

Alzheimer's Disease

Q. What should I do if I suspect that I might have Alzheimer's disease?

A. If your memory loss does not interfere with your activities of daily living, you probably do not have the disease. All of us forget things once in awhile and some slowing of memory is a normal consequence of aging. Ninety percent of individuals past the age of 65 do NOT have Alzheimer's disease. However, if you have doubts or concerns, discuss them with your doctor.

Q. How is a diagnosis made?

A. There is no single definitive test for this disease. Before a diagnosis of Alzheimer's disease is made, other illnesses and adverse drug reactions that may cause memory loss must be ruled out since many of these disorders can be treated. Comprehensive physical, neurological, and psychiatric evaluations are done. After other diseases are ruled out, a diagnosis of Alzheimer's usually can be made based on medical history, mental status, and the course of the illness.

Q. What treatments are used for individuals with this disease?

A. There is no prevention or cure for this disease, but proper care can reduce some of the symptoms. The person should stay under the care of a physician who can monitor the course of the disease and treat any other ailments that could complicate the disease.

The U.S. Food and Drug Administration has approved two drugs to treat Alzheimer's: Cognex® (tacrine) and Aricept® (donepezil). Though not cures, these drugs relieve some of the memory impairment and other symptoms associated with Alzheimer's in some patients. Patients or their caregivers should weigh the benefits versus the potential side effects: liver damage, nausea, vomiting, diarrhea, abdominal pain, indigestion, and skin rash. Other medications may help reduce anxiety and depression and improve sleep patterns. In addition, preliminary studies suggest that estrogen therapy may improve memory and attention span in women with Alzheimer's. Other studies indicate that vitamin E and the Parkinson's disease drug selegiline hydrochloride can slow the progression of the disease.

Proper nutrition and fluid intake are important, but special diets and supplements usually are not needed. Activities should be kept as close to normal as possible. A constant environment may help decrease the effects of memory loss. As the disease progresses and the individual needs more care, a nursing home setting may be necessary.

Family and friends should maintain contact with the doctor so they can know how to best support the Alzheimer's patient. Family members also may benefit from support groups for families and friends of people with Alzheimer's disease.

Important Questions to Keep in Mind

Note: The following questions may be appropriate for the caregiver rather than the victim.

- Are regular checkups needed, or should I see my doctor only when I am having a problem?
- What can I do to slow the disease's progress? What should I eat? Should I exercise?
- What medications will I be taking? How long will I need to take this drug(s) before I feel its effects? Will this drug affect the other drugs I take? How?
- Are there any new treatment options we could try? What are the benefits? Risks? Costs?
- How can I make my home/environment safer?
- What support groups or organizations are available to help me (or the family) cope with Alzheimer's disease? How can I contact them?
- What happens if I do nothing? What are the risks? Are there any benefits to this approach?

245

Arthritis

· ·

Every minute, two more people are diagnosed with arthritis. That translates into more than a million new cases every year. The Arthritis Foundation estimates that 37 million Americans suffer from arthritis, a disabling disease that strikes half of people aged 65 or older.

Arthritis is a disease as old as mankind, but one thing is certain: Exercise, weight management, and drug therapy all can work together to ease the pain of this condition and increase mobility and flexibility in those with the disease.

While it may seem natural for you to have the blues and to feel down if you have arthritis, in one or more of its various forms, it's not healthy when depressive symptoms are more severe, longer lasting, and more disabling. Frustration at not being able to perform your usual activities may cause you to withdraw from them entirely. This sense of isolation can be increased if you also are facing depression. The good news is that depression can be successfully treated. See "Depression," pages 264-265.

Q. What is arthritis?

A. Arthritis is an inflammatory disease of the joints. There are more than 100 different kinds of arthritis. The most common are:

- **Osteoarthritis** occurs when the cartilage surrounding a joint breaks down. Most people feel osteoarthritis in the knees and hips, but it can affect the back and fingers as well. Individuals who have spent a career overusing one or more of their joints (e.g., construction workers, athletes, dancers, miners) have a greater chance of developing osteoarthritis than the rest of the population does.
- **Rheumatoid arthritis** is less common and more baffling than osteoarthritis. The disease can appear at any age, but most new patients are women between the ages of 20 and 50. Unlike osteoarthritis, rheumatoid arthritis is a disease of

the immune system. The body's defenses attack tissue surrounding the joint; the body then replaces it with new, different tissue that can eventually lock up the joint.

- **Gout** is caused by a buildup of uric acid crystals in the fluid that bathes the joint, causing severe pain and swelling in that joint.
- **Ankylosing spondylitis** is a degeneration of the joints that support and are part of the spinal column.

Q. What causes this disease? How will I know if I am at risk for arthritis?

A. Arthritis is an inflammation of the joint. In osteoarthritis, the inflammation is caused by the overuse or abuse of joints over a period of time. In rheumatoid arthritis, the immune system plays a role. Certain foods and hormonal changes can trigger arthritis also. Much is still to be learned about exactly how all these factors work together to cause this disease. Heredity seems to be a factor because arthritis seems to run in families. Women are generally affected three times more often than men. Age also is a risk factor.

Q. What are the common symptoms of arthritis?

A. The symptoms of arthritis are clear: stiffness, difficulty moving joints through their full range of motion, and swelling or redness in affected areas. Rheumatoid arthritis sufferers also may have extreme fatigue, weight loss, increasingly more deformed joints, and loss of appetite.

Q. What do I do if I suspect I have arthritis?

A. The symptoms may be relieved by getting enough rest, doing stretching and range of motion exercises each day, and maintaining your ideal weight. Aspirin and hot and cold treatments can relieve minor discomfort.

Arthritis

You should call your doctor if you have arthritis pain with fever, if there is sudden unexplained swelling, redness or pain in any joint, if the pain is so great that you cannot use the joint or if it limits your regular activities, or if the problem does not get better after five to six weeks and home care is not working. Also, don't be afraid to ask your care provider to review the self-care options listed above in greater detail.

Q. What are the common diagnostic tests for arthritis?

A. A diagnosis of arthritis is made by physical examination of the joints, a history of arthritis-like symptoms, X-rays, examination of joint fluids, and, for some forms of arthritis, blood tests.

Q. What treatment options are available to me?

A. Fortunately, the three most common prescriptions for arthritis cost very little. Losing weight takes stress off of affected joints. Exercise—even just walking for half an hour every day—can strengthen muscles around the joints and can improve joint motion dramatically, particularly in those with knee osteoarthritis. And the drugs of choice—aspirin, ibuprofen (e.g., Advil®, Motrin®)—cost just pennies a day. Over-the-counter preparations containing capsaicin, camphor, or menthol may help relieve minor joint pain and stiffness. For more severe cases, doctors may recommend corticosteroid injections to fight inflammation. As well, research indicates that an intake of at least 386 units of vitamin D each day can keep knee osteoarthritis in check.

Sometimes people with rheumatoid arthritis find that more rigorous drug therapy or surgery is necessary to slow the progression of the disease and ease pain. Drugs that regulate the immune system, along with corticosteroids, often are prescribed, but their side effects can be serious.

Immune-regulating drugs can suppress the entire immune system, leaving individuals at risk for other infections. Corticosteroids administered over a long period of time can cause bone to thin and can increase the incidence of diabetes and cataracts. Promising research offers hope: Tests have demonstrated that two experimental drugs have provided relief to rheumatoid arthritis sufferers by inhibiting the action of a substance that is released by inflammatory cells in the body and that causes severe pain and swelling.

Unfortunately, a $1 billion "quack cure" industry attracts many arthritis patients. Radon gas treatments, copper bracelets, and electric wands are only a few of the unproven—sometimes even potentially dangerous—treatments every arthritis patient should avoid.

Important Questions to Keep in Mind

- What side effects should I watch for with the medications prescribed for arthritis pain? Do I need to take them with food?
- Is it important to limit or avoid drinking alcohol when taking some of these medications? Why?
- Are creams effective for relieving the pain of arthritis? How do they work? What are the advantages and disadvantages of creams over oral medications? Are they right for me?
- What other things can I do to relieve the pain of arthritis aside from taking medications?
- When is physical therapy helpful? Are there things I can do on my own that also will help?
- What is the best exercise to help my arthritis? How much? How often?
- Where can I get information to help me eat a healthy diet and manage my weight?
- If joint replacement surgery is recommended, what should I expect?
- What assistive devices are available (e.g., canes, faucet turners, extended handles on tool, etc.) to help me with daily activities and to take pressure off my affected joints?

247

Asthma

Asthma is a chronic, life-threatening illness that kills more than 5,000 people each year and affects more than 12 million people in the United States. Over the past decade, asthma cases have been on the rise, particularly among children and teen-agers younger than age 18. Though it cannot be cured, asthma is a chronic condition that can be controlled. It's important for asthma sufferers to work with their doctor to develop a treatment plan that prevents or relieves symptoms. The alternative is to risk a potentially fatal episode. *It's a good idea to carry medical identification such as a medic alert bracelet or wallet card at all times.*

Q. What is asthma?

A. Asthma is an upper respiratory condition caused by a tightening of the muscles and swelling of the lining in the small breathing tubes (bronchioles) of the lungs. This tightening, called bronchospasm, causes labored breathing as the airways become narrowed and restrict air flow. Also, the inflamed breathing tubes produce excess mucus, which further restricts breathing.

Q. What causes asthma?

A. Asthma symptoms usually are triggered by agents that a person is sensitive to. Common triggers include infections such as the common cold and influenza, things a person is allergic to (e.g., pollens, molds, dust, animal dander, certain foods), cold air, tobacco smoke, strenuous exercise, air pollution from industrial and auto emissions, pesticides, chemical fumes, drugs (e.g., aspirin, heart medications), and stress. Roach infestation also has been linked to asthma attacks.

Q. Who is at greatest risk for asthma?

A. Asthma is more common in children than adults, with about 30 percent of children outgrowing this problem before they reach adulthood. Also, asthma seems to run in families. The most important thing to remember is that asthma at any age is a serious health condition that requires a doctor's care.

Q. What are the common symptoms of asthma?

A. Symptoms of an asthma attack may start immediately or take a long time to develop. In turn, symptoms can be severe, moderate, or mild. Typical symptoms of mild to moderate asthma attacks include labored breathing (wheezing), shortness of breath, tightness in the chest, coughing, and spitting up mucus. When an attack happens, it's important to take asthma medication and watch your symptoms. If symptoms do not clear up in the time your doctor has told you they should, or your symptoms get worse, call your doctor.

In the case of a severe attack, symptoms may include the inability to catch your breath or feeling breathless, you may have a hard time talking, fingernails may be bluish or grayish, neck muscles may be tight, and the chest muscles (between the ribs) may feel sucked in and tight. If you experience these symptoms of a severe attack, it's important to take asthma medication immediately and seek emergency medical care as soon as possible.

Approximately 12 to 15 percent of the general population experience exercise-induced asthma (EIA), a condition in which an increase in air resis-

Asthma

tance occurs after a few minutes of exercise. Common symptoms of EIA include tightness in the chest, shortness of breath, wheezing, coughing, fatigue, and difficulty recovering after exercise. However, EIA should not be a reason not to exercise since physical activity helps build and maintain lung function. In fact, many professional and Olympic athletes have EIA and with proper medical supervision have excelled in their respective sports.

Q. What do doctors mean by "the second wave"?

A. The second wave is a condition in which the air tubes continue to swell, even without symptoms for some people, after an initial asthma attack has eased. This reaction can last for days or for weeks and make the lungs more sensitive to triggers. A second-wave attack can be more severe and life-threatening than the first attack. Medical supervision may be required in order to monitor the condition and avoid a more serious attack.

Q. How is a diagnosis made?

A. If you or a family member has any sign of an asthma attack, it's important that you see your doctor. Your doctor will take a medical history to see if you have another health problem that may mimic asthma, such as allergies or an upper respiratory infection. Other tests that usually are done include a physical exam with lung function tests that measure your "breathing efficiency." Lab tests might include chest X-rays, further pulmonary tests, blood work (e.g., complete blood count), urinalysis, sputum test, or other evaluations such as allergy tests (if there's an indication of an allergic attack).

Q. How can an asthmatic monitor his or her condition?

A. Outside of symptoms, an asthma sufferer can tell if his or her airways are narrowing before an attack by using a peak flow meter. This hand-held device measures lung efficiency. By blowing into the device, a user can tell if his or her "lung power" is decreasing, thus signaling a potential asthma attack.

Q. What is available to treat asthma?

A. There is no cure for asthma, but day-to-day management can help prevent or reduce symptoms. First, it's important that individuals be under their doctor's supervision because asthmatic attacks can be life-threatening if left untreated. Depending on the severity of symptoms, there are many treatment options:

• **You can reduce your exposure** to agents that trigger asthmatic attacks. This may include allergens or environmental agents such as smoke, solvents, and air pollution.

• **Medications** such as cromolyn and nedocromil or corticosteroids are anti-inflammatories and help prevent asthmatic attacks from occurring. These drugs are dispensed through inhalers, pills, or shots. Another class of drugs—bronchodilators—are used to help relax bronchial tubes after an asthma attack has begun, thus making breathing easier. These drugs are available as pills or inhalers or come in liquid form.

For severe attacks your doctor may give you an injection of epinephrine (adrenaline), which provides short-term relief. Your doctor also may teach you how to self-administer epinephrine at home in case of emergency.

• **Self-care practices,** such as drinking plenty of water or breathing in warm, moist air, can relieve breathing problems. Regular aerobic exercise such as brisk walking and swimming can help build lung capacity. However, medications may need to be taken before exercising to help open up airways.

- **Hyposensitization therapy** (allergy shots) exposes a person to certain allergens in small amounts over a number of years. The person's system becomes less sensitive to certain allergens, thus reducing the chances of an asthmatic attack.

- **Counseling and stress management techniques** can help individuals whose asthmatic attacks are triggered or complicated by emotional triggers. Medications can be prescribed to reduce agitation, anxiety, and unpredictable behavior as well as to improve sleep.

Q. If I have asthma, what's the best way to control it?

A. The American Lung Association recommends three things:

1. See your doctor on a regular basis. Share with him or her any changes in your symptoms, reactions to your medications, and any new triggers that cause symptoms.

2. Take your asthma medications as directed by your doctor. *Don't stop taking your medication, even if you feel well.*

3. Stay informed about asthma. Learn about asthma triggers and how you may avoid them. Also, be sure that your family understands what asthma is, its symptoms, and how to provide emergency care if you cannot do it yourself.

Important Questions to Keep in Mind

- What agents or situations trigger my attacks?
- How can I avoid these triggers?
- What do I need to do when an asthma attack occurs?
- What medications should I carry at all times?
- Are my symptoms caused by certain allergens? What are they?
- If I'm allergic to certain things, should I consider hyposensitization therapy?
- What medications will I be taking? How should they be taken? What are the possible side effects? Will this drug affect the other drugs I take? How?
- How do I use a peak flow meter to monitor my condition? What are indication measures of a potential attack?
- How long does each drug take to relieve my symptoms? What should I do if my symptoms don't go away in the expected time?
- I hear that exercise is good for me, yet I have trouble breathing when I work out. What do I need to do in order to make exercise safe? For example, do I need to take medication before I start exercising?
- Where can I get information on how to make my home and environment safer for me?
- What support groups or organizations are available to help me cope with asthma? How can I contact them?

Back Pain

B ack pain is a common health problem. It's estimated that 70 to 80 percent of all adults have had at least one episode of back pain in their lives. Each year, 100 million people in this country suffer from back pain. In fact, backaches are one of the most common reasons for a visit to the doctor.

Q. What places a person at risk for back pain?

A. There are a number of factors that increase risk: a sedentary lifestyle, being overweight, heavy tobacco use, disc degeneration, stress, poor work posture, poor lifting techniques, vibration from vehicles and machinery, and aging.

Q. What causes back pain?

A. Back problems can involve the discs (cushioning pads between the vertebrae), back muscles, or ligaments. Most lower back pain is due to the spasm of the muscles that support the spinal column. Overstretching these muscles can strain them. Very few back problems are caused by a "slipped disc," where the disc bulges out and irritates the nerve roots.

In the older adult, back pain also can be caused by arthritis (see pages 246-247) or osteoporosis (see pages 273-274).

Q. Am I likely to experience any symptoms other than pain in my back?

A. Symptoms may range from aching and soreness to severe pain which may limit your ability to move and perform your daily activities. Arthritis pain may be a steady ache. Pain from strains and sprains to your back are acute and sharp. Osteoporosis pain usually has a quite sudden onset. There may be no clear reason for or incident that may have caused the pain.

Q. What should I do if I experience back pain?

A. First, there are several things you should NOT do. In most cases, excessive bed rest (i.e., more than two days) usually is the worst thing you can do. The second is excessive use of prescription medications (such as Percodan® or Percocet®) for pain management. More than half of back injuries heal within one week, and more than two-thirds in one month. You may get well if you do nothing more than do simple back exercises, control your activity (e.g., avoid lifting and twisting), and limit medication use.

However, there are times when you should consult your doctor for your back pain, such as if you:

- **sustain an injury from a fall or being hit in the back and are unable to move your legs (stay still and call for emergency help).**
- have pain or numbness that moves from your back into your leg or foot.
- have pain that is severe even though you can still move.
- experience low back pain that happens with other physical symptoms such as painful or frequent urination, flu, gastrointestinal distress, or abdominal pain.
- feel low back pain associated with loss of control of bladder or bowels.
- have tried self-care procedures and they fail to provide relief after 72 hours.
- find that your low back pain is associated with weakness of any muscles in the leg or foot.

Q. How can the doctor know what is causing my back pain? Will tests be done to find out the cause?

A. The doctor will ask you questions about your symptoms—what they are like, how and

251

when they started—as part of a comprehensive medical history. The doctor also may do a physical exam focusing on the back and spine. You may be asked to show how much range of motion you have. If you have symptoms such as weakness, numbness, or tingling in your extremities, the doctor also may perform a neurological exam such as testing the reflexes in your lower extremities. Finally, X-rays may be done to help the doctor diagnose the cause of your back pain.

Q. How is back pain treated?

A. The best way to treat back problems is to prevent them in the first place. Back problems can be avoided through good lifting techniques, sleeping on a firm mattress, maintaining good posture, controlling your weight, not smoking, participating in regular exercise, and doing regular stretching exercises.

If back pain does not require a doctor's attention, self-care treatments may include limiting activity, resting on a firm surface with your back flat, applying ice packs, and taking aspirin or ibuprofen as directed to reduce pain and inflammation.

Your doctor also may prescribe muscle relaxants, anti-inflammatory drugs, and pain relievers, or refer you to a physical therapist for a series of treatments.

Only a small percentage of patients require back surgery, such as the removal of a herniated disc. If surgery is recommended, it is important to ask sensible questions about available options and the costs, benefits, and risks of each option. Also, a second opinion from another specialist may be advisable before consenting to surgery.

Important Questions to Keep in Mind

- What are the options for treating my back pain? What are the risks of each? Benefits?
- If surgery is indicated in my case, what are the benefits of having this procedure done? Are there risks? What is the cost? Success rate? Must it be done immediately or can it be delayed? How long? What will happen if I choose not to have surgery?
- Will I need rehabilitation? How much and how long? Will I have to eliminate or change the level of activity in my life?
- How much medication is too much? How will I know if I am taking too much?
- Is exercise helpful for my back pain?
- What can I do to prevent episodes of back pain from recurring?
- Where can I get help for making lifestyle changes such as weight control, exercise, stress management, or stopping smoking?
- What happens if I do nothing? What is the likelihood of the back injury healing itself or of the pain going away? How long might this take?

Back Care

· ·

Did you know that four out of five people experience some sort of back pain during their lifetime?

Back injuries can be caused by overexertion, poor posture, jarring from motor vehicles, slips and falls, stress, excessive body weight, and lack of exercise. The leading cause of back injuries is improper lifting techniques.

The following ideas and exercises will help you keep your back healthy and, if you have a back problem, will help you manage it. *(If you do have a back problem, consult with your doctor before you try any of the exercises on page 255.)*

Ideas that Work

- **Improve your backspring: stay active.**
  - Try to exercise three to five days per week, with aerobic activities such as brisk walking, swimming, cycling, and jogging. See "Walking," pages 6-7.
  - Keep your abdominal and lower back muscles strong. See page 255.
  - Warm up with simple stretches before you do lifting or twisting movements. See the exercises on pages 10-12.
- **Take off that extra weight, especially around your middle.** Maintain your ideal weight by eating less fat and staying active. See "Watching Your Weight" on pages 22-23.
- **Relax.** Learn and practice relaxation techniques to help prevent or reduce stress and tension. See pages 33-34.
- **Sleep on a firm mattress.** If your mattress is too soft, try putting a sheet of plywood under it or purchasing an orthopedic mattress.
- **Reduce your load.** Avoid lifting and carrying loads that are too heavy, especially if the object is bulky and hard to keep close to your body. Lighten the load and take more trips, use a hand-cart, or ask for help.

- **Take a break.** If you sit or stand for extended periods of time, take hourly stretch breaks.
- **Proper lifting:**
  - When you're carrying a load, turn your whole body in the direction you need to go. Avoid twisting or jerking movements.
  - Stack material you're carrying in such a manner that your view is clear while you're carrying it.
  - If the load to be lifted weighs more than 30 pounds, use two people to make the lift or use mechanical means (hoist, etc.).
  - If the two-man load weighs more than 70 pounds, hand holds should be provided for accomplishing the lift.
  - When two people carry a long object, they should hold it at the same level and on the same side of the body.
  - Setting the load down is just as important as picking it up. Lower the load by bending your knees, keeping your back straight.
  - Avoid strain when lifting by storing heavy objects at least 12 inches above the floor.
  - Don't overreach or overstretch to reach objects stored overhead. This can result in strains or falls.
  - Wear shoes with firm, slip-resistant soles.
  - Never hurry or run when you're carrying a load.
  - Use mechanical aids such as hand carts if appropriate.
  - When wearing gloves, make sure you have a firm grip before trying to lift.
  - Consider wearing a lifting belt that supports the lower back.

253

Back Care

The Basics of Proper Lifting

1. Kneel with one foot slightly in front of the other. This helps broaden your base of support.
2. Try to keep the load between your knees, close to your body.
3. Keep your head and back straight.
4. Get a firm, secure grip. Be especially cautious if you're wearing work gloves—they weaken your grip and the load could drop.
5. Always use your legs to lift, not your back or arms. Slowly straighten your legs. Keep the load close to your body.
6. Putting a load back down requires you to do the opposite of lifting—keep the load close to your body, keep your head and back straight, bend at the knees, and slowly place the load down between your knees.

A final word: If the load is too heavy or hard to handle, use a handcart or get help.

LIFTING IN AWKWARD SITUATIONS

1. **Odd-size loads.** Long objects can be hard to carry. Don't "hug" them to your body. Instead, support them on your shoulder, keeping the front end higher than the rear.

2. **Overhead loads.** These can be difficult to lift. If the object is above shoulder level, use a ladder to prevent overreaching. If it's under 25 pounds, slide it to you and hug it to your body as you descend.

3. **Reaching into a bin.** Stand with your feet shoulder-width apart, bend your knees, and squat, bending at your hips, not at your waist. Slide the object as close to your body as you can and raise yourself up using your leg and hip muscles. Tighten your stomach muscles as you lift and rest your knees against the side of the container. Avoid reaching in and jerking the object out.

Back Care

Abdominal Curls

- Lie on your back.
- Keep heels flat, knees bent, and buttocks 12 inches from heels.
- Cross arms across chest with chin tucked close to your chest.
- Slowly bring head and chest up toward your knees until your shoulder blades are off the floor. Breathe out as you come up.
- Slowly return to resting position.
- Do 15 to 20 repetitions. Repeat two to three times.

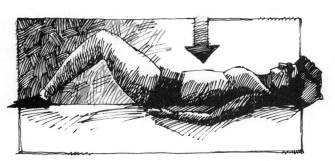

Single Knee to Chest Stretch

- Lie on your back.
- Keep heels flat, knees bent, head and back to floor.
- Grab left leg just below knee.
- Slowly pull knee toward chest.
- Hold for 15 seconds.
- Repeat two to three times with each leg.

Back Press

- Lie on your back.
- Keep heels flat, knees bent.
- Place hands on stomach or at your sides.
- Slowly press the small of your back against the floor. Breathe normally.
- Hold for six seconds, then relax.
- Repeat three to five times.

Back Extension

- Stand with feet shoulder-width apart.
- Place hands on small of lower back.
- Slowly extend your shoulders back.
- Move to a point of tension. Hold for six seconds, relax.
- Repeat three to five times.

Breast Cancer

Breast cancer remains the most common and second most deadly form of cancer (lung cancer is the deadliest) in women. One out of every eight women can expect to get breast cancer at some point in her life. There will be an estimated 180,000 women diagnosed with breast cancer in the coming year. More than 40,000 women will die from this disease this year.

Yet, when tumors are detected very early, the survival rate is about 90 percent. Therefore, it is especially important to know the facts about breast cancer and early detection of this disease.

Q. What is breast cancer?

A. Lumps, thickening, or tumors in the breasts can be malignant (cancerous) or benign (non-cancerous). Breast cancer cells spread throughout the breast tissue, into the lymph nodes, and finally, through the remainder of the body. Cancer cells interfere with and overrun the functioning of normal body cells. Without treatment, cancer cells continue to grow, crowding out and replacing healthy cells.

Q. What causes cancer?

A. For many years, researchers have tried to find out what causes a normal cell to turn into a cancer cell. Discoveries in recent years point to changes in genes as a way for cancer cells to begin to grow. The process by which cancer develops in the body usually takes years. However, there are some factors that increase the risk for cancer.

Q. What factors can increase the chance of getting breast cancer?

A. Risk factors include having one or more close relatives who have had breast cancer, a personal history of breast cancer or abnormal biopsy, being over 50 years of age, giving birth after age 30, never having given birth, a long menstrual history, and being very overweight.

As well, research indicates that drinking alcohol triples the levels of circulating estrogen in postmenopausal women taking oral estrogen. (Alcohol does not change the level of natural estrogen.) Because both estrogen replacement therapy and alcohol consumption have been shown to increase the risk of breast cancer, this combination may increase the risk more than either would alone.

Women at high risk for breast cancer may want to talk to their doctor about the use of tamoxifen or raloxifene to prevent the onset of the disease. It's important to weigh the potential benefits and risks carefully.

However, about 75 percent of all breast cancers diagnosed each year are among women with no known risk factors. That's why it is important to have regular exams.

Some good news: Studies suggest that physical activity is associated with a reduced risk of breast cancer. Researchers in one study found that the risk of breast cancer was lowest in lean women who exercised at least four hours per week.

Q. What signs of breast cancer should I be looking for?

A. Symptoms of breast cancer include:
- lump, thickening, or swelling in the breast
- dimpling or puckering of the skin (orange peel texture)
- change in skin color or feel
- pain or tenderness
- change in shape of breast
- discharge from nipple
- pulling in of nipple
- scaly skin on or around nipple

Breast Cancer

. . . .

Q. What should I do if I suspect that I have one or more symptoms of breast cancer?

A. See your doctor right away. The earlier breast cancer is caught, the better your chances for survival.

Q. How is breast cancer detected and diagnosed?

A. First of all, YOU should take responsibility for following a three-pronged strategy for early breast cancer detection:

1. **Perform a monthly breast self-exam (BSE).** See p. 45.
2. **Have a regular physical examination** performed by a health professional: At the time of your Pap test and pelvic examination if you're under age 40, or every year from age 40.
3. **Have a mammogram.** The recommended schedule for mammograms is every year or two after age 40. However, younger women with a family history of breast cancer or other risk factors should talk to their doctor about beginning mammography earlier.

Mammography is a procedure in which very low dose X-rays are taken of the breasts. The X-rays, called mammograms, are taken with a machine that flattens the breast and holds it still so details can be seen. Usually two views are taken of each breast, one vertical and one horizontal. Mammography can detect cancer in its earliest stages, two to five years before it can be detected by a regular exam. But it's still critical to continue the monthly BSE: About 10 to 15 percent of cancers that can be felt do not show up on a mammogram.

Q. How is breast cancer treated?

A. When tumors are detected early, many women with breast cancer have treatment choices. In addition to mastectomy (removal of the entire breast), women who meet certain criteria may have the option of breast conservation therapy (BCT), which involves removal of just the area of cancerous tissue with follow-up radiation therapy. In 20 years of comparison studies between BCT and mastectomy, the survival rates are the same. The medical follow-up is generally the same for both procedures. A woman will meet with the medical personnel involved in her care—often the surgeon, a medical oncologist, and a radiation oncologist for BCT—every three to six months. She'll continue breast self-exam and mammography, and the physician may recommend other tests and treatments as well.

While it may seem natural for a breast cancer patient to have the blues and feel down, it's not healthy when depressive symptoms are more severe, longer lasting, and more disabling. Breast cancer patients may become clinically depressed—an estimated 25 percent of cancer patients do—and feel isolated from family and friends. In turn, depression can make battling cancer far more difficult, as it tends to sever a woman's ties to the people and things she cares about. The good news is that depression can be successfully treated. See "Depression," pages 264-265.

Important Questions to Keep in Mind

- How should I do a monthly breast self-exam?
- Should I consider preventive therapy?
- Should I begin mammography? What does mammography consist of? How reliable are the results?
- What factors should I consider if I have a choice between BCT and mastectomy? What follow-up procedures will I need?
- What side effects can I expect from my treatment?

Cancer

Did you know that even though health care in general is improving and most average Americans seem to be living longer, your chances of developing and dying from cancer actually seem to be increasing? The number of new cancer cases has risen 15 percent over the last 15 years. One out of every four Americans now living will get some form of cancer at one point in his or her life. One out of every five will die from it.

We don't know why more people are developing cancer. Many experts feel that cancer-causing chemicals and dangerous lifestye habits such as smoking, sun exposure, or a high-fat diet contribute to the increase in the development of cancer. The greatest increase in cancer cases has been in malignant melanoma, a form of skin cancer caused by excessive exposure to the sun. Approximately 30 percent of cancer deaths are linked to smoking and another 35 percent are associated with diet. Cancers that have been on the rise include lung cancer in women (500 percent increase since 1950), prostate cancer in men (46 percent increase in 15 years), breast cancer (up 23 percent), and brain cancer (2 percent per year increase since 1973).

The good news is you can reduce your risk of getting cancer or dying from it by changing lifestyle habits and taking advantage of early detection and screening programs.

Q. What is cancer?

A. Cancer is the uncontrolled growth and spread of abnormal cells in the body. The abnormal cells grow and divide to create other abnormal cells. Without treatment, these cells continue to grow and crowd out and replace the healthy cells. They also may metastasize or spread to other parts of the body. Although all cancers have similar characteristics, each is different in its own way. Some are easy to cure, others are not. Some are slow growing, others rapidly take over the body.

Q. What causes cancer? How will I know if I am at risk for this disease?

A. Researchers have been trying to determine what causes cancer. According to recent discoveries, cancer is the result of changes in genes. Some genes stimulate cells to start dividing, others halt this process. Usually both types work in balance so that healthy cells can divide and replace dead or defective cells. In cancer, this process is upset, and abnormal cells grow out of control.

Many factors can influence a person's risk for developing cancer. Heredity accounts for about 10 percent of all cancers. Race also is a factor: African-Americans have a higher rate for some cancers than Caucasians. Viruses may cause certain leukemias and lymphomas, cancer of the nose and pharynx, liver cancer, and cervical cancer. About 5 percent of all cancers might be caused by radiation. Many chemicals used in industry also are carcinogens. Smoking, excessive exposure to sun, overuse of alcohol, and a high-fat diet also can increase the risk of developing some types of cancer.

Q. Are there any common symptoms for cancer that I should look for?

A. Yes. The American Cancer Society lists the following warning signs for cancer:
- change in bowel or bladder habits
- sore that does not heal
- unusual bleeding or discharge
- thickening or lump in breast or elsewhere
- indigestion or difficulty swallowing
- obvious changes in a wart or mole
- nagging cough or hoarseness

Q. What should I do if I suspect something may be wrong?

Cancer

....

A. Contact your doctor and discuss your concerns.

Q. How is cancer diagnosed?

A. Because you know your body better than anyone, you should screen yourself for the changes described on page 258. Women should do monthly breast self-exams; men should do frequent testicular self-exams. (Refer to page 45.) Watch for changes in size, color, number, and thickness of moles. (Refer to page 179.)

Also, follow the American Cancer Society's and your doctor's recommendations for cancer screening. Men and women over 50 should have sigmoidoscopy to examine the large intestine every three to five years and a stool sample for a fecal occult blood test every year. African-American men and men with a family history of prostate cancer may want to consider beginning PSA (prostate-specific antigen) testing and getting an annual digital rectal exam (DRE) before age 50. All men over 50 should discuss the need for regular PSA testing and DREs with their health care provider. A woman's doctor will recommend the frequency of a Pap test and pelvic exam—typically, every one to three years. Mammograms should be done every year or two for women age 40.

If signs and symptoms of cancer seem to be present, your doctor may order a biopsy or tissue sample of the area to be examined under a microscope to look for the presence of abnormal cells.

Q. What treatment options are available to me?

A. The best treatment is prevention. Maintain a healthy weight. Eat a diet low in fat and high in foods that are rich in fiber and vitamins A and C. Eat more vegetables and less foods that are salt-cured, are smoked, or contain nitrites. Limit alcohol consumption. Don't smoke or use smoke-less tobacco. Avoid excessive exposure to sunlight and radiation.

Medical treatment options for cancer are expanding rapidly. Treatments will vary by type of cancer; however, they may include surgery, radiation, chemotherapy, bone marrow transplant, or cryosurgery (tissue destruction using extreme cold). Promising research into the next-generation of cancer treatments includes therapies that help the immune system recognize cancer cells as harmful, "starve" tumors by inhibiting new blood vessel formation (anti-angiogenesis), and mend faulty genes or introduce genes that make cancer cells sensitive to drug therapy.

Finally, cancer patients may become clinically depressed—an estimated 25 percent do. In turn, depression can make battling cancer far more difficult, as it tends to sever a person's ties to the people and things he or she cares about. See "Depression," pages 264-265.

Important Questions to Keep in Mind

- Females: How do I do a breast self-exam?
- Females: Does the hormone replacement therapy I take increase my risk for cancer?
- Males: How do I do a testicular self-exam?
- What level of sunscreen should I use? How do I screen for skin cancer? What should I look for?
- At my age and with my family history, what cancer screening tests should I have? How often?
- If I have cancer, what stage is it in? What does this mean in relation to my treatment options and survivability?
- If I have cancer, what are my treatment options? What are the benefits and risks of each option?
- After my initial treatment, what follow-up will I need in the way of tests and other treatments?
- How can I learn more about a specific cancer and available treatment options?
- If I (or my partner) have cancer, where can I find support groups to help me cope?

259

Cataracts

....

As part of the normal aging process, changes in the eye and vision occur by age 50 for most individuals. You may notice a gradual decline in your ability to read small print or to focus on close objects (particularly in surroundings where the lighting is not bright), that your vision is less sharp, and that you have difficulty differentiating between certain colors such as blue and gray.

Although these are normal changes to expect in your vision as you grow older, there are other more serious eye conditions, such as cataracts, that require immediate attention and professional health care. In fact, cataracts are relatively common in older adults. Ninety percent of people over age 75 have some type of cataract.

Q. What is a cataract?

A. The lens of the eye is like the lens of a camera. It is the part that light passes through. The normal lens of your eye is clear or transparent. With cataracts, the lens becomes thick, cloudy, and hardened. The cloudy lens blocks or distorts the amount of light entering the eye just as a smudge on a camera lens would decrease the amount of light coming into the camera to expose the film.

Q. What causes cataracts?

A. Some types of cataracts are caused by normal changes in the aging eye. Cataracts also can be caused by overexposure to sunlight, an injury or blow to the eye, chemical burns, electrical shocks, certain drugs, or radiation. Certain individuals such as smokers, Native Americans, individuals who have taken steroids, and people with diabetes also are at increased risk for developing cataracts.

Q. What symptoms would alert me to the possibility that I might have a cataract?

A. Cataract symptoms develop gradually and painlessly in one or both eyes. They can include:
- hazy, blurry, fuzzy vision
- difficulty seeing at night
- problems compensating for glare
- double vision
- lights may appear to have a halo around them
- lens appears milky; vision greatly reduced (later stages)

Q. What should I do if I think I may have a cataract?

A. The best protection always is early detection: The U.S. Public Health Service preventive care guidelines recommend vision exams every two to four years for adults between the ages of 50 and 60 and every two years for people over the age of 60. If you are experiencing blurry or fuzzy vision, or if you are having trouble seeing at night, you should see a health professional.

Q. How are cataracts diagnosed?

A. Cataracts can be diagnosed by an ophthalmologist (a medical doctor who specializes in disorders of the eye). He or she will do a comprehensive eye exam, which will include looking at the lens and inside of your eyes with an instrument called an ophthalmoscope. You would not want to go to an optometrist (O.D.)—who does eye examinations and prescribes corrective lenses—or an optician—who makes eyeglasses and fills prescriptions for corrective lenses—since cataracts are a medical concern needing attention by a medical doctor.

Cataracts

Q. What treatment options are available to people with cataracts?

A. Surgery is the only effective treatment for cataracts. In the past, surgery was delayed until the cataract was very cloudy. Now, surgery is usually recommended much earlier—as soon as vision impairment becomes a problem. There is a high success rate for this procedure (approximately 95 percent). The procedure takes less than an hour, and usually is done under local anesthetic on an outpatient basis.

The diseased lens is removed and compensation is made with a replacement lens. This may be a contact lens, glasses, or an intraocular lens, which is implanted directly into the eye. Prior to surgery, you and your surgeon should discuss your options and decide which technique is best for you.

There are some things that you can do to help compensate for changes in your vision. Be sure to have plenty of light indoors, especially on steps and stairs where falls can occur. Use more than one light in a room; standard lights seem to work better than fluorescent. Cut down on glare by using blinds or shades on windows; when outdoors, wear yellow-tinted lenses and a large hat or sun visor. Position your TV screen so it doesn't reflect glare. Large-print books and newspapers and magnifying glasses or lenses can help you read better.

Important Questions to Keep in Mind

- What treatment options are there for cataracts? Must I have surgery? When is the best time to have the surgery? What happens if I decide not to have surgery for my cataracts?
- How can I best prepare for the surgery?
- How can I decide which option is best for me after the cataract is removed: contact lens, glasses, or intraocular lens? What are the risks and benefits of each?
- What can I expect during the normal recovery process after surgery? How soon will my eye sight return to "normal"?
- Are there any danger signs that I should watch for after this procedure? What are they? What should I do if they occur?

Chronic Obstructive Pulmonary Disease

Chronic obstructive pulmonary disease (COPD) includes emphysema and chronic bronchitis. These two separate but closely related and usually co-existing conditions damage the lungs and prevent them from doing their job of bringing oxygen to the body and getting rid of carbon dioxide. COPD is characterized by a progressive limiting of the air flow into and out of the lungs.

More than 10 million Americans suffer from chronic obstructive pulmonary disease, many of them smokers or former smokers. And, over 60,000 die each year as a result.

Q. What is emphysema? What is chronic bronchitis?

A. Emphysema is the limitation of air flow in and out of the lungs as a result of changes in the lung tissue caused by the disease. It affects the smallest air passages: tiny air sacs in the lungs called alveoli. Eventually, many of these air sacs are destroyed and the lungs are less able to bring in oxygen and get rid of carbon dioxide from the body. In addition, the heart has to work harder to deliver the oxygen to the body.

Chronic bronchitis occurs when the bronchial tubes in the lungs become inflamed. This inflammation thickens the walls of the bronchi and increases the production of mucus. This results in a narrowing of the air passages.

Q. What causes chronic obstructive pulmonary disease?

A. Cigarette smoking is the major cause of COPD. Seventy-five percent of individuals with chronic bronchitis have a history of heavy smoking. Exposure to air pollution can irritate the lungs, also. And, exposure to both air pollution and smoking is particularly harmful. Although any of these may cause COPD, together they have a synergistic effect—their combined effects are stronger than exposure to each one separately.

Other risk factors include gender (men are more susceptible than women), family history of the disease, and age.

Q. What are the symptoms of COPD?

A. Symptoms may appear gradually. Early signs include mild shortness of breath, a slight cough, especially in the morning, wheezing, and greenish sputum when you have a cold.

Signs of more advanced stages of the disease include severe breathlessness, fatigue, chest pains, palpitations, bluish skin and lips, insomnia, headache, impaired thinking, and irritability.

Q. How do I know when to get help?

A. You should contact a health professional if you have a sudden increase in shortness of breath; sharp chest pain with coughing; a productive cough with green, yellow, or rust-colored sputum; wheezing; changes in the nature of your cough; a cough that is so severe it is exhausting; or a cough that lasts longer than seven to 10 days without improvement.

Q. How will my physician make a diagnosis of COPD?

A. Your doctor will gather a thorough history of your symptoms, including a history of your smoking habits if applicable. You may undergo various lung function tests that measure the volume of air expelled in a single breath, the force with which air is expelled, the amount of air expelled in a second, and the amount of air remaining after exhaling. Tests also may be ordered to monitor the levels of oxygen and carbon dioxide in the blood.

Chronic Obstructive Pulmonary Disease

Q. How is chronic obstructive pulmonary disease treated?

A. Treatment focuses on two areas: slowing the progress of the disease and relieving the symptoms. Practices such as not smoking, avoiding polluted air or environments where the air is too hot, too cold, or too thin, and taking precautions to protect oneself against respiratory infections can help slow the advance of the disease.

Antibiotics can control respiratory infections; corticosteroids and bronchodilators can be prescribed to prevent respiratory attacks and improve air flow. And, increasing fluid intake will thin mucus secretions.

Respiratory therapy techniques such as "percussive massage" (clapping the chest and back, while lying in certain positions) and controlled coughing techniques assist in bringing up secretions from the lungs. Physical conditioning can tone respiratory muscles and slow the respiratory rate. Learning correct breathing techniques helps make the best use of limited lung capacity. Oxygen therapy may be needed in advanced stages of the disease.

Finally, as are patients with any chronic illness, COPD patients are susceptible to depression. Be alert for the signs and symptoms. See "Depression," pages 264-265.

Important Questions to Keep in Mind

- Can this disease be cured? What can I do to slow the progress of this disease? Which options are most effective? What are the disadvantages to each?
- What specific things can I do at home to make myself more comfortable? Breathe easier?
- What tests will be ordered? What does each do? How often will I need to have these tests? How will they help my treatment?
- What can I do to help protect myself against respiratory infections?
- Should I wear a surgical mask to help reduce respiratory complications when in public places or when doing yard work?
- Will I be on medications for this condition? How will they help me? What will happen if I choose not to take them? Will it make the condition worse? Will I feel worse? What side effects can I expect?
- What should I do on "bad air" days to help breathe easier?
- Do I need respiratory therapy? How will it help me? What will happen without it? Can I learn to do some of it myself?

263

Depression

More than 15 million Americans suffer from depressive illnesses, which can appear at any age. One in four women and one in 10 men will develop it during their lifetime. And more than half of the people who have had one episode of major depression will have another at some point in their lives. Left untreated, symptoms can linger for months, years, or a lifetime.

Nearly two-thirds of depressed people do not get appropriate treatment because their symptoms are not recognized, they blame the illness on their own weakness, they are unable to seek help, or they are misdiagnosed. The nature of the disease can interfere with a person's ability to seek help. The support of family and friends is critical.

The good news is that depression is one of the most treatable of all mental illnesses. Eighty percent to 90 percent of people respond to therapy by the end of one year of treatment. Early intervention increases the chances for successful treatment.

Q. What is depression?

A. Depression is not a sign of personal weakness and it's more than the blues. A person does not snap out of it. Depression affects a person's moods, thoughts, body, and behavior.

There are three main types of depression, though within each the number of symptoms, their severity, and their persistence vary by individual. **Major depression** includes a combination of symptoms that interfere with a person's functioning. Episodes can occur once or several times within a lifetime. Seasonal affective disorder (SAD) is a subtype of major depression. SAD appears to arise from a person's sensitivity to the limited amount of daylight that corresponds with seasonal changes. Symptoms typically begin in the fall, worsen in the winter, and improve in the spring.

Dysthymia involves chronic symptoms that don't disable but prevent a person from feeling good. However, a person with dysthymia can have episodes of major depression as well.

The third type is a **bipolar disorder** (formerly known as manic-depressive illness), characterized by cycles of extreme "highs" and "lows."

Q. What causes depression?

A. There is no single cause. Genetic factors (more so with bipolar disorders), imbalances of neurotransmitters (natural substances that enable brain cells to communicate), abnormal hormone functioning, physical illness, and/or certain medications (e.g., those for anxiety and hypertension) can be responsible. Some episodes appear for no reason. Some depressive episodes are triggered by a stressful event, such as the death of a loved one, divorce, a job promotion, or a health problem.

In the case of a health problem, it's important not to accept depression as a natural outcome of the illness. If you do, you may worsen your health condition and be less likely to take care of your physical, mental, and emotional needs. Bring any depressive symptoms to your doctor's attention and be assertive about getting treatment for depression, independent of the health problem.

Q. What are the symptoms of depression?

A. According to the National Depression Screening Project, there are nine symptoms that characterize clinical (meaning it requires treatment) depression:
- Depressed mood
- Diminished interest or pleasure in activities
- Significant change in appetite and/or weight
- Sleep disturbances
- Restlessness or sluggishness
- Fatigue or loss of energy
- Lack of concentration or indecision

Depression

- Feelings of worthlessness; inappropriate guilt
- Thoughts of death or suicide

A person with clinical depression will have at least one of the first two symptoms and four of the remaining seven; symptoms will last for two weeks or more, and the person's functioning will be impaired.

A person with a bipolar disorder will have cycles of depression (with symptoms as shown on the previous page) and mania. During the manic episodes, the person will:
- Have an excessively "high" mood
- Be irritable
- Have increased energy
- Have a decreased need for sleep
- Have grandiose notions
- Be easily distracted
- Have racing thoughts

Q. How is depression diagnosed?

A. A complete physical and/or psychiatric examination must be conducted to eliminate other diseases that might result in similar symptoms. A family history of health problems is taken as well.

Q. How is depression treated?

A. Medication is the most common form of therapy, and is essential for severely depressed people. These include heterocyclics, selective serotonin re-uptake inhibitors, MAO inhibitors, and lithium. A physician may try different dosage levels and combinations of medications to see what works best for an individual.

Psychotherapy ("talk therapy") helps people deal with psychological or social problems related to their illness. Psychotherapy is effective alone for many mildly to moderately depressed people and sometimes is used with medication therapy.

Some people with seasonal affective disorder (SAD) have success with light treatments. Typically, the patient sits for 30 minutes a day in front of a special diffused fluorescent light.

Because more effective medications have been developed, electroconvulsive therapy (ECT) has become a treatment of last resort. ECT affects the same neurotransmitters that medications do. With ECT, a small amount of electricity is applied to electrodes that have been placed on the head. These treatments continue two or three times a week until the patient improves or it becomes clear that it is ineffective.

Finally, you should practice positive lifestyle habits such as getting regular physical activity, eating right, getting enough sleep, avoiding alcohol, not smoking, and maintaining social contacts. These can help prevent and treat mild episodes of depression. For instance, moderate physical activity such as brisk walking or jogging for 30-40 minutes has been shown to help prevent and manage episodes of mild to moderate depression.

Important Questions to Keep in Mind

- Could my symptoms be the result of a physical illness?
- Could my symptoms be related to seasonal changes, indicating SAD?
- Can my family physician treat my illness? If not, can he or she recommend a specialist?
- Could I try psychotherapy alone (without medication) to treat my illness?
- If a medication(s) is prescribed, how long will I need to take it? What are the side effects? Can other medications be considered? What foods and other medications should I stay away from?
- What are the risks of electroconvulsive therapy?
- Will my treatment change as my condition improves?
- After treatment, am I likely to have another episode?

Diabetes

More than 100 million people around the world have diabetes mellitus. In this country, approximately 15 million Americans have diabetes and about half of these have not been diagnosed as having this disease. Diabetes is a complex disorder of body chemistry, but it can be managed if properly understood. *It's a good idea to carry medical identification such as a medic alert bracelet or wallet card at all times.*

Q. What is diabetes?

A. Normally, the body breaks down the components of foods (carbohydrates, fats, and proteins) into glucose, which the body then uses as an energy supply. In a person with diabetes, the hormone (called insulin) that helps change the glucose into energy is either underproduced or is prevented from working as it should. In either case, glucose levels in the blood rise to unacceptable levels.

There are two types of diabetes mellitus:

1. **Insulin-dependent diabetes mellitus** (IDDM) may be an autoimmune disorder where the body accidentally attacks the insulin-producing cells found in the pancreas. Also known as Type 1 diabetes, IDDM usually develops during childhood or young adulthood. But, it can develop at any age.
2. **Non-insulin-dependent diabetes mellitus** (NIDDM) usually develops in people over 40 years of age. NIDDM, also called adult-onset diabetes, is strongly associated with obesity. Excess fat is believed to interfere with insulin's role in changing glucose to energy. This type of diabetes also is sometimes known as Type 2 diabetes.

Q. What are the risk factors for diabetes?

A. If you have two or more of the following risk factors, you are at increased risk for developing Type 2 (NIDDM) diabetes:
- age 45 or over
- obesity
- family history of diabetes
- of African-American, Hispanic, or Native American descent
- a sedentary lifestyle
- personal history of diabetes in pregnancy, or of giving birth to a baby weighing more than nine pounds

Q. What are the symptoms of diabetes?

A. Common symptoms of diabetes include frequent urination, excessive thirst, weight loss, blurred vision, fatigue, and loss of muscular coordination. Other symptoms may include increased appetite, skin infections, slow-healing wounds, recurrent vaginitis, difficulty with erections, and tingling or numbness in the hands or feet.

Q. What should I do if I suspect I might have diabetes?

A. Know the signs. Be aware of the symptoms of diabetes, listed above. Consult your doctor if these symptoms begin and seem to persist or get worse over a few days. Early diagnosis and treatment is important to prevent serious complications. Left untreated, diabetes can leave you at increased risk for damage to blood vessels, kidneys, eyes, and the nervous system. The person with diabetes is at higher risk for stroke, atherosclerosis, hypertension, heart disease, kidney failure, visual problems such as blindness, and loss of a limb.

Also, you should be alert to the signs and symptoms of depression, which occurs three times

Diabetes

more often in diabetic patients than it does in the general public. See "Depression," pages 264-265.

Q. How can diabetes be diagnosed?

A. Testing for diabetes can be done by measuring sugar levels in the blood or the urine. The glucose tolerance test is among the most reliable: It measures blood sugar levels before and after the person drinks a specific dose of liquid glucose. If you have a level:
- of 126 mg/dl or higher on two different days, you have diabetes.
- between 110 and 125 mg/dl, you have a greater risk for diabetes.

Below 110 mg/dl is normal.

The American Diabetes Association now recommends that all Americans 45 and older be screened for diabetes with a blood sugar test every three years. Your doctor may recommend earlier and more frequent screening if you are at increased risk (e.g., if you have a family history).

Q. Is diabetes treatable?

A. Type 1 diabetes treatment includes daily injections of insulin or the use of an insulin pump to keep blood sugar levels under control, combined with a modified diet, moderate exercise, and regular monitoring of blood sugar, all under a doctor's supervision.

People with Type 2 diabetes or NIDDM generally don't have to take insulin. Treatment includes a carefully planned diet, weight loss, moderate exercise (20 minutes of walking for a minimum of three days per week), regular monitoring of blood sugar and, in some cases, medication. This may be insulin or medications taken by mouth to lower blood sugar (oral hypoglycemic agents).

Research has shown that for every incremental decrease in blood sugar, the potential complications of diabetes decrease.

Important Questions to Keep in Mind

- What is a normal blood sugar level? What are my risks if it is too high or too low? What should I do if I think my blood sugar is too high or too low? How do I monitor my blood sugar?
- How reliable is a glucose tolerance test? Blood glucose tests? What are the risks and benefits of each? Are there other test options that will tell me the same thing?
- What type of treatment option is best for my condition: insulin injections? insulin pump? oral hypoglycemic medication? What are the risks and benefits of these treatment options? Are there any alternatives? What may happen if I do nothing?
- Why is foot care important to diabetics? How should I be taking care of my feet? What danger signs should I watch for? What should I do if I think I have a problem?
- How should I treat common wounds (e.g., cuts and sores)? What are the warning signs that I need to be aware of?
- How often should I get my eyes checked? What may happen if I do not follow the recommendations for eye checkups?
- Should I modify my diet? Why? How? What improvements in my health can I expect from changing my diet? What will happen if I keep my current diet?
- How will exercising help with my diabetes? How does it affect my blood sugar level? Do I need a doctor to monitor my exercise?

Heart Disease

The statistics about heart disease are heartbreaking. More than 63 million Americans suffer from some form of cardiovascular illness. Nearly one out of every two adults dies of heart-related disorders. It is our nation's No. 1 killer.

The heart is the pump of life, pumping 75 gallons of blood every hour out into a circulatory system of arteries and veins that is 12,400 miles long. Your heart and circulatory system feed and nurture every system, organ, and cell in your body. Your body's heart is its key to life. Disorders of the heart can develop slowly and undetected. Yet, if not diagnosed and treated, they may develop into life-threatening problems.

Your heart's health depends on you—through the choices you make, the habits you adopt, and the lifestyle practices you follow. The outcome of heart disease can depend on you, as well: knowing when to get medical attention and how you and your medical professional can decide on options for your care.

Q. All these terms are confusing. Exactly what is heart disease?

A. Coronary heart disease occurs when the blood vessels that supply blood to the heart itself become blocked. The heart is a muscle, and like any other muscle, it needs a constant supply of oxygen and nutrients to function. The coronary arteries surround the heart like a "crown." When they become partially blocked, chest pain or angina results. If these arteries become totally blocked, that part of the heart muscle receives no oxygen and dies. This is known as a myocardial infarction or heart attack.

Q. What causes heart disease?

A. The primary cause underlying heart disease is atherosclerosis. Atherosclerosis is the gradual buildup of fat and cholesterol deposits in the arteries. These deposits slow the passing of blood through the vessels. Scar tissue and debris build up behind these fatty deposits, creating areas of plaque. The walls of the arteries grow thick and irregular and the opening narrows further. A blood clot can get caught in this narrowed channel and block it, or, over time, the deposits can completely block the passage.

Atherosclerosis can occur in any artery in the body. When blood flow to the brain is blocked, a stroke can occur (see pages 281-282). It also may occur in the arteries in the legs, producing a condition called peripheral vascular disease. When it happens in the coronary arteries supplying blood to the heart—called arteriosclerosis—it can cause angina and heart attacks.

Q. Are there any risk factors that make someone more likely to develop heart disease?

A. There are risk factors for heart disease that you can control and those you can't. Factors you can't control include a family history of heart disease, age (almost four out of five people who die of heart attacks are over age 65), and gender (men have a higher incidence of cardiovascular problems, although women may be catching up).

Controllable risks that contribute to the development of disease include lack of exercise, cigarette smoking, high blood pressure, high cholesterol, diabetes, excessive weight, and stress.

Q. What symptoms are common to heart disease?

A. Heart disease usually does not produce any symptoms until the artery is at least two-thirds blocked. Angina is a dull, sometimes crushing pain beneath the breastbone, usually after physical activity, which increases the heart's need for oxygen. It lasts from a few minutes to as much as 20 minutes and is nearly always relieved by rest. A heavy squeezing or crushing pain or dis-

Heart Disease

comfort in the center of the chest, which may last for several minutes; pain that may radiate to the shoulder, arm, neck, or jaw; anxiety, sweating, and nausea or vomiting; shortness of breath; and dizziness or fainting may indicate a heart attack. Also, see "Chest Pain" on page 127.

Q. What should I do if I think I may be having angina or a heart attack?

A. Take one aspirin and call for emergency help in the case of severe chest pain. You also should call for emergency help if the chest pain does not go away with rest or after taking any medications that may have been prescribed for it (such as nitroglycerine); if the chest pain radiates to the arm, elbow, shoulder, back, or jaw; or if the chest pain is accompanied by shortness of breath or difficulty breathing; rapid, irregular pulse; sweating; nausea or vomiting; or dizziness and confusion.

Q. What are the common diagnostic tests for heart disease?

A. There are numerous diagnostic tests available. Your doctor may evaluate your heart by using a stethoscope to listen to your heart and lung sounds and taking your pulse and blood pressure. He or she may order an X-ray to check for heart enlargement and/or blood enzyme tests to determine the amount of damage to the heart muscle from a heart attack. Other common tests used to diagnose heart disease include:

- The **electrocardiogram** (ECG/EKG) records the electrical activity of the heart, which can show irregular heart rhythms and provide information on the extent of injury to the heart tissue produced by a heart attack. An exercise ECG (stress test) is done while an individual walks or jogs on a treadmill. The ECG monitors the heart's response to the stress of exercise to determine whether any specific areas of the heart muscle are not getting enough oxygen.

- In **Transesophageal echocardiography,** a probe is inserted into the esophagus to produce ultrasound images of the heart as it beats. Another similar test involves inserting a small ultrasound probe in a small catheter into the blood vessels so cross-sectional images of the coronary arteries can be seen to measure the degree of blockage.

- **Thallium or nuclear scanning** uses radioactive isotopes that are injected into the bloodstream. A special camera picks up the rays given off by these isotopes, while a computer is used to translate these signals into images of the heart as it beats.

- **Coronary angiography** is the most accurate diagnostic test. A thin tube or catheter is threaded through the blood vessels of the heart. A radiopaque dye is injected through the catheter, and X-rays are taken to determine if there is any blockage of the arteries that supply oxygen to the heart muscle.

Q. How is heart disease treated?

A. Several options for treatment exist, depending on the location and severity of the problem. Some coronary heart disease can be treated through a combination of drug therapy and lifestyle changes. In fact, recent research shows that aggressive diet changes, regular exercise, and stress management can reverse coronary disease in some individuals. In turn, experts now recommend that adults with coronary artery disease and/or a strong positive family history take aspirin—81 mg every day and a bi-monthly booster of 325 mg—as a preventive measure. However, check with your doctor first, especially if you take another anti-coagulant drug or have a history of gastrointestinal bleeding.

For postmenopausal women, more and more research is pointing to the heart-protective benefits of hormone replacement therapy (HRT). Many women are concerned, justly, that HRT will

269

increase their risk of breast cancer. However, because heart disease strikes one in two post-menopausal women while breast cancer affects one in eight women at some time during their life-time, the risks and benefits must be carefully weighed. (Note: Estrogen also helps slow bone loss and may improve memory and attention span in postmenopausal women with Alzheimer's dis-ease.) The pros and cons should be carefully weighed with one's doctor.

Also, women should not ignore potential warning signs of heart disease or a heart attack—seek medical care immediately. Finally, women need to be assertive when discussing treatment options with their health care providers. Studies show that women are generally treated less aggres-sively than men, such as in receiving coronary artery bypass graft (CABG).

Another option is balloon angioplasty. The blocked coronary artery is opened by an inflatable balloon that is positioned into the artery through a catheter that is inserted and "snaked" through either an artery in the leg or in the arm.

The major option for treating severe blockage of the coronary arteries of the heart and its associ-ated symptoms (e.g., chest pain and shortness of breath) is through a CABG. Through this proce-dure, the surgeon bypasses the blockage in the coronary artery by taking a vein from the leg or the mammary artery from the chest and con-necting it above and below the blockage. This allows blood and oxygen to reach areas of the heart muscle that had been impaired by the blocked blood flow.

Of course, the best option is prevention. The lifestyle recommendations that doctors prescribe after surgery are the same methods that help pre-vent heart disease in the first place.

Finally, you should be aware during the treat-ment process that depression is a common com-plication of heart disease. An estimated 18 to 20 percent of heart disease patients who have not had a heart attack develop depression, and 40 to 65 percent of heart attack survivors develop some form of depression. What's more, depressed heart disease patients are 70 percent more likely to have a heart attack than those who are not depressed. Both for the sake of your heart and the quality of your life, seek treatment for depression. See "Depression," pages 264–265.

Important Questions to Keep in Mind

- If I have heart disease, can I be treated with more conservative approaches such as physical activity, dietary management, relaxation exer-cises, and drug therapy?

- Is coronary angiography accurate? How will the results affect my treatment options? What risks are involved? Are there less risky tests that can determine the same thing? What are the conse-quences if I delay or don't have this test?

- What specific drugs will I need to take to treat my condition? How does each work? How much and how often do I need to take them? What will happen if I stop taking them? What are the possible side effects of each? Will this drug(s) affect any other medication I am taking? Are there any dietary restrictions?

- Females: Should I consider HRT? What are the benefits and risks for me, given my lifestyle and family history?

- Do I need to be on a special diet to lower my cholesterol? What kinds of foods should I be eating? What foods should I eat less of or avoid? Do I need to take cholesterol-lowering drugs?

- When is CABG appropriate? When should other treatments, such as lifestyle modification or balloon angioplasty, be used? What are the ben-efits of CABG? What are the risks? How long will recovery take? What can I do to speed my recovery?

- Should I be taking aspirin every day to help prevent heart attack?

- What is the likelihood of needing CABG or angioplasty again?

- I'm recovering from a heart attack. When can I resume sexual intimacy?

High Blood Pressure

The two most common forms of cardiovascular disease in this country are high blood pressure (hypertension) and coronary heart disease (see pages 268-270). More than 50 million Americans have high blood pressure that is severe enough to require monitoring and treatment; 75 percent do not have their blood pressure under adequate control.

High blood pressure, although a common medical condition, can have serious consequences if left untreated, including coronary artery disease, stroke, and kidney failure. Even borderline hypertension can contribute to damage of the heart and blood vessels and increase the risk of heart attack.

Q. What is high blood pressure?

A. Blood pressure is the amount of force blood exerts against artery walls as it flows through them. It is measured and recorded as two numbers: systolic pressure, the peak force when the heart beats (contracts) and diastolic pressure, the force against the artery walls when the heart is at rest or between beats.

A blood pressure level of 120/80 mmHG is considered optimal. People with high blood pressure (140/90 or higher) or with readings in the "high normal" range (a systolic reading of 130 to 139 or a diastolic reading of 85 to 89) should take steps to manage it.

Q. What is the cause of high blood pressure?

A. Ninety percent of the time, the cause of high blood pressure cannot be determined. This type of high blood pressure is referred to as "essential hypertension." The remaining 10 percent are caused by such conditions as kidney disease and tumors.

Q. Are there any risk factors that make it more likely that I could develop high blood pressure?

A. Risk factors for high blood pressure fall into two categories—those you can control and those you can't. Risk factors you can't control include previous family history, gender (affects more males than females), race (affects African-Americans more than other ethnic groups), and age (high blood pressure occurs most often in men over age 35 and women over age 45). Risk increases with age.

Factors over which you have control are smoking (narrows your blood vessels and makes the heart beat faster, causing your blood pressure to rise), excessive weight, stress, lack of exercise (regular exercise tones your heart, blood vessels, and muscles and keeps your blood pressure lower), alcohol consumption, and excessive sodium (salt) consumption.

Q. What are the symptoms of high blood pressure?

A. Most people with high blood pressure have no symptoms. The only way you can tell if blood pressure is high is to have it checked.

Q. What should I do if I think I might have high blood pressure?

A. Since hypertension usually has no symptoms, the best way to keep track of your blood pressure is to have it checked once a year by a health professional.

Q. Will I have to go through a lot of tests to find out if I have high blood pressure?

A. Blood pressure is easily measured by a pressure cuff, gauge, and stethoscope, or by a computerized instrument. Also, home test kits can be purchased for home monitoring. The American Red Cross or your health care provider can teach you the proper way to measure your blood pressure. If you do measure your blood pressure yourself, don't forget to have it checked once a year by a health professional also.

Q. How is hypertension treated?

A. If you are diagnosed with hypertension or are in the high normal range, your doctor will recommend lifestyle changes. These include:
• maintaining your recommended weight
• exercising three to five times per week
• quitting smoking
• avoiding eating prepared, high-sodium foods
• eating a diet that is low in fat and rich in vegetables, fruits, fiber, and low-fat dairy products. Foods rich in potassium (bananas, oranges, potatoes, and green vegetables) seem to offer protective value as well.

Lifestyle changes can have a significant impact: Research has shown that by losing weight and/or cutting back on salt, older people in particular can end their need for blood pressure medications.

Your doctor will consider how high your blood pressure levels are and how many other cardiovascular risk factors (e.g., smoking, high blood cholesterol, family history, age older than 60 years, diabetes) you have in order to determine whether your condition should be treated with

medication, and, if so, which kind. You may begin by taking a small dose of a specific anti-hypertensive drug or drugs. You and your doctor will monitor blood pressure changes and any side effects carefully. Standard hypertensive drugs include diuretics (which increase urination), beta blockers, calcium channel blockers, alpha blockers, and angiotensin-converting enzyme (ACE) inhibitors. If you are put on a medication schedule, don't change your treatment without your doctor's approval. Be sure to take your medication as prescribed. Tell your doctor about any side effects such as headaches, fatigue, and extra or skipped heartbeats.

Important Questions to Keep in Mind

• Can diet and lifestyle changes help to control my high blood pressure? If so, what can I do?
• Do I need to limit my sodium intake? How much? What foods should I eat? What should I avoid?
• How does increasing my calcium and potassium intake help to control blood pressure? How can I increase my intake?
• How often should I get my blood pressure checked? Should I check it myself? Or should I have a health professional check it?
• Will medication help to control my hypertension? What type of drug will work best for me? How does it work? What side effects can I expect? Should I take it with food? Do I have to take it at the same time each day?

Osteoporosis

Osteoporosis is an extremely debilitating bone condition that affects 28 million Americans and is particularly common in the elderly. Its impact on health, lifestyle, and emotional well-being can be far reaching. As a matter of fact, some health professionals feel that osteoporosis is reaching epidemic proportions. It is the major form of bone loss in postmenopausal women. About one in two women and one in four men over the age of 50 will have an osteoporosis-related fracture.

Q. What is osteoporosis?

A. When levels of calcium and phosphorus—the minerals essential to bone formation—are insufficient, bone mass is lost. This causes bones to become dry and brittle. Osteoporosis results from:
• aging
• diminished estrogen after menopause
• improper intake of vitamins such as vitamin D
• inadequate calcium levels
• poor physical conditioning and development
• use of tobacco and caffeine
• excessive use of alcohol

Q. Who is at risk?

A. Women are much more likely than men to develop osteoporosis. Women as a group have lighter bones and less total calcium. And estrogen loss after menopause accelerates the loss of calcium. Smoking interferes with calcium absorption, putting smokers at greater risk. Other risk factors include family history, race (Caucasian and Asian women are more susceptible), low calcium intake, inactive lifestyle, a petite body frame, smoking, and excessive alcohol use.

Q. What are the symptoms? What should I do if I have these symptoms?

A. Sometimes the first sign of osteoporosis is a loss of height or the beginnings of a humped back caused by a collapse of weakened vertebrae. However, usually there are no symptoms until a fracture occurs. The first sign may be sudden pain in the back or hip, or painful swelling of a joint after a minor fall.

You should see a health professional if any of these symptoms occur, if a sprain does not improve after four days of home treatment, or if there is a lot of swelling or bruising after even a minor fall.

Q. Can osteoporosis be prevented?

A. The two major strategies for helping reduce the risk of osteoporosis are proper nutrition and regular weight-bearing exercise. Men and pre-menopausal women should consume a minimum of 1,000 mg of calcium per day. Postmenopausal women should increase their daily calcium intake to 1,500 mg. Excellent sources of calcium include skim milk, low-fat yogurt, chopped collards, broccoli, and canned sardines with bones. See page 17.

The second defense against osteoporosis is daily weight-bearing exercises that place stress on the major joints, thus encouraging bone growth. Excellent exercises include walking, jogging, aerobic dance, and tennis. Recent studies also suggest that weight training also may help maintain bone density.

Q. How is it diagnosed?

A. Diagnosis usually occurs after a fracture when an X-ray reveals osteoporosis. An X-ray of normal bone shows a very white, harsh image. But in a bone with too little calcium, this white color is

273

noticeably washed out. The calcium content of bone (typically in the spine and hip) can be measured by dual-energy X-ray absorptiometry (DEXA), in which the absorption of low-level radiation is measured and assigned a number based on the bone's density. This can be done prior to a fracture as well to determine future fracture risk. When the density drops 30 percent below that of healthy people in their 30s, osteoporosis is diagnosed. Newer, and less expensive, options include portable bone scanners that measure bone in the heel or calf using high-frequency sound waves. These measurements are used to estimate fracture risk in other locations.

Q. How is it treated?

A. Scientists are not sure whether you can slow or prevent further degeneration. But treatment options can minimize the negative effects of osteoporosis.

First, maintaining a balanced diet (with adequate levels of calcium) and exercising regularly may provide benefit to those already suffering from osteoporosis.

Hormone-replacement therapy (HRT) has been shown to be an effective treatment for preserving bone density. However, there's evidence that hormone replacement therapy may increase breast cancer risk, as well as complications such as breast tenderness, breakthrough bleeding, and bloating. Another option is treatment with selective estrogen-receptor modulators (SERMS). SERMS (e.g., raloxifene) increase bone formation without some of the side effects of estrogen-replacement therapy. It's important to talk to your doctor about the benefits and risks of these therapies.

Another treatment approach is the use of prescription medications that are used to slow the rate of bone loss in women who have significant osteoporosis. Alendronate (Fosamax®) has been shown to increase bone density and prevent fractures. Calcitonin (Calcimar® and Miacalcin®) has been shown to only reduce bone loss.

Hip replacement surgery is a common treatment for degenerated hips. With hip replacement, complications are markedly reduced and independence improved. This is especially important since the complications from hip fractures among elderly adults can be very serious.

Finally, because osteoporosis can be painful and can rob people of their independence and self-esteem, victims can become isolated and depressed. Be alert for the signs and symptoms of depression. See "Depression," pages 264-265.

Important Questions to Keep in Mind

- Can osteoporosis be prevented? How? Is it too late to start?
- Should I be screened (DEXA) for osteoporosis if I have a family history?
- How can I increase my consumption of calcium-rich foods? Are calcium supplements helpful? How much? How often? Any precautions?
- What side effects can I expect from HRT? What are the risks of breast cancer?
- Is alendronate or calcitonin appropriate for me? How do I take it? How effective is it? What are the risks? Side effects? Are there alternatives?
- When is hip replacement surgery indicated? What are the risks? What benefits can I expect? What do I need to do to prepare for this procedure? What kind of recovery period can I expect? Will I need rehabilitation? What kind? How long? What if I refuse to have the surgery?
- How do I develop an exercise plan that will be effective against osteoporosis?

Parkinson's Disease

Parkinson's disease is a progressive disorder caused by the degeneration of specific cells within the brain. In these cells, the neurotransmitter dopamine is no longer produced. Dopamine is needed to transmit the signals that control body movements to and from the brain. That's why the disease is characterized by rhythmic tremors, rigid muscles, and loss of reflexes.

Parkinsonism usually occurs between the ages of 40 and 70, although Parkinson's disease in individuals under the age of 50 is rare. This disease affects more than one million Americans and is a major cause of disability. Individuals with Parkinson's disease can have difficulty living independently as the disease progresses because of significant physical and intellectual symptoms. Home treatment, medication, lifestyle modifications, and appropriate medical care can help slow the progress of the disease.

Q. What causes this condition?

A. The origin of this disease is not yet known.

Q. What are the risks to my health if I develop Parkinson's disease?

A. Since this is a chronic, incurable, progressive disease that affects the nervous system, movement, and communication ability, your ability to live and care for yourself independently may decrease to the point where you may not be able to live alone. Stiffness and changes in balance may put you at increased risk for injury from falls. In severe and late stages of the disease, you may become immobile and require constant nursing care.

Q. What are the symptoms of this disorder?

A. The early symptoms of Parkinsonism often are mild and may go unnoticed. They include mild tremors (usually in the hands), stiffness, and fatigue. As the disease progresses, tremors increase and posture becomes stooped—pitched forward—resulting in a shuffling and unsteady gait. Joint and muscle stiffness increase. Movements become slower. It becomes more difficult to change direction and to start and stop movements. Salivation and drooling may increase. Blinking of the eyes decreases, resulting in a fixed stare. The face may have a fixed, mask-like expression.

Q. What should I do if I suspect I may have Parkinson's disease?

A. You should make an appointment to see your health care provider, even if symptoms are mild. Recognizing and treating Parkinson's disease in the early stages may help slow its progression and help you live a more comfortable and independent life for a longer period of time.

Q. How is a diagnosis of Parkinson's disease made?

A. Your doctor will begin by doing a complete health history and physical exam. If your symptoms warrant it, a thorough neurological exam also will be done. Additional tests and procedures may be done based on the results of these examinations. No specific lab work is significant in making a diagnosis of Parkinsonism; the diagnosis is based on what your doctor finds during the exam. Special note would be made of the symptoms mentioned earlier.

Q. What treatments are available to me?

A. Although there is no known cure for Parkinson's disease, your doctor may recommend medication as well as diet and exercise

Parkinson's Disease

regimens to help slow the progression of the disease. You should control your stress, eat regular and well-balanced meals, and get regular exercise, based on your doctor's recommendations.

Medications may include drugs that contain levodopa such as Dopar®, Larodopa®, or Sinemet®. However, levodopa drugs can cause severe side effects. Sometimes a drug called deprenyl is prescribed with the levodopa to decrease the side effects. In fact, some tests indicate that deprenyl alone can slow the effects of the disorder.

Researchers are continuing to look for other treatments to slow the progression of this disease and to lessen the symptoms. Shock therapy has been tried with some success. Fetal brain cells have been transplanted in the brains of some patients to replace the dopamine no longer made; this, too, has lessened symptoms. Electronic devices also have been implanted in the brains of some individuals with Parkinson's disease, with promising results. This method lessens the involuntary movements, tremors, and rigidity that accompany this condition.

Important Questions to Keep in Mind

- How often should I see my doctor if I have this disease? Should I schedule regular checkups or wait until I have a problem or my condition changes?
- What symptoms would require an immediate visit to my doctor?
- What can I do in my daily life and activities to slow the progression or lessen the symptoms of this disease? How should I exercise? What should I eat? Is there anything I can do to lessen the stiffness, tremors, and lack of balance? How can I modify my living environment to make it safer if I fall?
- What medications will I be taking? When? How? What are the side effects? How can the side effects be lessened? Will these drugs affect any other drugs I might be taking? How?
- Are there any new treatment options for this disease (e.g., medications, electronic implants)? How successful have they been in cases like mine? What are the benefits, risks, and costs? Is there any new research that could change the way this disease is treated?
- If my condition worsens and I can no longer live alone or without assistance, where can I get assistance? What are my home care options?
- What happens if I do nothing and accept the progression of this disease? Are there any risks to my health and well-being? Are there any benefits to doing nothing? If I change my mind later, will it be too late?
- Are there any home treatments that can help me deal with the changes I will experience as the disease progresses?
- How will the progression of this disease affect my communication skills? How can I get help in coping with decreased verbal ability? What communication aids are available?

Periodontal Disease

Periodontal or gum disease is the main cause of tooth loss in older adults. Most of the estimated 25 million Americans who have lost all of their teeth are the victims of periodontal disease. More than 40 percent of people over age 65 are missing all of their teeth. Only two percent of older people still have all 28 of their own permanent teeth. Approximately another 94 million suffer from lesser consequences of this condition. Nearly half of all older adults show signs of gum disease.

And the consequences of gum disease can go beyond your mouth. The bacteria associated with periodontal disease can travel into the bloodstream to other parts of the body. Gum disease may:

- **Contribute to the development of heart disease.** In one theoretical scenario, a person with gum disease injures the gum tissue by chewing or brushing. Bacteria enter the bloodstream. The accumulation of these bacteria on heart valves then can lead to a fatal infection if left untreated. In another scenario, bacteria in an oral cavity may enter the bloodstream, attach to fatty plaques, and contribute to the formation of clots. Blood clots block blood flow, depleting the heart of nutrients and oxygen.

- **Increase the risk of preterm, low birth-weight babies.** Gum disease in a pregnant woman may trigger a rapid increase in two fluids that normally induce labor.

- **Pose a threat to people with diabetes.** Research has shown that diabetics are more likely to have gum disease. Now it appears that severe gum disease may be an important risk factor for the progression of diabetes.

- **Pose a threat to people with respiratory diseases.** Bacteria in the throat and mouth can be inhaled and drawn into the lower respiratory tract. This can cause infections, such as pneumonia, or worsen existing lung conditions, such as chronic obstructive pulmonary disease (COPD).

Q. What is periodontal disease?

A. Periodontal disease attacks the structures that support the teeth and keep them in place. In the beginning stages, the gums become inflamed. Then, as the disease progresses, the underlying bone also degenerates. The teeth, having nothing to be anchored to, grow loose and fall out.

Q. What causes it?

A. Periodontal disease is caused by a buildup of plaque and bacteria around the teeth and gums. The main culprits are infrequent brushing, failure to floss regularly, and not seeing a dentist for regular checkups. Bacterial buildup creates a film on your teeth called plaque. Plaque attracts sugars that in turn produce acids that inflame the gums or degrade the supporting bone.

Q. Who is at risk?

A. Those with poor dental hygiene, individuals with diabetes, and those who smoke or chew tobacco also are at increased risk for periodontal disease.

Q. What are the symptoms?

A. Bleeding gums are an indication of periodontal disease. Signs also include reddened, swollen gums, loose teeth, and bleeding upon brushing. In addition to getting regular dental checkups (every six months), you should consult your dentist if your gums are red and swollen, if your gums bleed when you brush your teeth, if your teeth are loose or seem to be moving apart, or if there are changes in the way your dentures fit.

Periodontal Disease

Q. How is it diagnosed?

A. Your dentist will determine if you have periodontal disease based on his or her visual examination of your teeth and gums. This may include some probing to detect bleeding or pockets along the gum line. An X-ray may be taken to detect bone loss in advanced stages of the disease.

Q. How is it treated?

A. Early stages of the disease can be treated with correct brushing and flossing of the teeth every day and can be monitored by dental checkups every six months. At these checkups, a professional cleaning of your teeth will be done to remove plaque and calculus (hardened bacterial plaque). Your dentist also may prescribe a mouthwash containing chlorohexidine (e.g., Peridex®, Perioguard®) to treat symptoms.

More advanced periodontal disease may be treated by either eliminating the pockets of diseased tissue or by cleaning the affected tooth roots using a process known as scaling and root planing. If your dentist suggests surgery first, ask about scaling or planing. Surgery may be used in some instances.

Important Questions to Keep in Mind

- Can periodontal disease be slowed or reversed? How? What can I do to prevent further disease?
- Will changing the type of foods I eat help prevent this condition?
- Is brushing with a fluoride toothpaste helpful in preventing periodontal disease?
- How should I be brushing and flossing my teeth? How often? Do I need a special brush or floss?
- How often should I have a dental checkup if I have this condition? What will happen if I don't see a dentist regularly? What will be done at these checkups?
- What will be my options if the disease worsens? Is scaling and planing an option for me? What are the benefits? Risks? What will happen if I do not have this procedure done? When is dental surgery appropriate?

Prostate Problems

The prostate—a doughnut-shaped gland that surrounds the bladder opening and urethra in males—is located at the bottom of the bladder, about halfway between the rectum and the base of the penis.

Common prostate problems in older men include prostatitis or infection of the prostate, benign prostatic hypertrophy (BPH) or non-cancerous enlargement of the prostate gland, and prostate cancer. Enlargement of the prostate is a common condition in men over 60 years of age. Cancer of the prostate is as common as lung cancer among males and claims about 42,000 lives a year. Less than one percent of men under age 50 have any detectable forms of prostate cancer, but after age 80, more than 50 percent of males have been shown to have some stage of prostate cancer.

Q. What causes these conditions?

A. Prostatitis, particularly chronic prostatitis, frequently accompanies a urinary tract infection. After age 40 the prostate enlarges. This condition is called benign prostatic hypertrophy and it occurs to some degree in every man as he ages. The cause of prostate cancer, as with other cancers, is uncertain. However, risk factors for prostate cancer include family history of the disease, age, smoking, and a high-fat diet. Men may be able to reduce their risk by taking vitamin E supplements: Male smokers who took 50 mg every day for five to eight years reduced their risk of developing or dying from prostate cancer in one study published in the *Journal of the National Cancer Institute*.

Q. What are the symptoms of these conditions?

A. Symptoms of prostatitis include pain and burning on urination and ejaculation, frequent urges to urinate but only being able to pass a small amount of urine, and, occasionally, blood in the urine.

BPH symptoms include decreased force of the stream of urine, difficulty starting and stopping urination, increased urinary frequency (especially at night), and incomplete emptying of the bladder.

Prostate cancer is a slow-growing cancer and many men die from other causes before the cancer advances to the stage where it causes noticeable symptoms. As in BPH, symptoms may include decreased force of the stream of urine, problems starting and stopping the stream, and frequent urination. Hip or lower back pain, blood or pus in the urine, and painful urination also may be noticed.

You should contact your doctor if any of these urinary symptoms occur for more than two weeks, or sooner if there is blood in the urine, pain, fever, chills, or abdominal pain.

Q. How are problems of the prostate diagnosed?

A. Diagnostic tests may include a complete history of symptoms, blood and urine tests, a digital exam of the prostate in which the doctor inserts a finger into the rectum and feels the prostate for enlargement and abnormal growths, X-ray of the urinary tract system, and tissue biopsies.

The PSA (prostate-specific antigen) test screens for prostatic abnormalities. It detects a protein in the blood when there is a tumor, infection, or non-cancerous enlargement of the prostate. Once the PSA test detects elevated levels, your doctor can then use other exams to determine the specific problem. Because BPH and prostatitis can elevate PSA levels, this test is not a definitive indicator of the absence or presence of prostate cancer, but rather a method to assess the risk. For example, for men with slightly elevated PSA levels, the chance of prostate cancer is 20 to 50 percent.

The American Cancer Society recommends that African-American men and men with a family history of prostate cancer consider beginning PSA testing and getting digital rectal exams (DRE)

Prostate Problems

before the age of 50. All men over 50 should discuss the need for regular PSA testing and DREs with their health care provider.

Q. What treatment options are available?

A. Prostate infections usually respond well to antibiotic therapy. Also, your doctor may advise you to avoid alcohol, coffee, tea, and spicy foods; increase your fluid intake; and manage stress. Soaking in a warm bath also seems to help.

BPH usually is not a serious problem unless urination becomes extremely difficult or the incomplete emptying of the bladder causes bladder infections or kidney problems. Surgery is a common treatment for BPH. The most common procedure is transurethral prostatectomy (TURP), in which the core portion of the prostate is removed to relieve the obstruction. In some cases, the best treatment is no treatment (watchful waiting). And, medications (e.g., finasteride, alpha-adrenergic blockers) can improve the symptoms of BPH. Currently, there are a number of other surgical options under investigation that include the use of ultrasound, vaporization, microwaves, lasers, and shunts to treat BPH. Your doctor can discuss the various treatment options available for your particular situation.

Treatment options primarily are based on how far the disease has spread. Radical prostatectomy—complete removal of the prostate—is effective for cancer contained within the gland. Radiation treatment through external beam radiation or implants is used when the cancer is contained or has spread only slightly. Hormone therapy or removal of the testicles—both of which stop the supply of testosterone the cancer needs to grow—is used when the cancer has spread widely. With these last two techniques, impotence is a side effect. Cryotherapy, a method that freezes the prostate and kills the cancer cells, is currently being used and assessed.

Finally, watchful waiting and monitoring a small tumor carefully through regular exams and screening is another option.

When considering treatment options, men need to carefully assess the risks and benefits of each procedure and weigh them against other factors such as age, stage of disease, and quality of life. For instance, incontinence and/or impotence are two major risks associated with radical prostatectomy, radiation therapy, and hormone therapy. The good news is that new surgical techniques that spare delicate nerve connections are getting better at reducing these risks.

Note: An estimated 25 percent of cancer patients develop clinical depression. Depression can make battling prostate cancer far more difficult, as it tends to sever a man's ties to the people and things he cares about. Refer to pages 264-265.

Important Questions to Keep in Mind

- How often should I—given my age, family history, and any symptoms—get a PSA test and a digital exam to screen for prostate cancer?
- If I have a prostate infection (prostatitis), what antibiotics will be prescribed? Is there anything else I can do to feel better?
- When should I be concerned about BPH? Is no treatment the best option for me? What should I do if the symptoms get better? Worse? Can I take medication to treat my symptoms of BPH?
- When is surgery appropriate for BPH? What are the risks? Benefits? Could another treatment option be as effective? How successful is this procedure? How long is the recovery period?
- If I have been diagnosed with prostate cancer, what treatment options are recommended for my condition? What are the risks, benefits, success rates, and major side effects of each?
- When is "watchful waiting" an appropriate option? Is it the best option for me?
- What other factors do I need to think about when considering treatment options (e.g., stage of disease, age, other health problems)?

Stroke

Stroke is a serious medical emergency that affects more than 500,000 people each year. Stroke ranks third, after heart disease and cancer, as a cause of death. This condition kills more than 150,000 Americans each year. The good news is that almost four million Americans have survived strokes.

For many years, the number of strokes per year declined. However, recently the numbers have begun to rise. Some experts think this is because more Americans are living longer, medical care is helping more people survive heart disease, and doctors are better able to diagnose and detect strokes.

It is important to understand what stroke is and how it can be prevented and treated. Also, stroke appears to be a triggering event for people whose genes predispose them to Alzheimer's disease.

Q. What is a stroke?

A. A stroke is the death of an area of nerve cells in the brain, occurring when the blood supply to the area is blocked. Sometimes a person also will suffer transient ischemic attacks (TIAs) or "little strokes" that cause less damage but can serve as a warning sign that a more serious stroke could occur. One of three people who have TIAs will have a stroke within the following five years if they do not get treatment.

Q. What causes this condition?

A. A common cause of stroke is blockage of a brain artery by a clot. Clots can form around deposits sticking out from the arterial wall. Sometimes a clot in the blood stream becomes lodged in one of the cerebral arteries, completely plugging it (cerebral embolism). A stroke also can be caused by the bursting of a diseased artery in the brain (cerebral hemorrhage).

TIAs usually are caused by a narrowing of blood vessels in the neck (carotid arteries) because of a buildup of plaque. (See pages 268-270.)

All of these conditions cause a decrease in blood flow—and, therefore, oxygen—to the brain. Brain tissue, like the heart muscle in a heart attack, begins to die when it does not get enough oxygen.

Q. Do certain things increase my risk for having a stroke?

A. Again, individuals experiencing TIAs are at increased risk for stroke. After TIAs, the most important risk factor for stroke is high blood pressure. Other risk factors include: heart disease, age, gender (men are more susceptible), family history, race (African-Americans are more vulnerable), diabetes, high level of red blood cells, sickle cell disease, smoking, stress, and obesity.

In addition, a study that received a lot of media attention showed a higher prevalence—most notably in men—of stroke in people with migraine than in those without migraine. While some experts believe it's difficult to isolate and quantify the risk, they do recognize that there may be a slightly elevated risk, particularly among those who do not receive therapy for their migraines. The recommendation for migraine sufferers is to undergo treatment for their migraines and to reduce their risk factors for stroke.

Q. What are the symptoms?

A. Warning signs of a stroke include:

- sudden blurred or decreased vision in one or both eyes
- numbness, weakness, or paralysis of the face, an arm, or a leg, on one or both sides of the body
- difficulty in speaking or understanding
- dizziness, loss of balance, or an unexplained fall
- difficulty swallowing
- headache that is severe and comes on abruptly, or unexplained changes in a pattern of

Stroke

headaches

Do not ignore these signs, even if they seem temporary. They may be a TIA—a warning of a stroke to come. A TIA lasts only a few minutes and symptoms usually disappear within 24 hours. **You should get emergency medical assistance if any of the symptoms listed on page 281 occur.**

Q. How is this condition diagnosed?

A. Your doctor can diagnose narrowing of the carotid arteries, which can be the cause of TIAs, by feeling and listening to the arteries, through ultrasound, by measuring the pressure or circulation rate from the carotids to the eyes, or by arterial angiography (injection of dye into the arteries as X-rays are taken). Your doctor may diagnose a stroke through physical examination, medical history, electroencephalogram (EEG), and CAT scanning (computerized axial tomography).

Q. What treatment options are available?

A. Urgent action is critical. People with stroke caused by arterial blockages (80 percent of strokes are this kind) who receive tissue plasminogen activator (t-PA) within three hours of the beginning of stroke symptoms are 30 percent more likely than those who don't receive t-PA to recover completely or with minimal disability.

To diminish the risk of future strokes, aspirin or other blood thinners (e.g., heparinoids) may be prescribed. Aspirin can cut in half the risk of strokes caused by blood clots traveling from the heart to the brain and has proven to be as effective as medications such as warfarin, which inhibits the clotting ability of the blood.

In the case of blocked carotid arteries, surgery—called carotid endarterectomy—may be done to remove excess fatty plaques (atherosclerotic plaque buildup). Also, a new, experimental technique called cerebral angioplasty is being used to treat some cerebral vascular problems. With this procedure, balloons, stents, and coils are used to hold the artery open.

Depending on the amount of damage, physical, occupational, and speech therapy may help the stroke survivor deal with any limitations.

Finally, because a stroke often is disabling and the rehabilitation process difficult, victims may become depressed, and feel further isolated from family and friends. In fact, 10 to 27 percent of post-stroke patients suffer from depression, and another 15 to 40 percent show less severe forms of depression within the two months following a stroke. The good news is that depression can be successfully treated. See "Depression," pages 264-265.

Important Questions to Keep in Mind

- How often should I have my blood pressure checked? Why? Do I need to see a doctor each time? Can I monitor my blood pressure myself?
- If I am having TIAs, how can I tell if this means I am going to have a stroke? What should I do?
- What diagnostic tests are appropriate for my condition? How reliable are the results? Is a CAT scan needed?
- Is there a medication to help prevent a stroke? Improve my current condition? What will they do? How effective are they? What are the risks and side effects? When would I have to take them? Are there any incompatibilities with medications I am now taking?
- Will I need rehabilitation? What kind? How long? What is the success rate for these treatment options?
- What kind of adaptive devices are available to help me maintain daily activities?
- What type of support and assistance is available for those who will be helping me care for myself? How can these services be located and accessed?

Appendix: Family Medical Records/Resources

By using this section you will learn:

- How to maintain a medical record-keeping system for you and your family members.

- How to record and track medication use for you and your family members.

- How to contact organizations that can provide more information on a specific health topic.

Personal Medical Record

PHOTOCOPY THE FOLLOWING PAGES FOR EACH FAMILY MEMBER AND FILE IN A SAFE PLACE. KEEP THESE RECORDS UP-TO-DATE AND TAKE THEM WITH YOU WHEN YOU CHANGE DOCTORS.

Family member's name: _____

Date of birth: _____

Problems at birth: _____

_____

Blood type:_____   Rh factor: _____

CHILDHOOD DISEASES

Chicken pox   Date _____

Measles   Date _____

Mumps   Date _____

Whooping cough   Date _____

Rubella (German measles) Date _____

OTHER ILLNESSES:

Illness: _____ Date: _____

Comments _____

_____

284

Illness: _____ Date: _____

Comments _____

_____

Illness: _____ Date: _____

Comments _____

_____

Illness: _____ Date: _____

Comments _____

_____

Personal Medical Record

ALLERGIES:

Type: _____   Medication _____
Allergic to what?   _____
                           _____
                           _____

Type: _____   Medication _____
Allergic to what?   _____
                           _____
                           _____

Type: _____   Medication _____
Allergic to what?_____
                           _____
                           _____

HOSPITALIZATIONS:

Reason _____ Date _____ to _____
Doctor _____
Hospital   _____
Comments: _____
                _____
                _____

Reason _____ Date _____ to _____
Doctor _____
Hospital   _____
Comments: _____
                _____
                _____

Personal Immunization Record

FAMILY MEMBER'S NAME: _____

Date of birth _____

IMMUNIZATION	DATE	DOCTOR'S NAME	COMMENTS
Diphtheria Pertussis Tetanus (DPT)	_____	_____	_____
	_____	_____	_____
	_____	_____	_____
	_____	_____	_____
	_____	_____	_____
Adult Diphtheria and Tetanus	_____	_____	_____
	_____	_____	_____
Oral Polio (OPV)	_____	_____	_____
	_____	_____	_____
	_____	_____	_____
	_____	_____	_____
Chicken pox	_____	_____	_____
Measles, Mumps and Rubella (MMR)	_____	_____	_____
	_____	_____	_____
	_____	_____	_____
Hemophilus B	_____	_____	_____
	_____	_____	_____
	_____	_____	_____
Influenza	_____	_____	_____
	_____	_____	_____
Pneumonia	_____	_____	_____
Hepatitis B	_____	_____	_____
	_____	_____	_____
	_____	_____	_____
TB Skin Test	_____	_____	_____
Other	_____	_____	_____

NOTE: Keep separate record for each family member.

Medication Use Record

....

Make a photocopy of this form and take a copy with you whenever you visit your doctor. If a prescription or over-the-counter medication is recommended, have your doctor fill out the information below. Be sure you understand the instructions. Do not change your treatment schedule without first consulting your doctor. Keep this form in a safe place.

FAMILY MEMBER'S NAME: _____

Name of drug? _____

Date prescribed? _____

M.D.'s name? _____

Used to treat what problem? _____

How much?_____

How many times a day? _____

For how long? _____

With food or on an empty stomach?_____

Fluids recommended? _____

Alcohol prohibited? _____

Do not take with other drugs? _____

What foods/drinks to avoid? _____

What do I do if I miss a dose? _____

Name of drug? _____

Date prescribed? _____

M.D.'s name? _____

Used to treat what problem? _____

How much?_____

How many times a day? _____

For how long? _____

With food or on an empty stomach?_____

Fluids recommended? _____

Alcohol prohibited? _____

Do not take with other drugs? _____

What foods/drinks to avoid? _____

What do I do if I miss a dose? _____

Resources

AIDS

National AIDS Information
Clearinghouse
P.O. Box 6003
Rockville, MD 20849-6003
(800) 458-5231
http://www.cdc.nac.org

Pediatric, Adolescent and
Maternal AIDS Branch
Center for Research for Mothers
& Children
National Institute of Child
Health and Human Development
6100 Executive Blvd.
Room 4B11
Rockville, MD 20852
(301) 496-7339

Alcohol/Drug Abuse

AA—Alcoholics Anonymous
General Service Office
P.O. Box 459
Grand Central Station
New York City, NY 10163
(212) 870-3400
http://www.aa.org

Al-Anon/Alateen Family Group
Headquarters
1600 Corporate Landing Parkway
Virginia Beach, VA 23454-5617
(757) 563-1600
http://www.al-anon.alateen.org

Cocaine Anonymous
World Services Center
3740 Overland Ave. , Suite H
Los Angeles, CA 90034
(800) 347-8998
(meeting referrals)
(800) COCAINE (hotline)
http://www.ca.org

Pills Anonymous
P.O. Box 248
New York, NY 10028
(212) 874-0700 (hotline)

Narcotics Anonymous
P.O. Box 9999
Van Nuys, CA 91409
(818) 773-9999
http://www.wsoinc.com

National Clearinghouse for
Alcohol and Drug Information
P.O. Box 2345
Rockville, MD 20847
(800) 729-6686
http://www.health.org

National Institute on Alcohol
Abuse and Alcoholism
600 Executive Blvd.
Suite 401
Bethesda, MD 20892-7003
(301) 443-3860
http://www.niaaa.nih.gov/

National Institute on Drug Abuse
Parklawn Building, Room 10A39
5600 Fishers Lane
Rockville, MD 20857
(301) 443-4577
(800) 622-HELP (hotline)
http://www.nida.nih.gov/
NIDAhome.html#Communications

Allergies

American Academy of Allergy,
Asthma, and Immunology
611 E. Wells St.
Milwaukee, WI 53202
(800) 822-2762
http://www.aaaai.org

National Institute of Allergy and
Infectious Diseases
Building 31, Room 7A50
Bethesda, MD 20892
(301) 496-5717
http://www.niaid.nih.gov

Alzheimer's Disease

Alzheimer's Association
919 N. Michigan Ave.
Suite 1000
Chicago, IL 60611-1676
(800) 272-3900
http://www.alz.org/

Alzheimer's Disease Education &
Referral Center
P.O. Box 8250
Silver Spring, MD 20907-8250
(800) 438-4380
http://www.alzheimers.org/adear

Arthritis

Arthritis Foundation
1330 W. Peachtree St.
Atlanta, GA 30309
(800) 283-7800
http://www.arthritis.org

National Institute of Arthritis and
Musculoskeletal and Skin Diseases
Information Clearinghouse
1 AMS Circle
Bethesda, MD 20892-3675
(301) 495-4484
http://www.nih.gov/niams/

288

Resources

....

Asthma

Asthma and Allergy Foundation
of America
1125 15th St., N.W.
Suite 502
Washington, DC 20005
(202) 466-7643
http://www.aafa.org

National Asthma Education
Program
NHLBI Information Center
P.O. Box 30105
Bethesda, MD 20824-0105
(301) 251-1222
http://www.nhlbi.nih.gov/
nhlbi/nhlbi.htm

Breast-feeding

LaLeche League International
P.O. Box 4079
Schaumburg, IL 60168-4079
(800) LA-LECHE
http://www.lalecheleague.org/

Cancer

American Cancer Society
1599 Clifton Road, N.E.
Atlanta, GA 30329
(404) 320-3333 or
(800) ACS-2345
http://www.cancer.org

National Cancer Information
Center
National Cancer Institute
9030 Old Georgetown Road
Building 82
Bethesda, MD 20892
(301) 496-7403
http://www.nci.nih.gov

Skin Cancer Foundation
245 Fifth Ave.
Suite 2402
New York, NY 10016
(212) 725-5176

Child Care

Child Care Aware
2116 Campus Drive S.E.
Rochester, MN 55904
(800) 424-2246
http://www.childcarerr.org

National Child Care
Information Center
301 Maple Ave. W.
Suite 602
Vienna, VA 22180
(800) 616-2242
http://ericps.crc.uiuc.edu/nccic/
nccichome.html

Children's Health

American Academy of Pediatrics
Department of Publications
141 N.W. Point Blvd.
Post Office Box 927
Elk Grove Village, IL 60007
(800) 433-9016
http://www.aap.org

Maternal and Child Health
Center Clearinghouse
2070 Chain Bridge Road
Suite 450
Vienna, VA 22182
(703) 821-8955
http://www.circsol.com/mch

National Institute of Child
Health and Human Development
Building 31, Room 2A32
Bethesda, MD 20892
(301) 496-5133
http://www.nih.gov/nichd/

Diabetes

American Diabetes Association
1660 Duke St.
Alexandria, VA 22314
(800) 232-3472
http://www.diabetes.org

National Institute of Diabetes and
Digestive and Kidney Diseases
Information Clearinghouse
1 Information Way
Bethesda, MD 20892-3560
(301) 654-3327
http://www.niddk.nih.gov

Dental Health

American Dental Association
211 E. Chicago Ave.
Chicago, IL 60661
(312) 440-2500
http://www.ada.org

National Institute of Dental
Research
31 Center Drive
Building 31, Room 2C35
MSC 2290
Bethesda, MD 20892
(301) 496-4261
http://www.nidr.nih.gov

Resources

Environmental Health

Environmental Health
Clearinghouse
2605 Meridian Parkway
Suite 115
Durham, NC 27713
(800) 643-4794
http://infoventures.com/e-hlth/

National Institute of
Environmental Health Sciences
P.O. Box 12233
Research Triangle Park, NC 27709
(919) 541-3345
http://www.niehs.nih.gov

U.S. Environmental
Protection Agency
401 M St., S.W.
Washington, DC 20460
(202) 260-2080
http://www.epa.gov

Exercise/Fitness

American Alliance for Health,
Physical Education, Recreation
and Dance
1900 Association Drive
Reston, VA 22091
(703) 476-3437
http://www.aahperd.org

American College of Sports
Medicine
P.O. Box 1440
Indianapolis, IN 46206
(317) 637-9200
http://www.a1.com/sportsmed

President's Council on Physical
Fitness and Sports
HHH Building, Room 738H
200 Independence Ave., S.W.
Washington, DC 20201
(202) 690-9000
http://www.dhhs.gov/progorg/
ophs/pcpfs.htm

YMCA of the USA
Health and Physical Education
101 N. Wacker Drive
14th Floor
Chicago, IL 60606
(800) USA-YMCA
http://www.ymca.net

Family Health

Family Resource Coalition
200 S. Michigan Ave.
16th Floor
Chicago, IL 60604
(312) 341-0900
http://www.famres.org

National Domestic Violence
Hotline
3616 Far West
Suite 101-297
Austin, TX 78731
(800) 799-SAFE
http://www.usdoj.gov/vawo

National Council on Family
Relations
3989 Central Ave., N.E.
Suite 550
Minneapolis, MN 55421
(612) 781-9331
http://www.ncfr.com

General Health

American Academy of Family
Physicians
Foundation Library
8880 Ward Parkway
Kansas City, MO 64114
(816) 333-9700
http://www.aafp.org

American College of Preventive
Medicine
1660 L St., N.W., Suite 206
Washington, DC 20036
(202) 789-0033
http://www.ngaus.org

American Heart Association
7272 Greenville Ave.
Dallas, TX 75231
(800) 242-8721
http://www.amhrt.org

American Lung Association
1740 Broadway
New York, NY 10019
(212) 315-8700
http://www.lungusa.org

American Medical Association
515 N. State St.
Chicago, IL 60610
(312) 464-5000
http://www.ama-assn.org

American Public Health
Association
1015 15th St., N.W.
Third Floor
Washington, DC 20005
(202) 789-5600
http://www.apha.org

Resources

American Red Cross
1730 D St., N.W.
Washington, DC 20006
(202) 737-8300
http://www.redcross.org

National Health Information
Center
P.O. Box 1133
Washington, DC 20013
(800) 336-4797
http://nhic-nt.health.org

National Heart, Lung,
and Blood Institute
Education Programs Info. Center
P.O. Box 30105
Bethesda, MD 20824-0105
(301) 251-1222
http://www.nhlbi.nih.gov/nhlbi/
nhlbi.htm

National Multiple Sclerosis
Society
733 Third Ave.
New York, NY 10017
(800) 532-7667
http://www.msaa.com

National Osteoporosis
Foundation
1150 17th St., N.W.
Suite 500
Washington, DC 20036
(800) 223-9994
http://www.nof.org

National Self-Help Clearinghouse
City University of New York
Graduate Center
25 W. 43rd St., Room 620
New York, NY 10036
(212) 354-8525
http://www.selfhelpweb.org

Hearing

National Institute on Deafness
and Other Communication
Disorders
One Communication Ave.
Bethesda, MD 20892-3456
(800) 241-1044 (voice)
(800) 241-1055 (TTD/TTY/TT)
http://www.nih.gov/nidcd

Immunizations

Centers for Disease Control
and Prevention
National Immunization Program
Mail Stop E05
1600 Clifton Road, N.E.
Atlanta, GA 30333
(404) 639-8200
http://www.cdc.gov/nip/home.htm

Infertility

American Society for
Reproductive Medicine
1209 Montgomery Highway
Birmingham, AL 35216-2809
(205) 978-5000
http://www.asrm.com

RESOLVE
1310 Broadway
Somerville, MA 02144-1731
(617) 623-0744
http://www.resolve.org

Medications

American Pharmaceutical
Association
2215 Constitution Ave., N.W.
Washington, DC 20037
(202) 628-4410
http://www.aphanet.org

Center for Drug Evaluation
and Research
Food and Drug Administration
5600 Fishers Lane, Room 1471
Rockville, MD 20857
(301) 594-1012
http://www.fda.gov/cder/

Mental Health/Stress

American Institute of Stress
124 Park Ave.
Yonkers, NY 10703
(800) 24-RELAX
http://www.stress.org

American Self-Help
Clearinghouse
St. Clare's Riverside Medical
Center
25 Pocono Road
Denville, NJ 07834
(201) 625-7101
http://www.cmhc.com/selfhelp/

Grief Recovery Helpline
(800) 445-4808

National Clearinghouse on
Family Support & Children's
Mental Health
1912 S.W. Sixth Ave.
Room 120
Portland, OR 97201
(800) 628-1696

National Institute of
Mental Health
5600 Fishers Lane, Room 7C02
Rockville, MD 20857
(301) 443-4513
(800) 421-4211 (depression
awareness hotline)
http://www.nimh.nih.gov/

Resources

National Mental Health
Association
1021 Prince St.
Alexandria, VA 22314
(800) 969-6642
http://www.nmha.org

Panic Disorder Information Line
(800) 64-PANIC

Neurological Disorders

National Institute of Neurological
Disorders and Stroke
31 Center Drive, MSC 2540
Building 31, Room 8A06
Bethesda, MD 20892-2540
(800) 352-9424
http://www.ninds.nih.gov

National Stroke Association
8480 E. Orchard Road
Suite 1000
Englewood, CO 80110-5015
(800) STROKES
http://www.stroke.org

Nutrition

American Dietetic Association
National Center for Nutrition
and Dietetics
216 W. Jackson Blvd.
Chicago, IL 60606
Consumer Nutrition Hotline:
(800) 366-1655
http://www.eatright.org

Center for Food Safety and
Applied Nutrition
Food & Drug Administration
200 C St., S.W., HFF-11
Washington, DC 20204
(202) 205-4317
http://vm.cfsan.fda.gov/list.html

Food and Nutrition Information
Center
Department of Agriculture
National Agricultural Library
10301 Baltimore Blvd.
Room 304
Beltsville, MD 20705
(301) 504-5719
http://www.nal.usda.gov/fnic

Pregnancy

Healthy Mothers,
Healthy Babies Coalition
409 12th Street, S.W.
Washington, DC 20024-2188
(202) 863-2458

March of Dimes Birth Defects
Foundation
1275 Mamaroneck Ave.
White Plains, NY 10605
(914) 428-7100
http://www.modimes.org

International Childbirth
Education Association
P.O. Box 20048
Minneapolis, MN 55420
(800) 624-4934
http://www.icea.org

Pacific Postpartum Support
Society
1416 Commercial Drive
Suite 104
Vancouver, B.C. V5L 3X9
(604) 255-7999
http://www.postpartum.org

Primary Care

National Clearinghouse for
Primary Care Information
2070 Chain Bridge Road
Suite 450
Vienna, VA 22182
(800) 400-BPHC
http://www.bphc.hrsa.dhhs.gov

Safety

Consumer Product Safety
Commission
4330 East-West Highway
Bethesda, MD 20814
(800) 638-2772
http://www.cpsc.gov

National Center for Injury
Prevention and Disease Control
Centers for Disease Control
1600 Clifton Road, N.E.
Atlanta, GA 30333
(404) 639-3311
http://www.cdc.gov/ncipc/
ncipchtm.htm

National Fire Protection
Association
P.O. Box 9101
Quincy, MA 02269
(800) 344-3555
http://nfpa.org

National Highway Traffic Safety
Administration
400 Seventh St., S.W.
Washington, DC 20590
Auto Safety Hotline:
(800) 424-9393
http://www.nhtsa.dot.gov

Resources

National Institute of
Occupational Safety and Health
(NIOSH)
4676 Columbia Parkway
Cincinnati, OH 45226-1198
(800) 35-NIOSH
http://www.cdc.gov/niosh/
homepage.html

National Safe Kids Campaign
1301 Pennsylvania Ave., N.W.
Suite 1000
Washington, DC 20004
(202) 662-0600
http://www.safekids.org

National Safety Council
1121 Springlake Drive
Itasca, IL 60143-3201
(800) 621-7615
http://www.nsc.org

Sexually Transmitted Diseases (STDs)

American Social Health
Association
P.O. Box 13827
Research Triangle Park, NC 27709
(919) 361-8400
http://sunsite.unc.edu/ASHA

Centers for Disease Control and
Prevention
National Center for HIV, STD,
and TB Prevention
1600 Clifton Road, N.E.
Mailstop E02
Atlanta, GA 30333
(404) 639-8260
http://www.cdc.gov

STD National Hotline
(800) 227-8922

Senior Support

Administration on Aging
Department of Health and
Human Services
330 Independence Ave., S.W.
Room 4646
Washington, DC 20201
(202) 619-0641
http://www.aoa.dhhs.gov

American Association
of Retired Persons
601 E St., NW
Washington, DC 20049
(800) 424-3410
(202) 434-2479 (TTY)
http://www.aarp.org

National Council on Aging
409 Third St., S.W., Suite 200
Washington, DC 20024
(202) 479-1200
http://www.ncoa.org

Sleep

The American Sleep Disorders
Association and the Sleep
Research Society
1610 14th St., N.W.
Suite 300
Rochester, MN 55901
(507) 287-6006
http://www.asda.org

The Better Sleep Council
P.O. Box 19534
Alexandria, VA 22320-0534
(703) 683-8371

Vision

American Foundation
for the Blind
11 Penn Plaza
Suite 300
New York, NY 10001
(800) 232-5463
http://www.afb.org/afb

National Eye Institute
Building 31, Room 6A32
Bethesda, MD 20892
(301) 496-5248
http://www.nei.nih.gov

Work and Family

The Women's Bureau
U.S. Department of Labor
200 Constitution Ave., N.W.
Room S-3002
Washington, DC 20210
(800) 827-5335
(Request "Work and Family
Resource Kit")
http://www.dol.gov/dol/wb/

Family and Work Institute
330 Seventh Ave.
14th Floor
New York, NY 10001
(212) 465-2044
http://www.familiesandwork.org

Index

A green entry indicates a medical emergency.
A bold entry indicates primary discussion in the self-care pages and/or Q&A section.

Index

A green entry indicates a medical emergency.
A bold entry indicates primary discussion in the self-care pages and/or Q&A section.

Index

A green entry indicates a medical emergency.
A bold entry indicates primary discussion in the self-care pages and/or Q&A section.

Index

A green entry indicates a medical emergency.
A bold entry indicates primary discussion in the self-care pages and/or Q&A section.

Index

A green entry indicates a medical emergency.
A bold entry indicates primary discussion in the self–care pages and/or Q&A section.